BROKEN

Broken

The Failed Promise of Muslim Inclusion

Evelyn Alsultany

NEW YORK UNIVERSITY PRESS

New York

NEW YORK UNIVERSITY PRESS
New York
www.nyupress.org

Parts of chapter 1 were previously published as Evelyn Alsultany, "The Cultural Politics of Islam in U.S. Reality Television," *Communication, Culture and Critique* 9:4 (December 2016): 595–613; and Evelyn Alsultany, "Real Time with Bill Maher and the Good Muslims of Liberal Multiculturalism," in *Muslims and U.S. Politics Today: A Defining Moment*, ed. Mohammad Hassan Khalil (Cambridge, MA: Harvard University Press, 2019), 83–103. An earlier version of chapter 3 was published as Evelyn Alsultany, "How Hate Crime Laws Perpetuate Anti-Muslim Racism," *Meridians* 20:2 (Fall 2021), 414–442.

References to Internet websites (URLs) were accurate at the time of writing. Neither the author nor New York University Press is responsible for URLs that may have expired or changed since the manuscript was prepared.

Library of Congress Cataloging-in-Publication Data
Names: Alsultany, Evelyn, author.
Title: Broken : the failed promise of Muslim inclusion / Evelyn Alsultany.
Other titles: Failed promise of Muslim inclusion
Description: New York : New York University Press, [2022] | Includes bibliographical references and index.
Identifiers: LCCN 2022030947 | ISBN 9781479823963 (hardback) | ISBN 9781479805136 (paperback) | ISBN 9781479853540 (ebook other) | ISBN 9781479857746 (ebook)
Subjects: LCSH: Muslims--United States--Social conditions. | Arabs--United States--Social conditions. | Islamophobia--United States. | United States--Ethnic relations. | United States--Race relations. | Multiculturalism--United States. | Social integration--United States. | Arabs in mass media. | Islam in mass media.
Classification: LCC E184.M88 A47 2022 | DDC 305.6/970973--dc23/eng/20220701
LC record available at https://lccn.loc.gov/2022030947

For Benefo

I enclose the term in quotes because the very term "diversity" prevents people from thinking seriously and deeply about the extent to which our institutions are thoroughly saturated with racism, sexism, homophobia, class bias, and xenophobia.
—Angela Y. Davis, *The Meaning of Freedom: And Other Difficult Dialogues*

CONTENTS

Introduction

How Muslims Get Included through Crisis Diversity

As an Arab American Latina Muslim first-generation college student and daughter of immigrants at the University of Michigan in the early 1990s, I felt alienated in my classes and understood why my brother had dropped out of college. Everything changed for me when an academic advisor, a white man who advised underrepresented students, encouraged me to take Introduction to Women's Studies. Women-of-color feminism rocked my world. Patricia Hill Collins's *Black Feminist Thought* and Cherríe Moraga and Gloria Anzaldúa's concept of a "theory of the flesh" in *This Bridge Called My Back* made my life come into focus: women of color can build knowledge—epistemologies—based on their experiences. Our personal experience offers vital clues into the social and political world. This was everything to me. My profound feeling of alterity finally made sense. I came to understand how my sense of isolation around my identity was not unique but shaped by social and political forces that have valued certain identities (white, Christian) over others. But I longed to see my experiences as Muslim and Arab (and multiethnic) reflected in women-of-color feminist or ethnic studies courses. Where could I go to learn about why being Arab and Muslim felt loaded, marked, and far from normative concepts of identity?

I yearned for a course on Muslims in the US or Arab Americans to gain perspective on my histories and experiences. Courses were available about Arabs in Middle Eastern studies or about Muslims in religious studies departments, but not about the histories and experiences of Muslims in the US or the experiences of Arab Americans vis-à-vis US racial politics. Efforts to decenter Europe from educational curricula at the time did not include learning about Arabs or Muslims in ethnic studies. This is because the US Census classifies people from

Southwest Asia and North Africa as "white" despite the fact that Arab American organizations have been lobbying for a Middle Eastern/ North African (MENA) census box for the last three decades. Furthermore, diversity initiatives tend to focus on established race and ethnicity categories (Black, Native, Asian, and Latinx) and not on religious identity (Muslim).

In 1999, when I applied to PhD programs in American studies and ethnic studies, I proposed bringing Arabs into conversations about race in ethnic studies, but my advisor strongly recommended that I change my topic. She was concerned that I would spend years pursuing a topic for which there would be no jobs. Then 9/11 happened. Suddenly, I was told repeatedly that my topic was cutting-edge. A national-turned-global crisis in "terrorism" that led to the surveillance, detention, and deportation of Arabs, South Asians, and Muslims in the US simultaneously produced an interest in these communities and professional opportunities. Granted, most focused on national security and terrorism; however, at the same time, Arabs and Muslims were included for the first time in national conversations about racial profiling, racism, and discrimination, and also in ethnic studies conversations about racialization.

After earning a PhD in 2005, I was hired by the Department of American Culture at the University of Michigan, where I collaborated with my colleague Nadine Naber to create an Arab and Muslim American Studies program as part of US Ethnic Studies.[1] Undergraduate students from Southwest Asia and North Africa, as well as South Asian students— many of whom were Muslim—flocked to our courses eager to make sense of their experiences, especially in a post-9/11 context in which they were perceived as the enemy, and to connect with Nadine and I personally, as we were two of a very small number of Arab faculty. At the time that the program was created, the University of Michigan became one of only three universities that offered a minor or dedicated curriculum on Arabs and/or Muslims in American studies. As paradoxical as it seemed in many ways, the events of 9/11—specifically the government policies that demonized Arabs and Muslims and increased hate speech and hate crimes—made this possible. At least some portion of the public recognized a crisis in the demonization of Muslims, considering the US-led wars in Muslim-majority countries (Afghanistan and Iraq), the opening of Guantanamo Bay prison to indefinitely detain Muslim men, and the passing of the USA PATRIOT Act that eliminated due process for Muslims (and consequently many others) in the name of national security.

The program was formalized in 2015, after nearly ten years, thanks to my department chair's advocacy and renewed recognition across campus (and the world) of "Islamophobia" as a global problem. Many point to 2015 as the apex of anti-Muslim racism, as seen in a marked increase in hate crimes and mosque vandalism.[2] The year saw not only Muslim-led violent attacks in Paris and San Bernardino, but also the murder of three Muslim students in Chapel Hill, North Carolina—Deah Barakat, Yusor Abu-Salha, and Razan Abu-Salha—as well as the arrest of fourteen-year-old student Ahmad Mohamad for making a clock that his teachers mistook for a bomb. It was also in 2015 that media coverage of such events increased, the term "Islamophobia" went mainstream,[3] and Donald Trump first uttered his idea for a "Muslim ban."[4] The ten-year lull in establishing the Arab and Muslim American Studies program is significant and speaks to an institutional pattern —one of crisis, response, and then inertia until the next crisis, what I term "crisis diversity."

In hindsight I realize how thoroughly Nadine and I fell into the all-too-common trap of underrepresented faculty doing unacknowledged diversity work for the university. Even when the program became official, its relatively low status as an ethnic studies program was starkly illustrated by its funding relative to that of other programs. Crucially, however, none of this affected the public relations value of the program for the university. Many universities promote diversity as a social value, but when underrepresented groups do the work of helping institutions to "do diversity,"[5] they often receive little to no financial benefit. After all, they are told, their work is for the social good. Universities and corporations, on the other hand, can then include diversity as part of their branding—a near universal practice today that is profoundly lucrative. As scholar of higher education Toby S. Jenkins writes, "Budgets are moral documents that reflect institutional priorities."[6] She points to how universities affirm a commitment to diversity but allocate very little money to it. From 2014–2015 to 2018–2019, universities increased their diversity, equity, and inclusion budgets by 33.7 percent.[7] However, even after this substantial increase, such budgets account for less than

1 percent of university spending. While spending on diversity initiatives remains low, this minimal expense pays off; it has a substantial impact on recruiting and retaining students, faculty, and staff, especially from underrepresented backgrounds, and therefore positively impacts university budgets. Furthermore, studies have shown that diversity initiatives disproportionately burden faculty from underrepresented groups who are tasked with serving as mentors to underrepresented students, sponsoring student groups, and serving on a range of committees to ensure diverse representation.[8] Referred to as a "minority tax," this invisible service work often comes at the expense of research and promotion[9] and leads to burnout.

My educational and professional history marks how things have changed over time: from an absence of conversations about Arabs and Muslims vis-à-vis racial politics to building an educational program to address this; from being discouraged from my topic to being hired for my precise topic; and from a general lack of interest to a sudden demand for talks, workshops, and trainings on "Islamophobia," accompanied by a notable increase in the number of scholarly books and articles on Islamophobia.[10] Sociologist Louise Cainkar points out that it took four decades to include Arabs and Muslims and now Iranians in ethnic studies conversations because Arab Americans were seen as white given census categorizations (and some identify as white), and religious groups were not seen as part of an ethnic studies framework, producing "a misalignment with dominant paradigms and scholarship on race."[11] Arabs and Muslims went from being excluded from discussions about campus diversity to being included in such endeavors—most visibly when there was some sort of emergency situation or increased national debate about anti-Muslim racism. Crises can lead to recognition of a long-standing problem, professional opportunities marked by uncompensated overwork during the period of crisis, opportunities to advance conversations and initiatives to address the newly recognized problem, and co-optation by institutions who use diversity for profit in an era in which diversity is valued.

This book traces the cultural politics of Arab and Muslim identities as they are included in diversity initiatives by media, hate crime laws, corporations, and universities. It examines my repeated surprise at what happened during the late-stage War on Terror from the Obama administration through the Trump administration, 2008–2020: that "Islamophobia" came to be recognized as a social and political problem; that media representations expanded beyond those of Muslims proving their US patriotism, first to a focus on secular Muslims and then to a wider field of possibilities; that certain hate crimes against Muslims became headline news; that journalist Juan Williams was fired by NPR for anti-Muslim speech; and that Arab, North African, Southwest Asian, and Muslim students are being included in DEI initiatives on some college campuses. Yet I wondered if such inclusion was effectively solving the problem of anti-Muslim racism. Government surveillance practices, policies like the "Muslim ban," and US-led wars in Muslim-majority countries continue to severely impact the lives of Muslims in the US and around the globe, even as diversity initiatives expand to include Muslims and seemingly recognize anti-Muslim racism for the first time. As Nadine Naber has put it, "Together, the U.S. state and media have reproduced the historical contradictions of U.S. racial formations that fuel hate violence, while at the same time promoting tolerance and diversity"[12] Given this paradox, we need to ask what exactly it means to "do diversity" and what we should expect as a result.

In what follows, I elaborate on the book's central foci—the *what, who, when,* and *where* that will organize and inform my discussion.

The "What": Diversity and Anti-Muslim Racism

To investigate how Muslims came to be included (however problematically) in how we currently approach diversity in the US, we need to establish first an understanding of "diversity" as an ongoing project, and of anti-Muslim racism, the phenomenon that makes Muslim inclusion in that project necessary. In the simplest terms, diversity is promoted as a social good that ensures a wide range of issues and identities are represented in the policy, practice, or institution in question. The idea that diversity is a goal not yet realized rests upon a recognition that hierarchal systems of race, gender, class, ability, and sexuality, among others, continue to structure access to resources and power in our society. Increasing the diversity of people with access to those resources and power is thus argued to be an important step in rectifying society's inequalities.

Not everyone embraces diversity as the solution to racism and other forms of discrimination. Political conservatives tend to be harsh critics of diversity initiatives. Right-wing media pundit Tucker Carlson sees efforts toward diversity as destroying a system of meritocracy in the US.[13] He argues that true equality will be achieved by embracing meritocracy, which he claims was in place in the US until it was destroyed by diversity initiatives that seek to place particular identities in certain positions. While some deny historic inequality, others acknowledge it but deny that inequality persists today. Philosopher Stephen Paul Foster writes that diversity "is a euphemism for 'more blacks needed.'"[14] He says that "accusations" of racism and systemic racism are from people who want white people to be morally indebted to Black people "one hundred and fifty years after hundreds of thousands of white people killed each other putting an end to slavery." According to Foster, the term "racism" is now used to insist on payback for a grievance resolved over a century ago.

Leftist activists and scholars also tend to reject diversity initiatives but for completely different reasons. Activists for social justice see diversity initiatives as window dressing that does little to impact structural change. Therefore, they argue for defunding the police, prisons, and Immigration and Customs Enforcement in order to reduce the role of policing in society and bolster providing communities with mental health, providing community fridges and pantries to combat food insecurity, and other kinds of support. They argue for ending state violence on the US's own domestic communities and abroad by ending war. Ethnic studies scholars, of which I am one, similarly tend to question the effectiveness of diversity approaches to addressing longstanding issues of white supremacy and US imperial projects. Ethnic, gender, and sexuality studies scholar Roderick A. Ferguson argues that institutions have appropriated and institutionalized social movements of the 1960s and 1970s that sought racial, gender, and sexual justice.[15] Institutions like the university and corporations co-opt and contain minority difference to absorb it and thus regulate it.

Diversity became an increasingly popular discourse and project in the 1980s and 1990s as an alternative to affirmative action, which was a post–civil rights movement approach to rectifying enduring inequality. As time has passed, however, and as backlash has developed among those groups whose dominance is threatened by diversity initiatives, the term itself has become a heavily loaded catchphrase and buzzword whose meaning depends very much on who is using it and how (e.g., sincerely or cynically). It became formalized as "diversity, equity, and inclusion" (DEI) in specific institutional contexts in the 2010s, in continued response to a fierce backlash against affirmative action, resulting in further divestment from a civil rights model that seeks to rectify inequality in favor of a neoliberal vision that benefits everyone and promotes one's marketability.[16]

As already noted, the inclusion of Muslims in diversity initiatives is a relatively recent development in the US, marked by the events of 9/11 and their varied aftermath. It may seem obvious now to point out that Muslims' inclusion in diversity initiatives rests on the recognition of anti-Muslim racism as both real and problematic, but this was not always the case. Even establishing the term "anti-Muslim racism" has been—and, indeed, continues to be—a contested process. Anti-Muslim racism, as defined by Junaid Rana and Nadine Naber, is the "interpersonal, media, and state-based targeting of [. . .] those who are Muslim and those perceived to be Muslim."[17] This point is crucial, as they elaborate: "The targeting often relies upon the assumption that 'Muslims' are enemies of, and pose a threat to, the US nation." It is important to understand anti-Muslim racism as produced at the intersection of enduring white supremacy[18] and the US endeavor to maintain a position of global supremacy. By "white supremacy" I am referring to the history of the US creating systems to maintain the superiority of people of European descent, and more specifically of placing white heterosexual cisgender Christian men at the center of rights, privileges, citizenship, and personhood. By "US global hegemony," I am referring to the ways in which the demonization required of Arabs and Muslims to justify war cannot be understood separate from the history of US imperial interests and interventions abroad.

The term "Orientalism" is helpful to understanding how white supremacy and US global supremacy intersect and have impacted Arabs and Muslims.[19] Edward Said's book *Orientalism* (1978) named a particular form of racism that had previously been unnamed, a form of "knowledge" that authorizes and justifies assertion of Western power over the East. This "knowledge" frames "the Orient" as inferior and uncivilized while defining the West as its opposite: superior and civilized.

Orientalism, as a precedent to anti-Muslim racism, has shaped it. Orientalism helps us understand not only the connection of anti-Muslim racism to white supremacy, but also to the global project of US hegemony. Orientalism provided the logic necessary to invade and colonize large swaths of the Middle East (Southwest Asia and North Africa). The decline of European colonialism in the Middle East in the first half of the twentieth century was replaced by the US becoming a global power in 1945 at the end of World War II and the beginning of the Cold War. Since the US emerged as a global power in 1945, it has sought to maintain that position through wars (e.g., the War on Terror), proxy wars (e.g., the Cold War), and interference in the domestic affairs of other governments (e.g., Iran, 1953). The logics that legitimized colonialism—that Arabs are uncivilized and need intervention to become civilized—morphed into neocolonialism, in which Arabs and Muslims are a barbaric threat to civilization.

Anti-Muslim racism operates, in many respects, like other forms of racism and discrimination in the US, but the ways in which it differs are crucial to its definition. Cultural and political historian Melani McAlister has shown that US domestic politics must be understood as co-constituted with and through its foreign policies, particularly when it comes to US interests in the Middle East.[20] Transnational American studies scholar Alex Lubin writes that the War on Terror "is not just about vanquishing the perpetrators of the September 11, 2001, terrorist attacks on the United States, it is also, and much more so, about securing the global politics of the United States and the multinational corporations that US power is meant to secure."[21] What stereotypes people have about Muslims, who is even considered a Muslim, and how and why Muslims move into or out of the public spotlight—all these phenomena may play out within the US, but their dynamics are shaped by global economic and political concerns. When we understand anti-Muslim racism in the US context as produced at the intersection of white supremacy and US global supremacy, then it becomes clear that to solve the problem we need to address the national security machine that produces and justifies it. Diversity initiatives tend to chime in to acknowledge discrimination and injustice and attempt to "include" Muslims. However, because they usually do not take on the structural or root-cause issues around the US's foreign wars, they tend to provide feel-good Band-Aid solutions that do not solve the problem in a substantial way. I say these are feel-good approaches because it feels good to finally be recognized and included in media representations and in conversations about diversity, equity, and inclusion.

It is a misconception that anti-Muslim racism is exclusively promoted by the political right and challenged by the political left. Lubin traces a continuum between the Bush, Obama, and Trump presidencies, pushing back against the notion that Bush and Trump were bad for Muslims but that Obama was good. While Obama criticized the Bush administration's use of torture and vowed to close Guantanamo Bay prison (he did not), he revised the Bush administration's torture program into a targeted assassination program.[22] On the one hand, Obama insisted on the rule of law, complying with the Geneva conventions, and that those who are convicted of terrorism should be allowed to have a fair trial. On the other hand, his administration was responsible for a drone strike program abroad that killed thousands of people, many of whom were children and civilians in Pakistan, Yemen, Somalia, and Afghanistan.[23]

Islamophobia itself is far from new—scholars trace forms of Islamophobia as far back as the seventh century, with the very establishment of Islam as a religion—but the term found new popularity in the late twentieth century. Many point to the 1997 report published by the Runnymede Trust in the UK as the first influential use of Islamophobia, but the term did not enter the US lexicon until about a decade after 9/11.[24] Definitions have varied, but are fairly well represented by that offered by the Center for American Progress: Islamophobia is "an exaggerated fear, hatred, and hostility toward Islam and Muslims that is perpetuated by negative stereotypes resulting in bias, discrimination, and the marginalization and exclusion of Muslims from America's social, political, and civic life."[25] The term has numerous limitations, however, ranging from its implied reduction of the phenomenon to an individualized fear, to its limited ability to capture the unique processes that frame Muslims as not simply a religious group, but a racialized one. What is particularly useful about the term "Islamophobia Industry" as opposed to "Islamophobia" is that it highlights how it is produced by people in power (e.g., politicians, scholars, artists, religious institutions, educational institutions, the media) and not the result of sheer ignorance (similar to how

Edward Said explained Orientalism). One drawback of the term is that this industry is easily misunderstood as being solely composed of the political right that seeks to malign Islam, thus overlooking the ways in which it is deeply embedded in not only white supremacist logics, but also foundational tenets of Western liberalism. For these reasons, I and a number of other scholars, particularly in ethnic studies and sociology, prefer "anti-Muslim racism" and agree with the argument that racism and racial thinking, particularly white supremacy, are so foundational to the US that it is not possible to understand "Islamophobia" outside of this history of racial logics.[26]

Theorizing about Arab American racialization in the 1980s and 1990s laid the foundation for what would become theorizing around anti-Muslim racism.[27] Scholars who use the term "anti-Muslim racism" are expanding our understanding of racism by revealing how racial thinking is transferable to conceptions of culture and nation. Feminist sociologist Sherene Razack has written about how "race thinking" applies to Muslims as "the belief that Muslims carry the seeds of fanaticism and irrationality in their culture."[28] As Naber has also detailed, a wide range of signifiers can be interpreted as symbolizing Muslims' threat to US security and values—from names (e.g., Muhammad) to brown skin (a range of ethnicities), particular forms of dress (e.g., hijab), particular nations of origin (e.g., Iraq, Pakistan), language (e.g., Arabic), and criticisms of US empire (e.g., criticisms of US or Israeli government policies). These signs are then used to justify airport profiling, surveillance, detention, deportation, and banning entry to the US.[29] Muslim racialization is also gendered. At the beginning of the War on Terror, First Lady Laura Bush in a radio address to the nation stated that "the fight against terrorism is also a fight for the rights and dignity of women," thus powerfully linking "the oppression of Muslim women" to the need for military intervention in Afghanistan.[30] Muslim men are seen as exceptionally violent against women and LGBTQ+ people and such discourses are used to justify both repressive policies and as litmus tests for including "exceptional Muslims."[31]

However, the use of "anti-Muslim racism" should not give the false impression that Muslims comprise a "race." Islam is a religion, not a racial category. Rather, "anti-Muslim racism" highlights that Muslim othering has involved racialization. It seeks to capture the sheer vastness of the demonization, marginalization, and violence to which Muslims are subjected. The term thus encompasses not only individuals' acts but large-scale practices and policies with domestic and global roots and ramifications. But who are these Muslims and how do we identify them?

The "Who": Muslims, Arabs, Iranians

Scholars of anti-Muslim racism point out that it is not only Muslims who are impacted, but also those who are *perceived* to be Arab/Middle Eastern/Muslim, such as Arab Christians, Iranian Jews, Indian Sikhs, Latinos, and Black Americans. The construction of an Arab "look" that comes to stand in for Muslims is an important feature of this form of racialization. As the late mass communication studies scholar Jack G. Shaheen copiously documented, Hollywood's Arab has dark features (skin, hair, and eyes), a distinctive hooked nose, "exotic" clothing (veils, belly dancing outfits, keffiyehs, etc.), and conforms to a limited number of cultural tropes (greedy, rich, corrupt oil sheik; fanatic with violent religious beliefs; terrorist; etc.).[32] Postcolonial and media studies scholar Ella Shohat demonstrated that Arabs have been racialized via visual representations, troping, and narrative positioning with Eurocentric storylines.[33] The US media has produced an Arab look that is both narrow enough to mark Arabs for exclusion and discrimination yet inclusive enough to erroneously include Indians, Pakistanis, and Iranians—as evidenced by misdirected hate crimes during the Gulf War and after 9/11. Anti-Muslim racism today is entwined with anti-Arab and anti-Iranian racism.[34]

One of the challenges in talking about anti-Muslim racism is defining the group impacted by this problem. By Muslim, do we mean only those who identify with the religion of Islam, or also the ethnicities equated with Islam and racialized accordingly, such as South Asians, Arabs, Iranians, and others from Southwest Asia and North Africa? Such questions are critical when dealing with a group of people who have been racialized in imprecise, conflated, and paradoxical ways. Sociologist Erik Love notes that there is no adequate or singular term that captures the full range of people impacted by Islamophobia as with Arab, Muslim, Sikh, South Asian, or Middle Eastern Americans, and therefore this group is often insufficiently referred to as Muslim or Middle Eastern.

Literary scholar Carol Fadda acknowledges the shortcomings in how terms like Arab, South Asian, and Muslim tend to flatten identity categories and overlook the "immense range of ethnic, racial, national, and religious affiliations" contained *within* each of those groupings.[35] Yet she also notes that the terms serve a purpose, namely, they "underscore the interconnections and differences between these identity categories, which are racialized in similar ways," and as such can also serve as the basis for organizing and solidarity.[36]

Some Muslim activists have expressed frustration at the coupling of anti-Arab and anti-Muslim racism. Lawyer Namira Islam criticizes terms used to describe those impacted by Islamophobia like "MASA" (Muslim, Arab, South Asian) and "AMEMSA" (Arab, Middle Eastern, Muslim, South Asian) for treating Islam as a cultural or ethnic identity.[37] She says that such terms make Muslim synonymous with Arab and South Asian, erasing other Muslim identities from the conversation. Similarly, Margari Hill argues that such an approach erases Black American Muslims from conversations about Islamophobia and civil liberties.[38] Muslims are racialized, but they are not all racialized in the same way. Islam racializes differently for white, Arab, and Black Muslims. And as detailed above, anti-Muslim racism and anti-Arab racism are hard to disentangle from each other given that Arab and Muslim identities have not only been historically conflated in US discourses, but have also been co-constituted in their racialization. No terminology is perfect and it is therefore important to acknowledge the complexity and debates surrounding terminology.

While admittedly imprecise and imperfect, I use a range of terms to capture the scope of conflated representations in US politics and culture —"Arab and Muslim," "Arab, Iranian, and Muslim," "Arabs and others from Southwest Asia and North Africa." I refer to "Arabs and others from Southwest Asia and North Africa" to be inclusive of Iranians, Turks, Kurds, Copts, Chaldeans, and others who trace their roots to the region and to avoid the term "Middle East" because of how it normalizes Eurocentrism.[39] At times I use Middle Eastern/North African (MENA) because it is the term that is used in Hollywood, universities, and other institutions to include these identities. I also use "the figure of the Muslim" to signal the construction of this conflated category. I trace the proliferation of discourses that have given meaning to Muslims in twenty-first century US politics and culture, particularly a massive increase in representations and writings that give contemporary meaning to the concept of the Muslim and, more often than not, attach the figure of the Muslim to Arabs, Iranians, and South Asians. Furthermore, diversity initiatives that emerge in response to anti-Muslim racism often increase visibility for Arabs and others from Southwest Asia and North Africa. If this naming strategy strikes some readers as circular, that's because it is. Indeed, only by attending to the slippages of anti-Muslim racism can we account for the changing conceptualizations of Muslims over time and across institutional contexts.

The "When": Crisis Diversity and the Temporality of Inclusion

Crises create conditions to think about Muslims—in good ways and bad. There have been countless crises regarding Muslims over the last two decades in the US and around the globe: the USA PATRIOT Act; Special Registration; the US invasions of Afghanistan and Iraq: the Abu Ghraib prison scandal; the continued existence of Guantánamo Bay prison; the practice of extraordinary rendition; the legalizing of torture; the Countering Violent Extremism program; the emergence of the Islamophobia Industry; Sharia law panics; Burn-a-Quran Day; the rise of ISIS; the Charlie Hebdo attack in Paris and other coordinated attacks by ISIS in France; the Danish cartoons controversy; the Boston Marathon bombing; the San Bernardino shooting; the Pulse Nightclub mass shooting in Orlando; the mosque shootings in Christchurch, New Zealand; the Syrian refugee crisis; the hijab and burqa bans across Europe; Hindu nationalism in India; violence toward the Rohingya people in Myanmar; internment of the Uighur population in China; Islamophobic rhetoric from government officials; the surveillance of mosques and Muslim students; rampant hate crimes; and the "Muslim ban." This list is not exhaustive.

The rapid succession of crises involving and affecting Muslims has shaped public perceptions. US citizens today are divided on their perception of Islam. A 2018 poll showed that 56 percent of the US public believe that Islam is not compatible with US values, with that number rising to 71 percent among Republicans.[40] An analysis of reporting on

Muslims in the *New York Times* from 1990 to 2014 reveals that 57 percent of the stories associate Muslims with bearing collective responsibility for terrorism.[41] Dominant US discourses have constructed a binary between US values defined as freedom, democracy, and equality and Muslim values figured as repressed, authoritarian, and fanatical. One great irony of the unquestioned assumption that all Muslims are immigrants and that Islam is a foreign religion is that it ignores the long history of Islam and Muslims in the US, particularly among Black Americans.[42] Another irony is that these US values or ideals have never applied to all US-Americans, given the history of racial, gender, and sexual inequality. To many, Islam is seen not as a religion protected by the First Amendment right to freedom of religion, but rather as a religion of terrorism, anti-Americanism, antisemitism, misogyny, and anti-LGBTQ+ animus.[43] Some even refuse to recognize it as a religion but disparage it as an extremist ideology.[44]

Crisis also comes in a variety of forms. Some crises are violent acts committed by Muslims. Some are policies that purport to combat terrorism but implicate all Muslims and fail to address root causes. And some are hate crimes or mass shootings against Muslims and those mistaken for Muslim. These events are global. In the case of events defined as "terrorism," one can even identify a typical cycle, beginning with some sort of violent event, then a government response that codes the event as a crisis and frames it using Islamophobic political rhetoric, followed by government policies that target all Muslims and fail to address the causes of the event, followed by an increase in anti-Muslim racism more broadly and a spike in discrimination and hate crimes against Muslims. Next, there is a counter-response as various communities, institutions, and corporations argue against blaming all Muslims for the actions of a few, and push for recognition of "Islamophobia" as a local and global predicament.

The problem with this cycle is the assumption that the story begins with terrorism or with Islam and not with US foreign policy and intervention; or that terrorism originates in religion rather than being a response to political situations. As a result, most US policies do not actually address the root causes of Muslim-led acts of violence. As scholar of anti-Muslim racism Arun Kundani points out, "Rather than reducing violence, the War on Terror intensified conflict [. . .] because its architects never grappled with the root causes of 'jihadist' political violence: the US's propping up of authoritarian regimes such as in Pakistan, Saudi Arabia, and Egypt; support for Israel's military occupation of Palestine; and US direct warfare in Iraq, Afghanistan, Pakistan, and so on."[45] It might appear that "terrorism" perpetrated by Muslims leads to policies that make all Muslims suspect, Islamophobic political rhetoric, and hate crimes. But surprisingly, studies have shown that hate crimes against people perceived to be Muslim tend to increase not so much in response to Muslim-led violence, but in response to the political rhetoric that uses "Islam" to explains those events.[46] Assumptions about cause and effect are further complicated when we consider the high incidence of white males responsible for mass shootings in the US, without any parallel increase in discrimination, fear, and/or violence directed toward all white men as a category. It is this distinction in the responses to and consequences of violence committed by different groups that signals that it is not the violence per se that is the problem.

The ostensible cycle of violent event, government responses, hate crimes, and counter-responses leads to what I refer to an *crisis diversity*. Crisis diversity is when a crisis event or series of events produce a domino effect of responses: the general public becomes aware of a long-standing problem (anti-Muslim racism); people of that particular identity group (Muslims and experts on Islam) are called upon to urgently educate the public and advise leaders on how to make changes; media conglomerates, corporations, universities, organizations, and other entities respond by issuing statements or embarking on new diversity initiatives. The crisis moment then passes and there is little attention paid to the issue until the next crisis emerges, restarting the cycle. How much social change is accomplished through these crises/responses is varied and debatable.

Crisis diversity is not a response solely to anti-Muslim racism. One need only look at how the police killing of George Floyd in the spring of 2020 led to widespread national protests, reigniting public debate about police brutality and putting anti-Black racism firmly on the agenda of not only the criminal justice system, but also that of universities and a wide variety of corporations and industries.[47] All of a sudden, government officials, media pundits, journalists, and much of the US public talked about racism—a problem with a centuries-old pedigree—as if it had only recently been discovered. In similar, yet distinct ways, anti-Muslim racism is seemingly discovered anew each time an instance of it manages to capture public attention. The larger point is that crisis temporality shapes the ways in which various forms of racism are perceived and responded to. Of course, not every national protest produces a crisis that leads to a response that seeks to repair or rectify the problem. But it is precisely because the responses to crises are varied that paying attention to the temporality and rhythms of when anti-Muslim racism moves into or out of the spotlight is so important. Moreover, understanding how crisis shapes anti-Muslim racism and the responses to it helps to account for its limitations.

The Where: How Different Institutions "Do Diversity"

Diversity as a "business necessity" has proved itself more compelling to a broader audience than the logic of social justice per se.[48] Starting in the 1980s, corporations started to see underrepresented groups as consumers and believed that having underrepresented employees might help them reach those consumers. A 1998 survey showed that 75 percent of Fortune 500 companies had a diversity program,[49] and a 2001 survey found that 75 percent of Fortune 1000 companies had a diversity manager.[50] A 2007 survey based on 265 HR professionals with companies with an average of ten thousand employees found that 55 percent had a diversity department and over 80 percent offered mandatory or voluntary diversity training for employees.[51] And studies have shown that diversity is good for business.[52] Part of the corporate influence on the development of diversity is that it has become cast as a valuable business skill or competency, a form of training that will make one more effective in a globalized world.[53] Hence there has been a shift toward corporations "valuing diversity" as part of their ethos in the 1980s and 1990s as distinct from legal compliance with the Civil Rights Act.[54]

By the 2010s, when Muslims were included under the mantra of diversity, Muslim women attained a new commodified visibility. *Playboy* featured its first Muslim woman in a hijab, Noor Tagouri (2016, she was fully clothed). *Sports Illustrated*, famous for its "swimsuit issues," featured the Somali American model Halima Aden, wearing a hijab and burkini for the first time (2019).[55] CoverGirl launched its first Muslim woman in a hijab, Nura Afia, as a brand ambassador (2016).[56] Nike launched its Pro Hijab (2017), a headscarf for Muslim women athletes, and Olympic medalist Ibtihaj Muhammad became its model. Muhammad also served as the inspiration for the first Muslim Barbie doll (2017). For the first time, Muslim women were recognized as constituting a profitable US market and as marketable commodities themselves.[57] However, corporations including Muslims in their marketing is a form of (neoliberal) social progress that raises important questions about the ways in which anti-racism gets turned into diversity-for-profit and also about the limits of diversity work when mediated by corporations.

Of course, corporations are not the only institutions that have been shaped by and have participated in shaping conceptions and approaches to diversity. Today, it is common practice for corporations, universities, the media, and (some, but not all) legislators to promote diversity as a core value. DEI programs and initiatives are the new buzz phrase at universities, where conversations about diversity have become commonplace. But how exactly do US institutions "do diversity" in an era in which there is both a greater commitment to diversity and a backlash against it?[58] What are the limits and possibilities of diversity practices, be they representational inclusion in the media to firing public figures for anti-Muslim speech? By tracing the operations of diversity's intersection with anti-Muslim racism across these institutional landscapes, this book seeks to identify how institutions and their specific logics shape—and delimit—how we address racism. My purpose is not to criticize various institutions for their efforts to be more diverse and inclusive. Instead, I interrogate how we think about and approach diversity at this current historical moment, so we are aware of the normalized and often invisible logics that influence our thinking in ways that appear to be promising but can be disappointingly limiting. In many respects, the institutional and corporate embrace of diversity as both a term and a goal is not surprising. Feminist scholar Sara Ahmed points out that "diversity becomes a positive tool for social action because of its status as a positive term."[59] In other words, using "diversity" instead of "rectifying racism" or ensuring equal opportunity "has less negative connotations, providing a cushion, that diversity, at least for some practitioners, is a starting point, a way of getting through people's defenses."[60] Diversity, in short, is a "feel-good" solution.[61]

The result, Ahmed notes, is that diversity initiatives are often superficial or work as rapid damage control in response to a situation potentially damaging to an institution's image, like racial or sexual harassment.[62] Legal scholar Nancy Leong similarly cautions against institutions that create superficial images of diverse identities (often using Photoshop) to promote themselves as prioritizing diversity.[63] So-called "diversity-speak" tends to bracket or not deal with the problems posed by enduring white supremacy or the national security state that justifies war in Muslim-majority countries—hence, why broader solutions offered by leftist activists that include calls to end US-led wars and/or support Palestinian self-determination, for example, do not gain traction in conversations about diversity. All too often, there is a particular way of "doing diversity" and addressing inequity in liberal multiculturalism that "divert[s] social energy from other political and social forms and imaginaries."[64] Understanding how diversity has developed to replace more effective approaches to rectifying inequality requires discussion of two things: (1) what came before diversity was so widely popularized—namely, its predecessor, affirmative action, and the subsequent backlash against it; and (2) the neoliberalization of the corporate and institutional contexts in which diversity is now pursued.

Efforts to address inequality in the US from the 1960s to the early 2000s focused primarily on the numeric underrepresentation of minorities—understood at the time as African Americans, Latinos, and Native Americans—and white women in positions of corporate and institutional leadership, and in the educational and employment pipelines that lead to such positions. Affirmative action, the solution introduced in 1965 to address this problem and lambasted by some ever since, was rooted squarely in a civil rights framework: minorities and women were being denied access to opportunities and thus denied their constitutional rights. The story of affirmative action's demise is simultaneously the story of diversity's rise and its neoliberal appropriation. These dynamics were vividly illustrated by the landmark *Grutter v. University of Michigan* case (2003) in which Barbara Grutter, a white woman, sued the University of Michigan, claiming that she had been discriminated against based on her race when she was denied admission to the University of Michigan Law School despite a stellar GPA and LSAT score.[65] Grutter argued that the university's use of affirmative action had violated the Fourteenth Amendment and Title VI of the Civil Rights Act of 1964; in short, she argued, the university had enacted precisely the kind of racism it purported to reject. When the case went to the Supreme Court, the University of Michigan prevailed—but at a significant cost. Sociologist Ellen Berrey argues that UM won the case precisely because it did *not* cite the goal of remedying historic inequality, but instead emphasized that a diverse educational environment was beneficial to all. That position, Berrey points out, marked a lasting shift away from a civil rights framework to a distinctly neoliberal justification that she calls the "diversity rationale."[66]

Building on the works of theorists Howard Winant, Jodi Melamed, and Wendy Brown's conceptualization of neoliberalism and neoliberal multiculturalism, my use of the term "neoliberalism" signifies three key points.[67] First, it indicates that corporations are taking an increasingly prominent role in addressing social inequality. Rather than it being addressed by courts and the law, universities, corporations, and the media become the arbiters, or shall I say social influencers, in promoting or contesting diversity as a social value. Second, neoliberalism refers to how corporations turn diversity into something profitable that can be bought, sold, consumed, and monetized. Neoliberal multiculturalism's approach to diversity involves including groups regardless of context or purpose of inclusion,[68] using crises as opportunities to add or include a targeted group, and turning crisis diversity into a lucrative endeavor. Third, it refers to a trend in addressing racism and other forms of discrimination as a problem that exists on the individual level, as opposed to an institutional one. Thus, it tends to individualize racism rather than addressing root causes.

Given the disposition to ignore the institutionalized dimensions of inequality and exclusion built into the very operations of neoliberal capitalism, it is all the more ironic that it is institutions and corporations that have emerged as the primary "actors" shaping and directing the project of diversity today. Contradictions, not surprisingly, proliferate. Various forms of media can offer Muslims more visibility and representation than ever before, but continue to do so in ways that are predetermined by the very stereotypes they seek to oppose, or are compromised by a lack of knowledge about Muslim communities within the industry. Law enforcement can punish individual perpetrators of hate crimes, but not address how state violence against Muslims perpetrates hate crimes. Corporations can fire public figures for anti-Muslim speech and present themselves as anti-racist heroes, as if racism is an individual problem as opposed to an institutional one. And universities can include Muslim students in diversity initiatives but marginalize those same students when they participate in activism for Palestinian self-determination. Each chapter of *Broken: The Failed Promise of Muslim Inclusion* examines a different institution to trace how each addresses anti-Muslim racism by including Muslims in diversity initiatives. Chapters 1 and 2 focus on how Hollywood has diversified its representations of Muslims, from 2010 to 2015 and from 2015 to 2020, respectively. Through analysis of two reality TV shows, *All-American Muslim* and *Shahs of Sunset*, and a political talk show, *Real Time with Bill Maher*, chapter 1 explores the development of normative or acceptable Muslim figures by tracking various iterations of the "good Muslim" and by parsing the contours of the nominal Muslim who purportedly, unlike other Muslims, is uniquely capable of adopting the liberal values of individual rights, equality, and pluralism. I highlight how the production of normative Muslims is limited by how these figures are shaped in response to negative stereotypes. By contrast, chapter 2 focuses on a range of factors that converged to produce an expansion of representations of Muslims beyond those responding to stereotypes. The chapter introduces the Obeidi-Alsultany Test, a test I co-authored with Sue Obeidi of the Muslim Public Affairs Council's (MPAC) Hollywood Bureau. We show that the expanded representations are promising and significant, yet some efforts are compromised by a focus on metrics as opposed to substance, the recycling of old tropes like Orientalism or terrorism, and other factors.

Chapter 3 turns to law enforcement, with studies of two cases in which Muslim youths were murdered, yet authorities refused to classify the murders as hate crimes. The cases I examine are the 2015 murders of Deah Barakat, Yusor Abu-Salha, and Razan Abu-Salha in Chapel Hill, North Carolina, and the 2017 murder of Nabra Hassanen in Reston, Virginia. I approach the denial of hate crime classification as a form of *racial gaslighting* and parse why simply acknowledging violence against Muslims as a hate crime does not solve the problem of hate crime violence. Chapter 4 focuses on two cases in which public figures were fired for anti-Muslim speech: National Public Radio's (NPR) firing of journalist

Juan Williams in 2010 and the Entertainment and Sports Programming Network's (ESPN) firing of sports analyst and former Major League Baseball player Curt Schilling in 2015. The chapter analyzes the trend of firing public figures for racist speech and considers the consequences of addressing racism through purging individuals from the social order. Chapter 5 traces how universities—and one in particular, the University of Michigan—have been pioneers in including Muslim (and MENA) students in their diversity initiatives, yet those efforts often crash and burn when it comes to Palestinian rights activism on campus. Universities may adopt a flexible and all-inclusive approach to diversity in an effort to be apolitical, but I emphasize how ignoring power dynamics only leads to further marginalizing of Muslim and MENA students. The epilogue briefly considers how the US government has become more diverse with the election of the first two Muslim women to Congress, Ilhan Omar and Rashida Tlaib, and contemplates alternatives to crisis diversity.

Each chapter explores and develops a particular concept—stereotype-confined expansions, diversity compromise, racial gaslighting, racial purging, and flexible diversity, respectively—that are not necessarily unique to the case of Muslims or exclusive to the approach to diversity of a particular institution, but are thrown into sharp relief by the cases I examine. These are modes or strategies of inclusion that reveal both the potential and the limits of "doing diversity" within a neoliberal system without simultaneously recognizing racism in all its historic and ongoing, interpersonal and systematic, domestic and global forms.

My contemporary cultural politics methodology involves taking a snapshot of the discursive field involving Muslims during a period of time and tracing the process of racialization—how race and othering is made and challenged. To that end, I have assembled an archive of materials that reflect the cultural politics regarding Muslims in the US from 2008 to 2020. My sources are uniquely composed of representations of Muslims in US television, corporate and university statements, hate crime cases, hate speech cases, news reports, op-eds, and Twitter and Facebook posts. While this approach risks not having the benefit of hindsight, it involves reconstructing the field of meaning by assembling a range of materials that illustrate how Muslims are being vilified, debated, and incorporated. As a cultural studies scholar, I utilize critical discourse analysis to identify the competing meanings produced about Muslims in representations and political discourses, highlighting how logics that justify inequality are produced and resisted. Ultimately, this book examines the processes by which the media, corporations, universities, and arms of the government have acknowledged, in one way or another, the realities of anti-Muslim racism and have responded in kind. It is about institutionalization as a procedure that gives meaning to Muslims as a racial category.

Whether we opt to call it "Islamophobia" or "anti-Muslim racism," we now have a name to describe and address an important social and political problem. When Hollywood seeks to increase and improve representations of Muslims, when law enforcement denies a hate crime classification but convicts the perpetrator of that crime to life in prison, when corporations fire public figures for Islamophobic speech, and when Muslims are included in university diversity initiatives, what happens to anti-Muslim racism? Is it adequately addressed and combated? Does it result in Muslims and others impacted by Islamophobia being more included in US society? *Broken: The Failed Promise of Muslim Inclusion* offers an analysis of how diversity is "done," and how Muslims specifically are included in these projects. As such, it continues a movement in ethnic studies to bring Arabs, Iranians, Southwest Asians, North Africans, and Muslims into the conversation about racial politics in the United States.

1

Stereotype-Confined Expansions

Shortly after September 11, 2001, Mahmood Mamdani, scholar of global politics, highlighted a distinction made by President George W. Bush in his post-9/11 speeches between "good" and "bad" Muslims.[1] The default assumption was that all Muslims were "bad" (potential terrorists) unless they proved their allegiance to the United States and its War on Terror. At the same time, however, and largely in response to this assumption, a number of alternative categories of "good" Muslims emerged who could prove their worth in various ways—e.g., by placing a high value on community service to prove moderation,[2] by seeking to demonstrate Islam's compatibility with American values,[3] by making their religion look more like American civil religions,[4] or by modifying the expression of one's Muslim identity, to name but a few.[5]

The *patriotic Muslim* emerged as one of the most popular pathways to inclusion in liberal multiculturalism. Muslims eager to differentiate themselves from terrorists can display US flags,[6] publicly affirm their commitment to the United States and its values, and even enlist in the military, thus demonstrating their willingness to perform the highest form of service, namely, dying for one's country. Post-9/11 media saw an uptick in the number of patriotic US Arab and Muslim characters on TV.[7] One of the significant changes was the standardization of Arab American and US Muslim patriotic characters depicted as working for the CIA or FBI in terrorist-themed shows like *24* (Fox, 2001–2014).[8] These characters function to prove that Arabs and Muslims are patriotic US-Americans, as opposed to foreign threats to national security, and therefore worthy of recognition and acceptance in the US. These figures also function to circumvent potential critiques of perpetuating stereotypes by civil rights groups like the Council on American-Islamic Relations by including an Arab and/or Muslim character who is not a terrorist.

Regarding the "good Muslim," historians Abdullah Al-Arian and Hafsa Kanjwal write that they must be:

> uncritical of empire, liberalism, and neoliberal economic policies. [...] In the US context, a "good" Muslim overlooks the role that US policies have played in political and socioeconomic developments in Muslim societies and instead situates blame entirely on *other* Muslims' understanding or interpretation of Islam.[9]

What is important to note is that, even when proven otherwise, one's status as a "good Muslim" can be easily revoked. As religious studies scholar Edward E. Curtis shows, even when patriotic Muslims in the military give the ultimate blood sacrifice, they are still not fully incorporated into the US national imaginary.[10] Similarly, moderate Muslims must not only endure but also participate in endless discussions about how they are against extremism and terrorism.[11] Furthermore, the continual positioning of both moderate Muslims and native informants as useful for national security actually has the effect of stigmatizing them as less than American.[12] Lauding them, for example, as "our eyes and ears on the front lines" as Hillary Clinton did in 2016, ensures that even "good" Muslim Americans are indelibly linked with terrorism in the popular imagination. Muslims, it seems, cannot be imagined as having any other relation to the US state.

Although the figure of the "good Muslim" represents a departure from stereotypical representations of harem girls, oppressed veiled women, rich oil sheiks, and terrorists, it continues to define Arabs and Muslims as being "good" or "bad" in the context of terrorism and presents a limited notion of patriotism—namely, that Arabs and Muslims can be patriotic only by wholeheartedly supporting and serving the US government. This strategy is a form of "simplified complex representation" that is now commonly used by television producers and writers to give the impression of a complex representation, yet effected through markedly reductive and predictable means. In the two decades since 9/11, terrorist themes have persisted in stories that include Muslim identities (e.g., *London Has Fallen*, 2016; *Bodyguard*, 2018), and even though patriotic Muslim characters are now included in these stories (e.g., *24*; *Homeland*,

2011–2020; *Jack Ryan*, 2018) these seemingly positive figures remain limited in that they are confined by their response to the stereotype.

This chapter reflects on the cultural phenomenon of *normative Muslims* as an umbrella category that includes all the ways in which Muslims in the US can (at least try to) prove themselves as "good Muslims"—from the aforementioned *patriotic Muslim* to variants such as the *moderate Muslim* and the *native informant* to a more recent variation, the *nominal Muslim*. The nominal Muslim is someone who is born into a Muslim family and maybe raised Muslim, but who is not religious and identifies as a cultural or secular Muslim as opposed to a religious Muslim, if they identify as Muslim at all. The nominal Muslim, more than their other normative counterparts, makes clear that Muslims can be included in liberal multiculturalism on the condition that they leave behind or shed the thing that marks them *as* Muslim, namely, Islam. I track these categories as they have developed over time by looking at representations from roughly 2010 to 2015, focusing on "reality"-based television, then in chapter 2 on the period from roughly 2015 to 2020, during which time Hollywood writers and producers sought to respond to the "Muslim ban" proposed by President Trump in 2016 and to the impact of the Trump presidency more broadly. These periods of 2010–2015 and 2015–2020 are analytical constructs; they speak to certain trends, but are not meant to demarcate beginnings and endings in any sort of neat or definitive way.

The temporality of these shifts in representation are important, especially when changes come in response to perceived crises. The patriotic Muslim, moderate Muslim, and native informant emerged as acceptable Muslim figures in the aftermath of 9/11-as-crisis and as a response to the subsequent crisis: the notion that all Arabs and Muslims are terrorists, religious extremists, and threats to US national security. Nominal Muslims emerged in the second decade of the War on Terror during the Obama presidency, which was marked by the "ground zero mosque" controversy and the flourishing of the Islamophobia Industry.[13] During the 2008 US presidential campaign, right-wing activists accused Barack Obama of being a closet Muslim, a secret Muslim, and a sleeper cell agent.[14] "Once a Muslim, always a Muslim," declared conservative political commentator Debbie Schlussel.[15] The Clarion Fund, a right-wing nonprofit organization whose mission is to educate the public about the radical Islamic threat, distributed twenty-eight million copies to US mailboxes of a film, *Obsession: Radical Islam's War against the West*, months before the election in an attempt to associate Obama with terrorism.[16]

Alienating and racializing Muslims in the name of US national security is a widespread practice that was not spared during Obama's administration, marked by the Countering Violent Extremism (CVE) program, surveillance of Muslim students, and secret drone strikes in Yemen, policies that would set the stage for Trump's crass approach to Muslims. Scholar of Muslim cultural politics Moustafa Bayoumi points out that during the Obama administration's drone strike program, all military-aged men who were killed were counted not as civilians, but rather as combatants, designating them as terrorists by virtue of being a Muslim man of a certain age and thus justifiably killed.[17] The NYPD surveilled mosques and Muslim students as a terrorism-prevention strategy, assuming that students and religious services are ripe for "terrorist" conversion. This approach to national security has also led to detaining Muslims at Guantanamo Bay prison indefinitely just in case they might become "terrorists."[18]

Hate crimes against persons perceived to be Muslim also continued during Obama's presidency.[19] In August 2010, a passenger stabbed a New York City cab driver when the latter confirmed that he was Muslim.[20] A few months later, slices of bacon arranged to spell the words "pig chump" were left on the tile walkway to a mosque.[21] In March 2011, a Muslim woman wearing a hijab was removed from a Southwest Airlines flight because the flight attendant deemed her suspicious.[22] And in May 2011, two Muslim clerics traveling to North Carolina for a conference on Islamophobia were escorted off an Atlantic Southeast airlines flight in Tennessee after the pilot expressed discomfort at their presence.[23] This list, unfortunately, could go on and on, but my point here is simply to insist that our discussion of cultural representations remains tethered at all times to the "real world" conditions of racialized violence perpetuated by both the state and individuals in which those representations are produced and consumed.

The increase of both Middle Easterners and Muslims in reality television is demonstrated by two shows: TLC's *All-American Muslim* (2011–2012) and Bravo's *Shahs of Sunset* (2012–present). A comparison between the two shows illuminates the shift in representations during 2010–2015 from patriotic Muslims to nominal Muslims. I then turn to a specific and now (in)famous 2014 episode of *Real Time with Bill Maher*, which clearly elucidates the nominal Muslim category but also illustrates the debate surrounding this figure and alternative ones, namely, the heroic Muslim and the sandwich-eating (or ordinary) Muslim.

It is important to note that it was the protest of civil rights organizations like the Council on American-Islamic Relations and the American-Arab Anti-Discrimination Committee that led to standardizing the patriotic Arab/Muslim character in terrorist themed shows.[24] The government's and media's construction of the figure of the Muslim-as-terrorist was protested by these civil rights organizations and led to the message that some are patriotic Americans. In 2010, when the Cordoba Initiative announced plans to build a Muslim community center in an abandoned building two and a half blocks away from "ground zero" in New York City, right-wing activist Pamela Geller dubbed it the "ground zero mosque" to give the impression that Muslims were literally building a mosque on the actual site of the former World Trade Center as a victory dance, such national controversies along with the rise of the Islamophobia Industry that insisted that Sharia law was a threat to the US constitution led to the nominal Muslim as a counternarrative, a nonreligious Muslim who embraces the very tenets of freedom and liberalism argued as defining (North) America.

Much of the problem rests in the reactive nature of responses to cultural crises. When categories of normative Muslims emerge under crisis conditions, representations expand but more often than not do so in ways that adhere to stereotypes, even when their avowed purpose might be to the contrary. Whereas the patriotic Muslim figure was a response to government discourse and media portrayals framing Muslims as a threat to US national security in the immediate wake of 9/11, the nominal Muslim figure emerged as a response to the political right's subtle shift in rhetoric that framed Muslims not as terrorists per se, but as incompatible with, and opposed to, US freedom and liberal values. But in both cases, precisely because they developed as reactions to negative representations, the new categories tend to be as one-dimensional and limiting as those they are meant to counter. The content of portrayals might shift, but the underlying parameters of portrayal remain intact.

Muslims are still confined to binaries of good and bad, patriotic and dangerous. So even though both the patriotic and the nominal Muslim seem emancipatory because they are new forms of Muslim representation, they raise important questions about the kinds of Muslims who can and cannot be included in (neo)liberal multiculturalism.

How are Muslims made acceptable for television programming? How does one go from a terrorist threat and oppressed "veiled woman" stereotype to a patriotic or nominal Muslim—a trajectory that on the surface appears to be a notable improvement? The prevalent media strategy, as I will show, creates normative versions of "Muslim-ness" that, when read critically, reveal the possibilities and limits afforded within a (neo) liberal framework. The work of cultural studies scholars like Herman Gray and Stuart Hall has shown that simply including representations of underrepresented groups in the media does not solve the problem of stereotyping. Gray writes that "media discourse about racial and ethnic difference produces normative subjects of diversity." Similarly, Hall points out that the spaces "won" for difference are "very carefully policed and regulated . . . [such] that what replaces invisibility is a kind of carefully regulated, segregated visibility."[25]

I would like to clarify the use of terms in this chapter, particularly liberalism, liberal multiculturalism, neoliberalism, and neoliberal multiculturalism. My use of liberalism refers to the long-standing political philosophy that claims universality, open-mindedness, tolerance, and freedom at its central tenets.[26] My understanding of liberalism, however, also recognizes the historical contradiction at its center, which many commentators fail to mention in their definitions—namely, that its principles of freedom were cultivated while slavery, colonialism, and inequality were entrenched in the formation of US democracy.[27] Liberalism promotes equality, freedom, and tolerance while at the same time historically it has restricted access to such ideals to certain identities, namely, white cisgendered heterosexual able-bodied middle- or upper-class Christian men. When I refer to liberal multiculturalism, I am referring to the limited form of multiculturalism that emerges from liberalism's contradictions. My objective is to think through permissible forms of being Muslim—the range of normative Muslims—given the conditions of liberal multiculturalism and its terms of inclusion in the US. My use of neoliberalism refers to the specific form of liberalism that can be traced to the 1980s Reagan era, which was characterized by widespread economic privatization of public institutions such as education, prison, and the military, and the parallel increase in corporate influence and autonomy.[28] Neoliberal multiculturalism is when the project of civil rights and anti-racism become deprioritized in favor of the economy.[29] Paradoxically, neoliberal multiculturalism also accounts for the way in which representation of marginalized groups can sometimes expand when the idea, if not the actual realization, of "diversity" becomes profitable. As the chapter will show, the dynamics of crisis diversity make only limited forms of inclusion possible—forms of inclusion that can be hugely profitable and that can be pointed to as evidence of liberalism fulfilling its ideals. The production of normative Muslims in response to crisis leads to stereotype-confined expansions: the patriot in response to the terrorist and the nominal in response to the extremist who is incompatible with liberal values. A stereotype-confined expansion is an expansion in representations defined and confined by the stereotype to which it is responding. There is an expansion in representations, but a very specific, conditional, and limited one. Furthermore, Muslim inclusion is delimited by the contradictions embedded in liberalism and the profit motive embedded in neoliberalism. Put another way, liberalism and neoliberalism produce acceptable Muslim subjects that reveal the limits and possibilities of not only Muslim inclusion, but also of liberalism and neoliberal multiculturalism themselves.

Middle Easterners and Muslims on Reality TV

There has been a noticeable increase in Muslims and Middle Easterners on US reality television since 2010. To list just a few: In 2010, Rima Fakih was the first Arab American Muslim to win the Miss USA pageant. She went on to train to be a professional wrestler on the USA network's reality show *WWE Tough Enough* (2011), and then appeared on FOX's dating game show *The Choice* (2012). In 2010, Sahar Dika was the first Arab American Muslim to be cast on MTV's *The Real World*. In 2013, Arab American Muslim Selma Alameri was on the cast of ABC's *The Bachelor*. And from 2010 to 2013, formerly married Paul Nassif and Adrienne Maloof, both Arab American Christians, were cast members on Bravo's *The Real Housewives of Beverly Hills*. In addition to an increase in cast members of Middle

Eastern descent on reality television, there has also been an increase in reality television shows that feature Middle Eastern identities. Whether or not Armenians identify as Middle Eastern is up for debate, but the most famous reality TV stars, the Kardashians on E!'s *Keeping Up with the Kardashians* (2007–2021), are Armenian and at times have identified as Middle Eastern.[30] This section focuses on two such shows: TLC's *All-American Muslim* (2011–2012),[31] which chronicled the everyday lives of five middle-class Lebanese American Muslim families in Dearborn, Michigan, and Bravo's *Shahs of Sunset* (2012–2021),[32] which follows six affluent Muslim and Jewish Iranian American friends in Beverly Hills, California. This increase in Muslims and Middle Easterners on reality television being exemplified by a wrestler, a pageant queen, a dating show contestant, and a rich consumerist speaks to the possibilities of inclusion in neoliberal multiculturalism.

On the surface, reality TV's promise to show "real" people in their "real" lives seems to make it the perfect antidote to stereotyping. Considering the overwhelming Orientalist history of representing Muslims, Arabs, and Iranians through tropes of exoticism, oppression, and violence,[33] surely programs that present such people "as they really are" and allow them to speak for themselves have the potential to challenge stereotypes and expand the representational field. But as the past few decades of this form of programming have revealed, reality shows, like other genres of television, center around narratives of conflict and are somewhat scripted and highly mediated. Far from providing accurate depictions, reality TV offers the kinds of representations and storylines to which audiences are deemed most likely to respond—as reflected in nine seasons of *Shahs of Sunset* and the one season of *All-American Muslim*.

In what follows, I provide a brief overview of TLC and Bravo's branding formulas to understand how *All-American Muslim* and *Shahs of Sunset* fit within their respective network contexts. I then examine the emergence of the figure of the nominal Muslim in contrast to the patriotic Muslim; I examine the ways in which Islam is represented (or not represented) in each show to unpack how the cultural politics of Islam in the US play out on reality television and are delimited by both stereotype-constrained expansions and neoliberalism's consumerist objectives.

All-American Muslim was broadcast on The Learning Channel (TLC), while *Shahs of Sunset* was broadcast on Bravo. Both networks have re-branded themselves over the last few decades. From 2000 to 2005, TLC was known for shows that focused on making over one's home, wardrobe, and fashion sense (e.g., *Trading Spaces*, 2000–2011; *What Not to Wear*, 2003–2013). In 2005, following the success of *Jon & Kate Plus 8* (2007–2009), a show featuring a couple with eight children, TLC re-branded itself by offering family-centered series that focused on atypical families or extreme family situations.[34] Produced by Dearborn native Mike Mosallem, *All-American Muslim* was part of this larger theme of atypical families, as was its lead-in show, *Sister Wives*,[35] which follows a polygamous Mormon family. According to media research company SNL Kagan, around the time of *All-American Muslim*'s airing, TLC was available in ninety-nine million homes in the United States.[36] The network's key demographic is women aged eighteen to thirty-four,[37] and its viewers tend to skew slightly to the right of the political spectrum.[38]

Though some of TLC's shows are critiqued as presenting nonnormative people and lifestyles as "freaks," Howard Lee, the network's senior vice president of production and development, disputes this. He describes the network as "captur[ing] the imagination of our public by showing you how other people live."[39] Amy Winter, general manager of TLC, in an interview about *All-American Muslim*, stated that "TLC has a track record of going into communities that people know very little about and opening them up for our viewers to experience."[40] TLC tried to promote the show as part of a broader strategy of supporting marginalized lifestyles, including those of polygamous Mormons (*Sister Wives*), the Amish (*Breaking Amish*, 2012–present), and people with dwarfism (*Little People, Big World*, 2006–present). Nonetheless, although *All-American Muslim* premiered to 1.7 million viewers, those numbers dropped to 900,000 by the finale.[41] In contrast, *Sister Wives*, still airing and in its sixteenth season in 2022, was averaging 2.1 million viewers in 2012. *All-American Muslim* was not renewed for a second season; it lasted only eight episodes.[42]

If TLC's shtick is normalizing the "abnormal," then Bravo's not-so-subtle strategy is presenting rich and glamorous lifestyles that the audience is often invited to "love to hate." When *Shahs of Sunset* premiered in 2012, Bravo's programing explored five main "branches": food, fashion, design, lifestyle, and pop culture.[43] Some of Bravo's other reality show hits are *Top Chef* (2006–present) and *The Real Housewives of Orange County* (2006–2014). Bravo executives have coined the term "affluencers" to describe their audience and its appetite for elitist characters.[44] In 2012, when *All-American Muslim* and *Shahs of Sunset* were both airing, the network was reaching eighty-eight million households and attracting an audience composed primarily of educated women and gay men with professional success and expensive taste.[45] Bravo's audience is among the most educated and affluent in the US and they tend to vote Democrat.[46]

One of Bravo's promotional strategies is to create like-minded programs that define its brand. *Shahs of Sunset* follows a very similar theme and format to the *Real Housewives* franchise and other Bravo reality television shows.[47] *Shahs of Sunset* is produced by Ryan Seacrest, who is known for producing *Keeping Up with the Kardashians* and its spin-off shows, and for being the host of Fox's *American Idol* (2002–present). In addition to being compared to Seacrest's *Kardashian* franchise, *Shahs of Sunset* is also frequently likened to other successful reality shows such as *The Real Housewives* franchise, as mentioned above, and MTV's *Jersey Shore* (2009–2012). Brand strategy advisers from Truth Consulting say that *The Real Housewives* franchise is successful because "people want to watch rich girls behaving badly."[48] *Shahs of Sunset* appears to be tapping into this audience.

Understanding the network contexts is important to recognizing how each show fits its network's brand, particularly how that network brands and markets diversity. TLC's brand of normalizing "atypical families" is a diversifying mission that engages with a wide range of typically marginalized identities. While the mission of normalizing the abnormal inadvertently reinscribes notions of "normal" and "abnormal" identities, it nonetheless provides an opportunity for audiences to see and learn about people not usually represented on television and thus, arguably, challenges stereotypes. Bravo's brand—of elitist lifestyles that we love to hate—diversifies by showcasing obnoxiously rich Black women in Atlanta, as it does with *The Real Housewives of Atlanta* (2008–present), and obnoxiously rich Iranians in Los Angeles, as it does with *Shahs of Sunset*. In a strategy not without irony, wealth and narcissism serve as vehicles for inclusion through envy: "they" are as awful as "we" are!

Jodi Melamed argues that "liberal antiracist terms of difference have restructured and maintained systems of heteronormativity, political economic normativity, and US national cultural normativity by limiting which social representations of difference have appeared reasonable, possible, or desirable."[49] The forms of difference that are advanced and made acceptable, usually in response to crisis, through reality television's articulation of "alternative lifestyles" or "atypical families" maintain systems of normativity in the act of diversifying. Gray says that the recognition afforded under racial neoliberalism does not seek to remedy, rectify, or repair the white supremacist logics that produce exclusion.[50] Rather, marginalized groups are included by constructing narrow normative categories that are used to assess, in this case, Muslim acceptability. In doing so, "the cultural politics of diversity seeks recognition and visibility as the end itself."[51]

While Islam is a religion, not a race, and comprised of people of all ethnic and racial identities, it has long been racialized by US media and political discourses and policies. Like homonormativity—the process by which LGBTQ+ people use the norms of heterosexual culture, such as marriage and monogamy, to negotiate their terms of inclusion[52]—racial normativity involves negotiating the terms of a historically marginalized group's inclusion based on white norms and the specific logics of the out-group's racialization. Muslim normativity, as with other forms of racial normativity, involves proving that the racialized discourses used to justify one's exclusion are not true. If debunking the exclusionary logics is not possible for the group in question, then categories of exception must be created.

Thus, when the dominant discourse frames Muslims as terrorist threats to national security and posits that being both Muslim and American is an oxymoron, then negotiating the terms of inclusion involves proving that one is not a threat and that one exemplifies patriotism (in the most narrow sense of the term). The patriotic Muslim who is willing to fight and die for the US is the normative Muslim, who is both acceptable and exceptional. When Muslims are cast as religious extremists, the moderate Muslim responds. When Muslims are cast as antisemitic, then other Muslims must demonstrate their capacity to love Israel or Israelis. When Islam is cast as incompatible with liberalism and against free speech and LGBTQ+ and women's rights, then the nominal Muslim who is not religious is the perfect antidote. Gray refers to this process of racial normativity as one of subjugation because it only reacts to dominant discourses and, worse, it does so within their discursive terms, rather than critiquing the logics of exclusion they inscribe. Conforming to normative versions of being Muslim might seem like it increases acceptance, but at what cost?

Wrapping Muslims in the American Flag: The Case of *All-American Muslim*

Premiering on TLC in November 2011, *All-American Muslim* chronicled the everyday lives of five Muslim families in Dearborn, Michigan. The show was unprecedented in its representation of Muslims on US television, particularly in the ways it attempted to expand the representation of Muslim identities. For one, it offered the possibility of moving away from representing all Arab and Muslim characters in contexts exclusively focused on terrorism. Second, it portrayed Arabs and Muslims in leading roles, rather than their more frequent supporting or inconsequential roles. Third, it included an array of Muslim identities that ranged from more to less conservative: two people had tattoos, one was scantily clad while another decided to don the hijab, and one was marrying an Irish American. Almost as soon as it aired, *All-American Muslim* kindled unexpected controversy. Many Muslims had criticisms of the show. Some claimed that the cast was not composed of "real Muslims" because some had tattoos. Others claimed the show portrayed one Muslim community (Lebanese Shia) as representative of all Muslims in the US. One Muslim commenter on the entertainment website IMDb stated that the show "is a joke and utter insult to the diversity that is Islam" and should be renamed "All-Lebanese American Shia Muslim."[53] Such critiques served to highlight the impossible pressure on a single show to undo over a century of stereotypes.[54] Hussein Rashid, scholar of Islam and popular culture, says that, given the vast diversity of the Muslim community, it is not possible for one show to represent every

US Muslim's experience and that such criticisms from the Muslim community negatively impacted the reception of the show.[55]

Less surprising were the negative responses from other kinds of viewers. It was precisely the show's effort to offer a more nuanced and positive picture of Muslims in the US that drew the ire of some, most notably the Florida Family Association (FFA) run by David Caton, a right-wing activist known for his anti-gay agenda. Anti-gay and anti-Muslim organizing converged, targeting the channel one media studies scholar refers to as "the compulsory heterosexuality channel"[56] for its focus on heterosexual families. In December 2011, the FFA organized an email campaign that protested the show's "deceptive" portrayal of Muslims as non-terrorists and called on advertisers to withdraw their sponsorship. As there are no terrorists on the show and Muslims are depicted as ordinary people, Caton charged that *All-American Muslim* was propaganda "attempting to manipulate Americans into ignoring the threat of jihad."[57] Soon after the FFA's campaign, the retailer Lowe's Home Improvement and the travel website Kayak.com pulled their commercials.

Apparently, even this modest expansion in representing Muslims disturbed those who saw the show as denying the essential incompatibility of Islam and America. Even the *Wall Street Journal* faced the wrath of this audience when an article on the controversy described the show as reflecting the reality that "Islam in America today is a story of rapid assimilation and even secularization, not growing radicalism."[58] Online reader responses to the article included the following:

I will happily sing the praises of middle class American Muslims as soon as middle class American Muslims denounce the jihad their brethren are leading against the rest of us. Until then, they are suspect.[59]

The Koran is not a book compatible with American middle-class values. Nor is the life of Mohammed.[60]

I wonder if the media will ever stop trying to brainwash us. Now, the drumbeat telling us Muslims are just nice American people trying to live normal lives. And we are being unfair . . . Sorry, but they are not ordinary Americans. They are engaged in a global religious war against us . . . we must be vigilant to not allow them to spread their violent religion and Sharia law in this our great and free nation.[61]

Such responses revealed the existence of an audience for whom *any* representational strategy that did not condemn all Muslims as inherently anti-American was unacceptable. It is important to note, however, that this controversy also generated a sizeable backlash, with people critiquing Lowe's and Kayak.com for their decision to withdraw sponsorship. A national Lowe's boycott campaign was launched and hip-hop mogul Russell Simmons offered to purchase any remaining advertising space on the show.[62]

For all its effort to provide a more nuanced portrayal of Muslims, *All-American Muslim* relied in other ways on narrow representational strategies that have become standard fare in TV dramas since 9/11—namely, the focus on Muslims as patriots and victims that have become stock normative Muslims.[63] Among the people featured on *All-American Muslim* are a police officer, a football coach, a county clerk, and a federal agent, mirroring the now-standard inclusion of "patriotic" US-American Muslim characters on fictional television shows. These portrayals, while certainly "positive," reflect the ongoing demand for US Muslims to continually prove their patriotism. Victims also appear on *All-American Muslim*, but to a much lesser extent than those cloaked in the trope of patriotism. We witness discrimination and harassment when one of the married couples leaves Dearborn to visit a neighboring town, only to be ignored at a restaurant while other customers are offered seating,[64] and when high school students recount being called "camel jockeys" by students at other schools.[65] The emphasis here is on the innocence of Muslims, thus assuring viewers that not all Muslims are threatening.

These representations of "patriots" and "victims" are undoubtedly improvements over the constructed figure of the Muslim as terrorists, oil sheiks, belly dancers, and oppressed, veiled women. Nonetheless, these "improvements" reveal an equally narrow and one-dimensional script of representation. By attempting to make Islam seem less frightening and more familiar through association with occupations and leisure activities that emphasize US citizenship, *All-American Muslim* adopts a strategy of *normalization*—producing normative Muslims who are patriotic US citizens—that distinguishes it from the other portrayals of alternative lifestyles and atypical families on TLC—and may help to explain why, in the end, the show failed to attract viewers.

The most obvious comparison is with the show *Sister Wives*. In *Sister Wives*, the Brown family members are portrayed as unjust victims of prejudice given the stigmatization of their lifestyle in mainstream society. They cannot legally marry since polygamy is illegal, and they must hide their identity as a polygamous Mormon family from the general public and from the community in which they live. But while the Brown family is burdened to prove that they are simply living a nonnormative lifestyle and are not perverted religious fanatics, their religious difference does not demand that they *also* prove their patriotism or citizenship. In contrast, *All-American Muslim*'s focus on its cast members' patriotism marks the show as distinct and reveals that Muslim identity, unlike Mormon identity, necessitates a framework that proves its protagonists are not just unfairly stigmatized, but also really and truly *American*.

To this end, *All-American Muslim* features "normal" people living a "normal" middle-class life with very little conflict. The ironic result: the show was widely perceived as boring. The "difference" of being Muslim is featured—we see, for example, a twelve-year-old girl putting on the hijab for the first time, an Irish American Catholic converting to Islam for marriage, conflict over having a dog as a domestic animal, and special accommodations at the high school for football training during Ramadan—but the insistence on US patriotism as a normalizing device neutralized its representational potential. Discussing the show online, viewers seemed unanimous: Where were the exciting scenes of drunk people and screaming fights that characterized other reality shows? On the *Hollywood Reporter*'s website, for example, viewers commented: "watched it once and was bored to death"; "It shows everyday people doing what . . . people do everyday. I don't watch TV for that."[66]

Arguably, the show's poor reception could be attributed to this relative normalcy and lack of melodrama. And if we were comparing *All-American Muslim* only with *Shahs of Sunset* and the kinds of shows featured on Bravo, this argument might make sense—but recall that TLC's particular reality television brand is not about drunken brawls or narcissists with abundant wealth. Rather, the focus is on marginalized and misunderstood lifestyles, and other TLC reality shows using this formula have been successful; the failure of *All-American Muslim* is thus somewhat puzzling. Since reality television excels at selling lifestyles, not citizenship, perhaps *All-American Muslim* would have done better to follow the *Sister Wives* model of showcasing a marginalized religion and "atypical lifestyle" rather than attempting so earnestly to prove its cast members' patriotic citizenship.

As the show's title and its portrayal of the protagonists' religious beliefs and practices demonstrated, the inclusion of Muslims that the producers were promoting sought a delicate balancing act that embraced religious difference—specifically, Islam—as normal. While the term "all-American" showcased the producers' efforts to evoke the framework of patriotism, the term "Muslim" dared to foreground, rather than downplay, religious identity. This was a risky representational strategy that inadvertently revealed the limits of US multiculturalism in 2011—an idealized form of inclusion that was ambivalent at best, especially when it came to Islam. In other words, *All-American Muslim* amplified the patriotic American version of the normative Muslim, a Muslim who works for the police, FBI, or as a football coach. In doing so, the producers sought to use the terms of their exclusion to negotiate their inclusion.

Individualism, Consumerism, and Freedom (from Islam): The Case of *Shahs of Sunset*

Shahs of Sunset is a significant development when considering the history of negative portrayals of Iranians in Western media. The films *Not Without My Daughter* (1991) and *Argo* (2012) both portray Iranians as a fanatical, irrational, and anti-American people consistent with the history of representations of Muslims, Arabs, and people from Southwest Asia and North Africa in US media. *Shahs of Sunset* should be understood in relation to an increase in more positive and/or less stereotypical portrayals of Iranians in Western media. It is reflective of media producers seeking to promote a diversity of representations and part of a larger trend that includes, for example, *Girlfriends' Guide to Divorce* (2014–2018), *The Bisexual* (2018), and *The L Word: Generation Q* (2019). *Girlfriends' Guide to Divorce*, broadcast on Bravo, included the Iranian

American high-powered lawyer Delia Banai, played by Necar Zadegan. *The Bisexual*, broadcast on Channel 4 in the UK and on Hulu in the US, is written by and stars Iranian American Desiree Akhavan. It is about Leila, an Iranian American living in England, who discovers that she is bisexual after breaking up with her longtime girlfriend. The cast of Showtime's *The L Word: Generation Q* includes the character Gigi Ghorbani, played by Sepideh Moafi.

While *All-American Muslim*'s title puts Islam front and center and attempts to announce its incorporation into a multicultural America, *Shahs of Sunset*'s title sidesteps Islam and plays into Orientalist discourse by evoking associations with royalty, rather than religion. The names of both shows and their promotional materials (see figures 1.1 and 1.2) immediately communicate certain expectations to viewers. One promotional image for *All-American Muslim* shows a heteronormative family with the father wearing his police uniform in front of their suburban house (see figure 1.1), while the promotional image for *Shahs of Sunset* conveys glamour and wealth (see figure 1.2). In the case of *Shahs of Sunset*, viewers are invited to gaze upon vaguely Oriental others (the relations and distinctions between Iranians, Arabs, and Muslims being lost on most Americans) and provided with a familiar Bravo structure of feeling (characters you "love to hate") through which to funnel any negative emotions.

Shahs of Sunset focuses on six Iranian American friends who met while students at Beverly Hills High School. Their families left Iran after the 1979 Islamic Revolution and moved to Los Angeles, sometimes referred to as "Tehrangeles" because of its large Iranian population. When the show first aired in 2012, the cast members were in their mid- to late thirties, single, and mostly employed in real estate; they are portrayed as rich, obnoxious narcissists. The season 1 trailer features Golnesa saying, "There are two things I don't like. I don't like ants, and I don't like ugly people," and Mike saying, "We don't work in buildings, we own them."[67] In the season 1 premiere, Golnesa says: "Looking good, and not repeating outfits, is imperative" and "I am a thirty-year-old and my only paycheck is from my daddy."[68] Reviews and viewer comments focus on how shallow the show is and how despicable they find the cast, but *Shahs of Sunset* has, nonetheless, been popular. Whereas the *All-American*

Figure 1.1. One of the families featured in *All-American Muslim*, TLC, 2011.

Figure 1.2. Promotional image for *Shahs of Sunset*, Bravo, 2012.

Muslim viewership and ratings did not merit a second season, *Shahs of Sunset* was renewed for nine seasons, with viewership consistently in the millions.[69]

The show has not been without controversy, particularly regarding the extent to which it perpetuates stereotypes of Iranians as rich and materialistic, and whether these stereotypes are "better" than that of Iranians as religious fundamentalist terrorists. Some critics say that the focus on rich, materialistic people actually normalizes Iranian identity. The *Boston Herald*'s Mark Perigard states that the show "proves that materialism is an insidious infection in this nation, vanity crosses every culture and just about everyone behaves like a moron when a camera is pointed in their direction."[70] Similarly, Pete Vonder Haar for the *Houston Press* writes that "the lesson of *Shahs of Sunset*, it would seem, is that the repulsiveness of rich people knows no ethnic or cultural boundaries."[71]

Whereas these "endorsements" are cynical, the cast members themselves are more optimistic about the show's portrayal of Iranian Americans. Reza, a gay man from a Muslim and Jewish background, and the most frequently interviewed cast member, merges patriotism with consumerism and wealth when he states:

> I would rather be associated with a stereotype like loving gold, loving Mercedes, loving columns. For me, personally, those things are all true. I don't want to be associated with a stereotype that I like blowing things up, that I'm a terrorist, that I'm militant, all the stereotypes that most of the United States think we're associated with. Because we're not. I love this country. I am so proud to call myself an American. I worship the ground that I walk on here and I don't take it for granted one minute. If I'm going to personify a stereotype, absolutely let me personify a harmless one that's accurate as opposed to a toxic one that's completely false.[72]

Still, the most vocal concerns regarding *Shahs of Sunset* have come from the Iranian American community itself. Shortly after the show premiered, petitions began circulating among the Iranian American community to get the show taken off the air. One petition, which collected five hundred signatures on Change.org, protested the show's promotion of stereotypes. Jimmy Delshad, an Iranian American and former mayor of Beverly Hills, expressed concern that the show would "take us back and make us look like undesirable people."[73] The city of West Hollywood passed a resolution condemning *Shahs of Sunset* for perpetuating negative stereotypes.[74]

Yet, as numerous cultural theorists have pointed out, debating whether one stereotype is better or worse than another is not particularly productive.[75] A negative stereotype is defused not with a "better" stereotype, but with a diverse field of images. For the purposes of this chapter, the more pertinent question is not so much how *Shahs of Sunset* presents Iranian Americans, but how (or, indeed, whether) *Shahs of Sunset* presents *Muslim* Americans. The answer is complicated and warrants further elaboration, which I provide in the following section. On the one hand, *Shahs of Sunset* largely avoided the topic of Islam until season 3; on the other hand, whether avoiding Islam or addressing it directly, the show figures Islam as the binary opposite to American freedom. As a result, the cast of *Shahs of Sunset* is, ironically, read as "more American" than the cast of *All-American Muslim*.

Shahs of Sunset is consistent with the "rich bitch"[76] genre of reality television that focuses on wealthy, narcissistic cast members and invites viewers to judge them. At the same time, the show pushes boundaries with its portrayal of interracial, interfaith, and gay relationships, but the one boundary it is careful not to push too much is that around the cultural politics of Islam. Unlike the people featured in *All-American Muslim*, the cast members of *Shahs of Sunset* are not focused on proving their citizenship or patriotism. Nonetheless, certain markers are used to provide just such proof—namely, binary discourses about American freedom in comparison to Iran's lack of freedom. When Asa is about to have her first musical performance, she reflects on the significance of the event happening in the US, as opposed to Iran:

> My mom says, "We left Iran so you can be free and you don't have to wear chador." Being free and not wearing a chador has a huge meaning. It's not just a physical thing you wear. It's being able to express yourself as being a woman, even being an artist. Being who I am. I couldn't be me in Iran. Look at me. I would be an entirely different person.[77]

In season 3, Asa says that you can get killed for being gay in the Middle East,[78] and in other episodes she describes being "born

Muslim" as a way to indicate that she is not a practicing Muslim. Like "patriotism" in *All-American Muslim*, discourses about "freedom" in *Shahs of Sunset* indirectly and critically reference Islam, and it is this feature of freedom that serves as a proxy for one's "Americanness." In this way, *Shahs of Sunset* departs from *All-American Muslim*'s strategy of normalization through a narrow conception of patriotism and middle-class life. By seeking to present its protagonists not as "regular people," but as Others who are exoticized as much by their wealth as their ethnicity, *Shahs of Sunset* represents its cast members as assimilated in all the ways that matter—or more accurately, the one way that matters most. This strategy of assimilatory exoticization portrays the cast as exotic—in that they sprinkle their English with Farsi words like *joon* (dear) and *heyvoon bazi* (animal style)—but assimilable Others, for whom Islam is not central part of their identity and who are openly critical of Iran. They are nominal Muslims who are avid consumers, making them an ideal expression of neoliberal multiculturalism.

Extravagant and conspicuous consumption is portrayed as central to the cast members' identities and lifestyles—a strategy that cultural theorists such as Inderpal Grewal have highlighted for its ability to produce liberal subjects and American studies scholar Ida Yalzadeh says promotes Persian exceptionalism and capitalist multiculturalism.[79] Multiculturalism operates as a technology of hegemony, offering opportunities for racialized and gendered subjects to be interpellated into American identity through consumerism and consumer culture's emphasis on "choices."[80] According to Grewal, American identity, especially the notion of the American Dream, is deeply bound to consumer culture. The very phrase "American Dream," she argues, "connotes much more explicitly the close relationship between American national identity and consumer culture, as well as the ways in which American identity [is] a form of consumer nationalism."[81] In *Shahs of Sunset*, we see the cast members embrace the American Dream and become ideal subjects of US neoliberal multiculturalism through consumerism, secularism, and disavowal of Islam. Diversity is accomplished through assimilatory exoticization—portraying an exotic Other who is secular and invested in consumption, representing the upward mobility of the American Dream.

The cast members who are Muslim do not observe Muslim holidays. When Islamic observance is mentioned, it is part of one's background or heritage, but not part of their current lives. In contrast, Jewish holidays are observed and viewers have the opportunity to attend Shabbat dinner at Mike's parents' house and Reza's father's house. Jewishness is normalized, yet there are no parallels with Islam. It is as if the cast members left their "Muslim-ness" in Iran with the revolution. Coming to America is portrayed as the realization of a dream about freedom—the freedom to drink, the freedom to be sexually promiscuous, the freedom to have interfaith, interracial, and gay relationships, the freedom to be a rich consumerist narcissist, and perhaps most importantly, the freedom to practice one's Muslim faith as one wishes or, better yet, not at all.

Interestingly, despite the show's efforts to avoid or absent Islam for the first two seasons, some viewers still imposed this lens—with surprising results. A moderator on Bare Naked Islam, an anti-Islam website with the tagline "It isn't Islamophobia when they really ARE trying to kill you," actually defended Shahs of Sunset, initiating a debate while arguing that the cast members laudably refer to themselves as American and their Islam is downplayed:

> Yes, most of them are rich and spoiled (like the Housewives casts) but you never think of them as Muslims, only Americans of Iranian/Persian descent. The women wear sexy clothes, they play music, dance, sing, have sex, and drink liquor often. The character Reza is gay and one of the women said about him, "If Reza lived in Iran now, they would kill him for being gay." I said it after I saw the previews of this show and I can confirm it now, if all Muslims in America had the attitudes of these people, blogs like this one would not exist.[82]

Apparently, for the moderator, drinking, dancing, having sex, and wearing provocative clothing signify "American freedom" and thus operate as a proxy for "American patriotism" in the context of Islam. Some members of the site reacted with surprise that the moderator would actually praise a show that contains Muslims:

> you cannot trust any muslim and should not affiliate with any of them. . . . and all their "places of battle" aka mosques / aka masjids should be razed

to the ground in this and every country. let them live in a little sand patch isolated from civilization somewhere where they have no interaction whatsoever to do with any of US. honestly, when i read this article . . . i'm wondering is this site hacked.[83]

The Bare Naked Islam moderator elaborated:

It is a chance to see at least a few Muslims who don't consider themselves Muslims first and Americans last. They have embraced an American life-style where religion doesn't dictate every move they make. They dress like Americans instead of 7th century throwbacks, they have fun like Ameri-cans, and don't force little girls to cover their heads, or think that the way Americans dress is immoral. And you can bet they have a few pet dogs in the family. I doubt they are demanding special treatment and accom-modations for their religious needs from non-Muslims. There's even a storyline about a romance between a Muslim woman and a Jewish man. If they get serious, I doubt we'll see the Jewish man converting to Islam.[84]

With these implicit references to *All-American Muslim*—which showed, as mentioned earlier, a twelve-year-old girl putting on the hijab for the first time, an Irish American Catholic converting to Islam for marriage, conflict over having a dog as a domestic animal, and spe-cial accommodations at the high school for football training during Ramadan—the moderator makes clear that while the cast members of *All-American Muslim* are a threat to the US because they are observant Muslims, the cast members of *Shahs of Sunset* are acceptable Americans because Islam is insignificant to their lives.

Such notions reflect contemporary liberalism's reliance on a basic op-position: "the opposition between those who are ruled by culture, totally determined by the life-world into which they were born, and those who merely 'enjoy' their culture, who are elevated above it, free to choose their culture."[85] Slavoj Žižek elaborates that, in liberalism, culture is privatized, becoming "an expression of personal and private idiosyn-crasies."[86] In this way, the individual is prioritized over the collective. In both *All-American Muslim* and *Shahs of Sunset*, cast members negoti-ate this tension between individual and collective identities and desires. For example, in *All-American Muslim*, we watch Shadia's fiancée convert to Islam, and in *Shahs of Sunset*, we watch Mike's girlfriend prepare to convert to Judaism. However, in *All-American Muslim* religion moves beyond a private idiosyncrasy when the football team's practice schedule changes during Ramadan or when a woman cast member is unable to open a nightclub. In contrast, the cast members of *Shahs of Sunset* embrace individualism over the collective and are positively portrayed as being "above" religion. *Shahs of Sunset* cast members, while they often state that family is the most important thing and that family comes first, embrace consumerism, secularism, and free choice; culture is a vehicle to build a community, but it does not rule their choices or take priority over their individuality. Muslim normativity—and more specifically the nominal Muslim as normative—is constructed through consumerism, individualism, and, most importantly, secularism.

When *Shahs of Sunset* finally does address Islam explicitly, it does so in ways that reveal its deep ambivalence. This does not happen until season 3 and is confined to two episodes in which the cast members travel to Turkey.[87] Most of the cast members have not returned to Iran since they fled the country as children as a result of the 1979 revolution, nor have they traveled to any Muslim country. Each cast member has a different reaction to being in Turkey, seeing women in hijabs and niqabs, and hearing the call to prayer. These episodes finally provide an opening for a conversation about Islam and feature a range of reactions on the part of the cast members. The dominant message, however, remains consistent: Islam is essentially unfree and incompatible with American values.

At one point, the three women cast members are moved when they hear the call to prayer and connect with it as something beautiful.[88] MJ acknowledges that embracing being a nominal Muslim has been the path to acceptance for her in the US. She says:

> When you're a Muslim kid in America and you look like this, you hide it. When I'm asked if I'm Muslim, I respond yes, *but*. I always said yes, *but* I'm not practicing. Yes, *but* I'm not Islamic. Yes, because I'm afraid that I'm gonna be labeled as a terrorist. And for the first time in my life there was no shame attached to being a Muslim.

Golnesa is moved to tears by the call to prayer. She says: "In Iran, every day you hear that prayer everywhere. And that sound, it knocked the wind out of me." Asa connects deeply with the call to prayer as part of her heritage, and the three women stand outside of the mosque together with tears in their eyes.

However, this profound moment of portraying the Muslim call to prayer as beautiful is quickly tempered by Reza's and Mike's reactions. Echoing some of the most common, monolithic portrayals of Islam in the US, Reza reads the call as representing a culture that is anti-gay, while Mike reacts to it as antisemitic:

Reza: Hearing the call to prayer was jarring. I was worried that I'm a gay man standing outside of a mosque hearing this call to prayer and I'm thinking, if these people had X-ray vision and knew who I really was, would they start throwing stones at me?

Mike: No disrespect to Muslims but it scared the hell out of me. People are just rushing into the mosque. I got this overwhelming feeling inside of me that I couldn't help. I felt like a little kid that had lost his mom and dad and was looking for them. It was really weird. . . . At this very given moment, I'm feeling more Jewish than I am feeling Iranian. Because of my religion, I could have left Iran and went to Israel if I chose to because they would have taken me in. My country didn't want me, but my religion does. If I had to fight for one or the other, I would fight for Israel.[89]

Reza's comment underlines the notion that Islam is against freedom and that it is only in the United States that he can be himself as a gay man (putting aside the fact that public opinion on LGBTQ+ identities remains contested in the US). Similarly, Mike's comments affirm the idea that the US and Israel are closely aligned because they share values that are incompatible with "the Muslim world." The US and Israel thus represent freedom and democracy while the Middle East represents their opposite.

In addition to affirming the notion that Islam is anti-gay and antisemitic, these episodes of *Shahs of Sunset* also affirm the image of Islam as oppressive to women. Asa, MJ, and Golnesa are moved by the call to prayer—until they enter the mosque. There, they respond to gender segregation with disappointment and alienation. The association of Islam with the oppression of women continues during a conversation about the hijab (headscarf) and niqab (face veil). Reza states that the niqab freaks him out,[90] while Golnesa and Asa try to offer a more nuanced point of view, noting the niqab's cultural significance and critiquing only its mandatory imposition. But Reza remains adamant:

> No. I don't like it aesthetically. I don't like it symbolically. I don't like it religiously. I don't like it oppressively. I don't like anything it stands for. It separates people. It's such an in your face: We are this way, you guys are that way. I hate that.[91]

Reza then draws an analogy between the niqab and living one's life in the closet—further conflating Islam with an anti-LGBTQ+ disposition.

Reza's positionality is important to consider, not least because, as noted above, he is the most frequently interviewed and popular cast member. He also embodies what Jasbir Puar refers to as homonationalism[92] and what Ali Behdad and Juliet A. Williams refer to as neo-Orientalism.[93] He produces an ideology within his gay subjectivity that replicates dominant discourses about Islam that justify US intervention and invasion. Given that he is a native informant, his narrative of US progress and modernity in opposition to Iran and Islam holds "authenticity" or credibility. In this case, Reza, our homonationalist, is of Iranian Muslim/Jewish descent and his explicit disavowal of Islam is a crucial component to establishing his homonormativity and Americanness. His performance of nationalism positions him as a "real American" by delineating which kinds of Muslims should and should not be included in the land of the free. The season ends with Reza proposing marriage to his gay partner, the ultimate sign of homonationalism and American freedom.[94] Reza embodies Americanness in his affirmation of Orientalist discourses about the backward nature of Islam and his embrace of American sexual freedom and consumerist lifestyle.

A similarly heated debate takes place during season 6 when Reza plans a trip to Israel.[95] While Reza and Mike paint a rosy picture of Israel, insisting that it is a place of peace and unity, Golnesa and Shervin have hesitations regarding the extent to which they would feel welcome in Israel as Iranian Muslims. Reza insists that the choice to go to Israel is devoid of politics.

REZA: Are you in?

GOLNESA: What about like Tahiti?

REZA: No, here is another reason why I wanna go—gay people are like accepted there.

GOLNESA: They're cool with gays but not Palestinians.

REZA: No dude, they just don't like the ones that wear bombs.

GOLNESA: They wanna bomb Iran.

REZA: We're just going on a vacation. Fuck Iran.[96]

In a separate interview commenting on their conversation, Golnesa elaborates: "That is a very extreme statement to make because guess where you're from, homie. You represent being Persian but you say fuck yourself as well. You're like a walking oxymoron right now." Reza continues the conversation: "We're not trying to make a political statement. We're just going on a vacation." Then, in an interview about the conversation, Reza says: "Don't get me wrong, I love the Iranian people. My anger is with the government: you can't be different, you can't be gay. And I cannot wait until they're gone." In this debate, Golnesa defends her Iranian Muslim identity and challenges Reza's binary attitude. These debates are important moments in the show that not only offer insight into different perspectives and experiences of being Iranian and Muslim, but challenge Reza on his anti-Muslim racism.

This debate continues in Israel, where Reza and Mike describe and experience Palestinian people and areas as violent and unruly, but describe Israeli people and areas as peaceful, orderly, and full of love.[97] Golnesa challenges them on this and says that their attitude toward Muslims is offensive. Despite such debates, Israel is portrayed as a place where this groups of friends can drink, party, and have a good time. The way in which Israel is ultimately figured as a welcoming place further operates to code the cast of *Shahs of Sunset* as the right kind of Muslims. The right kind of Muslim agrees to visit Israel and accepts it as a place of peace, coexistence, and love; the right kind of Muslim understands that Israel's safety is threatened by Palestinians (figured as Muslim) who have hate in their hearts; the right kind of Muslim gets that Israel is a place where one can debate freely, be openly gay, and drink and party; the right kind of Muslim agrees to go to Israel and does not attempt to go to Gaza or the West Bank. While Golnesa adamantly defends Islam and even questions the Israeli government's treatment of Palestinians, the word "occupation" is never uttered.

A Muslim's relationship to Israel plays a significant role in crafting the acceptable Muslim. In *Shahs of Sunset*, Muslim (and Iranian) cast members' relationship to Israel is negotiated through an actual trip to Israel in which the normative acceptable nominal Muslim is also importantly a supporter of the Israeli government. *All-American Muslim* also has an episode in which Muslim cast members articulate their friendliness to Israel. In one episode, two cast members—Bilal and Shadia—travel to New York to visit the site of the 9/11 attacks as part of their expression of US patriotism. While there, they have tattoos done by famous Israeli tattoo artist Ami James, star of the reality show *NY Ink*.[98] Bilal is concerned that because James served in the Israel Defense Forces and was stationed in Lebanon, their visit might be tense when James sees Bilal's tattoo of the Lebanese flag. Instead, the two end up having a conversation about how politics interferes with peace and coexistence. James says that his Israeli passport bars him from visiting many countries from Egypt to Ireland and that he cannot expect to be safe there. He also says that it is a shame that they have to leave their countries to become friends, and he jokes (with no acknowledgement of the politics of cultural appropriation) that the only war there should be between Jews and Muslims is over who makes a better falafel. Both Bilal and Shadia say that they were enlightened by their conversation with James. They show that they are the right kind of Muslims who can be friends with Israelis, even those who have served in the Israel Defense Forces and participated in the destruction of Lebanon, their home country. This tense interaction with a happy ending gives the impression that (Arab) Muslims and (Ashkenazi) Jews ordinarily cannot be friends because of interpersonal differences, overlooking that the issue is not an interpersonal one but about the illegal Israeli military occupation of Palestine.

It is important to emphasize, however, that what makes *Shahs of Sunset* both popular and (problematically) powerful is not its overtly anti-Iran and/or anti-Muslim moments, but its delivery of such sentiments through the discourse of liberal multiculturalism. Transnational media studies scholar Raka Shome writes that a "striking thing about the narrativization of multiculturalism in public discourses in

the United States [. . . is how it] is often used as evidence of its tolerance and openness in relation to many 'other worlds'—today, especially
Muslim worlds—whose cultures are dismissed as monolithic, rigid,
backwards, and closed."[99] Both Sara Ahmed and Žižek point out that
the logic of multiculturalism allows racism to be articulated, under the
guise of free speech, as signifying freedom in a democratic system.[100]
Reza and Mike exemplify this double move of multiculturalism. On
the one hand, they are incorporated into neoliberal multiculturalism
as subjects of difference, epitomizing US multicultural exceptionalism.
On the other hand, they represent ideal subjects of both liberal multiculturalism and neoliberal multiculturalism. Their expression of anti-
Muslim racism and disdain of the collective in Islam positions them as
ideal liberal subjects. As an Iranian Muslim/Jewish and Iranian Jewish
Other, respectively, their inclusion as acceptable is leveraged against
the imagined intolerance of those *other* Iranian/Muslim Others whose
identities and affinities challenge the limits and expectations of liberal
multiculturalism. Their disavowal of Islam coupled with their embrace
of Israel are central elements to constructing their normativity. They are
ideal subjects of neoliberalism both because of their consumerism and
as people who have leveraged their Iranian identity for monetary gain
through reality television. They have successfully capitalized on their
exotic difference and made it consumable to a broad audience.

In season 6, Reza plans a "Gaza Strip, Peace in the Middle East Halloween Party" to celebrate their upcoming trip to Israel. He astutely describes his friends as follows:

> At this Halloween party we're representing both Jews and Muslims and
> my crew breaks down like this: You've got swervin' Shervin who's Muslim
> but drinks more alcohol than any Irishman I've ever met. Then we have
> our fair Golnesa who is covered head to toe in biblical Arab Allah tattoos
> which really doesn't go along with your Muslim heritage. Then there is
> MJ who is as frugal as my half Jewish side but she is pure Muslim. And
> then we have Asa who is the most Muslimey-Muslim of the Muslims.
> And then there is Mike who is 100 percent Jewish, wants his wife to be
> Jewish and his kids to be raised Jewish but he'll eat a shrimp in a hot
> minute. And then there's me. I'm half Muslim, half Jewish, and all gay. So
> I'm all confused.[101]

These words are spoken over a montage of images that include Shervin drinking and partying, Golnesa wearing a bikini in a hot tub with her Arab-style tattoos showing, MJ bargaining at a store, Asa dressed in a chador on the streets of LA as part of an artistic project, Mike praying and eating shrimp, and Reza kissing his husband. This is the brand of acceptable Americanized Islam that is promoted; the normative Muslim drinks, parties, has sex, is an avid consumerist, and most importantly, either disavows Islam or engages with Islam peripherally. In addition, as we will see with Bill Maher's nominal Muslim, this nominal/normative Muslim is Islamophobic, casting Islam as not tolerant when it comes to women and LGBTQ+ people, and embraces Israel as a nation that promotes peace, coexistence, and liberal values.

In the shifting context of the cultural politics of Islam in America, same-sex, interfaith, and interracial relationships are portrayed as symbols of American freedom and progress in contexts referencing Islam, eliding the contestation of such issues within the US itself. In a sense, *Shahs of Sunset* succeeded and *All-American Muslim* did not because of how each engaged with the tension between being Muslim and being American. It seems that, in the 2010–2015 period, Muslims could be included in (neo)liberal multiculturalism only when and if Islam was, at minimum, not that important to their identity, and ideally, completely irrelevant. To put it more bluntly, while *All-American Muslim* failed in its attempt to make Islam palatable by wrapping it in a patriotic American flag, *Shahs of Sunset* won viewers and approval by driving away from Islam in a Mercedes-Benz.

Real Time with Bill Maher's Incompatible Muslims

In this next part of the chapter, I offer a close reading of an episode of *Real Time with Bill Maher*, in which the eponymous host argues that—with the singular exception of the nominal, explicitly nonreligious Muslim—almost all Muslims are incompatible with the liberal values of individual rights, equality, and pluralism. The nominal Muslim was already being popularized on *Shahs of Sunset*, but Bill Maher's show articulated the category explicitly and related it to supposedly liberal (and thus, according to the show's logic, American) principles. On October 3, 2014, Bill Maher's panel included *New York Times* bestselling author and key figure in the New Atheism movement Sam Harris, actor and filmmaker Ben Affleck, Pulitzer Prize–winning journalist Nicholas Kristof, and former chairperson of the Republican National Committee Michael Steele.[102] During the panel's discussion, both Bill Maher and Sam Harris asserted that Islam fundamentally clashes with liberal principles like freedom of speech and equality for women and LGBTQ+ people, yet liberals in the US fail to point this out because of their commitment to political correctness. The only solution to this problem, Maher and Harris argued, was for the West to throw support behind "nominal Muslims"—Muslims in name only, not in practice—in the hopes of effecting reform within Islam to make it more compatible with liberal values. The other panelists challenged these comments, characterizing them as Islamophobic, and the whole episode soon went viral, prompting yet another cycle of op-eds[103] and news coverage[104] in which Islam's diversity or lack thereof was debated.

My point is not to argue that *Real Time* promotes noninclusive or illiberal values; to the contrary, I find Maher and Harris's arguments to be entirely consistent with Western liberalism, its checkered history, and internal contradictions. Instead, I seek to unpack the implications of their arguments, paying particular attention to the limits of neoliberal multiculturalism they reveal and the reductive and contradictory categories of Muslims they construct. To simply write off Maher and Harris's comments as Islamophobic or blanket generalizations misses the nuance and complexity that makes such statements repugnant, yes, but also resilient.

The discussion relevant to this chapter lasted approximately ten minutes. Maher begins it as follows:

> Liberals need to stand up for liberal principles [. . .] like freedom of speech, freedom to practice any religion you want without fear of violence, freedom to leave a religion, equality for women, equality for minorities including homosexuals. These are liberal principles that liberals applaud for, but then when you say in the Muslim world, this is what's lacking, then they get upset.

Sam Harris chimes in, agreeing and stating that liberals have "failed on the topic of theocracy" because they do not want to criticize the

Figure 1.3. From left to right: Ben Affleck, Sam Harris, and Bill Maher on *Real Time with Bill Maher*, HBO, October 3, 2014, photo by Janet Van Ham, Associated Press.

failure of liberal principles within the Muslim world. Any criticism of Islam, he argues, gets conflated with criticism of the people and unproductively labeled as Islamophobia. Ben Affleck, clearly offended by their line of thinking, asks if they are questioning whether Islamophobia is a real thing (see figure 1.3). Bill Maher replies, "Well, it's not a real thing when we do it." The audience laughs at this seemingly facetious response, but a serious Maher repeats, "It really isn't." Harris acknowledges that some people are bigoted against Muslims but argues that he and Maher are simply making the point that bad ideas should be subject to criticism—and that "Islam at this moment is the mother lode of bad ideas."

The discussion becomes heated as Affleck describes their argument as racist and offensive. Nicholas Kristof points out that the image Maher and Harris are painting is "hugely incomplete"—that ISIS might fit that profile, but not those Muslims who fight for liberal principles like Muhammad Ali and Malala Yousefzai. Affleck interjects, "Or how about the over a billion people who aren't fanatical, who

don't punch women, who just want to go to school, have some sandwiches, pray five times a day, and don't do any of the things that you're
saying?" Michael Steele agrees with Kristof and states that voices challenging extremists do not get heard or receive the same platform as
extremists. He cites the example of clerics in Australia, Europe, and
the US who have risked their lives to take a stance against ISIS, but
have not received media coverage. Maher retorts that it is not about a
platform, but that Muslims are too scared to speak out because they
will be killed "if you say the wrong thing, draw the wrong picture, or
write the wrong book."

Throughout the discussion, both Maher and Harris insist that while
only a minority of Muslims are violent extremists, the majority hold
extremist views that are in opposition to liberal principles. Maher cites
a Pew poll showing that 90 percent of Egyptians believe that death
is appropriate for those who leave the religion. When Affleck challenges Harris to provide a solution, however, Harris seems to contra-
dict this point by saying, "There are hundreds of millions of Muslims
who are nominal Muslims, who don't take the faith seriously, who don't
want to kill apostates, who are horrified by ISIS, and we need to defend
these people, prop them up, and let them reform their faith." Nonetheless, both Harris and Maher end by reaffirming that extremists are not
a minority; as Maher puts it, "In the Muslim world, it [extremism] is
mainstream belief."

The debate on *Real Time with Bill Maher* reveals that the level of conversation about Islam in the US is less than rudimentary and in urgent
need of remediation. Under what conditions can accurate statements
be made about 1.8 billion people? While Maher and Harris's views seem
to blend into one voice on the show, their approaches are actually distinct from one another. Maher tends to present the world's Muslims
as being essentially the same: against liberal principles like freedom of
speech and freedom of religion and against equal rights for women and
LGBTQ+ people. In contrast, Harris (both on the show and in his writings) conceptualizes Muslims in concentric circles with "jihadists," like
ISIS and al-Qaeda, at the core, followed by Islamists who are politically
motivated but not violent. He says that these two circles comprise 20
percent of Muslims, and he adds that 20 percent is a conservative esti-
mate. The next concentric circle comprises Muslims who support violent

jihad in some way but would not be personally involved. The next circle he describes in his 2015 book with Maajid Nawaz, *Islam and the Future of Tolerance*:

> Finally, one hopes, there is a much larger circle of so-called moderate Muslims, whether they would label themselves that way or not, who want to live by more modern values. Although they may not be quite secular, they don't think that groups like [ISIS] represent their faith. Perhaps there are also millions of truly secular Muslims who just don't have a voice.[105]

According to Harris and Nawaz, those who are violent or support violence are at the center of Islam while those who are not oriented toward violence are farther away; all ultimately exist within a spectrum of one's closeness to or distance from violence. On the show, Harris says, in agreement with Maher's larger argument, that Muslims who are not jihadists nonetheless hold problematic views on human rights, women's rights, and gay rights, and "keep women and homosexuals immiserated in these cultures." Thus, he concludes, "we have to empower the true reformers in the Muslim world to change it and lying about the link between doctrine and behavior is not going to do that."[106] In other words, Muslim moderates are problematic because they believe in the doctrine while secular Muslims (that is, nominal Muslims) are the true hope because they are presumably not religious.

In his 2004 book *The End of Faith: Religion, Terror, and the Future of Reason*, Harris argues that there are problems inherent to all faiths and that religious moderates get in the way of understanding those problems. Such moderates, he states,

> are themselves the bearers of terrible dogma: they imagine that the path to peace will be paved once each of us has learned to respect the unjustified beliefs of others. . . . [T]he very ideal of religious tolerance—born of the notion that every human being should be free to believe whatever he wants about God—is one of the principle forces driving us toward the abyss.[107]

While Harris is critical of all religious moderates, he reserves his harshest criticisms for Muslim moderates. It is this perspective that he was promoting on *Real Time with Bill Maher* and is the reason why Maher, who identifies as an atheist, invited Harris on his show: to bolster and add credibility to his own position that all religious Muslims pose a danger to liberalism and that nominal Muslims are needed to reform Islam.

On the one hand, there was nothing surprising about the discussion.[108] As is common in conversations about Islam in the United States, Islam is figured as a foreign religion but not a domestic or historic part of the US (aside from Nicholas Kristof's passing reference to Muhammad Ali). Similarly and depressingly familiar, too, were the invocations of women's rights and LGBTQ+ rights as the purported litmus tests of Western liberalism—invocations that, as usual, elided any opposition to or ambivalence regarding such rights within the US.[109] In addition, Islam is discussed as if there are no debates or internal disagreements, as if Western interference—in this case propping up nominal Muslims—is necessary to bring about social change within Islam.[110] These are common themes that several scholars and civil rights groups have identified in news media and dominant discourses that produce and justify anti-Muslim racism. For example, in their examination of op-eds published in the *Wall Street Journal*, Suad Joseph and Benjamin D'Harlingue find that Islam is portrayed as incompatible with modernity and as linked to fanaticism and terrorism.[111] Similarly, media studies scholar Deepa Kumar points to Western representations of Islam in the media as a monolithic, uniquely sexist, and inherently violent religion.[112]

On the other hand, it was the consistent reoccurrence of this approach to Islam on *Real Time with Bill Maher*—a show (and host) generally considered left-leaning—that struck many as surprising, thus fueling the episode's "viral" popularity. For many on the political left, Islamophobia is understood as perpetrated by those on the political right. Among right-wing commentators, the very notion of Islamophobia is often derided as a politically correct way to shut down legitimate criticism of Islam, hindering rational efforts to confront real problems like "terrorism." What was so notable about Maher's arguments was their resonance with this logic and their identical denial of any kind of bias or racism.

When it comes to Muslims, however, it is not unusual to find ideological convergence between the political left and right. Steven Salaita has written extensively on how the left promotes anti-Muslim racism, revealing that such ideologies are not unique to the right.[113] Arun Kundnani identifies a "liberal form of anti-Muslim racism" that uses the language of "values" rather than race or ethnicity. Like Maher, its proponents rationalize it as "no more than criticism of an alien belief system—hostility to religious beliefs rather than to a racial group—and therefore entirely distinct from racism."[114] But as Kundani points out, such arguments merely use religious belonging as a proxy for racial difference, thus producing a form of anti-Muslim racism entirely consistent with liberal principles. Indeed, I would argue that it is liberal principles—or at least a particular vision of liberal principles—that unites such anti-Muslim racist arguments on both sides of the political spectrum.

To be sure, not all criticisms of Islam fall into the category of anti-Muslim racism. However, what makes Maher a promoter of this form of racism is his essentialist approach to Islam and Muslims. Harris, meanwhile, contributes to anti-Muslim racism through his simplistic understanding of terrorism and religious extremism. In *The End of Faith*, he states that 9/11 happened because the Muslim men involved believed that they would go to paradise for doing what they did. Echoing Bernard Lewis's seminal text "The Roots of Muslim Rage," Harris writes that we can understand terrorism not through the optics of grievances with Western imperialism, but through understanding Muslims as fearing Western contamination and being wrought with feelings of humiliation because the West has surpassed them as a great empire. He states that bin Laden's grievances with US support of Israel and US troops in Saudi Arabia are religious in nature, not political, that they derive from scripture.[115] Ultimately, he is claiming that the key to understanding terrorism is understanding Islam. This is a very dangerous and misleading approach that dismisses the complex factors that contribute to Muslim-led violence in the Middle East region, from Western foreign policies to failed Arab governance and social and economic factors that produce social alienation.[116]

Religious studies scholar Mohammad Hassan Khalil takes on Harris's arguments about Islam and Islamic scripture, pointing out the many flaws in his assessments: that he is unfamiliar with modern Muslim scholarly arguments against the practice of aggressive jihad, that he overlooks the many Muslim leaders and scholars who condemn terrorism, that he ignores the many Muslims in the West who are active and proud citizens, and that he pays no attention to the fact that countless religious Muslims have lived peacefully with people of all faiths. Khalil writes, "All things considered, most Muslim theologians would likely balk at [Harris's] claim that the non-Muslims who died on 9/11 were all simply 'fuel for the eternal fires of God's justice.'"[117] While Harris's approach to Muslims might seem more nuanced than Maher's, he nonetheless echoes and bolsters Maher's argument about the fundamental incompatibility between Muslims and liberal society.

Philosopher Falguni Sheth provides a useful definition of liberalism as "a political philosophy that identifies the rational individual as the primary political unit in society."[118] Central to this political approach is the freedom of the individual to govern their affairs, limited interference from the state, and a commitment to the rule of law and pluralism demonstrated through the toleration of cultural, ethnic, religious, and other kinds of "difference."[119] This political philosophy is promoted as civilized, especially in contrast to other political orders that are doomed illiberal and thus barbaric.[120] Both political liberals and conservatives embrace liberalism as a political philosophy, though they disagree on the role of the government in solving social problems and the extent to which forms of "difference" should be "tolerated."

What I want to highlight here is liberalism's reliance upon and reinforcement of monolithic oppositional binaries—freedom/non-freedom, modern/antiquated, civilized/barbaric, tolerance/intolerance, and so on. Of course, such binaries are not new to liberalism, but central to Eurocentrism, nationalism, and other hierarchical ideologies, and numerous scholars have shown liberalism's historical role in legitimating imperial and colonial projects. American studies scholar Lisa Lowe argues that "liberal philosophy, culture, economics, and government have been commensurate with, and deeply implicated in, colonialism, slavery, capitalism, and empire."[121] Sheth writes that "[t]he British and American empires promoted the ideal vision of liberalism at the same time that they were engaged in extremely destructive and violent expansionism. [. . .] In fact, a great deal of insight can be gained by understanding how the ideal vision of liberalism and empire were working hand-in-hand."[122] As such, it is not the exception, but the rule in liberalism that humanity is denied to some, whether based on race, religion, or in this case, the racialization of religion.

The purported elements that make Muslims incompatible with liberalism—delineated by Maher and Harris as the inability to appreciate the importance of free speech, hostility toward women's rights and LGBTQ+ rights, support of the death penalty for apostates—are presented as fact through racializing discourses. The categories of acceptable Muslims who are "moderate" or "nominal" shows that there is a path to inclusion available if one sheds or modifies their religious identity. Sociologist Mitra Rastegar shows that marking certain Muslims as tolerable retains their association with a potential threat.[123] She demonstrates that discourses of tolerance provide variables of assessment to ascertain the potential threat of Muslims. Thus, even those deemed patriotic, moderate, or compatible with liberal values are susceptible to losing their status; the same standards used to deem some Muslims as worthy of tolerance can then be used against them.

There is, in fact, a long history of media portrayals of Muslims who "revert" to their essential barbaric nature. In the 1921 film *The Sheik*, Rudy Valentino's character exhibits a capacity for rational thought as a European, but also brutishness as a Westerner "gone Arab/Muslim." If we fast-forward to the 1991 film *Not Without My Daughter*, we are introduced to an Iranian American doctor who is a kind husband and father in Michigan but then transforms into an abusive husband upon arrival in Iran, as if regressing and revealing his "true" Muslim essence.[124] In the FX series *Tyrant*, the longer Westernized Barry (aka Bassam) stays in Abuddin, the more he becomes a dictator.[125] The paths available for Muslim inclusion in liberalism tend to be precarious. Furthermore, liberalism itself purports to be inclusive, yet the productions of racialized discourses to justify exclusion are central to liberal ideologies. Given that liberalism has been implicated in slavery and colonialism, and continues to be implicated in interventionist policies, it is not inconsistent for it to exclude Muslims today. And as liberalism has developed into neoliberalism, the same exclusionary principle stands. As Grewal writes, "Neoliberalism relies on racial, religious, and gender exclusions as much as did liberalism."[126]

Furthermore, the position of religious Muslims as incompatible with liberal principles is not unique. Catholics, Jews, Mormons, atheists, and other religious minorities have been historically excluded from US conceptions of Americanness despite a commitment to liberalism as an ideal political system.[127] Liberalism should be understood as rooted in a paradox of inclusion and exclusion, equality and inequality. Thus, Maher and Harris's argument dehumanizing observant Muslims exemplifies this paradox in which exclusion is consistent with liberalism, not exceptional to it. Indeed, Joseph Massad, scholar of Arab politics, argues that Islam has been central to the formation of liberalism as an ideology and political identity in the same way that Edward Said describes Orientalism[128] as central to the formation of European identity in the nineteenth century, in that Islam became the Other through which Western liberalism would define itself. Massad points out how Western liberalism has constructed Islam as its Other—opposed to "freedom, liberty, equality, the rights-bearing individual, democratic citizenship, women's rights, sexual rights, freedom of belief, secularism, rationality, etc., in short as a pathology."[129]

The racialized assumptions of liberalism are thus built into the terms of "liberal" debate itself, regardless of whether or not one identifies as being on the political left or right. Most remarkably, liberal values can be used to justify their own suspension. Consider Maher's invocation of the common argument in liberal multicultural societies that there ought to be a limit to liberalism's tolerance—that is, liberalism cannot and should not tolerate intolerance.[130] By painting Islam and thus all religious Muslims as intolerant, Maher rationalizes their derogation as reasonable criticism of "bad ideas." It is precisely his self-identified commitment to liberal values that enables Maher to insist that he is not being racist and that it is not Islamophobia "when we do it." Maher touts statistics to justify the dehumanization of Muslims and to exempt himself from being a promoter of anti-Muslim racism similar to how racial scientists have used "facts" throughout history to justify racism and inequality.[131] The tautology of the argument immunizes the liberal subject (read: Maher) from critique, while stripping its target (read: Muslims) of reason and thus humanity. For if Muslims were capable of reasoning, they would embrace liberal principles; but because religious Muslims reject liberal principles *by definition*, they cannot be capable of reasoning and therefore are not deserving of respect or human dignity.[132]

Maher does not mention that the same Pew poll he cites that finds that 90 percent of Egyptians agree that death is the appropriate response to those that leave Islam also finds that the majority of Muslims favor religious freedom for people of other faiths, favor democracy over authoritarian rule, and see no inherent tension between being religiously devout and living in a modern society.[133] This complex portrait depicted in the Pew poll is overlooked. Furthermore, a 2017 Pew poll showed that Muslims in the US have become more accepting of homosexuality—52 percent say homosexuality should be accepted by society.[134] Among Americans, the findings are not drastically different: 55 percent have a favorable view of gay men and 58 percent have a favorable view of lesbian women.[135] Evangelical Christians oppose homosexuality by larger margins.[136] Among the other findings were that 64 percent said that there is more than one way to interpret Islamic teachings, 69 percent said that working toward social justice is part of the faith, and 75 percent said that targeting civilians can never be justified for a religious or political cause. These findings are a direct challenge to Maher and Harris's claim that Muslims are incompatible with liberal values. Given the essentialized portrait of Islam commonly promoted in US media and political discourses, it is no surprise that the poll also revealed that half of American Muslims have experienced at least one form of religious discrimination in the last year.

Though the October 3, 2014, episode of *Real Time with Bill Maher* became a viral sensation, given its seeming revelation of anti-Muslim racism "even" on a show with a progressive reputation,[137] what made it most interesting was not the repetition of old stereotypes, but the articulation of new categories of Muslims—namely, the nominal Muslim, the heroic Muslim, and the sandwich-eating Muslim. Though clearly related to their predecessors, the nominal and heroic Muslim categories offer new insights into the contradictions of liberal inclusion, while Ben Affleck's sandwich-eating Muslim opens a space for Muslim Americans in the popular imagination predicated on their common humanity, rather than their difference.

In defining the nominal Muslim, Harris, as quoted above, says, "There are hundreds of millions of Muslims who are nominal Muslims who don't take the faith seriously, who don't want to kill apostates, who are horrified by ISIS, and we need to defend these people, prop them up, and let them reform their faith." Harris assumes that the prevailing interpretations of Islam are threatening and thus that the entire religion needs reform. Who should lead this reform movement? Nominal Muslims—those who are Muslim in name only but not in practice; those who were raised Muslim but for whom Islam is insignificant in their lives.

Here we see the continuation of an age-old colonial strategy of using particular groups of "natives" to assimilate others. It assumes that Muslims have no capacity for agency unless it is activated and directed by the West. In addition, Muslims who are not religious or who have left Islam are embraced or propped up as those who should reform the religion. Where is the line between the nominal Muslim and other kinds of "good Muslims," such as the moderate Muslim? It seems that the nominal Muslim is not the same as the moderate Muslim. The moderate Muslim can still be Muslim but knows to keep their religion private (and to cooperate with the government in counterterrorism endeavors). The nominal Muslim, however, is either no longer a practicing Muslim or has left the religion entirely. In other words, this version of the "good Muslim" is no longer Muslim; they are cultural Muslims as opposed to religious Muslims. Unlike the moderate Muslim, nominal Muslims "don't even take the faith seriously." Nominal Muslims are essentially not Muslims, but they can still be referred to and activated *as* Muslims by a West seeking to reform Islam from within. This crucially leaves agency not with the Muslims, but with those who know how to prop them up to serve Western interests. If the nominal Muslim who is a cultural Muslim, not a religious Muslim, is the answer, then according to this logic, Muslims are acceptable in neoliberal multiculturalism as long as they are not religious.

Maher and Harris position themselves as courageous for speaking out despite the norms of political correctness. They also position nominal Muslims as courageous for risking their lives to speak out against Islam. The use of the language of courage and bravery serves to co-opt courage. This is a common tactic used by those in the Islamophobia Industry in promoting anti-Muslim racism—to present individuals and their arguments as courageous instead of racist.[138] Courage also plays a central role in Kristof and Steele's disagreement with the portrait of Islam promoted by Maher and Harris. They do not see Islam as incompatible with liberalism, and to make their point, they list courageous Muslims who fight for humanity and speak out against injustice. According to Kristof and Steele, there are Muslim heroes who present a more diverse portrait of Islam. These are Muslims who have been victimized—like Malala Yousefzai—and who have fought for their rights and for the rights of others—like professional boxer and civil rights activist Muhammad Ali. Kristof (on the show and then in an op-ed that elaborated on his position) gives the examples of Mohammad Ali Dadkhah in Iran, who has been in prison for years for defending Christians, and Rashid Rehman, who was killed in Pakistan for defending people accused of apostasy. What is important here is that Kristof and Steele are challenging Maher's depiction of Muslims as having no agency unless activated by the West. They are showing that Muslims do have agency and do fight for liberal principles and risk their lives doing it. It is an important challenge, but it also reinscribes the notion that to be Muslim is essentially to be a victim, unless one has the courage to be a hero. Most of the examples of heroic Muslims are outside the US, thus once again marking Islam as a foreign religion. The things heroic Muslims have done are truly extraordinary in the sense that they are not ordinary, everyday actions. Most of them end up dead, seriously injured, or in prison, making them martyrs of a sort. Thus, a doomed form of heroism is possible for a small number of people. This narrative reinforces the notion that only a small minority of Muslims are "good," in this case as heroes.

And then we have Ben Affleck's challenge to Maher and Harris, which oddly ends up being the most astute criticism in this debate. I say oddly because the film *Argo*, which Affleck produced and in which he stars, is an exercise in monolithic portraits of Islam. Covering the events of the 1979–1980 Iran hostage crisis, it portrays Iranian Muslims as threatening, irrational, and incapable of individual rational thought.[139] Affleck, as quoted above, says, "How about the over a billion people who aren't fanatical, who don't punch women, who just want to go to school, have some sandwiches, pray five times a day, and don't do any of [those] things?" He importantly criticizes Maher and Harris for painting a monolithic image of Islam as fanatical and unreasonable and challenges it through the "ordinary Muslim" who wants to eat sandwiches. He is asking, what about Muslims who are just people living their lives—who are not heroes, or nominal, or patriotic, or defectors? In the political climate in which we live, where remediation is needed in conversations about Islam, such a banal statement becomes a significant intervention into this debate. In other words, "sandwiches" is not radical in itself. But given the context in which Muslims come in predetermined categories that deny their humanity, "sandwiches" and Affleck's invocation of "over a billion people" becomes an important intervention in this conversation.

The Nominal Muslim and the Limits of Inclusion

Expansions to liberal multiculturalism occur through crisis, leading to the creation of specific types of acceptable Muslims. In examining efforts to expand representations of Muslims between 2010 and 2015, I am seeking to illustrate that such efforts can instead produce restrictive categories of what constitutes a "good Muslim." I have considered the various kinds of "good Muslims" that liberal discourses have promoted since 9/11 to highlight the limited ways in which Muslims can be imagined and thus the limits of liberal multiculturalism. The new category that promises inclusion in 2010–2015, the nominal Muslim, is predicated on not being a religious believer. Maher's commitment to liberal values enables him to exclude religious Muslims while arguing for inclusive ideals. It is assumed in this logic that to be in favor of liberal principles as a Muslim is possible only if Islam is religiously insignificant or irrelevant to one's life. Otherwise, the Muslim must pass a slew of litmus tests in advocating for women's rights, LGBTQ+ rights, and free speech (litmus tests to which other Americans are not subjected) or be designated a lesser human who deserves to be dehumanized.

At first glance, the very existence of *All-American Muslim* and *Shahs of Sunset* is a signifier of multicultural progress in their representation of Muslims as Americans during a time when the place of Muslims in the US remains, in *real* reality, deeply contested. Examination of these two shows reveals the limits of liberal multiculturalism. Both series demonstrate, in different ways, how multiculturalism tames difference rather than celebrates it, produces consumerism over rights, and operates to promote the US as exceptional. Just because Muslims are incorporated into reality television does not necessarily signify progress toward racial justice. The creation of specific types of acceptable Muslims is shaped by neoliberal commodity culture that appropriates and commodifies the Other. In the case of TLC's *All-American Muslim*, viewers refused to "eat the Other" because it did not spice up one's life as promised.[140] The focus on producing Muslim normativity led to losing the spice. While it might have satisfied the requirements of liberal multiculturalism through producing patriotic Arab-Muslims who could be included in the US national imaginary, it did not satisfy the requirements of neoliberal multiculturalism's consumerism and profit objectives. In contrast, *Shahs of Sunset* on Bravo was able to make money from the nominal Muslim who also fit into their "rich bitch" genre. Bravo proved that the nominal Muslim was marketable, especially in embodying the consumer-extraordinaire and just the right amount of ethnic difference to enable audiences to "eat the Other." It seems that secularism and consumerism have become prerequisites to including Muslim difference in US neoliberal multiculturalism in the late-stage War on Terror.

In addition to arguing that crisis diversity at this particular moment results in a limited expansion in representations that are confined and defined by their response to a particular stereotype, I broaden the frame to show that the limits to inclusion are a core feature of liberalism. The types of normative Muslims that emerge for inclusion in response to crisis are direct responses to images that justify exclusion. The patriotic Muslim is offered as the antidote to the figure of the terrorist and the nominal Muslim as the antidote to the figure of the religious fanatic Muslim who presumably seeks to install Sharia law in the US. The popularization of the nominal Muslim as an alternative to the patriotic Muslim in the 2010s, and by US Muslim writers themselves like Aziz Ansari, with *Master of None* (2015–2021), or Kumail Nanjiani, with *The Big Sick* (2017), still positions Muslims as needing to prove their humanity and belonging. Expanded representation is not in itself better representation. Insisting on this distinction is not "nitpicking" or failing to appreciate those relative gains that have been made. It is, rather, a continued demand for abundant, well-rounded, and historically and regionally accurate portrayals that reflect Arabs', Iranians', and Muslims' full diversity and humanity. While the nominal Muslim signifies one way Muslims get included in diversity politics and highlights the operations of stereotype-confined expansions in response to crisis, the next chapter will show that the field of representations and parameters of potential inclusion shift depending on the political moment defined by the next crisis.

2

The Diversity Compromise

In 2018, Leila Fadel at NPR reported that Hollywood was having a "Muslim moment," marking more representations of Muslims and more nuanced representations.[1] The news story mentions *East of La Brea*—a short-form digital show about a friendship between two twenty-something-year-old women, an African American Muslim and a Bangladeshi American Muslim—and *Ramy*, a Hulu comedy that features an Arab American Muslim family, the first television show to do so. Fadel described this increase in popular cultural representations of Muslim characters as reflecting a defiant Hollywood's response to Donald Trump's Muslim ban. Writers and producers disturbed by the increase in overt white supremacist ideology that accompanied the Muslim ban, and the Trump presidency in general, were inspired to do their part in fostering a more socially inclusive nation. When Fawzia Mirza, for example, a writer for the TV show *The Red Line*, was asked about a queer Indian Muslim character she created, she explained that originally there was no such character in the show, but the creators "were thinking, 'How do we take this story to another level?', especially living in the political climate of a time where our president wants to ban Muslims and Muslims are deeply vilified by every aspect of this system. They thought, 'What if we made him Muslim?'"[2] Another writer, Marc Guggenheim, added a Muslim computer hacker superhero, Zari Adrianna Tomaz (played by Tala Ashe), to the show *DC Legends of Tomorrow* in 2017 after his Muslim sister-in-law shared with him how difficult it was to be Muslim given the political climate.[3] And when the *New York Times* hosted a roundtable discussion with five showrunners about representations of Muslims on TV, two weeks after the election of Donald Trump, Joshua Safran of the TV show *Quantico* said he did not want to see any more shows about terrorism during the Trump administration because it was more important to provide hope during dark times.[4]

Donald Trump first announced his idea for a Muslim ban while on the campaign trail by releasing a statement in December 2015. It stated:

Donald J. Trump is calling for a total and complete shutdown of Muslims entering the United States until our country's representatives can figure out what is going on. According to Pew Research, among others, there is great hatred towards Americans by large segments of the Muslim population. Most recently, a poll from the Center for Security Policy released data showing "25% of those polled agreed that violence against Americans here in the United States is justified as a part of the global jihad" and 51% of those polled, "agreed that Muslims in America should have the choice of being governed according to Shariah." Shariah authorizes such atrocities as murder against non-believers who won't convert, beheadings and more unthinkable acts that pose great harm to Americans, especially women.

Mr. Trump stated, "Without looking at the various polling data, it is obvious to anybody the hatred is beyond comprehension. Where this hatred comes from and why we will have to determine. Until we are able to determine and understand this problem and the dangerous threat it poses, our country cannot be the victims of horrendous attacks by people that believe only in Jihad, and have no sense of reason or respect for human life. If I win the election for President, we are going to Make America Great Again."—Donald J. Trump[5]

Trump's statement was met with enthusiasm from his supporters and outrage from others. One supporter stated, "I think that we should definitely disallow any Muslims from coming in. Any of them. The reason is simple: we can't identify what their attitude is."[6] Former president Barack Obama, however, described the ban as "totally contrary to our values as Americans." Many Republicans also criticized Trump's statement. Republican senator Lindsey Graham said that Trump is "putting our troops serving abroad and our diplomats at risk." Former vice president Dick Cheney said that banning Muslims overlooked the importance of religious freedom in the US.[7]

Despite such initial criticisms, during his first week in office, on January 27, 2017, Trump signed Executive Order 13769, Protection of the Nation from Foreign Terrorist Entry into the United States, which suspended the entry of refugees from seven Muslim-majority nations: Iraq, Syria, Iran, Sudan, Libya, Somalia, and Yemen. As he signed the order, also referred to as Muslim Ban 1.0, he said it was intended to "keep radical Islamic terrorists out of the United States of America" and that "we only want to admit those into our country who will support our country and love deeply our people."[8] In response, the American Civil Liberties Union filed a lawsuit and masses of people protested at airports across the US where Muslims were being detained. Despite being challenged, the Supreme Court upheld President Trump's Muslim Ban 3.0 on June 27, 2018.

Many members of the entertainment industry reacted to the Muslim ban with outrage.[9] The actors' union, SAG-AFTRA, issued a statement: "SAG-AFTRA's membership includes creative professionals from all over the world. This union values equality of opportunity regardless of race, gender, creed, disability, sexual orientation or country of birth. Any public policy that enacts discrimination based on religious or national background runs absolutely counter to those values and will be vigorously resisted. This immigration policy is misguided and we will support our fellow artists every step of the way."[10] The Directors Guild of America issued a similar statement.[11] Actor Marlon Wayans tweeted, "To my Muslim people deeply sincerely apologize for this disgusting act of hate exhibited by our so called president. This is #unAmerican."[12] Director Rob Reiner tweeted, "Along with liar,racist,misogynist,fool,infantile,sick,narcissist-with the Muslim ban we can now add heartless & evil to DT's repertoire."[13] Writer and actor Issa Rae tweeted, "This #MuslimBan is disgusting and disturbing. #MakeAmericaHateAgain."[14] According to news reports, "Hollywood is hiring way more Muslim actors than ever before . . . and President Trump might very well be the one to thank." Why? Because "Hollywood power players, most of whom are vehemently anti-Trump, are pushing back against what they see as his exclusionary policies."[15] Journalist Sam Asi wrote that "Muslims and Middle Easterners may finally be in line for the same Hollywood inclusion which previously benefitted other discriminated minorities such as blacks and LGBT"[16] (see figures 2.1 and 2.2).

Figure 2.1. News story covers an increase in opportunities for Muslim actors during Trump's presidency: "Muslim Actors Scoring More Roles in Hollywood . . . Take That, Prez Trump?," *TMZ*, March 21, 2017.

Figure 2.2. News story covers Hollywood's challenge to Trump's Muslim ban: Sam Asi, "No Ban Here: Hollywood (Finally) Embraces Muslim and Middle Eastern Talent," *Golden Globes*, March 7, 2017.

Whether manifested through increased representations or the eschewing of old tropes, we do indeed seem to be experiencing an encouraging "Muslim moment" in popular culture—from Aziz Ansari's Netflix comedy show *Master of None* (2015–2017) to Netflix's comedic political talk show *Patriot Act with Hasan Minhaj* (2018–2020), Emily V. Gordon and Kumail Nanjiani's romantic comedy film *The Big Sick* (2017), and Tan France as a cast member of Netflix's *Queer Eye* (2018–present). New regular and recurring characters were added to the cast of some TV shows, such as Dr. Dahlia Qadri (2017–2019) on *Grey's Anatomy* and Alison Abdullah (2017–2019) on *Orange Is the New Black*.[17] Freeform's *The Bold Type* (2017–2021) includes the first lesbian Muslim character on network television. In 2017, NBC's *Blindspot* created the character Afreen Iqbal, an Indian Muslim FBI lab technician who wears the hijab. That same year, LL Cool J's character, Sam Hanna, came out as Muslim on CBS's *NCIS: Los Angeles*, and in 2019, Special Agent Fatima Namazi, who wears a hijab, was introduced.[18] The Amazon show *Jack Ryan* includes Black Muslim FBI Agent James Greer (2019–present). The rapper Common plays an imam on Lena Waithe's Showtime drama, *The Chi* (2018–present). Fox's *9-1-1: Lone Star*, a fire department drama, includes firefighter Marjan Marwani (2019–present), a Muslim woman who wears the hijab. Writers and producers reacted to Trump's "Muslim ban" by creating an array of Muslim characters, often notably in stories having nothing to do with terrorism, many of whom are women who wear the hijab, queer, and/or Black. Furthermore, Muslim men are being featured in leading roles for the first time. In addition to Hulu's *Ramy* (2019–present), the first TV series in the United States to focus on an Arab American Muslim family, CBS's *FBI* (2018–present) co-stars Zeeko Zaki, who plays Special Agent Omar Adom, "O.A." Zidan is a co-lead, making him the first Egyptian-born Muslim actor on a major network to play a TV protagonist (see figure 2.3). NBC's *Transplant* (2020–present) is about Dr. Bashir Hamed, a Syrian refugee doctor, played by Hamza Haq (see figure 2.4). In 2021, NBC Universal's streaming platform, Peacock, premiered the UK Channel 4's music comedy *We Are Lady Parts*, which focuses on five UK Muslim women in a punk rock band (see figure 2.5).

This Muslim moment extends to awards recognition. Riz Ahmed was nominated for an Academy Award for his leading role in *Sound*

Figure 2.3. Promotional image for *FBI*, CBS, 2018.

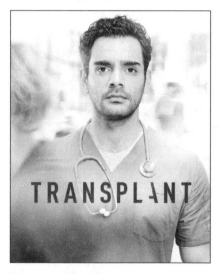

Figure 2.4. Promotional image for
Transplant, NBC, 2020.

Figure 2.5. Promotional image for *We Are
Lady Parts*, Peacock, 2021.

of Metal.[19] While the character Ruben Stone is not Muslim, Ahmed is the first Muslim to be nominated in the Oscars' Best Actor category. He also won Outstanding Lead Actor in a Limited Series for *The Night Of* (2017). Mahershala Ali won Best Supporting Actor for *Moonlight* (2017)—thereby becoming the first Muslim actor to win an Oscar—and *Green Book* (2019). Aziz Ansari won Primetime Emmy Awards for his show *Master of None* in 2016 and 2017. While some perceive Muslims playing non-Muslim roles as progress, colorblindness is not the most effective solution to the problematic of stereotyping. Rather, Muslim visibility in a wide range of roles is a more effective solution.

Representations matter. They influence how we see each other, public opinion, and policies. Studies show that repeated exposure to representations of Muslims as terrorists leads to public support for civil restrictions of Muslims and for wars in Muslim countries.[20] Another study shows that when a Muslim commits an act of violence it is reported on 357 percent more than violence committed by a white person.[21] Cultural representations also impact one's self-esteem and the extent to which we feel part of the collective nation. It is not "just entertainment" Riz Ahmed, in a 2017 speech to the UK parliament about why diversity matters, stated, "People are looking for the message that they belong, that they are part of something, that they are seen and heard and that despite, or perhaps because of, their experience, they are valued. They want to feel represented. In that task we have failed."[22] Ali Nahdee, creator of the Aila Test to measure representations of Indigenous women, says that "Native girls deserve to have characters to identify with" and to say "I want to be like her when I grow up."[23] Even institutions like Disney are embracing the perspective that representations matter. Their Stories Matter website, initiated in 2020 to educate viewers on the problems with stereotypes and why they are using disclaimers with their older content, explains, "Stories shape how we see ourselves and everyone around us. So as storytellers, we have the power and responsibility to not only uplift and inspire, but also consciously, purposefully and relentlessly champion the spectrum of voices and perspectives in our world."[24]

Hollywood responded to the Muslim ban crisis by expanding representations of Muslims and people from the Middle East and North Africa (MENA). Members of Hollywood responded heroically, yet without necessarily acknowledging the long history of anti-Muslim

and anti-MENA racism over the last century, shaped in part by stereotypes they produced.[25] Despite decades of the American-Arab Anti-
Discrimination Committee and the Council on American-Islamic
Relations protesting Hollywood's stereotypes, it was this moment
with the Muslim ban that produced a recognized crisis and concerted
effort to change representations. In this chapter, I ask: How can we
understand a century of denial about the harm in propagating stereotypes turned into action-oriented awakening? What can we learn
from the "Muslim moment" about the strategies media professionals
use to diversify representations? What do these strategies reveal about
the limits and possibilities of Muslim representation in the US at this
time? And who benefits when Hollywood includes Muslims in diversity initiatives—who profits and does it matter? This last question is
particularly important, if unpopular. It interrupts the positive narrative of Hollywood simply becoming more inclusive and concerned
with social justice to ask such questions. And yet it would be naïve to
deny that the entertainment industry is capitalizing on the diversity
imperative by turning historically marginalized identities into valued
commodities. While racial capitalism has historically been central to
systems of slavery, segregation, property ownership, and citizenship
rights in the US,[26] it has taken on new forms in the twenty-first century, blending easily with logics of diversity and multiculturalism.[27]
My use of "racial capitalism" relies on legal scholar Nancy Leong's
definition and formulation. Leong defines racial capitalism as "the use
of nonwhite people by corporations and institutions to make money
or boost their brand" or "the process of getting some sort of social
or economic benefit from someone else's racial identity."[28] Many in
Hollywood have capitalized and profited on diversity and emerged
as heroes.

The possibilities for marketable and profitable Muslim identities
are expanding beyond stereotypes like terrorists and oppressed veiled
women, and beyond recent "positive" representations like the "good"/
patriotic US Muslim and the nominal Muslim. Through marketization—
turning something or someone into a unit that is consumable and
profitable—racial commodification becomes a pathway to "diversity."
Scholar of race and media Anamik Saha's defines commodification as
"the conversion of a thing, a culture, or an aspect of life that does not

have an intrinsic economic value into a commodity to be bought and sold."[29] The expansion of diversity in representations within a capitalist, neoliberal society is structured by profit. Commodification and consumerism often tend to replace critiques of racism with celebrations of diversity.[30] Scholar of media and communications Sarah Banet-Weiser notes that visibility often becomes the end rather than the means to an end. In other words, "visual representation becomes the beginning and the end of political action."[31] Neoliberalism transforms the politics of visibility into an economic project that is deemed successful when it is trending.[32]

Crisis diversity in Hollywood, in this case Hollywood's response to Trump's Muslim travel ban, has led to an unprecedented expansion in representations of Muslims, but this expansion is at times hindered by what I refer to as "the diversity compromise." The diversity compromise is when Hollywood producers and writers make a concerted effort to challenge stereotypes but still fall flat in some way, whether big or small. It is when one important component of the problem in representing Muslims is addressed but others are ignored or insufficiently confronted. In this chapter, I will explore several common examples of the diversity compromise: prioritizing metrics over substance; recycling old tropes, particularly orientalism and terrorism; presenting Muslim characters as primarily religious or political beings; and making mistakes in representations that compromise the integrity of a Muslim character. I am not saying that all representations are compromised, but rather that many efforts get one important thing right but not another. For example, when *Orange Is the New Black* introduced Black Muslim prison inmate Alison Abdullah (played by Amanda Stephen) to the storyline, her backstory included that she was in a polygamous marriage and jealous of her husband's second wife.[33] While the NBC medical drama *Transplant* is groundbreaking in focusing on a Syrian refugee doctor remaking his life in the face of tragedy, loss, and trauma, the first scene of the series involves suspicion that the lead character is a terrorist. Furthermore, the lead character is played by a Pakistani Canadian actor—while this casting is certainly better than casting an actor of European descent (whitewashing) would have been, it continues to conflate Arab and South Asian identities. The fire department drama *9-1-1: Lone Star* includes as part of the team Marjan Marwani (played by Natacha Karam), an Arab Muslim firefighter who wears the hijab. However, in a two-to-three-second scene, the character is seen praying in the firehouse, but incorrectly, which led to a Twitter firestorm.[34] It is as if a new lens became available or recognized through which to challenge the history of stereotypical representations of Muslims, but it is only partially in use.

A wide range of compromises take place on this path to diversify representations, and this chapter explores some of the common forms the diversity compromise takes when it comes to expanding representations of Muslims during this unique "Muslim moment." If "simplified complex representations" characterized the post-9/11 expansion in representations of Muslims, the diversity compromise describes the post–Muslim ban moment. Simplified complex representations result when writers and producers try to make their characters or narratives more "complex" to avoid accusations of stereotyping but do so in a predictable, simple way, usually in the context of a storyline about terrorism (e.g., adding a patriotic Muslim character). The diversity compromise is a more expansive approach that is largely (but not entirely) a departure from terrorist themes. Put another way, while simplified complex representations result when storytellers are trying to avoid being accused of perpetuating stereotypes, the diversity compromise results from an interest in the project of diversification. While chapter 1 explored a limited expansion in representations from 2010 to 2015 that are confined and defined by a response to stereotypes and to producing acceptable Muslims, chapter 2 explores what happened next, from 2015 to 2020, in response to Trump's Muslim ban in which the representational field expanded beyond producing acceptable Muslims and responding to stereotypes with the introduction of Muslim doctors, superheroes, firefighters, and millennials. In what follows, I first explore various factors that converged with Trump's Muslim travel ban—such as the #OscarsSoWhite hashtag and impactful research studies about diversity in the movie and TV industry, aka "report cards"—which have contributed to crisis-response diversity in Hollywood. I consider how these various factors, including ones related to the box office and profit, together influenced Hollywood to take diversifying the industry seriously. Here, I caution that one possible outcome, reflective of the diversity compromise, is a focus on increasing numbers of underrepresented groups over substance. Second, I will consider how a variety of tests, including one that I co-authored, the Obeidi-Alsultany Test, offer important guidance on how not to sacrifice substance for metrics. Throughout, I argue that when Hollywood diversifies in response to crisis, it often results in the diversity compromise—unprecedented advancements compromised by a range of minor to major issues.

Hollywood Diversifies Its Representations in Response to Crisis

What prompts expansions in Hollywood's diversity practices today? While the Muslim ban was a key factor in the expansion of representations of Muslims and in including Muslims in conceptions of diversity in Hollywood, it is not the sole factor that produced crisis diversity. A range of factors converged that highlighted the exclusion of women, BIPOC, disabled, and LGBTQ+ people from Hollywood representations and from the industry more broadly. Trump's Muslim ban would not have yielded the unprecedented expansion in representations of Muslims that it did without the convergence of these other factors: #OscarsSoWhite and the use of social media to create controversy, the increasing influence of report cards published by university research centers and advocacy organizations, and the emerging idea that diversity is profitable. Hollywood responded to crisis with a sense of responsibility that is structured by financial concerns and that produced the capitalizing of underrepresented identities, or what Leong calls "identity capitalism."

There are various motives for making diversity an objective or value. Leong notes that "employers may believe that diversity actually leads to a better-functioning workplace, or they may believe that the appearance of diversity bolsters their standing among customers, or they may actually believe in the remedial value of hiring members of groups historically subject to discrimination but strategically couch their justifications in the language of diversity."[35] In the case of the entertainment industry, controversy generated by social media, "report cards," and the box office can motivate a sense of social responsibility and an increase in diversity. Intensifying at particular moments, controversy and crisis add a temporal dimension to diversity practices, hence the tendency for representational trends to come in waves and/or follow specific events. More often than not institutions correct, improve upon, or otherwise expand their diversity practices in a reactive, rather than proactive, manner. Without moments of disruption, racism would not be seen as a problem in need of a response in the first place.

As mentioned above, Donald Trump's explicit propagation of racism, sexism, anti-immigrant hostility, and white supremacist logics inspired some writers and producers to diversify representations in a gesture of social responsibility. It is not unusual for media executives to respond to social and political events. The terrorist attacks on September 11, 2001, led to Hollywood's capitalizing on this event by producing more stories about terrorism. Some sought to promote social responsibility after 9/11 (e.g., *The West Wing, 7th Heaven*[36]) by making explicit distinctions between Muslims and terrorists, and others, after being called out by the American-Arab Anti-Discrimination Committee and the Council on American-Islamic Relations, sought to avoid accusations of stereotyping and racism by inserting patriotic Muslims into storylines about Muslims as terrorists.[37] The Trump administration's normalization of white supremacy and promotion of inequality created a sense of social and political crisis to which media executives responded with a sense of social responsibility.

Social media has come to play a large role in pointing out the failures of writers and producers and holding them accountable. For example, when the Academy of Motion Picture Art and Sciences announced the nominees for the 2016 Academy Awards, the actors nominated in the top categories were all white, prompting the hashtag #OscarsSoWhite.[38] Beginning as a critique of Hollywood's casting practices—particularly that of "whitewashing" or casting white actors in non-white roles— the hashtag went viral and prompted a national conversation about the lack of diversity in Hollywood.[39] A number of high-profile casting decisions were called out as "whitewashing," such as Scarlett Johansson playing a mixed-race Japanese American character in *Ghost in the Shell* (2017), Tom Cruise playing the lead role in *The Last Samurai* (2003), Jake Gyllenhaal playing the lead in *Prince of Persia: The Sands of Time* (2010), and Christian Bale and Joel Edgerton playing Moses and Ramses, respectively, in *Exodus: Gods and Kings* (2014).[40] When *Exodus* producer Ridley Scott was challenged on his casting decisions, he bluntly responded: "[I cannot] say that my lead actor is Mohammad so-and-so from such-and-such. I'm just not going to get it financed."[41] While his comment was seen as derogatory toward Muslims, Scott was also arguably stating a hard truth based on extensive experience. Given how the Hollywood industry operates, recognizable white (and preferably male) actors are necessary to secure financing; using unknown non-white actors has not been profitable. The irony of Scott's statement is that, notwithstanding the valuable cultural capital attached to white men actors, none of the aforementioned films did well at the box office—some would argue precisely because of the controversy surrounding their casting.[42]

Such controversies combined with failed profits likely influenced Disney and other Hollywood corporations to take casting practices more seriously. Hollywood executives responded by promising to do better in diversifying representations.[43] In January 2016, Cheryl Boone Isaacs, former president of the Academy of Motion Picture Art and Sciences, vowed to double the number of women and people of color in the Academy's membership by 2020.[44] Social media can provide a vehicle for insightful criticism and also has the potential to influence audience opinions and whether or not they will spend their money on a film.

"Report cards" also play a role. Universities like the University of California, Los Angeles (UCLA) and the University of Southern California (USC), and organizations like GLAAD and the Geena Davis Institute, release annual reports on how well the media is doing at diversifying representations. Writers and producers pay attention to these report cards and are motivated to avoid being singled out as representing the worst network or film studio when it comes to diversity. The UCLA College of Social Sciences' Institute for Research on Labor and Employment released a series of annual reports from 2014 to 2018 assessing the relationship between diversity and box office success. The 2018 "Hollywood Diversity Report" indicates that, despite significant progress, minorities and women remain underrepresented as film leads, film directors, film writers, TV scripted leads, reality TV leads, and creators of media content. Their findings show that "America's increasingly diverse audiences prefer diverse film and television content."[45] The USC report "Inclusion or Invisibility? Comprehensive Annenberg Report on Diversity in Entertainment" ranks companies (e.g., Netflix, Hulu, Amazon, The Walt

Disney Company, 21st Century Fox) on their level of inclusivity on-screen and behind the camera. Based on data from 2014–2015, the USC report reveals that females comprise 28.7 percent of all speaking roles in film; that females (34.3 percent) are more likely than males (7.6 percent) to be shown in sexy attire; and behind the camera only 15.2 percent are women.[46] The report similarly uncovers that 28.3 percent of all speaking characters and 13 percent of all directors were from underrepresented racial/ethnic groups.[47] Regarding LGBTQ+ representation, it shows that 2 percent of all speaking characters across 414 movies, television shows, and digital series were identified as lesbian, gay, bisexual, or transgender.[48] The report also confirmed that the tendency to create white characters prevails: "Of characters with an ascertainable race/ethnicity, 70.7% were white, 12.1% Black, 4.8% Asian, 6.2% Hispanic/Latino, 1.7% Middle Eastern, <1% American Indian/Alaskan Native, <1% Native Hawaiian, and 3.9% Mixed Race or Other."[49]

USC's Annenberg Inclusion Initiative released a report in 2021 that examined representations of Muslims in the top two hundred movies released between 2017 and 2019 in the US, the UK, Australia, and New Zealand.[50] One hundred of these films were in the US and 1.1 percent of the characters in these films were Muslim and 25.5 percent of them were female. Regarding the data, Dr. Stacy L. Smith stated, "[Muslims are] 24% of the world population—that's greater than the United States population. And yet, in 181 films, they're erased."[51] The study also revealed that most portrayals of Muslims were set in the past as if Muslims are not part of modern society, and that 76.5 percent of the Muslim characters were of Middle Eastern/North African (MENA) descent, continuing a non-diverse portrayal of Muslims. Most of these MENA Muslim characters were foreign and one-third of them were instigators of violence. Furthermore, these Muslim characters tended to be secondary and served the needs of a white protagonist. This abysmal portrait of representations of Muslims on film is not reflected in television, where there has been a concerted effort to expand representations of Muslims. However, despite the better content, were a similar study conducted on television, the numbers themselves would likely be bleak too. Before this 2021 report, two significant reports were published in 2018: the MENA Arts Advocacy Coalition's "Terrorists & Tyrants: Middle Eastern and North African (MENA) Actors in Prime Time & Streaming Television" and the Pop Culture Collaborative's "Haqq and Hollywood: Illuminating 100 Years of Muslim Tropes and How to Transform Them."[52] The MENA Arts Advocacy Coalition was founded by actor-activist Azita Ghanizada in 2016 to educate the entertainment industry about MENA identity and advocate for better representations. The report it published demonstrates, based on data from 2015–2016, that 1 percent of series regulars are identified as Middle Eastern and/or North African and, of those, 78 percent are portrayed as threats.[53] Just as calling out studios on social media for their failure with diversity sparks controversy, so does doing badly on a report card. Thus, controversy is a motivating force in diversifying representations. The fact that not diversifying sufficiently is considered controversial is itself a big change from the days when comedian/actor/talk show host Ellen DeGeneres was ostracized and did not work for years after coming out as gay on her sitcom *Ellen* in 1997.

Of course, ratings and box office profits play a large role in when and how Hollywood studios take steps to diversify representations. The success of *Black Panther* (2018) and *Crazy Rich Asians* (2018) has been hailed as proving that stories about people of color are no longer the domain of small specialty theaters. Conversely, as noted above, "white-washed" films like *Exodus: Gods and Kings* and *Ghost in the Shell* did not do well at the box office and were criticized extensively. A business argument for diversity has emerged that, for better or worse, might prove to be even more effective than arguments based on rectifying inequality or social responsibility.[54] According to UCLA's 2019 diversity report: "Films with casts that were from 31 percent to 40 percent minority enjoyed the highest median global box office receipts, while those with majority-minority casts posted the highest median return on investment. By contrast, films with the most racially and ethnically homogenous casts were the poorest performers."[55] A 2019 white paper by Movio, a marketing data analytics company, shows that on-screen representation of minority groups leads to more attendance from those groups and "understanding how to drive attendance from diverse audiences can strengthen a film's box office returns and sustain the viability of theatrical release."[56] This report makes the case that for cinema to remain relevant, it must cater to the tastes of diverse audiences.

Such business arguments for increasing representations of historically marginalized groups are used to make the case for diversity, an otherwise potentially divisive concept, as attractive to broad audiences if achieved in a nonthreatening way. It is not necessarily about rectifying injustice. Studies tell us that diversity is good for business—it makes us better as institutions, organizations, and society as a whole. Scholar of business ethics Carl Rhodes writes that the "business case approach" to diversity argues that "it is for the purpose of commercial self-interest that forms of discrimination that impede diversity should be removed."[57] But when diversity is corporatized and profitable, it becomes entangled in a form of racial capitalism in which diversity becomes a commodity. In other words, a compelling argument about diversifying representations is made more palatable by severing it from any reference to the history of white supremacy and the marginalization of nonnormative identities. Diversity becomes a brand and a profitable one at that.

Farah Merani, actor, producer, and co-founder of Women on Screen—an organization whose mission is to promote a more dynamic representation of women in the entertainment industry—and former co-chair of the Diversity Committee at ACTRA Toronto stated in an interview with me that statistics from report cards can be useful to get projects funded. They can be used to convince high-level executives that a project will be financially successful if made more diverse or that the studio has an interest in avoiding a low score on such reports.[58] Merani says that diversity objectives in Hollywood when not driven by crisis can be like the action in a pinball machine: the issue is flung back and forth with no one assuming accountability and the ball can bounce only so many times before it gets dropped entirely. Film and television studios are increasingly creating "Diversity and Inclusion" teams to ensure that the ball is not dropped entirely.[59] When I interviewed Ghanizada—who lobbied the SAG-AFTRA organization and Hollywood executives to adopt a Middle Eastern/North African identity checkbox to track and increase MENA representation—she said that many studios have whole departments now tasked with "getting it right"—"it" being diversity.[60] This can mean many different things—from ensuring that a character with an accent sounds authentic to hiring advisors or offering feedback on casting decisions. But she cautions that the decisions ultimately lie with studio and network executives.

While the box office carries the most weight in considering all of these factors, the operating logic seems to be that there is no problem until there is a controversy or crisis, at which point some kind of action is taken to address it. The action can be small (including a "good" Muslim in a storyline about terrorism) or big (producing a show written by a Muslim about a Muslim family). That action then becomes symbolic of the media corporation's commitment to diversity, through which they garner social and economic benefits from representing historically marginalized identities. Leong gives the example of a nearly all-white law firm hiring a Latina. She says that "the firm derives economic benefits from her presence on an ongoing basis. It may improve relationships with its customers who value diversity, which yields economic benefits. It may be able to recruit other employees more successfully (both other employees of color and other employees of all races who care about diversity), giving it access to a broader talent pool and yielding further economic benefits. It may also be able to attract new clients through the enhanced trust and racial credibility it has gained by having a Latina employee—again yielding economic benefits." Leong further explains that "the law firm has used the commodity of racial identity acquired through hiring the Latina employee to derive surplus value by enhancing its own image as a diverse, tolerant, and nonracist institution."[61] Hollywood similarly derives economic benefits from diversifying representations. A particular media corporation can rebrand itself through racial commodification and in doing so improve its image with audiences and yield economic benefits as a result. Racial and other kinds of identity difference (religion, sexuality, gender identity) are valuable so long as they can be translated into monetary value.

Now that I have identified some triggers to diversifying representation, how does Hollywood respond? What are common ways that diversity is practiced? There are two common pathways toward diversifying media: diversifying casting and diversifying narratives, both of which are most successful when also linked to diversifying the production crew. Regarding diversifying casting, seeing oneself represented is cited repeatedly in scholarly literature as crucial to one's feeling of visibility (and not seeing oneself represented to invisibility).[62] Regarding diversifying narratives, increasing the stories written by and about Muslims (and other historically marginalized groups) is important—and thus so is increasing the number of Muslim writers, producers, directors, and showrunners. As Leong notes, there is a spectrum of approaches to doing diversity. She defines a "thin" and a "thick" approach. The thin approach to diversity focuses on numbers and appearances: "it is exclusively concerned with improving the superficial appearance of diversity." Furthermore, it is often motivated by circumventing criticism that one is perpetuating racism or stereotyping. In contrast, the thick approach is substantive because it "fosters inclusivity and improves cross-racial relationships, thereby benefiting institutions and individuals of all races."[63] In the realm of media representations, those that I have termed "simplified complex"[64] can be understood as a thin approach. Simplified complex representations appear to be complex and nuanced but are really quite simple and formulaic—e.g., inserting a patriotic Muslim American into a storyline about Muslim terrorism or inserting inconsequential background characters to create the appearance of diversity. Conversely, there are thick approaches in media representations of Muslim people. The TV show *Ramy* is written by and stars an Arab American Muslim. And, of course, there is a wide spectrum between thin and thick approaches to representations. Furthermore, Saha importantly points out that commodification is an ambivalent process.[65] In other words, while it often produces reductive representations, that is not always the case; Saha argues, "there are still moments and opportunities where the enabling properties of commodification can be harnessed by producers in order to make race in radical and subversive ways that contribute to its undoing."[66] Saha stresses that the process of racial commodification in the culture industries is "complex, ambivalent and contested."[67]

In addition to expanding casts, crews, and storyline, the sea change in diversifying Hollywood is illustrated in the use of disclaimers to signal racist depictions in past media productions, the use of consultants and community advisory committees to ensure accurate representations, and the newly devised Oscar criteria to promote diversity. When the streaming platform Disney+ was launched in 2019, certain films such as *Dumbo* (1941) and *Peter Pan* (1953) came with the following disclaimer: "This program is presented as originally created. It may contain outdated cultural depictions."[68] The disclaimer was well earned. *Peter Pan* includes stereotypical Native American characters, and *Dumbo* has long been criticized for the inclusion of a crow character—literally, Jim

Crow—who speaks with a stereotypical Black American voice. The disclaimer signals Disney's recognition that racist stereotypes once socially acceptable are no longer so. Critics pointed out the absence of similar disclaimers for other problematic movies like the animated *Aladdin* (1992) or *Pocahontas* (1995), revealing limits to that recognition.[69] Nonetheless, shortly thereafter, Disney expanded the disclaimer, applying it to more programming, including the 1992 *Aladdin*, and added a website, Stories Matter, to further educate their viewers on the problem with stereotypes. The revised disclaimer, which is twelve seconds long and cannot be skipped, states: "This program includes negative depictions and/or mistreatment of people or cultures. These stereotypes were wrong then and are wrong now. Rather than remove this content, we want to acknowledge its harmful impact, learn from it and spark conversation to create a more inclusive future together. Disney is committed to creating stories with inspirational and aspirational themes that reflect the rich diversity of the human experience around the globe."[70] On the one hand, the use of disclaimers and the efforts to update stories themselves reflects an important shift in social norms around race, gender, and sexuality. On the other hand, the uneven and reluctant nature of these efforts reveals a lack of agreement, evidences a steep learning curve on the parameters of what constitutes racism or "outdated cultural depictions," and is reflective of the diversity compromise.

Given my status as an analyst and critic of cultural representations of Arabs and Muslims in the US, I was asked to serve on the Aladdin Community Advisory Council and had the opportunity to attend two meetings while the film was in production. I am bound by a nondisclosure agreement (NDA) and unable to discuss the contents of the meetings (though I can discuss my take on the film, which I do below). One objective of an NDA is that the content of a media production is not leaked to the public before its official release, thus potentially compromising profits and viewer experience. However, the NDA does more than that. It operates to delimit speech about the content of the meetings after the media product has been released, raising important questions about how we can learn about and improve diversity approaches if such conversations are legally protected. Nonetheless, the fact that there was a Community Advisory Council comprising activists, scholars, and creatives from the Muslim, Arab, and South Asian communities, in addition to two consulting teams throughout the production process—the Hollywood Bureau at the Muslim Public Affairs Council (MPAC) and Sila Consulting—underscores Disney's desire to seek community input and avoid perpetuating offensive stereotypes (or, at the very least, avoid criticism for doing so). As culture journalist Ann-Derrick Gaillot points out, "the stakes for Disney are high in a time where online discussion helps consumers hold companies accountable for their laziness."[71] Using cultural consultants and consultants from underrepresented groups is a growing practice in Hollywood as the industry diversifies casts and storylines.

One of the most significant ways in which Hollywood is institutionalizing diversification is through new Oscar standards. The Academy of Motion Picture Arts and Sciences announced in 2020 that starting in 2024 new criteria would be introduced for movies to qualify for Oscar nomination consideration to encourage diversity.[72] Films will have to meet two out of four categories that delineate criteria designed to promote the diversification of on-screen representations and industry professionals as whole. The first of the four categories pertains to on-screen representation; the lead actor or a significant supporting actor must be from an underrepresented group, or 30 percent of actors in secondary or minor roles must be from at least two underrepresented groups, or the main storyline must focus on an underrepresented group to qualify for Oscar consideration. What constitutes an underrepresented group?

Underrepresented Group
- Women
- Racial or ethnic group
- LGBTQ+
- People with cognitive or physical disabilities, or who are deaf or hard of hearing

Underrepresented Racial or Ethnic Group
- Asian
- Hispanic/Latinx
- Black/African American
- Indigenous/Native American/Alaskan Native
- Middle Eastern/North African

- Native Hawaiian or other Pacific Islander
- Other underrepresented race or ethnicity

It is notable that Middle Eastern/North African is included as an underrepresented racial or ethnic group given that it has long been excluded from conversations about diversity. This inclusion is the result of the work of Ghanizada and the MENA Arts Advocacy Coalition. In 2017, the organization successfully lobbied the SAG-AFTRA union to include a MENA box as a casting category in theatrical contracts. Prior to 2017, MENA identity was not an acknowledged identity category used in casting or in identity accounting for diversity purposes.

The second criterion is that the film crew must have at least two members of underrepresented groups in leadership positions (producer, writer, casting director, cinematographer, composer, costume designer, makeup artist, etc.) and at least one of the two must be specifically from an underrepresented racial or ethnic group. Alternately, at least 30 percent of the film's crew must be from underrepresented groups. The third criterion is that there must be training and skills development opportunities for people in underrepresented groups to ensure advancement in the field. The fourth criterion relates to audience development and marketing—that the film be marketed to underrepresented groups.

This is a significant and important development that will lead to diversifying the entertainment industry in front of the camera and behind the scenes. However, it could lead to a number crunching approach to diversity to fulfill metrics. The film *American Sniper*, controversial for its anti-Arab and anti-Muslim racism, for example, would pass the criteria.[73] Goals and metrics play an important role in the project of diversifying. But the work cannot stop there. It is not enough to include a Black or queer or Muslim character, or a Black queer Muslim character. We also have to think about the specifics of how that character is drawn and presented. Crisis diversity approaches can easily slide into a numbers or metrics approach over a substantive one. As scholar-artist-activist Su'ad Abdul Khabeer writes, "being represented can merely result in just being a diversity box that gets 'checked off' rather than present a real challenge to a racist status quo."[74]

The use of disclaimers, consultants, and the new Oscar standards reflects a new way of thinking and commitment in Hollywood to rectify its history of excluding and demonizing many groups of people. The metrics offered by report cards and those set forth by the new Oscars criteria are important to the goal of diversifying representations. Numbers are important to give us a sense of the severity of the problem and the progress toward addressing it. However, there are crucial matters of content and quality that the metrics do not convey. Diversifying Hollywood will not be successful if the focus is solely on numbers. Focusing on numbers, statistics, or metrics while a vital part of the conversation becomes a neoliberal response to a deeply structural problem if it becomes the primary way in which diversity is rectified. Anti-racism becomes tokenized as diversity when it is dealt with as solely an issue of numbers—number of actors, number of students, number of faculty, number of employees, number of executives, number of media representations, etc.—at the expense of substance. In the next section, I explore the popularization of qualitative measures or tests created to expand representations of marginalized groups and I then turn to how the diversity compromise influenced the Obeidi-Alsultany Test.

The Obeidi-Alsultany Test

In 1985, cartoonist Alison Bechdel coined a test to assess the representation of women in media in her comic strip *Dykes to Watch Out For*; the criteria are as follows: (1) The movie has to have at least two women in it; (2) the two women must talk to each other; and (3) they must talk to each other about something besides a man.[75] In the 2010s, this test came to be called the "Bechdel Test," and it has been used to evaluate and challenge writers on their depictions of women.[76] Though criticized for establishing a very low bar for representations of women,[77] this cartoon strip–turned–evaluative criteria has sparked important conversations and inspired the creation of other tests, such as the DuVernay Test, the Russo Test, the Aila Test, the Riz Test, and the Obeidi-Alsultany Test. The DuVernay Test, devised in 2016 by *New York Times* film critic Manohla Dargis and named after African American director Ava DuVernay, aims to measure racial diversity in the media.[78] The DuVernay Test requires "African Americans and other minorities [to] have fully realized lives rather than serve as scenery in white stories."[79] Another test, this one created in 2019 by GLAAD and named after film historian of LGBTQ+ portrayals in Hollywood and GLAAD co-founder Vito Russo, offers criteria to assess LGBTQ+ representations. To pass the Vito Russo Test, a media production must contain an identifiably lesbian, gay, bisexual, and/or transgender character who is not solely defined by their sexual orientation or gender identity and "must be tied into the plot in such a way that their removal would have a significant effect."[80] The Aila Test was created in 2020 by Anishinaabe writer Ali Nahdee to assess representations of Indigenous women.[81] It consists of three questions: (1) Is the Indigenous or Aboriginal woman a main character? (2) Does she not fall in love with a white man? (3) And does she not end up raped or murdered at some point in the story?

Similarly, the Riz Test, coined in 2017 by Shaf Choudry and Shadia Habib in the UK and inspired by a speech actor Riz Ahmed made to the British House of Commons, proposes five criteria to measure representations of Muslims:

If the film/show stars at least one character who is identifiably Muslim (by ethnicity, language or clothing)—is the character . . .

1) Talking about, the victim of, or the perpetrator of terrorism?
2) Presented as irrationally angry?
3) Presented as superstitious, culturally backwards or anti-modern?
4) Presented as a threat to a Western way of life?
5) If the character is male, is he presented as misogynistic? or if female, is she presented as oppressed by her male counterparts?

If the answer for any of the above is Yes, then the Film/TV Show fails the test.[82]

In 2020, Sue Obeidi, director of the Muslim Public Affairs Council's Hollywood Bureau, and I teamed up to expand upon the Riz Test to address Hollywood's recent efforts to improve representations of Muslims explored in this chapter. We developed the Obeidi-Alsultany Test, published in the *Hollywood Reporter*, which offers the following criteria:[83]

1) The project that includes a Muslim character(s) does not reproduce or reinvent old tropes but rather explores new stories and contexts.
2) The project that includes Muslim character(s) has a Muslim-identifying writer on staff to ensure that Muslim cultures, religion, characters and storylines are being portrayed accurately and authentically.
3) The Muslim character(s) is not solely defined by their religion. Religion can be part of the character's backstory but should not be their entire story. Muslim culture and faith should be accurately delineated.
4) The Muslim character(s) has a strong presence and the character(s) is essential to the story arc and has a rich and clearly defined backstory.
5) The Muslim character(s) is portrayed with diverse backgrounds and identities.

In addition to report cards, these tests provide useful evaluative criteria and promote important conversations around representation. These tests as a whole broaden the conversation from quantitative metrics approaches to include qualitative and substantive considerations. At the same time, these tests do not and cannot in themselves resolve the problem of inequality in representations. We want easy ways to address diversity through numbers or a quick and easy test. The problem is that it is not an easy problem that can be solved simply by meeting certain metrics or criteria. When we create metrics and tests, then people focus on them and meet them in ways that can perpetuate the problem. Tools created to facilitate a solution can easily turn into simplistic and inadequate approaches. While the Obeidi-Alsultany Test seeks to broaden the conversation, it too is a conversation tool and not the end-all be-all of representation, especially since representations change over time and therefore assessments must change too.

Some of the above-mentioned reports also include suggestions for how to effectively diversify representations. Stacy L. Smith, who leads the Media, Diversity, and Social Change Initiative at the University of Southern California, penned an op-ed for the *Hollywood Reporter* in 2014 introducing the idea of an equity or inclusion rider—namely, that A-list actors could stipulate in their contract that certain provisions be set to ensure that underrepresented groups are represented on-screen and behind the camera. The 2018 report adds to this notion a recommendation that companies set target inclusion goals and craft plans to achieve those goals.[84] The MENA Arts Advocacy Coalition's report "'Ter-rorists and Tyrants" offers the following solutions: to stop limiting the portrayal of MENA characters to geopolitical contexts; to use the new MENA category to track diversity and stop categorizing MENA people as white; to hire and mentor MENA performers, writers, directors, and executives; and to hire consultants. The Pop Culture Collaborative's "Haqq and Hollywood" report offers the following solutions: "1. Un-derstand the diversity of Muslim communities—and frontline both their participation in and ownership of the creative process. 2. Build and expand creative and career pipelines for Muslim artists within the entertainment industry. 3. Invest in the Muslim communities' ability to advance long-term narrative change and participate in pop culture for social change field."[85] Obeidi identifies four ways to produce more diverse representations of Muslims: work collectively to produce bet-ter narratives; hire qualified consultants who can help provide accu-rate information about Islam and Muslims; be sure to include Muslim screenwriters on projects that include depictions of Muslims; have film departments at universities educate their students to do their research in creating stories.[86] Pillars Fund, a Muslim Philanthropic organization, re-leased "The Blueprint for Muslim Inclusion: Recommendations for Film Industry Professionals" in 2021. It offers the following recommenda-tions: move past terrorism tropes; invest in Muslim creators to increase the prevalence of three-dimensional Muslim characters; educate staff on Muslims; hire Muslim casting directors; seek out expert consultants to assess scripts; and others.[87]

Having more Muslim writers in writing rooms is repeatedly cited by Hollywood insiders as important to changing representations, in ad-dition to offering Muslims leading roles as opposed to supporting or background roles. In one interview, when asked what needs to be done to increase the representation of queer Muslim women, Nikhol Boosheri of The Bold Type replied that more queer, female, Muslim, and diverse people are needed in the writer's room and at executive decision-making levels.[88] Abdul Khabeer writes that being serious about diversity requires having Muslim writers and directors on set, not just as advisors. She says that this distinguished movies like Black Panther, Coco, and Crazy Rich Asians and made them successful.[89] Abdul Khabeer also encour-ages us to move beyond the project of humanizing Muslims by proving that Muslims are people too.[90] Similarly, Hussein Rashid points out that a common response to stereotyping is satire in which the absurdity of stereotypes is highlighted, for example, by mocking a character's fear of Muslims.[91] While this is an improvement over stereotypes, he insists that we must move beyond a focus on stereotypes too.

The Obeidi-Alsultany Test targets the limits in approaches to diversifying representations of Muslims in 2015–2020. The test acknowledges an unprecedented expansion in representations of Muslims, an expansion from the "good" patriotic Muslim and the nominal Muslim to a wider range of possibilities. But it also recognizes that these efforts often fall short because of an element that compromises the integrity of the character or storyline, what I call the diversity compromise—an approach that captures crisis diversity during the Trump presidency. I will now turn to an examination of the common mistakes that the test addresses by exploring one or two examples per criterion.

* * *

Criterion 1: The project that includes a Muslim character(s) does not reproduce or reinvent old tropes but rather explores new stories and contexts.

There are two common tendencies when it comes to expanding storylines and contexts pertaining to Muslims and MENA people. The first is the idea that portraying the Middle East in an Orientalist fashion is an improvement over portrayals of it as terroristic. This tendency is exemplified by Disney's 2019 *Aladdin*, which made strides not only in seeking out community consultants but also in resisting the tendency to whitewash the cast and characters. Nonetheless, it promoted Orientalism. The second tendency is to continue to tell stories about terrorism but to tell them in new ways by providing a complex backstory to explain the terrorist's motives or at times by revealing that white men are the ones behind the terrorist attack, aka flipping the enemy.[92] This tendency is exemplified by Amazon's 2019 *Jack Ryan*.

On May 24, 2019, Disney released its much-anticipated live-action remake of *Aladdin*.[93] In just one week, the film made over $817 million worldwide.[94] Writing for the *New York Times*, A. O. Scott argued that the remake was motivated by money and that Disney makes money by introducing new generations to its extensive catalog of stories that dates back to *Snow White and the Seven Dwarfs* in 1937. Disney's 1992 animated version of *Aladdin* was the first animated film to make $200 million.[95] Scott noted, however, that although reissuing Disney classics worked in the past, social norms have changed, making Disney's landmark white patriarchal princess stories less marketable today.[96] Well aware of this shift, Disney has not only been remaking its classic stories, but also updating them in an effort to make them more socially and culturally palatable to contemporary audiences.[97] In the 2019 version of *Aladdin*, the story has been updated to show Princess Jasmine not only selecting a husband, but also succeeding her father as the ruler of Agrabah.

Many critics writing about the 2019 *Aladdin* questioned Hollywood's motives. Aisha Harris, writing for the *National Post*, argued that "the shoehorned-in progressive messages only call more attention to the inherent crassness of Disney's current exercise in money-grabbing nostalgia."[98] Writing for *Brown Girl Magazine*, Raina Hasan offered a critical take on the movie's popularity: "The box office success exposes America for what it is: a capitalist economy that profits off of Middle Eastern and South Asian culture (i.e., hummus, henna and harem pants) while the political system remains incredibly Islamophobic, using our tax dollars to spy on our neighbors and drone their families abroad."[99] Others pointed out that the film was released during Ramadan—something that could have been avoided by waiting only ten days—making it clear that Disney's core concern is not sensitivity toward Muslims.[100]

How did the movie do in light of Disney's intentional attention to questions of diversity? Many hoped the movie would avoid and even rectify some of the problems with its animated predecessor, which was widely critiqued as reinforcing negative stereotypes about the Middle East. But while there are some improvements, the new *Aladdin* doesn't so much reject Orientalist tropes as simply recycle them. That the remake avoids associations of Arabs and Muslims with terrorism will undoubtedly be hailed as progress by some, but doing so fails to recognize the film's recourse to an older arsenal of Orientalist imagery. After 9/11, writers and producers employed a host of strategies to circumvent stereotyping. The strategy adopted in *Aladdin* was strangely familiar—a return to old Orientalist tropes of the exotic, romantic Middle East (see figure 2.6).

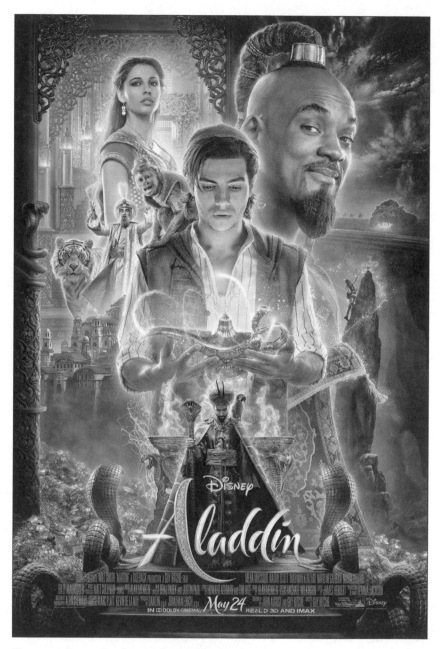

Figure 2.6. Promotional image for *Aladdin*, Disney, 2019.

This same move can be seen in other post-9/11 Hollywood films such as *Hidalgo* (2004), *Salmon Fishing in the Yemen* (2011), and *Victoria and Abdul* (2017). Operating under what one can only assume is a strange form of cinematic amnesia, there seems to be an assumption that depicting the Middle East as exotic and romantic is an appropriate correction. Surely, the implicit reasoning goes, it is an improvement over stories about terrorism. In *Hidalgo*, Frank T. Hopkins travels to the Arabian desert in 1891 to participate in a horse race where, in classic Orientalist fashion, he saves the rich sheik's daughter from the evil, power-hungry nephew. *Salmon Fishing in the Yemen* is about a Yemeni sheik who lives among Yemeni radicals; when he has the far-fetched idea of bringing salmon fishing to the country, he hires a firm in England to make his outlandish wish come true.[101] And *Victoria and Abdul* features an unlikely friendship between Queen Victoria and her Indian Muslim servant, Abdul Karim. Highlighting the inner workings of the diversity compromise, the story's criticism of racism and Islamophobia in nineteenth-century British high society is countered by the infantilized and exoticized portrayal of Karim.[102] All of these films rely upon and reinforce, however inadvertently, long-standing binaries contrasting the civilized West and barbaric East. Yet none of these films were released with a similar disclaimer about outdated tropes—reflecting the bizarre Hollywood assumption that an exotic Middle East is better than a terroristic Middle East.

What Hollywood seems to have forgotten, but many Arab and Muslim Americans have not, is that early Hollywood films, such as *The Sheik* (1921) and *Arabian Nights* (1942), regularly depicted the Middle East as a magical desert filled with genies, flying carpets, mummies, belly dancers, and harem girls. While arguably fun and charming, such representations reflect the logic of colonialism[103] and flatten out differences within and across Middle Eastern cultures. As Melani McAlister, professor of American studies, has detailed, a series of political events from the Arab-Israeli War of 1967, the Arab oil embargo of 1973, and the Iran hostage crisis of 1979–1980 to the Gulf War of 1990–1991 eventually led to such exotic and romantic images being replaced with ominous representations of violence and terrorism.[104] The late scholar of ethnic and racial stereotypes Jack G. Shaheen extensively documented how hundreds of Hollywood films over the last fifty years "regularly link the Islamic faith with male supremacy, holy war, and acts of terror, depicting Arab Muslims as hostile alien intruders, as lecherous, oily sheikhs intent on using nuclear weapons."[105]

Against this backdrop, the Orientalism of Disney's 1992 animated *Aladdin* was, in many ways, unsurprising. The opening song lyrics, for example, described a land "where they cut off your ear if they don't like your face," then declared, "It's barbaric, but hey, it's home!" At the same time, it is important to note that, despite the offensive stereotypes, the animated *Aladdin* holds a special place in the hearts of many Muslim, Arab, and South Asian Americans who were children in the 1990s, since it was the only time they saw a popular story, no matter how problematic, ostensibly about themselves.[106] When Shaheen and the American-Arab Anti-Discrimination Committee protested the lyrics, Disney removed the reference to cutting off ears in the home video version, but left the descriptor "barbaric" intact.[107] There was still an issue, however, with the racialized representation of "good" versus "bad" characters. As gender studies scholar Joe Kadi pointed out, "Aladdin presents dozens of 'bad' Arabs, all grotesque, ugly, and sinister, with huge noses and strong accents," while the "good" characters of Aladdin and Jasmine have "Caucasian features and white, middle-class American accents," making them for all intents and purposes white.[108] The film also continued the Orientalist pattern of erasing the specificities of distinct Middle Eastern cultures, presenting the fictional Agrabah (originally Baghdad but changed to avoid associations with the Gulf War) as a paradoxically homogeneous hodgepodge. That such representations matter was forcefully demonstrated when a 2015 poll by Public Policy Polling asked Republicans and Democrats if they would favor bombing Agrabah; seemingly oblivious to both the fictional nature of the city and the facetious nature of the question, 30 percent of Republicans and 19 percent of Democrats indicated their support.[109]

Aladdin is still Orientalist in spectacular ways—the desert, the magic, the mishmashing of cultures and accents. It is an Orientalist spectacle. Yet as popular culture critic for the *Los Angeles Times* Lorraine Ali points out about the 2019 version, "several aspects of the story were updated to avoid the barbarous, hook-nosed stereotypes of the original."[110] Tweaks were made to ensure that not only bad or inferior characters speak with accents and the opening song manages to avoid any offensive lyrics. Compared to its predecessor, the film is not blatantly offensive.

The 2019 *Aladdin* also reflects some progress vis-à-vis diversity in its casting. Controversy surfaced when light-skinned extras were made brown using makeup during filming, exposing an incredible depth of cluelessness when it comes to racial politics.[111] Ultimately, however, Disney largely avoided accusations of "whitewashing" by casting actors of MENA descent in most of the main roles. This diversified casting was the result of a controversy generated by the #OscarsSoWhite hashtag; as discussed above, controversy can fuel expansions in diversity practices. Historically, in films like *The Sheik* and *Road to Morocco* (1942), Arabs were played by white actors and occasionally by Mexicans—e.g., Anthony Quinn in *Road to Morocco*, *Lawrence of Arabia* (1962), and *Lion of the Desert* (1981). The 2019 *Aladdin*'s casting of Egyptian Canadian actor Mena Massoud as Aladdin was thus a huge win for the MENA community. As for the rest of the cast: Iranian American actor Nasim Pedrad plays Dalia; Marwan Kenzari, who is Dutch Tunisian, plays Jafar; the Turkish German actor Numan Acar plays Hakim; and Jasmine's father is played by Iranian American actor Navid Negahban. Given the long history of Hollywood whitewashing and the backlash against it by viewers, likely coupled with the disappointing returns from *Prince of Persia* and *Exodus: Gods and Kings*, Disney wisely chose to diversify its casting practices.

Casting British Indian actor Naomi Scott as Jasmine was controversial as many hoped to see an Arab or MENA actor in this role and questioned whether casting someone of Indian descent would simply reinforce notions of "Oriental" interchangeability.[112] As a result, there is an effort in the film to flag her South Asian heritage (the character's mother is from "another land"), but if you blink you will miss it. What is clear in the film about Jasmine is that her father is Iranian for anyone familiar with the accent. However, Julie Ann Crommett, vice president of multicultural audience engagement at Disney, says that Scott was cast as Jasmine because *Aladdin* is meaningful to many South Asians. She says: "there are South Asian individuals who associate with Aladdin and with Jasmine as well, and I think there was a sense of we should reflect some part of the community in the principle cast so that we're actually being inclusive of who sees themselves and identifies with this text. . . .

What we've done intentionally with Naomi's character as part of the plot is that her mother is actually from a different land, and it's very clear in the movie that her mother is from a different land that's not Agrabah and that's drawing on a lot of her motivations in terms of how she sees the future of Agrabah as a welcoming place that embraces people from other places because her mother was from somewhere else."[113]

While the modest expansion in diversity can be seen in its casting practices and even in the message that Agrabah will be an inclusive place under Princess Jasmine's rule, the same cannot be said about how the 2019 film rehabilitates an older form of Orientalism as if to counteract more recent terrorist stereotypes. Yes, there was an expansion in diversity because of the highly publicized #OscarsSoWhite controversy, but there was no equivalent controversy when it came to Orientalism. Orientalism remains marketable and profitable. And without the threat of reduced box office returns, Disney adopted the minimal strategy necessary to avoid being explicitly offensive to most at this particular cultural moment.

Some critics point out that it is not possible to remake *Aladdin* in a non-Orientalist way given the story's origins and the proven profitability of Orientalist tropes. Legal scholar Khaled Beydoun writes:

For Disney, *Aladdin* is far more than just a film. It is a multimillion-dollar franchise—one that encompasses television and film spin-offs, roller-coaster rides, Halloween costumes, and scores of trademarked toys, gadgets and other products that generate considerable revenue for the mass media and entertainment conglomerate. [. . .] *Aladdin*, the film and its aggregate franchise, is not only a material embodiment of Orientalism— the system that reduces the Middle East, and its elaborately diverse peoples, cultures and faiths, into a backwards monolith—but also an enterprise that generates extravagant profits from perpetuating these misrepresentations. Beyond problematic characters and themes, Aladdin's Agrabah, the fictitious Middle Eastern setting of the film, is a cartoon remake of the Orient, a fictive and distorted recreation of the Middle East itself. A made-up place based on a made-up place.[114]

One must recall that the original story of Aladdin is an Orientalist tale penned by a male European author in the eighteenth century. The character and story of Aladdin is from *1,001 Nights*, also known as *The Arabian Nights* or, in Arabic, *Alf Layla Wa Layla*, a collection of stories of Persian, Indian, and Arabic origin that likely evolved out of a tradition of oral storytelling. The name *1,001 Nights* derives from one particular story, that of Scheherazade. The stories were popularized when Antoine Galland, a French writer and archaeologist in the eighteenth century, translated a fourteenth-century Syrian manuscript.[115] Because the translation contained only about 280 stories, far from the titular "1,001," Galland created some of his own, including "Aladdin," "Ali Baba and the Forty Thieves," and "Sinbad the Sailor," which may have been incorporated into future Arabic translations[116] and led to these tales becoming incorrectly attributed to *1,001 Nights*.[117]

Hollywood has a lucrative history of trafficking in and profiting from Orientalist imagery, with films such as *The Thief of Bagdad* (1924), *Arabian Nights* (1942), *Aladdin and His Lamp* (1901, 1928), and others. But before its US iterations, Aladdin was first performed in London in 1788 and was a popular theater production in the nineteenth century. It was also in the nineteenth century (1885, to be exact) that Richard Burton published his sixteen-volume edition of the *1,001 Arabian Nights*, which embodied the Victorian values of the time.[118] This Eurocentric history has led one critic to state, "Aladdin is a white fantasy, and that's hardly surprising, because the film is basically some white guy's foggy notion of the Orient."[119] Another critic argues that casting in an ethnically appropriate way is not possible because "something like *accuracy* isn't exactly tenable for the reprise of a story with characters whose culture only exists in the white imagination."[120] Yet another critic puts it even more bluntly: "The story of 'Aladdin' is the story of Orientalism."[121]

Cultural studies scholar Amira Jarmakani has shown a long history of consuming and commodifying "the Orient" through world's fairs and cigarette advertisements from the end of the nineteenth century through the mid-twentieth century.[122] Orientalist images of exotic Arab women were consumed en masse during a period marked by nostalgia amid rapid developments in modernization and industrialization.[123] Jarmakani writes that Orientalism is cast as premodern and thus consumed through nostalgia for a premodern past. One could argue that the reversion to Orientalism in a film like the remade *Aladdin* could also be understood as a form of nostalgia, a longing among contemporary audiences for a time when the Middle East was a site of exoticism and not terrorism.

The biggest problem with the 2019 *Aladdin* is that it rehabilitates—and thus relegitimates and repopularizes—an older form of Orientalism as if it is an improvement over newer, terrorist iterations. It trades explicit racism for clichéd exoticism, so the means may have changed but the end results are largely the same.[124] Once again, characters with American accents are "good" while those with non-American accents are mostly (but not entirely) "bad." And audiences today will be as hard pressed as those in 1992 (or 1922, for that matter) to identify any distinct Middle Eastern cultures beyond that of an overgeneralized "East." Belly dance and Bollywood dance, turbans and keffiyehs, Iranian and Arab accents—all are seemingly interchangeable. At the same time, Aladdin distinguishes itself from *Hidalgo* and other films that employ this exoticizing strategy by at least not revolving around the experiences of a white protagonist. Jasmine is not simply seeking to choose her mate, as she was in the 1992 version; she is set to be the next ruler of the kingdom. Reflective of the #MeToo movement (without, of course, explicitly referencing it), Jasmine sings that she will not stay silent. In addition to reflecting changing conceptions of gender roles and the progress reflected in the casting of non-European actors, this social change happens even as the film perpetuates Orientalism, revealing that such change is rarely without compromise.

Aladdin importantly breaks the trend of whitewashing while still advancing Orientalism by portraying the Middle East as exotic. Writers and producers respond to a problem, such as whitewashing, and seek to rectify it while leaving other problems intact as if they too are not problems. *Aladdin*'s reversion to old Orientalism highlights a common approach to diversifying representations, the "diversity compromise." It involves making a minor or major tweak toward diversifying representations just enough to be profitable and avoid controversy, but not enough to shift the paradigm.

In addition to perpetuating Orientalist tropes, another tendency is to continue to tell stories about Muslims in the context of terrorism, but to take a new or fresh approach. It must be stated that terrorist-themed shows that depict Arabs and Muslims persist lest I inadvertently give the impression that the expansion in representations has meant a significant decline in terrorist-themed TV shows and films. The new post-9/11 terrorist drama is different from its predecessors. It no longer features one-dimensional Muslim terrorists (of course, blatant terrorist-themed dramas persist: *Iron Man*, 2010; *London Has Fallen*, 2016; *Bodyguard*, 2018). The new terrorism dramas usually include a patriotic Muslim character to counteract or defuse the terrorist stereotype, an example of what I have described as simplified complex representations. Today's terrorist dramas more often than not play on the assumption that Muslims commit acts of terror but then flip the assumption on its head by either revealing that the mastermind is a white man or by offering a backstory to explain that the Muslim became a terrorist not because of religion but because of the impact of US foreign policies on their life and livelihood.

Amazon's *Jack Ryan* is a good example of how Hollywood is telling a new kind of story about terrorism.[125] The Arab Muslim terrorist Suleiman (played by Ali Suleiman) lost his family in Syria to US drone strikes when he was a child. Everyone was killed except for him and his younger brother Ali (played by Haaz Sleiman). This tragic event does not turn them into terrorists. Rather, they grow up in Paris where there are limited opportunities for Arab immigrants. Suleiman is educated and brilliant but cannot get hired. In one scene, Ali is smoking pot and is harassed by the police. Since Suleiman loves his brother, he distracts the police so that his brother can escape and he gets arrested to spare his brother. Neither brother is religious. However, while Suleiman is in prison, he says that he never felt such a sense of belonging and he becomes "radicalized." The TV drama provides a lot of backstory to make Suleiman a three-dimensional character and explain why he became a terrorist. Thus, it is not unusual today for the figure of the Muslim terrorist to be humanized through a backstory, showing him in his familial relationships—protecting his brother, with children who love him. This practice of providing backstory is a significant development. Historically, terrorist dramas did not include any backstory or provided seconds of forgettable political context at the beginning of the film, leading viewers to conclude that terrorism is caused by Islam (e.g., *Black Sunday*, 1977; *The Siege*, 1998; *Argo*, 2012).

Other common devices involve inserting critiques of US imperialism and including a patriotic Muslim on the FBI or CIA team. In the case of *Jack Ryan*, the US is implicated as being part of the problem given the practice of drone strikes. Racism and the marginalization of people of color are also implicated as problems. In addition to CIA agent James Greer (played by Wendell Pierce) being a Black Muslim, Mena Massoud is on the CIA team as a background character, Tarek Kassar. In other terrorist-themed dramas, like Epix's *Condor* (2018) and Amazon's *Unlocked* (2017), there are Muslim terrorists in the background, but we discover that the masterminds are white men, often US government officials. Muslims are portrayed as innocent but used by the US as a cover, nonetheless perpetuating the depiction of Muslims as terrorists even if they are ultimately not the responsible parties.

* * *

Criterion 2: The project that includes Muslim character(s) has a Muslim-identifying writer on staff to ensure that Muslim cultures, religion, characters, and storylines are being portrayed accurately and authentically.

In addition to the examples cited above from *9-1-1: Lone Star* and *Orange Is the New Black*—which introduced unprecedented Muslim characters yet either made a mistake (e.g., praying incorrectly) or perpetuated stereotypes (e.g., polygamy) compromising the integrity of the Muslim character—Freeform's comedy-drama *The Bold Type* (2017–2021) perpetuates a similar error that compromises an otherwise unprecedented Muslim representation. Adena El-Amin, played by Iranian Canadian actor Nikohl Boosheri, is the first Muslim lesbian character on US network television. *The Bold Type* is about three twenty-something-year-old friends, Jane, Kat, and Sutton, all of whom work together at a fashion magazine, *Scarlet*. Adena is a feminist artist from Iran who becomes Kat's (played by Aisha Dee) girlfriend and helps her figure out that she is bisexual.

We are never told explicitly Adena's country of origin, but we are given the impression that it is a repressive Middle Eastern country, most likely Iran because Boosheri is Iranian and in later episodes we come to learn that Adena speaks Farsi. In one episode, Adena is detained in her country of origin because she is carrying vibrators, which are illegal, in her luggage.[126] Before she departs on her trip, Adena makes it clear that she does not respect that law and that she cannot be herself as a queer Muslim woman in her homeland. While the Middle East is figured as sexually repressive compared to a free US, *The Bold Type* complicates Adena's character and avoids easy binaries by also highlighting her precarious legal status in the US. She is seeking to renew her work visa, concerned about being deported,[127] and subject to anti-Muslim harassment on the street. While out walking with Kat, Adena receives a phone call from her mother and speaks to her in Farsi. A white male passerby says, "Why don't you speak English, bitch." When Kat challenges the man and demands that he apologize to Adena, the white man says, "I think your towel-head friend should speak English or go back to where she came from." Adena insists that they walk away. Kat then punches the man in the face and the police arrest her. During the arrest, Adena disappears. When Kat gets upset and argues that justice would have been served if Adena had only stuck around to explain the scenario to the police, Adena says that she is sorry but that she did not have a choice: "I'm a Muslim lesbian living in today's America. My choices are very limited. [. . .] It's obvious that we just come from completely different worlds." After speaking to Jacqueline Carlyle, the editor-in-chief of *Scarlet*, Kat comes to realize that Adena could have been deported had she been or rested. Some critics found this scenario unrealistic and pointed out Kat's status as a mixed-race Black woman in the US. Would she really need to be told about the unfairness of the US criminal justice system by Adena (a Middle Eastern Muslim woman) and Jacqueline (a white woman)?[128] Others, however, praised the episode for highlighting Adena's limited choices.[129] The episode ends with Kat going to Adena's apartment to apologize, which is when they have their first kiss.

Adena El-Amin is adored by some Muslims who deeply appreciate this unusual portrayal. A guest blogger on *Muslim Girl* writes, "as a Muslim girl growing up with little to no positive representation of herself, Adena is the best thing that's ever happened to me in the media."[130] She explains, "Adena is a real person, not just a stereotypical oppressed Muslim woman that mainstream media tend to capitalize off of."[131] On Twitter, some stated that it was refreshing to see not only a lesbian Muslim character on US television for the first time, but a character who is empowered and unapologetically herself as a queer Muslim immigrant woman: "This TV show introduced a queer, Muslim feminist, and she's badass."[132] The *Cut* published eight short interviews with young queer

Muslims talking about *The Bold Type*.[133] All of them found the representation extremely meaningful. One, Sofia, who identifies as a seventeen-year-old pansexual from Egypt, states:

> Adena's character is outstanding. Positive LGBT+ representation in general—on shows like *Orphan Black* and *Sense8*, and a YouTuber as well called Miles McKenna—helped me figure stuff out [about myself], so with the character being Muslim, it was amazing. I love that when Kat first tried to interview her and asked if she was scared to say that she's a lesbian, she replied that she has "Proud Muslim lesbian" in her Twitter bio. Truly iconic because I've never seen a positive Muslim LBGT representation on TV at all before. However, one thing that I disliked is the hijab representation, because that's not what a hijab is like at all. She's just covering her head, whilst hijab is about covering your whole body, including the neck and ears, not just the head.[134]

Another interviewee, Bahar, a nineteen-year-old pansexual from the Netherlands, shared her experience of watching Adena:

> My friend and I who watch it identified so much and it felt so safe for us, like we shouldn't be afraid of who we are. Because lots of times we feel so afraid and like we're doing something wrong, and they made us feel much safer. [. . .] She said she wears a hijab because it confuses people, so I wasn't really sure if she's wearing it because of the religion or just to make a statement. Also, she has open spots, like her arms and around her neck and upper part of her body. The people around me who wear hijabs—I don't—they are more closed. I think it's great she wears it how she wants, but if I look at it from my family's perspective they would say she's not entirely wearing clothes.[135]

Adena's hijab style is puzzling to many Muslim viewers. Adena wears a hijab, sort of. She wears the hijab in a variety of ways—sometimes in a loose style that shows her hair, sometimes in a style that covers all of her hair, sometimes in a turban-style, sometimes with sleeveless and lowcut shirts that expose cleavage—and sometimes not at all (see figure 2.7). Her engagement with the hijab diverges from traditional ways of wearing it. As a garment of modesty,

Figure 2.7. Adena El-Amin in *The Bold Type*, Freeform, season 3, episode 8, 2019, Panagiotis Pantazidis via Getty Images.

a traditional approach is to wear it in public and not at home unless there are male visitors present who are not family members. As a garment of modesty, this also means that women who wear the hijab would not wear revealing clothing that, for example, accentuates their cleavage or reveals much skin. It could be argued that, as a queer woman, Adena deliberately practices hijab wearing in a way that diverges from heteronormative societal expectations. However, given that there is no context to that effect, to many Muslim viewers it comes off as if the writers are clueless given that her hijab-wearing practices are inconsistent and not tied to modesty.

In a conversation, Kat asks Adena why she wears the hijab. "Isn't it kind of contradictory?" she asks, implying that surely Adena, a lesbian feminist Muslim, must find it oppressive. Adena replies, "I chose to wear the hijab. It does not oppress me but liberates me from society's expectations of what a woman should look like. People tend to get uncomfortable when they cannot put you in a box. But I've always liked to make people uncomfortable."[136] In an interview, Boosheri addresses how her character wears the hijab: "Adena likes to be provocative, she likes to make people question. [. . .] She doesn't wear a headscarf in a traditional way. She's someone who, back home where she grew up, stands out. I wanted to fit all those things in but for her still to seem to be relatable."[137]

The extent to which Adena is recognized as Muslim by Muslims has been debated on Twitter. Yet the show establishes that she is a practicing Muslim in various ways—i.e., through her own self-identifying statements, through wearing the hijab, by mentioning that she does not drink alcohol,[138] and, in one episode, doing her morning prayers. When Kat asks Adena if she prays regularly, Adena replies that sometimes she does pray five times per day.[139] A debate ensued on Twitter about the character.[140] Some Muslims said that the representation was offensive to Islam and that the character is not really Muslim: "Bold? As in disrespectful with no morals"; "She is not Muslim and she is not wearing a hijab"; "Please call her a different name but she's not to be called a Muslim."[141] To some, it does indeed come across as a contradiction to her Muslim identity that Adena frequents lesbian bars and clubs and has a very active sexual past. Of course, such Twitter debates devolved into statements about the oppressive nature of Islam: "These responses show me that Islam is mostly for close minded people, I am very sorry for the few nice ones, but even you can see this. [. . .] And you wondered why everyone hates Muslims";[142] "Yeah it sums it up, Islam is not compatible to be implemented with modern countries."[143]

Criticisms of Adena's inconsistent hijab-wearing practice can be read as reflective of Muslim rigidity and identity policing, and the responses that claim that one cannot be both queer and Muslim are certainly reflective of that. However, similar to how *Aladdin* made important strides in casting but then perpetuated Orientalism, *The Bold Type* offers an unprecedented lesbian Muslim character but then shows a lack of awareness when it comes to hijab-wearing practices among Muslim women. The apparent lack of understanding of the internal logics of Islam compromises Adena's impact for some Muslim audiences.[144]

* * *

Criterion 3: The Muslim character(s) is not solely defined by their religion. Religion can be part of the character's backstory but should not be their entire story. Muslim culture and faith should be accurately delineated.

Even when diversifying portrayals of Muslims, there can be a tendency nonetheless to portray Muslims and people from the MENA region as primarily religious or political beings. A month before Netflix's

January 2020 release of *Messiah*, its series about a mysterious Middle Eastern man who performs miracles and is being tracked by the CIA, a controversy erupted on Twitter.[145] Muslims were convinced that the Messiah would turn out to be the anti-Christ, aka Dajjal, further fueling anti-Muslim racism. One Twitter user summed up the sentiment: "Imagine Muslims ask for representations in media and you [. . .] receive a movie about Dajjal. We hate to see it."[146] Fortunately, the anxieties expressed on Twitter did not pan out. Nonetheless, the portrayal of Arabs and Iranians in *Messiah* fits a larger post-9/11 trend: representing (and conflating) Arabs, Iranians, and Muslims as more than simply bombers and belly dancers, but still as solely religious and political beings.[147]

Messiah sympathetically portrays Arabs as victims of, alternately, ISIS, a refugee crisis at the border of Israel, and US military interventions. We discover that the Messiah is not a terrorist and might actually be who he says he is. At the same time, none of the Arab, Muslim, or Iranian characters are developed enough for viewers to know who they are as people beyond their political and religious contexts. To be sure, this is a show about religion and politics. But the non-Arab and non-Muslim characters are not presented exclusively in terms of religion and politics. The American and Israeli characters have full lives in which religion and politics coexist among many other dimensions. By contrast, Arabs are either with ISIS, the Messiah, or another ideologue. They cannot think for themselves and can only subscribe to the rigid ideologies of their group.

The first episode, reminiscent of Moses in *The Ten Commandments*, frames the story around a supposedly Arab (who we later find out is Iranian but who is not believable as an Iranian) Moses-type character in the era of ISIS, a Syrian refugee crisis, and the ongoing War on Terror. Arabs yell and wave their guns in the air in the desert, a scene we have seen countless times portraying Arabs as violent and mob-like. As if that is not fueling stereotypes enough, in another episode the young Samer becomes a suicide bomber, reinforcing the pernicious idea that Islam is violent. Although the Messiah, aka al-Masih, aka Payam Golshiri (played by Mehdi Dehbi), is at the center of the story, the drama is fueled by our not knowing anything about him. This might be an effective dramatic device, but compare it to the depiction of the other central characters, Eva (the CIA officer tracking the Messiah, played by Michelle Monaghan) and Aviram (the Israeli Shin Bet officer, played by Tomer Sisley). While neither are particularly likable, we understand their backstories and how they became jaded through their life experiences. There is a fullness to these characters that is not afforded to any MENA character.

Similarly, Rebecca (the pastor's daughter) is a young person, but there is more to her than being young and vulnerable. By contrast, the two Arab youths, Jibran and Samer, present a wonderful opportunity for character development, but it is a missed opportunity. They are good because they are young, innocent, and vulnerable. But they do not have developed personalities beyond simply being innocent and vulnerable. Jibran and Samer are cast as pawns in the larger religious and political intrigues of ruthless leaders. Granted, neither of them actually adopts their elder's ideologies, but ultimately that is how Arabs are seen—as religious and political ideologues who indoctrinate their hapless youth.

To the writers' credit, political realities are cast as multidimensional. There is an unusual complexity to the portrayal of the Israeli-Palestinian conflict. While Palestinians are a problem, they are not portrayed as *the* problem. Israeli settlements and a harsh Israeli occupying military are a part of the problem. Another unusual highlight is when the Messiah meets the president of the United States; his big ask is to withdraw US troops from all over the world to bring peace. Despite the clear efforts by shows such as *Messiah* to not reproduce old stereotypes and to create new stories and contexts, it seems that Arabs, Iranians, and Muslims cannot be conceptualized as multidimensional human beings and thus efforts to diversify are compromised.

* * *

Criterion 4: The Muslim character(s) has a strong presence and the character(s) is essential to the story arc and has a rich and clearly defined backstory.

Hollywood commonly approaches diversity by adding a background character. It is a quick and easy way to address metrics as opposed to substance. Certainly, not all Muslim characters must be in leading or major supporting roles. However, the impulse to "do diversity" through background characters who are not essential to the storyline is not an effective approach to diversifying representations. *Grey's Anatomy*, known for having one of the most diverse casts on television, introduced Dr. Dalia Qadri, a hijab-wearing ER resident, in 2017 as a background character; she was fired from her position in 2019. We did not get to know Dr. Qadri's backstory, and while it was sad when she was fired, it did not have an impact on the storyline. It is important for viewers to have the opportunity to get to know underrepresented characters. Filling background characters with underrepresented identities easily devolves into a shallow diversity practice in which underrepresented people become mere window dressing.

* * *

Criterion 5: The Muslim character(s) is portrayed with diverse backgrounds and identities.

The fifth criterion seeks to signal that not all Muslims are Arab, Iranian, or South Asian and to encourage Hollywood to explore the stories of Black, Latinx, Indonesian, and other Muslims too. This is not to say that Arab, Iranian, and South Asian Muslims should not be portrayed but rather that the 1.8 billion Muslims of the world are an incredibly diverse group of people. Expanding storylines that includes Muslim characters requires reflecting the diversity of Muslim communities.

We are seeing more Black Muslims, queer Muslims, and hijab-wearing Muslim women represented on TV. Examples of Black Muslim characters include Jim Greer (played by Wendell Pierce) on *Jack Ryan*; Alison Abdullah (played by Amanda Stephen) on *Orange Is the New Black*; Rafiq (played by Common) on *The Chi* (2018–present); Sheikh Malik (played by Mahershala Ali, see figure 2.8) and Zainab (played by MaameYaa Boafo) on season 2 (2020) of *Ramy*; and Sam Hanna (played by LL Cool J) on *NCIS: Los Angeles* (2017–present). While Adena El-Amin is hailed as the first lesbian Muslim on US network television, she is not the only queer Muslim or hijab-wearing Muslim on TV. Examples of the increase in hijab-wearing women on TV include Raina on *Quantico* (2015–2018), Qadri on *Grey's Anatomy*, Fara Sherazi on *Homeland*, and the lead character in the 2019 movie *Hala* on Apple TV+. Adena also joins two real gay Muslim men on reality television: Reza Farahan

Figure 2.8. Ramy Youssef and Mahershala Ali in *Ramy*, Hulu, season 2, 2020, photograph by Craig Blankenhorn.

on Bravo's *Shahs of Sunset* and Tan France on Netflix's *Queer Eye*. On fictional television, there is Mohamad "Mo Mo" de la Cruz (played by Haaz Sleiman), the title character's best friend on the HBO show *Nurse Jackie* (season 1, 2009). Sammy Al-Fayeed (played by Noah Silver) on *Tyrant* (2014–2016) is the closeted gay teenaged son of Barry, aka Bassam Al-Fayeed, who left his ruling family in the fictional Arab Muslim country Abuddin, only to return after his father's death to help bring democracy to the country. Rasha Zuabi (played by Dalia Yegavian) is a Muslim Syrian refugee lesbian who appears during seasons 3 and 4 (2017) of the Canadian teen drama, *Degrassi: Next Class*, broadcast on Netflix in the US and Family (F2N) in Canada; she initially wears the hijab but then stops, presumably because she is "free" in Canada.[148] As noted above, CBS's *The Red Line* (2019) featured a Pakistani gay male character who was created by queer Pakistani Canadian writer Fawzia Mirza. Kumail Nanjiani and Emily V. Gordon's Apple TV+ series *Little America* (2020) includes an episode about a gay Syrian Muslim man (played by Haaz Sleiman) who seeks asylum in the US. Mike Mosallam's *Breaking Fast* (2020), an independent film, is a love story about a gay Muslim man in LA. Hulu's teen drama *Love, Victor* introduced the Iranian queer teen Rahim (played by Anthony Keyban) in season 2 (2021) and *Generation*

(2021) on HBO Max introduced the Egyptian queer teen Bo (played by Marwan Salama). These representations usually diverge from the deeply problematic handful of past representations of queer Muslim terrorists that suggested a connection between queer sexuality and terrorism. Salim on season 2 (2006) of *Sleeper Cell* is a repressed homosexual terrorist psychopath. He sleeps with a man at the gym but is wracked with intense feelings of shame and seeks fundamentalist teachings and terrorism to right his path. Mansour Al-Zahrani, who appears in season 1 (2011) of *Homeland*, is a Saudi diplomat and al-Qaeda contact who has three wives, ten children, and sleeps with men. His gay tendencies are framed as part of his corrupt lifestyle and culture.

The Obeidi-Alsultany Test does not include in the criteria anything about casting, a matter which is very important when talking about MENA characters and actors but not the same in the case of Muslims and religion. While ethnic casting is extremely important in challenging a history of whitewashing and ethnic interchangeability, and while having a Muslim actor play a Muslim character certainly helps, we did not deem religious matching in casting to be as important as matching ethnic and racial roles. What matters is Muslim visibility in a diversity of roles.

Diversifying Representations

What are we to make of this uneasy mix of triumphs and tradeoffs? Hollywood emerged as heroic in the Trump era as the industry made important strides in diversifying representations, leading to an unprecedented expansion in representations of Muslims between 2015 and 2020. To be clear, despite this important expansion, we have not yet arrived at the destination. Shows like *Ramy* and *We Are Lady Parts* are far from being the norm, but they raise the bar and pave the way to move past stereotypes entirely. Lasting change will come when Hollywood (and other industries) not only responds when there is a momentary crisis but when it is understood that the industry itself has participated in creating an ongoing crisis over the last century and thus that the crisis is enduring and there is no quick fix.

Muslim identities are becoming commodified and profitable as part of an imperative to diversify. At the same time, an expansion and a paradigm shift are not the same thing. As the examples above have illustrated, it is not usual for a compromise to take place in the process of diversifying, thus diminishing the impact and the possibility of a paradigm shift. The Obeidi-Alsultany Test and other tests, alongside report cards, create a path forward. Nonetheless, the solution to a history of white supremacy and Eurocentric depictions is not as easy as coming up with a three- or four-point plan. Rather, Hollywood executives, writers, directors, producers, and others in the industry need to acquire an understanding of the history of representations of various marginalized groups and their profound impact so as to change course and not repeat it. It is important to remember what is at stake here: the project is not just to diversify representations, but to repair a history of harmful stereotypes and misrepresentations.

The purpose of this chapter is not to nitpick or imply that the industry cannot get anything right. Rather, it is to highlight common pitfalls so that more of those involved become aware of them. Otherwise, small and sometimes large tweaks will be made to diversify, while simultaneously the problem is reinforced in other ways. As Rhodes points out, "while business approaches see diversity as just another means for securing commercial self-interest, social justice approaches claim a genuine ethical interest beyond business justification."[149] It has become common for diversity projects to essentially depoliticize the project of equality. To create diverse storytelling, Hollywood needs to become aware of this and figure out alternative pathways. Social justice, or rectifying the history of inequality, often gets lost in the project of diversity, especially when mediated through profit. Thus, the larger question that arises beyond practical suggestions is to figure out how to negotiate the relationship between corporate approaches to diversity that tend to depoliticize representations, focus on metrics, and make significant improvements that are compromised in other ways, and instead to focus on a paradigm shift capable of attaining social justice in storytelling and representations. Hollywood's commitment to "diversity" has to move beyond crisis response to understanding that the crisis is persistent and not the result of one policy like the Muslim travel ban or one Twitter firestorm like #OscarsSoWhite. Surely, Hollywood is creative enough to find a way forward.

3

Racial Gaslighting

On February 10, 2015, in Chapel Hill, North Carolina, Craig Stephen Hicks, a forty-six-year-old white male car-parts salesperson, murdered his neighbors, three Muslim students: Deah Barakat (age twenty-three); his wife, Yusor Abu-Salha (age twenty-one); and her sister, Razan Abu-Salha (age nineteen). He shot each of them in the head, execution-style. The FBI labeled the murders a parking dispute, not a hate crime, thus sparking a debate over the meaning of the latter. Hicks turned himself in and was charged with three counts of first-degree murder. His wife, Karen, insisted that the murders were not motivated by hatred, stating that his actions were motivated by "the longstanding parking disputes that my husband had with the neighbors. He often champions on his Facebook page for the rights of many individuals. Same-sex marriages, abortion, race, he just believes everyone is equal."[1] Hicks pled guilty to three counts of first-degree murder and in 2019, four years after killing Deah Barakat, Yusor Abu-Salha, and Razan Abu-Salha, he was sentenced to three terms of life in prison.[2]

Two years later, on June 18, 2017, in Reston, Virginia, twenty-two-year-old Darwin Martinez Torres, a construction worker and undocumented immigrant from El Salvador, killed Nabra Hassanen (age seventeen) in an incident law enforcement classified as road rage. At around 3:40 a.m. on a Sunday during the holy month of Ramadan, a group of fifteen teenagers were walking and bike riding from an IHOP restaurant back to the All Dulles Area Muslim Society (aka the ADAMS Center), where they were attending an overnight event. Some of the teens were on the sidewalk and others were on the road when Torres approached them in his car and got into an argument with them. He then got out of his car and chased them with a baseball bat. The teens ran away, but he captured seventeen-year-old Nabra Hassanen, hit her with the baseball bat, and then put her body in his car. After abducting her, he sexually assaulted

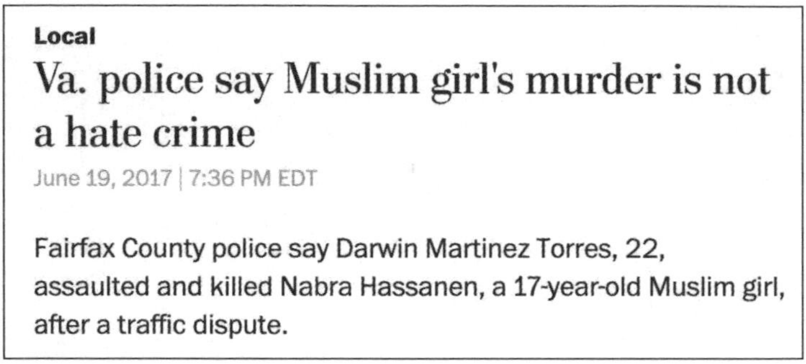

Local

Va. police say Muslim girl's murder is not a hate crime

June 19, 2017 | 7:36 PM EDT

Fairfax County police say Darwin Martinez Torres, 22, assaulted and killed Nabra Hassanen, a 17-year-old Muslim girl, after a traffic dispute.

Figure 3.1. Screenshot of a news story reporting that the police have indicated that Nabra Hassanen's murder was not a hate crime, NBC Washington, June 19, 2017.

her, murdered her, and left her body in a pond in Loudoun County, where the police recovered it.[3] Torres was officially charged with abduction with intent to defile, first-degree murder, and rape.[4] He pled guilty to the murder of Hassanen and, in 2019, was sentenced to eight life terms in prison.[5]

The police were clear in their statements that, despite the fact that a group of Muslim teens were attacked and that Hassanen was wearing a hijab at the time, this was not to be classified as a hate crime (see figure 3.1). Fairfax County police spokesperson Julie Parker said at a press conference that there was no evidence that the crime was motivated by race or religion and added that there was no evidence that Torres used any racial slurs as he chased the group of teens.[6] Tawny Wright, another spokesperson with the Fairfax Police Department said, "Everyone looks at this crime and thinks that because the victims were participating in activities at a mosque, they assume that's what it was [. . .] it seems like a guy got enraged and just went after the victim who was closest to him."[7]

In both this and the Chapel Hill case above, the Council on American-Islamic Relations (CAIR) and other civil rights groups challenged law enforcement's characterization of the incidents and insisted the events be investigated and classified as hate crimes. In the Chapel Hill case in 2015, over 150 civil rights groups signed a letter to Attorney General Eric Holder urging a hate crime investigation. In the Reston case in 2017, CAIR issued a public statement: "As we grieve for Nabra's loss, we also urge law enforcement authorities to conduct a thorough investigation of a possible bias motive in this case, coming as it does at a time of rising Islamophobia and anti-Muslim hate attacks nationwide."[8]

Debate ensued over whether the hate crime classification mattered. Michael McGough, writing for the *Los Angeles Times*, argued that, "[t]he killings in North Carolina were horrible if they were motivated by Islamophobia, but they were also horrible if they originated in equal-opportunity malice. Confirmation of the second scenario would not reflect disrespect for the victims or indifference to the targeting of people because of 'how they worship.'"[9] In contrast, Margaret Talbot, writing for the *New Yorker*, stated that even though a hate crime charge would not increase the penalty since the Durham County prosecutor was already seeking the death penalty, the designation would serve an important function. She wrote:

> hate-crime statutes are symbolic as well as instrumental: they exist not only to maximize punishment but also to underscore disapproval of bias, allowing us to name an ugly motivation and renounce it. To the families and friends of the victims, it was the naming of the crime, not the punishment, that mattered most.[10]

Why would law enforcement be reluctant to label cases in which Muslim youths are murdered as hate crimes? And what are the effects when the criminal justice system refuses to apply this category to instances of anti-Muslim racism? I contend that the denial of a hate crime classification in such cases contributes to the diminishment and denial of anti-Muslim racism and, as such, should be understood as a form of *racial gaslighting*—that is, a systematic denial of the persistence and severity of racism. Religious studies scholar Juliane Hammer, writing about these two murder cases, points to how the term "Islamophobia" itself contributes to understanding the murders as individual acts, focusing on individual culpability rather on the larger problem of anti-Muslim hatred that inspires such attacks.[11] As I explain in the introduction, I deliberately use the term "anti-Muslim racism" instead of "Islamophobia" to facilitate an analysis of systemic discrimination and to reject conceptualizing discrimination as located in the individual or as a phobia. I use ethnic studies scholars Nadine Naber and Junaid Rana's definition of anti-Muslim racism: the "inter-personal, media, and state-based targeting of [. . .] those who are Muslim and those perceived to be Muslim [. . .] [that] often relies upon the assumption that "Muslims" are enemies of, and pose a threat to, the US nation."[12] Anti-Muslim racism accounts for the dialectic between individuals and institutions[13] and the deep-rooted structures of white supremacy in US history that continue to shape and inform logics that legitimize exclusion today. Furthermore, it expands our understanding of racism to account for the ways in which it is based not only on phenotype, but in visual markers like the hijab or beard and how race thinking can be transferable to conceptions of culture and nation.[14]

While chapters 1 and 2 examine how Hollywood and the media respond to anti-Muslim racism by expanding the field of representations of Muslims, chapter 3 examines how law enforcement responds to the crisis of anti-Muslim racism when it comes in the form of civilian-enacted violence, or a hate crime. I conduct a critical discourse analysis of these murder cases that are not defined as hate crimes as they were covered in news reporting and police press releases, as well as responses in op-eds, on Twitter, and by civil rights organizations. I focus on these two cases because they, unlike other, similar cases, became newsworthy, and I am interested in exploring why that is so. In conversation with women-of-color feminist scholars advocating for rethinking the criminal justice system through prison abolition and restorative justice, seeking state recognition for hate crimes cannot provide justice because the state is responsible for constructing Muslims as a national security threat. Angela Davis, Ruth Gilmore, Mimi Kim, and others have underlined that prison and punishment are not the answer. They have called for rethinking the criminal justice system through prison abolition, restorative justice, and transformative justice.[15] In the case of redressing Muslims who are murder victims, a meaningful approach would not only address the state's responsibility in constructing anti-Muslim racism through a range of policies, but would also problematize a larger trend characteristic of a neoliberal era that involves investing in crime and punishment and divesting from civil rights.

Given that the criminal justice system is an important arm of the national security state that constructs the figure of the Muslim as a "terrorist" and is responsible for the widespread surveillance of Muslims in the US, these details cannot be bracketed out of the conversation about hate crimes against Muslims and anti-Muslim racism. Furthermore, given its role, the criminal justice system as currently configured cannot offer a meaningful resolution to victims of hate crimes or their families. Muslims in the US seek state recognition for hate crimes while the very same state subjects them to violence and surveillance. Muslim communities are under surveillance; mosques and even student groups like the Muslim Student Association on college campuses are infiltrated.[16] "Terrorism" is commonly understood as being caused by "Muslim extremists" without attention being paid to the role of US interventionist policies abroad.[17] The US employs secret drone strikes, targeted assassinations, military occupations, and the militarization of policing domestically in fueling the terror-industrial complex.[18] So to what extent can law enforcement be seen as an ally to US Muslims?

In 2016, several police officers in San Jose, California, posted private comments on Facebook that included "Black lives don't really matter" and "I say re-purpose the hijabs into nooses."[19] While these officers were placed on leave, their comments reflect the common tendency to individualize racism. The police chief assured the public that "any current employee involved with bigoted activity online will promptly be investigated and held accountable to the fullest extent in my power." However, these are not isolated or exceptional instances. In 2017, the Chicago Police Union president posted on Facebook, "savages they all deserve a bullet," referring to Muslims.[20] Police officers have been active on Facebook groups such as "Veterans Against Islamic Filth," "Americans against Mosques," "Death to Islam Undercover," and "Rage against the Veil."[21] In 2018, the New York Police Department reached a settlement in a lawsuit initiated by Muslim Advocates and the Center for Constitutional Rights for illegally spying on Muslims by placing informants in mosques and in Muslim student groups to prevent terrorism, an initiative that produced not even one intelligence lead.[22] Law enforcement engages in a continuum of violence against racialized communities that includes killing unarmed Black people and surveilling Muslim communities.

It is a difficult endeavor to write about hate crimes against Muslims that are not classified as such, thus gaslighting Muslim experiences with racism—a problem that is not solved by simply changing the classification to "hate crime." It is difficult because we, Muslims, want recognition of hate crimes. We want the racial gaslighting to stop. We want hate crime legislation and other measures to be taken to address the problem. We want recognition for the violence and pain experienced by our communities. However, if we bracket state violence from this conversation, then we will not find an effective solution to anti-Muslim racism. When addressing the problem of hate crimes, it is important to understand that the police and criminal justice system are part of the problem. While it is appealing to believe that law enforcement will ensure that justice is served through life-term prison sentences for individuals who kill US Muslims, we must also question whether it is possible for justice to be served by the same criminal justice system that subjects Muslims to surveillance, deportation, bans, and bombs. Racial profiling is mobilized to fuel a state-sponsored, ongoing "War on Terror" and inspires vigilante hate crimes. Expanding hate crime laws for greater recognition will not achieve justice; it will not end hate crimes or the project of US empire that results in countless deaths. In this chapter, I explore the denial of hate crime classifications and therefore the denial of anti-Muslim racism along with the importance of holding the state accountable for violence against Muslim communities. I do this by outlining three problematics that arise in thinking through the denial of hate crime classifications and therefore the denial of anti-Muslim racism. But first, what is gaslighting and racial gaslighting?

Gaslighting is a term adopted by psychologists that refers to psychological manipulation, originating in the 1938 play *Gaslight*, which was adapted into a film in 1944. The story centers around an abusive husband who intentionally drives his wife to question her sanity so that he can conceal his criminal activity from her. The specific term "gaslighting" refers to the husband's practice of dimming the gaslights in the house, only to deny doing so when his wife notices the change. He insists she is imagining things, making her question her own perception. Thus, "gaslighting" refers to manipulating someone and driving them to the point of questioning their own sanity by controlling their perception of reality. There was a surge in the popular usage of the term during the Trump presidency to refer to a range of his destructive behaviors, including, for example, his response when he was confronted about making fun of a disabled reporter—simply denying that he had done any such thing.[23]

Some journalists and bloggers have also used the term to describe the denial of racism effected when, for example, someone describes the Black Lives Matter movement as anti-white and/or anti-police, or responds with "all lives matter" or "blue lives matter" to deny the systematic dehumanization of Black life throughout US history. Referring to the country's long history of downplaying its roots in white supremacy, Rachel Bjerstedt writes, "White America has been gaslighting black Americans since our country was founded."[24] Greg Howard, writing for the *New York Times Magazine*, links gaslighting to racism by pointing to how common it is in US culture today to understand racism as an individual problem as opposed to a larger societal one:

> It's not that anyone denies that institutional racism once existed. But the belief now is that systemic racism is a national cancer that was excised long ago, in an operation so successful it didn't even leave lasting effects. All that remains is individual hatred in the souls of the most monstrous among us—or else, depending on whom you ask, in vengeful minorities who want to nurse grievances and see whites suffer for the sins of past generations. Through the willful perversion of shared history, whites have been able to appropriate the victimhood of minorities and, in an audacious reversal, insist that an obvious thing isn't real—otherwise known as gaslighting. And as in any case of sustained abuse, gaslighting is integral to institutional racism.[25]

Attempts to shine light on the intertwined histories of racism and white supremacy in the United States are frequently met with gaslighting. What I propose in this chapter is to use the concept of racial gaslighting to understand anti-Muslim racism—or, more accurately, denials of its existence. Understanding how denial operates reveals the normalization of racialized violence.

Refusing to designate murders of Muslim people in the US as hate crimes diminishes and denies anti-Muslim racism and thus operates as a form of racial gaslighting, or the systematic denial of the persistence and severity of racism (and other forms of discrimination). By upholding an extremely narrow and problematic definition of racism and thus what constitutes a hate crime, law enforcement adopts an approach to hate crimes that prioritizes punishment over social justice. Three problematics become apparent when we seek to understand how racial gaslighting operates in these murder cases and thus why seeking state recognition is not the answer. The first problematic is that the narrow definition of what constitutes a hate crime is itself a form of gaslighting anti-Muslim racism. The second problematic concerns the law enforcement rationale that a hate crime designation is not needed because justice will be served in the form of imprisonment, thus prioritizing punishment over civil rights. Muslim community advocacy for hate crime recognition highlights the third problematic, namely, the dilemma when state recognition for hate crimes comes at the expense of state accountability for anti-Muslim violence. Ultimately, the hate crime designation matters and has significant meaning for the communities involved, but seeking state enforcement of the designation is also not the answer. Rather, to end hate crimes against Muslims, the state must be held accountable for its role in producing anti-Muslim racism.

Why a Hate Crime Is Not a Hate Crime

Hate crime laws date back to the Civil Rights Act of 1968, which made it illegal to threaten or interfere with a person because of their race, color, religion, or national origin. Subsequently, hate crime legislation was passed in the 1990s and 2000s that required the attorney general to collect data on hate crimes annually, increased penalties for hate crimes, and expanded the identities acknowledged as targets of hate crimes to include sexual orientation, disability, and gender. Before President George H. W. Bush signed the first federal anti–hate crime law, the Hate Crime Statistics Act (HCSA), on April 23, 1990, which mandated that the FBI collect and disseminate data on hate crimes, there were four hearings to discuss which particular identities were vulnerable to hate crimes:[26] Crimes Against Religious Practices and Property (1985), Anti-Gay Violence (1986), Ethnically Motivated Violence Against Arab-Americans[27] (1986), and Racially Motivated Violence (1988).[28] The hearings as a whole identified white supremacy as the central cause of hate crimes and the need for state action to protect historically marginalized groups.[29]

Even though Arab Americans participated in the hearings that defined hate crime laws, they were not included in the FBI's annual hate crimes report (first published in 1993) until 2015.[30] At the 1986 hearing, prominent Arab Americans testified that Jewish extremist groups were targeting them for criticisms of Israel, highlighting the murder of Alex Odeh at the American-Arab Anti-Discrimination Committee (ADC) in 1985 as an example. They detailed incidents of violent intimidation, media discrimination, and political discrimination. They pointed to the FBI's own 1972 Operation Abscam (aka the Arab Scam or Abdul Scam), which involved people posing as rich Arab oil sheiks and offering bribes to US government officials in order to find corruption in the US Congress, as reinforcing anti-Arab prejudice. Most importantly, testimony linked US foreign policy in the Middle East to anti-Arab and anti-Muslim sentiment in the US.[31] Examples cited in the hearing included Arab American organizations, leaders, and families facing racist slogans like "Go back to Libya" and receiving death threats after the 1986 US bombing of Libya.[32] Hate violence was addressed as an obstacle to Arab American political and civic participation and both the government and media were implicated. Despite testimonies stressing that "state power and hate violence determine each other vis-à-vis U.S. foreign policy in the Arab nations and the rise of anti-Arab and anti-Muslim violence and bigotry in the U.S.,"[33] hate crimes came to be framed as an individual-level problem rather than a policy-level or systemic one, reflecting the neoconservative approach of the Reagan-Bush administration.[34] Maxwell Leung, researcher with the Islamophobia Research and Documentation Project at the University of California at Berkeley, argues that the hearings in the 1980s were integral to shaping hate crime definitions and legislation, focusing on hate as an individual problem, and directing resources toward a punitive criminal justice approach.[35]

In 1996, hate crime laws were expanded through the Church Arson Prevention Act (in response to a number of church burnings—most of them involving African American churches), which made it illegal to destroy someone's religious property or interfere with a person's religious practice. Hate crime legislation was amended once again in 2009 through the Matthew Shepard and James Byrd, Jr., Hate Crimes Prevention Act—so named in memory of James Byrd, Jr., a forty-nine-year-old African American man murdered by three white supremacists in Jasper, Texas, in 1998, and Matthew Shepard, a twenty-one-year-old white gay man murdered by two white men in Laramie, Wyoming, in 1998. This act was considered significant legislation; it made illegal crimes based on gender, disability, gender identity, or sexual orientation and also increased penalties for crimes motivated by race, religion, national origin, color, sex, sexual preference, disability, or age.[36] While these are federal hate crime laws, not all states have hate crime laws and thus some hate crimes will not be prosecuted as such.[37]

According to the FBI's website, "a hate crime is a traditional offense like murder, arson, or vandalism with an added element of bias."[38] The bias can be "against a race, religion, disability, sexual orientation, ethnicity, gender, or gender identity." The FBI also points out that "hate itself is not a crime" and that freedom of speech must be protected. Thus, a hate crime involves violence or the destruction of property and not hateful speech. For a crime to be classified as a hate crime, it needs to meet two specific criteria. First, the act needs to qualify as a crime. This might seem obvious, but the point of this criterion is to distinguish between illegal activity and hateful speech and actions that are protected by the constitution. Hateful actions, such as yelling racial slurs or spreading racist flyers, are protected speech and not considered to be crimes. In other words, the hate crime designation is applied only to existing/established crimes—e.g., vandalism, arson, murder—and is not a distinct category in itself.[39] It is worth noting that because a hate crime charge is used to enhance the penalty on an existing crime, many law enforcement officials do not see a hate crime designation as necessary in a murder case since murder usually involves the highest penalty anyway.

Second, once a particular crime has been confirmed, it can then be elevated to a hate crime if evidence suggests that the motive was hateful. But what determines a hateful motive? Did the attacker yell slurs, or otherwise say anything explicitly anti-gay or racist during the act? Does the attacker have a history, perhaps on social media or in other writings, of discriminatory ideas? If an attacker did not say something anti-Muslim while committing an attack against Muslims or if their Facebook profile does not exhibit anti-Muslim sentiments, then the act would not be classified as a hate crime. Law enforcement ask a series of questions about the perpetrator's motives, intent, and history before defining a hate crime as such.

There is abundant criticism of hate crime laws for a variety of reasons. Some argue that such laws should be abolished because they violate the First Amendment. Since the perpetrator must articulate overtly discriminatory language while committing a crime for it to constitute a hate crime, a fundamental contradiction exists in the criteria given that hateful speech is protected by the First Amendment.[40] Other critics argue that hate crime laws are counterproductive because they lead victims to perceive themselves as outside the mainstream of society, thus exacerbating identity politics and social divisions.[41] Another strand of criticism claims that hate crime laws amount to reverse discrimination, violating a person's right to equal protection under the law (under the Fourteenth Amendment) because some identities qualify for protection while others do not, and thus some are positioned as more worthy of protection than others.[42] These perspectives overlook the history of white supremacy in the United States and thus the need to protect historically marginalized identities. They also overlook the importance of hate crime laws in acknowledging the persistence of violence in and around marginalized communities. Much of the legal scholarship arguing the case against hate crime laws oddly contributes to racial and other forms of gaslighting: If hate crime laws are creating social divisions, then what are racism and anti-LGBTQ+ discrimination doing?

Ethnic studies and queer studies scholars have launched some important criticisms of hate crime laws. They point out that hate crime laws do not reduce or prevent the phenomena in question, nor do they account for the intersectionality of people's actual identities. But most importantly, hate crime laws only expand criminalization and penalization, and disproportionately impact poor people and people of color.[43] Over the decades, the Hate Crimes Statistics Act has become known for misrepresenting the prevalence of hate crimes because many agencies underreport or entirely fail to report hate crimes.[44] A 2016 investigation into the Chicago Police Department revealed that hate crimes often go unreported to the Civil Right Unit "because detectives minimize the seriousness of such crimes, saying things like, 'a crime is a crime,' or 'so they got called a name.'"[45] A report by the Bureau of Justice Statistics found that the majority of hate crimes (54 percent) went unreported to the police between 2011 and 2015.[46] Furthermore, it revealed that violent hate crimes reported to the police (10 percent) were three times less likely to result in an arrest than violent non-hate crimes reported to police (28 percent).[47] The discrepancy between hate crimes reported to civil rights groups and hate crimes documented by law enforcement reveals the institutional diminishment of the category in general.

Critics also state that hate crime laws are ineffective in reducing or preventing hate crimes.[48] One example is the case of thirty-seven-year-old

Khalid Jabara, who was shot and killed on August 12, 2016, by Stanley Vernon Majors, a sixty-two-year-old gay white man in Tulsa, Oklahoma. Jabara and his family, Orthodox Christians from Lebanon, were repeatedly harassed and called "Aye-rabs," "Mooslems," "dirty Arabs," and "filthy Lebanese" by their neighbor.[49] Jabara's murder was considered a hate crime because there was clear evidence of Majors's explicit racial and religious slurs. The fact that the Jabara family is not actually Muslim made no difference, as Majors's belief that they were was well established. What is particularly troubling in this case is that even though Jabara's murder was classified as a hate crime, repeated calls to the police and a restraining order did not prevent the murder.

In addition to the hate crime designation failing to protect Jabara, his death was not reported as a hate crime in official hate crime statistics, further revealing inaccuracies in hate crime data collection.[50] The Arab American Institute's 2018 report on hate crimes against Arab Americans found that any cases assigned Bias Motivation Code 31, indicating anti-Arab hate crimes, were excluded from official data collection from 1992 to 2015. The FBI had planned to publish anti-Arab hate crime data, but the Office of Management and Budget—notably, the same body that continues to classify Arabs (and others from Southwest Asia and North Africa) as white—recommended removing Bias Code 31 from the official data collection. So, even though thirty-two states reported over eight hundred anti-Arab hate crimes to the FBI prior to 2015, none of these were included in official statistics as Code 31 was rendered invalid. Some anti-Arab hate crimes were recorded under Code 33, "Anti-Other Ethnicity/National Origin," but it is difficult to disaggregate those that pertain to Arab Americans. Even after 2015, when the FBI reintroduced Code 31, anti-Arab hate crimes continued to fall through the cracks due to major discrepancies in data collection and reporting.[51] As the Arab American Institute's report states, just as Code 31 was rendered invalid, so too were victims of anti-Arab hate crimes rendered invisible.

While the FBI did not add an anti-Arab category until 2015, hate crimes against Muslims have been tracked since 1996.[52] Between 1996 and 2000, the FBI reported between 21 and 32 hate crimes against Muslims per year. There was a spike after 9/11 to 481 hate crimes in 2001, between 105 and 160 hate crimes annually through 2014, then another spike to 257 in 2015. However, given the underreporting of hate crimes, it is estimated that these figures are forty times less than the reality.[53] Even though the FBI is required to track and report on hate crimes annually as a result of the 1990 Hate Crimes Statistics Act, they cannot compel local law enforcement to collect and submit this data, leading to vast discrepancies.[54] Furthermore, if a community does not trust law enforcement, they might not report a hate crime at all. Maya Berry of the Arab American Institute writes, "of the hate crimes that likely occur each year in our country, only about 1 percent are reported in official federal statistics."[55] The flaws and exclusions of the hate crime designation itself reveal the limits of labeling and its ability to impact, let alone prevent, hate crimes. In addition, the criteria used to determine whether a particular crime is indeed a hate crime assume that racism is always necessarily overt, thus overlooking and even denying its varied manifestations.

The two cases of Muslim youths, which I examine below, whose murders were not labeled hate crimes are not the only murder cases that appear to be hate crimes but that are not designated as such. In April 2017, Bangladeshi imam Maulana Alauddin Akonjee (fifty-five) and his assistant Thara Uddin Miah (sixty-four) were shot in the head at point-blank range in Ozone Park, Queens, New York. They were dressed in religious garb as they left their mosque, Al-Furqan Jame Masjid.[56] Oscar Morel, a thirty-five-year-old Latinx maintenance worker for the New School University, was charged with first-degree murder, but the murder was not classified as a hate crime. Despite the Bangladeshi community's insistence that the crime be classified as a hate crime, law enforcement maintained that the motivation for the crime was unclear and thus that a hate crime determination could not be made. Morel's Facebook posts and interviews with friends did not reveal any animosity toward Muslims. The closest sign of anti-Muslim sentiment was his brother stating during an interview that they both felt hatred toward Muslims after 9/11, but he insisted that it was temporary.[57] Law enforcement stressed that Morel would face the harshest of penalties regardless of the lack of a hate crime classification. A year later, Morel was charged with first-degree and second-degree murder and sentenced to life in prison without parole. The motive was never identified.[58] The case did not make headline news.

Examining hate crimes in 2010–2018 that are not designated as such, one finds a number of cases in which murders of transgender youths are not recognized as hate crimes. Seventeen-year-old transgender Ally Lee

Steinfeld's 2017 murder was not classified as a hate crime despite the fact that she was stabbed in the genitals repeatedly by her four assailants.[59] Sheriff James Sigman and prosecutor Parke Stevens Jr. said that gender had nothing to do with Steinfeld's death.[60] Prosecutor Stevens stated that the reason the assailants have not been charged with a hate crime is because, according to Missouri law, hate crime charges cannot be added to first-degree murder as that charge already "carries the highest and most severe form of punishment in the State of Missouri."[61] Thus, he concluded, "murder in the first-degree is all that matters. That is a hate crime in itself."[62] Three out of the four assailants were charged with first-degree murder and one was charged with aiding in first-degree murder.[63] The Transgender Rights Project for Lambda Legal insisted that it be classified as a hate crime to shed light on violence against transgender people. Law enforcement classifications overlook the importance hate crime classifications serve in acknowledging and naming identity-based forms of violence. In this case, gaslighting operates by stating that gender identity has nothing to do with the murder, that the murder comes with the highest penalty and therefore that the hate crime designation is pointless, and by stating that murder is hateful in itself, thus diminishing the specific violence transgender people face as the result of anti-LGBTQ+ discrimination.

Similarly, in 2016, when sixteen-year-old African American, gender-non-binary Kedarie Johnson was murdered in Iowa, it was not classified as a hate crime. Johnson's mother described him as gender-fluid because he preferred the gender pronoun "he" but sometimes used "she." Johnson would sometimes dress in men's clothing and sometimes in women's clothing. He also dated both boys and girls and seemed to have a preference for boys. A New York Times article described him as popular at his high school.[64] On the day that he was murdered, he was wearing women's clothing. It is assumed that Johnson was approached by Jorge Sanders-Galvez (twenty-two) and his cousin, Jaron Purham (twenty-five), and that they thought that he was biologically female and killed him when they discovered that he was biologically male during a sex act. Johnson's body was found in an alley. He had been shot multiple times and a plastic garbage bag was wrapped around his head. Both men were found guilty of murder.[65] Given that, in Iowa, hate crime laws do not apply to transgender people, Kedarie Johnson's murder was not labeled as a hate crime. These examples demonstrate the multifaceted failure of hate crime laws and the pervasiveness of gaslighting identity-specific violence.

In the next section, I think through three problematics that arise when considering the murders of Deah Barakat, Yusor Abu-Salha, and Razan Abu-Salha in Chapel Hill, North Carolina, in 2015 and the murder of Nabra Hassanen in Reston, Virginia, in 2017. Given that these cases were defined as "not hate crimes," it appears that the solution to the problem would be changing the designation to one of "hate crime" and ensuring that they are statistically counted. On the surface, this would seemingly resolve the racial gaslighting. However, a hate crime designation does not resolve the issue because (1) the definition of hate crimes is narrow and flawed, (2) the neoliberal state has increasingly favored punishment over social justice, and (3) when Muslims seek state recognition for hate crimes, it tends to bracket state complicity with hate crimes from the conversation. Hate crimes must be understood as linked to rather than separate from state violence. Thus, asking the state for recognition through a hate crime designation absolves the state from being accountable for producing the conditions that fuel anti-Muslim violence.

Problematic 1: The Problem with Hate Crime Definitions

While Muslims of all genders are susceptible to hate crimes, women who wear the hijab tend to more often be the target of hate crime violence whereas Muslim men are more susceptible to government surveillance and government-sanctioned violence.[66] Many Muslims in the US argued that the murders in Chapel Hill were surely a hate crime given that Yusor Abu-Salha and Razan Abu-Salha both wore the hijab and were visibly Muslim. Their parents emigrated from Palestine, via Jordan, and Deah Barakat's family emigrated from Syria. However, insistence that this was a hate crime was countered with evidence to the contrary; most notably, those who objected to the label pointed out that Craig Hicks did not fit the profile of the standard "hater." His Facebook and other online posts revealed that he was an atheist, against all religion, regardless of whether it was Islam, Christianity, or Judaism. Alongside rants against religion, he had also expressed support for issues rarely seen as related, from freedom of speech and freedom of religion to the right to bear arms and gay marriage rights. An op-ed in the *Los Angeles Times* described him as a "militant atheist" and reported that his Facebook page included attacks on religion in general and a statement posted in 2012 that declared: "I hate Islam just as much as Christianity, but they have the right to worship in this country just as much as any others do."[67] His archived posts even included commentary on the 2010 "ground zero mosque" controversy, arguing that Muslims were entitled to the right to practice their faith and noting the importance of distinguishing between Muslims and Muslim extremists.

Offline, Hicks was described as a "known bully" in his neighborhood.[68] He had flashed his gun to his neighbors to warn them to keep the noise down and not to park in a particular spot that he claimed belonged to his wife. Given that North Carolina is an open-carry state, it is legal to carry a weapon. Neighbors who lived in the same apartment complex had complained to each other about Hicks's aggression.[69] However, on the day of the murder, none of the three victims' cars were parked in the disputed spot. Professor of psychiatry Jonathan Metzl writes that Hicks's masculinity—"an increasingly prevalent form of stand-your-ground masculinity"—provides insight into his actions, especially in light of his being a "self-appointed watchman" in the apartment complex, patrolling hallways and parking lots, monitoring noise levels, and checking whether cars showed the appropriate parking stickers.[70] As Metzl points out, "These actions went hand-in-hand with a complex psychological relationship to guns marked by disproportionate gun ownership."[71]

Nonetheless, in the eyes of many, Hicks's profile would not fit expectations regarding the kind of person likely to commit a hate crime—i.e., a white supremacist. It does not follow, however, that the killing of these three Muslim youths was therefore not a hate crime. Indeed, the varied ways in which Hicks defies popular expectations reveals the limits and problems with how racism is conceptualized—namely, as explicit, clear, individual, and aberrant. The rigid conception of hate crimes, and by default racism, individualizes racism and thus makes systemic racism invisible. Legal scholar and transgender activist Dean Spade notes that "the law's adoption of this conception of racism [. . .] make(s) it ineffective at eradicating racism and help(s) it contribute to obscuring the actual operations of racism."[72] Hate crimes law scholar Clara Lewis's work has likewise shown that hate crime coverage in the news focuses only on the most extreme cases like murder, thus reinforcing the impression that such crimes are exceptional events, committed by extremists who subscribe to views not shared by the general public. Hate crimes, as a result, appear completely disconnected from the culture at large, and only enter public consciousness as anomalies that can be collectively decried and disavowed. Because they hear only about such extreme cases, Lewis says that audiences get to feel that justice has been served and, indeed, that they have participated in this process, without implicating themselves or disturbing the social order.

So if hate crime designations (and the media coverage of them) portray racism as an individualized, extreme, and exceptional phenomenon, then what does it mean when the murder of a Muslim is denied that label, excluded from the category even with all its limitations? By not classifying these murders as hate crimes, racism becomes even further exceptionalized and rendered invisible. This classification conveys that even extreme individual violence doesn't constitute racism, and in doing so exceptionalizes Muslims' frequent exposure to hate crimes. In this case, "parking dispute" reclassifies reality through an act of labeling, coding a crime as race-neutral when it is anything but.

A key feature of racial logics today is the framing of racist incidents as having nothing to do with racism. Denials, reversals, and gaslighting are central to understanding how racism and other forms of discrimination operate.[73] Nathan Lean, scholar of Islamophobia, placing the Chapel Hill murders in the same frame as the countless police killings of African Americans such as Eric Garner, aptly summarizes:

> "Obesity." "Asthma." "Headlock." "Thuggery." "Troublemaker." And, now, "parking." We explain away violence that targets minority communities, and it has to stop. If we are serious about ending that violence, we'll examine the climate of prejudice that breeds it, and we'll quit looking for alternative explanations that make us feel better about the tragedies by placing partial blame on the victims.[74]

"Parking," a supposed dispute over it, Lean points out, becomes yet another codeword through which anti-Muslim hate gets described and ultimately deflected. Mohammad Abu-Salha, the father of Yusor and Razan Abu-Salha, and Farris Barakat, the brother of Deah Barakat, co-wrote an op-ed that was published in *Time* magazine. In it, they stated that the parking-dispute depiction "overlooks the fact that after Yusor moved in with Deah, Hicks repeatedly told her he did not like how she looked because of her headscarf."[75] They wrote that the refusal to acknowledge the anti-Muslim dimensions of the killing is akin to "re-telling the story of Rosa Park[s]'s civil rights struggle as an 'ongoing dispute over a bus seat.'" Abu-Salha and Barakat urged the federal government to classify the murders as a hate crime, pointing out that such action is not possible according to North Carolina laws, which cover "ethnic intimidation" but have no provision for hate crimes. The analogy between the 1956 case of Rosa Parks and the 2015 murder of the three Arab Muslim youths is less than perfect; there were no hate crime laws in 1956, and segregation and racial inequality were explicitly upheld by law. But the larger point the families were trying to make about gaslighting was that naming and recognition *matter*.

In the case of Darwin Torres, the murder of Nabra Hassanen was not classified as a hate crime because Torres did not have a social media presence that could prove he held anti-Muslim attitudes. Reports indicate that Torres accused one of the teens of blocking the road—the teen was riding his bike on the road—and that an argument ensued. The details of what was said are unclear, but what is clear is that law enforcement said that no racial slurs were uttered.[76] At a press conference regarding the murder of Hassanen, Fairfax County police spokesperson Julie Parker stated, "Nothing indicates that this was motivated by race or by religion. It appears the suspect became so enraged over this traffic argument that it escalated into deadly violence."[77] The police indicated that Hassanen's murder was the result of road rage: "[Torres's] anger over the encounter led to violence when he hit Nabra with a baseball bat. Torres then took Nabra with him in his car to a second location nearby in Loudoun County."[78] The press release also states, "If during the course of this ongoing criminal investigation, information or evidence later surfaces that would indicate this was hate-motivated, detectives would certainly ensure appropriate charges are filed."[79] The police were clear in their statements that, despite the fact that a group of Muslim teens were attacked and that Hassanen wore a hijab, this was not to be classified as a hate crime. To add insult to injury, a memorial for Hassanen created in DuPont Circle in Washington, DC, was vandalized and set on fire. Authorities stated that this was not a hate crime either.[80]

The failure to designate Hassanen's murder a hate crime was challenged in the news media and in op-eds that questioned in particular the logic that an act can be considered a hate crime only if racism is explicitly vocalized. Ibrahim Hooper of CAIR argued, "You can't just say, 'Oh, he didn't say anything against Islam, so no hate crime.'"[81] CNN legal analyst Danny Cevallos chimed in, "Hate crime legislation doesn't attack the underlying hatred; it only punishes those who were dumb enough to shout out racial or other epithets. It doesn't eradicate underlying motives of race or gender."[82] Others commented that the impact of the murder on the Muslim community was what mattered, and the impact was that of a hate crime, despite law enforcement's classification. A *Huffington Post* article quoted lawyer Frederick M. Lawrence, who noted how difficult it is to prove a person's hateful intent: "Even though it had the effect of a bias crime, it did not have the intent, at least according to the police."[83] Lawrence added that, whether it was motivated by hate or not, community members and Muslims across the nation deeply identified with the incident and would increasingly fear that they or their loved ones could be next. Petula Dvorak, writing for the *Washington Post*, similarly stated, "Even if this was not a hate crime targeting Muslims, it has the effect of one."[84] Other commentators specified the chilling message the murder had for Arab and Muslim women in particular. Azmia Magane wrote that "to deny that Islamophobia and anti-Muslim violence is a real—and dangerous—occurrence is to try and deny, discredit, and silence the experiences of Muslims—particularly women—in the West, who face violence *because* we are Muslim."[85] Journalist Mona Eltahawy called for Hassanan's murder to serve as a tragic "reminder that in the U.S. and other countries where Muslims live as minorities, the survival of visibly Muslim women is increasingly jeopardized by the brutal trifecta of Islamophobia, racism, and misogyny."[86]

Cases in which a murder appears to be a hate crime but is not classified as such involve a complex set of factors. On the one hand, law enforcement seeks certain criteria, most especially an overt verbal expression of hatred based on race or religion, in designating hate crimes. As a result, in addition to such cases being treated as isolated rather than as part of a larger systematic problem, the rigid definition and denial of racial hatred's varied manifestations actually furthers the denial of racism and thus its perpetuation.[87] On the other hand, Muslim community members insist on a hate crime designation in an effort to foreground how profoundly such crimes impact the community and signal a social crisis. The designation thus becomes important both practically and symbolically in acknowledging the existence and persistence of anti-Muslim racism. Despite the contradictions and failures of hate crime laws, they do serve an important purpose.[88] Language, as we know or certainly should know by now, has powerful affective and psychic dimensions. One cannot even begin to imagine tackling racism without naming and acknowledging it first. Refusing to do so denies the very real fear that racism and racist acts produce, suggesting to those who live with that fear that their feelings are irrational—the essence of gaslighting. Sociologist Jack Levin writes:

> Hate crime laws have important symbolic meaning. Hate crimes are message crimes—that is, they send a message not only to the primary victim but to every member of this group. [. . .] They send a message to two groups: They send it to the perpetrator, informing him that our community will not tolerate his intolerance. And then at the same time, they send a message to potential victims that they are welcome in our community.[89]

Thus, the denial of violence against marginalized communities and the refusal to classify such violence as racially motivated not only sends a message that such actions are tolerated, but gaslights victims of anti-Muslim racism.

It is also important to question the significance of calling this form of violence a "hate" crime. Hate crimes equate racism with hatred and hatred is understood as an extreme emotion. Both hate crimes and racism are thus framed as individual and exceptional, ultimately serving to reduce social accountability. The labeling itself frames racial violence as exceptional, as if it has not been part and parcel of the history and development of US "democracy." This legal designation serves to narrow and contain how we understand this violent act. Furthermore, the lack of classification means that it was neither hatred nor racism. Racism (and other connected forms of discrimination) are presented as an either/or option—either this is or is not a hate crime. Racial and other discriminatory epithets become barometers for discrimination and then feed into its denial. If there were no racial epithets used in the act of violence, then it is not a racial incident. Similarly, the perpetrator of violence either is or is not a racist. This binary approach to understanding racism narrows our understanding and thus our approach to racism. Understanding the logics of denial is necessary to understand racialized violence today and find a new paradigm to address violence against marginalized communities.

Problematic 2: The Problem with "Tough on Crime" Approaches

The second problem that becomes apparent when considering the complicated pros and cons associated with the hate crime designation—its intended effects versus its implications in action (or, more accurately, inaction)—is the risk of reinforcing a neoliberal logic that sees penalization as the solution to any and all social problems, also known as the "tough on crime" approach. Lewis argues that "[r]ising public recognition of hate crimes during the late 1980s and 1990s coincided, not accidentally, with the overarching ascendance of both neoliberalism and crime control culture."[90] In the 1980s and 1990s, a tough-on-crime approach emerged that led to an obsession with crime and punishment exemplified by the emergence of more cop shows and legal dramas like *Law and Order* and further development of the prison industrial complex. Lewis writes:

> neoliberal state policy and popular thought affected how hate crimes were understood. In this context, the condemnation of the individual hate crimes perpetrator took precedence over broader structural critiques [. . .] [and] the radicalism of civil rights lost ground to tough-on-crime sentiments and neo-liberal policies.[91]

The tough-on-crime approach coincides with the rise of neoliberalism, privatization, and deregulation, which led to a shrinking of the public sector, redirecting state policy away from social welfare and toward punishing crime.[92] During the Reagan administration in the 1980s, crime became understood as moral degeneracy and thus the focus turned to punishing individual offenders rather than addressing the causes of crime.[93]

This tough-on-crime approach, in turn, interacts in unexpected ways with the hate crime designation. While one might have expected the two to work in tandem, it is more often the case that one is used to downplay the other. In the case of Nabra Hassanen's murder, officials used press conferences to insist that her killer would be prosecuted to the fullest extent of the law and severely penalized, regardless of whether the hate crime designation was applied. Lieutenant Colonel Tom Ryan, deputy chief of the Fairfax County Police Department stated, "I can assure you that while justice will not bring Nabra Hassanen back, justice will be done as the suspect of this brutal attack is in custody and will be prosecuted to the fullest extent of the law."[94] Justice in the form of punishment is thus offered as the solution. I am not seeking to downplay the significance of holding perpetrators of murder accountable—especially in light of the rampant lack of accountability when Black people are killed by police officers—but what is problematic is how this assurance often comes at the expense of recognizing the racialized nature of the crime. There is, in a sense, a bait and switch: the authorities refuse to designate something as a hate crime, but attempt instead to appease the family members and communities in question by assuring them that penalties will nonetheless be severe, thus reinforcing the legitimacy of the neoliberal tough-on-crime approach.

In other hate crimes that I have investigated against Muslims (and also against transgender youths) that are not designated as a hate crime (and are not deemed newsworthy enough to make headline news), a few common gaslighting utterances emerge. Law enforcement often says things like "all murders are hateful"[95] or that the hate crime classification is irrelevant since the perpetrator will be prosecuted to the fullest extent of the law. The logic here is that, while a hate crime charge could increase the penalty if the crime was vandalism, it would not necessarily increase the penalty in a meaningful way in the case of murder, since murder already presumably comes with a significant penalty. Thus, some argue that seeking a hate crime charge in the case of murder is futile, or redundant even, while others say that it still has important symbolic meaning.

The debate over whether or not Hassanen's murder should be classified as a hate crime soon came to center, ironically enough, around the status of the assailant as a Latinx undocumented immigrant. Daniel Greenfield, writing for the right-wing *Frontpage Magazine*, stated that it was not Islamophobia that killed Hassanen, but "the left's own Illegalophilia."[96] In other words, the problem was not racism but undocumented immigrants, and the left was to blame for not seeing them as illegal and criminals. Greenfield insisted that "Nabra Hassanen was killed by the left's love for illegal aliens."[97] Far-right media pundit Ann Coulter echoed this line of thinking when she tweeted, "When a 'Dreamer' murders a Muslim, does the media report it?" not so subtly suggesting that the media (coded as left-leaning) would prefer not to discuss such a crime as it would undermine leftist arguments in support of immigration. Coulter's Twitter followers responded enthusiastically:

An illegal alien dreamer . . . Pres. Trump must do away with DACA!!!

Obviously "dreamed" to kill a young girl . . . such an asset to our community . . . wake-up America.

Leftist Ideology kills

Win/win situation.

Somehow the rabid Leftists will blame Trump. But the fact is the victim would be alive if her assailant was in Mexico where he belongs.[98]

Torres is not, in fact, Mexican, but El Salvadoran, yet commentators on the political right seized upon the idea that he was, strengthening the stereotype of Mexicans as criminals who make the US dangerous. Anti-immigrant discourses, in this case regarding undocumented immigrants from Central America, are unleashed while a range of emotions from remorse to ambivalence to celebration are expressed in relation to the murdered Muslim youths.

In addition to the racist assumption that undocumented immigrants are murderers, Greenfield also assumes that Torres was in a gang, stating that Fairfax "has become a magnet for the El Salvadoran MS-13 gang. It's unknown whether Torres was an MS-13 member, but his behavior matches the extreme brutality and fearless savagery that the group, which has been lethally active in Fairfax, is known for."[99] Follow-up police statements stated that there was no evidence that Torres was affiliated with a gang.[100] Despite the police saying that the murder was not gang related, the prosecutors in the case planned to introduce evidence that he was part of MS-13.[101] Torres was thus portrayed as already a criminal before committing a criminal act. In contrast, Torres's neighbors described him as "a quiet, a friendly, solicitous neighbor who gave people rides, helped women carry groceries up the stairs."[102]

What is crucial to see here is the way in which the tough-on-crime approach facilitates the mobilization of *other* racist discourses,[103] and pits different communities of color against one another. As Eltahawy aptly put it, "Racists in the United States will try to use the tragedy to turn people of color against each other. Already, my Twitter mentions are claiming that if Donald J. Trump had built a wall to keep Mexicans out as he promised during the campaign to become president, Nabra would be alive. That is as ludicrous as claiming that if Trump banned all Muslims from the U.S., it would save us from being murdered, as Nabra was." Given his undocumented status, Torres was held at an Immigration and Customs Enforcement (ICE) detention center before his trial and sentence.[104] And thus, communities that are themselves often treated with suspicion by immigration authorities find themselves looking to those same authorities to inflict penalties when one of their members is murdered for reasons purportedly having nothing to do with racism.

The cultural double standard is clear when we consider how white perpetrators are consistently talked about as individual aberrations or victims of mental illness, whereas a Latinx person who commits murder is portrayed as an "illegal alien" and gang affiliated, or a Muslim who enacts violence is framed as a "terrorist" motivated by Islam. Metzl highlights the double standard in how crimes are classified when the victims are people of color and when they are not. Writing about the murder of the three Muslim youths in North Carolina for MSNBC, he states:

> Yet regardless of whether the North Carolina shooting is categorized as [a hate crime], the immediate response to it illustrates a larger reality: when shooters are white, we as a society have an exceedingly difficult time ascribing political or racial motivations to their actions. This dynamic is

oftcn acutely seen in the aftermath of high-profile mass-shootings. Horrific crimes such as Newtown or Aurora would almost certainly be labeled as terrorism were they perpetuated by members of racial, ethnic, or religious minority groups. Our research shows, however, that when mass-killers are white, mainstream U.S. discourse goes to great length to define the crimes as isolated incidents that result from the actions of wayward individuals, or individually disturbed brains, rather than resulting from larger, communal etiologies.[105]

Metzl points to an important component to racial gaslighting: giving whites the benefit of the doubt when they are the perpetrators of crimes. Hicks as a white man is given the benefit of the doubt partly because his profile does not fit the narrow parameters of how racism is defined by law. Thus, his actions are discounted from being part of a larger pattern of anti-Muslim racism and seen as an isolated incident rooted in a parking dispute. In contrast, Torres was cast not as an individual but as reflecting a larger problem with illegal immigration and gang activity, amplifying his racialized criminality. Torres and Hicks are portrayed differently by the media and political commentators. Hicks "snapped"[106] and Torres was likely "in a gang." While both men will spend their lives in prison, Hicks received three life sentences for murdering three people while Torres received eight life sentences for sexually assaulting and murdering one person.

The gender and racial politics of anti-Muslim racism also shape who is deemed worthy of public grieving and sympathy. Hate crimes against Muslims rarely make headline news. Muslim death is not considered newsworthy unless it is to celebrate the murder of an alleged terrorist. Twenty-eight-year-old Somali Canadian Mustafa Mattan was shot dead in his apartment in Alberta, Canada, the day before the Chapel Hill murders, but it did not make headline news.[107] Even before the case of Barakat and the Abu-Salha sisters became headline news, Muslims commented on the jarring lack of coverage in the media, which stood in sharp contrast to the disproportionate attention given to cases in which people were killed by Muslims.[108] Nadia Ali tweeted, "No national media coverage on the #chapelhillshooting of a muslim family!!"[109] Samira tweeted, "The fact that the only info I am getting about the #ChapelHillshooting is via twitter showcases how permeating Islamophobia is in media."[110] And journalist Abdullah Azada Khenjani posted to Facebook, "Muslims are only newsworthy when behind a gun, not in front of it."[111] As if it were necessary to make them worthy of news coverage and public sympathy, when the media started to report on the Chapel Hill murders, the victims were immediately framed through the trope of the patriotic American. A CNN headline read, "Chapel Hill Muslim shooting victim said she felt blessed to be an American."[112]

Audiences are not primed to have sympathy for Muslim men and certainly not Black Muslim men. However, there is a history of sympathetic feeling for Muslim women, usually because they are perceived as oppressed.[113] However, in this case, the vulnerability and promise of these young women made them worthy of public sympathy. In addition, casting Yusor Abu-Salha as a patriotic American and highlighting her husband Deah Barakat's humanitarian work framed them as worthy of sympathy. Razan Abu-Salha at nineteen and Nabra Hassanen at seventeen were presented as innocent youth full of promise, ultimately making the US nation appear to care about Muslims amid rampant anti-Muslim racism. What was not part of the news coverage is the paradox at the center of this chapter: on the one hand, the state makes Muslims vulnerable to hate crimes and other forms of violence. And on the other hand, the state avenges the death of the vulnerable and appears like the guarantor of justice.

Spade cautions us to guard against simply tinkering "with systems to make them look more inclusive while leaving their most violent operations intact."[114] He argues that hate crime laws do not prevent violence against marginalized groups, but rather mobilize resources for criminal punishment systems. Thus, "investment in such a system for solving safety issues actually stands to increase harm and violence" because marginalized groups—trans people, Black people, Latinxs, Muslims—are frequent targets of criminal punishment.[115] The US approach to hate crimes perpetuates a disconnect between concern for crime and concern for social justice, revealing that ultimately it is not about combating racism and anti-LGBTQ+ discrimination, but rather it is about punishing individual civilian crime (not police crime), particularly extreme forms such as murder. So it does not matter from the perspective of law enforcement whether these cases are labeled as hate crimes or not. According to law enforcement, what matters is that the case is being taken seriously because the perpetrator was arrested and is being charged with murder.

Problematic 3: The Problem with Seeking State Recognition

The third and final problem that contributes to racial gaslighting when racialized murders are not designated as hate crimes has to do with seeking state recognition. Marginalized communities—in the cases I have discussed here, Arabs and Muslims—want their experiences of victimization to be recognized by one arm of the state, the criminal justice system, yet must wrestle at the same time with the ways in which they are subjected to violence and surveillance by both the criminal justice system and another arm, that of the national security state. When considering violence to which Muslims are subjected, we must think about a war on Afghanistan that has killed forty-three thousand Afghan civilians,[116] a war on Iraq that had nothing to do with 9/11 and has killed over two hundred thousand Iraqi civilians,[117] Guantanamo Bay prison, Abu Ghraib prison, extraordinary rendition, the USA PATRIOT Act, Special Registration, Countering Violent Extremism, and the "Muslim ban." Hate crimes are but one facet of the multidimensional violence that Arabs, Muslims, and those mistaken to be Arab or Muslim face today. And more importantly hate crimes are deeply connected and shaped by state policies. The "War on Terror" and USA PATRIOT Act, for example, convey that Muslims are a threat and un-American. Legal scholar Muneer I. Ahmad argues that individual hate crimes and governmental policies of racial profiling "mutually reinforce a shared racist ideology."[118] He says that government practices of racial profiling through airport profiling, secret arrests, and race-based immigration policies (like the Muslim ban) fortify the belief that all Arabs, South Asians, and Muslims are "terrorist suspects" and therefore legitimate targets of violence.[119]

Seeking state recognition is important; communities need to push back against gaslighting in order to have their experiences with discrimination recognized. But local and national conversations about hate crimes are rarely paired with discussions about other forms of violence to which Arabs and Muslims are subjected. Applying this concern to the case of Muslims leads to the following question: How can we think about requests for recognition by the state when the state sees Muslims through a lens of national security? Arab Americans and US Muslims are vulnerable to many forms of violence, yet hate crime debates give the impression that this is the primary form of violence. What about state violence? What about how state violence inspires hate crimes? What about how Muslims are most often framed either as "terrorist threats" to national security or useful for national security purposes?

Given that discourses around national security frame Muslims as good only when they are patriotic (in the most narrow sense) and support the state, it is not that surprising that the mosque in Virginia—the ADAMS Center—asked the community not to insist on a hate crime designation regarding Hassanen and to entrust law enforcement with the process. The statement read: "We request the community to not speculate on the motives and jump to conclusions. We thank both Fairfax County Police and Loudoun County Sheriff's departments for their diligent efforts in investigating and charging the suspect with Murder."[120] The ADAMS Center's statement assumes that law enforcement can and will resolve anti-Muslim racism, or at least bring justice in the case of this one particular murder.

In contrast, as mentioned above, a letter was sent to Attorney General Eric Holder organized by CAIR and signed by Arab, Muslim, Jewish, Sikh, Asian American, Latinx, LGBTQ+, and other civil rights groups urging a federal hate crime investigation in the case of the Chapel Hill murders.[121] The letter points to a larger context of Islamophobia to justify why these murders should be investigated as a hate crime. It reads:

> These killings come in the wake of a disturbing rise in especially threatening and vitriolic anti-Muslim rhetoric and activities. In recent weeks, after the release of the movie *American Sniper*, many tweeted hateful and deplorable messages demeaning to Muslims and Arabs. For example, one user tweeted that the film "makes me wanna go shoot some f**kin Arabs," while another stated that "American sniper made me appreciate soldiers 100x more and hate Muslims 1000000x more." On Saturday, January 17, 2015, outside a Muslim community event in Garland, Texas, hundreds of protesters shouted hateful messages and comments at attendees. Some of the protesters brandished guns, creating a threatening and hostile environment for families attending the event.[122]

The Council on American-Islamic Relations and other civil rights groups are at the forefront of criticizing government policies like the

USA PATRIOT Act, Special Registration, Countering Violent Extremism, and the Muslim travel ban. Furthermore, the Ethnically Motivated Violence Against Arab-Americans hearing in 1986 explicitly linked hate crimes to US government policies. However, the subsequent tough-on-crime approach has meant that Muslim communities seeking recognition from the state for hate crimes, with a focus on a climate of increased anti-Muslim racism, have had to accept the trade-off of silence regarding other violent state practices. Anti-Muslim racism is carefully limited to an individual problem that essentially advances the problematic that I outlined above concerning the conventional definition of hate crimes. In seeking recognition from the state, this letter embraces the definition of hate crimes and racism as an individual problem, but it does insist that it is not an exceptional problem, so it diverges from the conventional definition of racism in that way. Thus, in both examples of Muslim advocacy organizations responding to the "not a hate crime" classification of these murders, the problematic definition and approach to racism and hate crimes are embraced in pursuit of state recognition.

Sociologist Erik Love has analyzed the ways in which Muslim community organizations respond to Islamophobia, and particularly whether or not they articulate Islamophobia as a form of racism, which he terms the "racial dilemma."[123] Love says that many community organizations strategically avoid framing the problems they face as ones with racism and instead stress that they are Americans with First Amendment rights to religious freedom. Love writes, "The racial dilemma for these advocates is the choice of how to frame their efforts—whether they choose to represent themselves as marginalized communities of color struggling against racism, or position their communities as mainstream, regular Americans who just want to be treated equally."[124] In examining these responses to the murders of Muslim youths, an added dilemma emerges around whether or not to implicate the state; all too often, it seems that the safer strategy is not to criticize the state when seeking recognition from it. In other words, while CAIR usually critiques state violence, it is ignored in addressing this hate crime, and the ADAMS Center's message is to trust law enforcement. As Spade observes, "When advocates seek inclusion in institutions, they tend to lift up and valorize those institutions, which means ignoring and erasing the violent realities of those institutions."[125] And as critical policy

Figure 3.2. The #MuslimLivesMatter hashtag was used to protest the murder of Deah Barakat, Yusor Abu-Salha, and Razan Abu-Salha and the media coverage of it: "Hundreds march on media offices in New York to protest the #Chapel-HillShooting," September 14, 2015. Photo by Joe Catron, CC BY-NC 2.0.

studies scholar Nicole Nguyen aptly writes, "although these transactional agreements affirm Muslim cultural identities and facilitates their greater inclusion into U.S. society, they do not redistribute power or dismantle the institutions, discourses, and logics that criminalize Muslim communities."[126]

Other grassroots efforts have been more willing to highlight the systematic nature of violence against Arabs and Muslims, but the strategy was not without other problems. The hashtag #MuslimLivesMatter tried to connect the Chapel Hill murders to a larger systematic problem and to create solidarity with Black Americans as victims of violence (see figure 3.2). However, the hashtag was critiqued as appropriating the struggle of the Black community in the US, promoting a false equivalency with the struggles of Black people, overlooking that Black people are part of the Muslim community, and failing to acknowledge the ways in which non-Black Muslims have generally not acted in solidarity with and at times have acted directly against them.[127] Nonetheless, the debates that the hashtag ignited challenged the notion that racism is an individual problem and connected hate crimes to state violence.

Black Muslim author Anas White, writing for the Muslim Anti-Racism Collaborative (MuslimARC), criticized the Muslim community for appropriating the Black Lives Matter hashtag given a lack of solidarity and coalitional politics within the community.[128] He asked: "Where is the Muslim community in solidarity with a movement against these civil, and even human rights issues?" He noted that the lives of Barakat and the Abu-Salha sisters obviously mattered in the Muslim community, as they would be remembered in mosque sermons cross the country and beyond. But he highlighted the false equivalency between the murders in Chapel Hill and the violence faced by Black Americans: "The media is not painting their lives as criminal, in what little they are reporting. Their killer is not at home watching his face plastered on the news. There is no movement of people trying to justify the actions of the terrorist who killed these young Muslims." White challenged non-Black Muslims to "actually build a real relationship with a community, before you co-opt an expression many of you may have never even used." He encouraged readers to use the hashtag created by the Barakat and Abu-Salha families, #OurThreeWinners. Activist Linda Sarsour encouraged the use of #Justice4Muslims through Twitter, and others encouraged using #ChapelHillShooting or #TakeOnHate.

Lawyer Namira Islam, also writing for MuslimARC, highlighted the false equivalency in using #MuslimLivesMatter in relation to the murders in Chapel Hill, while also stressing that Muslims are not only victim to vigilante hate crimes, but also to state violence. She wrote:

> I am reminded daily that Muslim lives are considered less than and Muslim deaths do not matter in the eyes of our foreign policy and most of our media. But this was not an officer who murdered these beautiful young adults in Chapel Hill, nor, more importantly, do we have any reason to believe there will not be a fair trial (really, any trial) in which the killer will be held accountable for his actions. He is already in custody for first-degree homicide, which is far more a step towards some kind of justice than the loved ones of many Black victims will ever see.[129]

Others chimed in to criticize the appropriation of the Black Lives Matter hashtag in relation to the murders in Chapel Hill.[130] Writing for Al Jazeera, law professor Khaled Beydoun and executive director of

MuslimARC Margari Aziza Hill criticized the Muslim community for anti-Black racism, asking why the community did not mobilize after the murder of Mustafa Mattan, the Somali Canadian who was killed less than twenty-four hours before Barakat and the Abu-Salhas. They write, "In life and in death, Arab and South Asian Muslim lives seem to matter far more than the lives of black Muslims."[131] It is important to note that, in contrast to the North Carolina murders, the use of #BlackLivesMatter in relation to Hassanen's murder did not spark a similar debate on Twitter about appropriation. This is because Hassanen was from Southern Egypt and of Nubian descent. She was also part of a community in Virginia that is predominantly Sudanese (and Egyptian and Moroccan).[132] Thus she was read as Black. A BuzzFeed article reported that her cousins were critical of how Muslim groups focused on her Muslim identity and not on her racial identity, pointing to how her Black identity made her more vulnerable than her Muslim identity.[133] Both cases sparked important discussions about how conversations on anti-Muslim racism tend to focus on Arabs and South Asians and exclude Black Muslims.

Others defended the hashtag. Sofia Arias, writing for the *Socialist Worker*, responded to criticisms of the use of #MuslimLivesMatter, insisting that it be understood as an act of solidarity, not of co-optation.[134] She writes, "The reason the phrase 'Muslim Lives Matter' spoke to so many people after the Chapel Hill killing is because they saw it as *embracing* the struggle against racist violence against African Americans, and linking that to another fight against oppression and bigotry." Arias wrote that "Muslim Lives Matter" was a rejection of law enforcement's classification of the murders as a parking dispute and sought to connect to the resistance movement that developed after Ferguson. She linked the violence to which Muslims are subject not only to individuals who commit hate crimes, but to the US government, citing the attacks on civil liberties after 9/11, secret drone strikes in Yemen, and the way in which the government portrays itself as protecting Americans from a persistent Muslim threat. Regardless of one's position on the use of the #MuslimLivesMatter hashtag, the debate that ensued was one that productively considered a range of fundamental issues. It insisted on thinking about hate crimes in relation to state violence. It insisted on thinking about anti-Muslim racism in relation to other forms of discrimination and intersectionality. It included a criticism of racism within the Muslim community and the conspicuous absence of Black Muslims in many conversations about anti-Muslim racism. And it did not insist on criminal punishment as the solution to racism.

Fueling Gaslighting

The decision not to apply the hate crime designation to these cases is part of a larger trend in US politics to invest in criminal punishment instead of social justice. A label that has social justice significance is not used, but rather punishment of the violent perpetrator is affirmed as justice. The ultimate irony is that this conception of "hate"—racism equals hate, just not this kind of hate—exempts not only racist violence perpetrated by the individual, but also brackets state violence. Muslims are gaslighted, but their violent individual perpetrators are prosecuted to the fullest extent of the law. As critical theorist Elizabeth A. Povinelli writes, the state's embrace of liberal multiculturalism "make certain violences appear accidental to a social system rather than generated by it."[135]

What does one gain or lose through a "hate crime" classification? What are the limits to calling it hate? A hate crime classification would afford recognition for the racialized violence Muslims face. However, such recognition has a number of effects that continue violence against Muslims. Most importantly, Muslim communities lose out on addressing the root causes of hate crimes and anti-Muslim racism by not connecting hate crimes to state violence. Ultimately, it is not possible to prevent future hate crimes if the state is not held accountable for its role in racializing Muslims. The irony is that racial gaslighting operates both when the hate crime label is and is not applied. When it is not applied, there is no recognition of racialized violence, but criminal punishment is presented as justice from the state. When the hate crime label is applied, the racialized violence is acknowledged but as an individual problem that the state justly resolves while it is divorced from state complicity. This dilemma highlights a larger problematic with the neoliberal trend of divesting from civil rights and investing in the criminal justice system. Both options strengthen the criminal justice system and further the poverty in understanding and adequately addressing racism, whether systemic or individual.

In thinking about how state violence becomes invisible, it is also important to consider how the state is exempted from the rubric of hate crimes despite the surveillance of Muslims, deportation of Latinxs, and murder of unarmed Black Americans by law enforcement. American studies scholar Christina Hanhardt points out that "hate crimes are distinguished from acts that are lawful and [. . .] sanctioned state violence is intentionally left out of the definition because including the state would downplay the status of hate crimes as a category for state-administered condemnation."[136] Ahmad says that it is not entirely surprising that the state would charge perpetrators of hate crimes because it is in the state's interest to preserve its own monopoly on violence. Vigilante violence is thus punished because it is vigilante, not necessarily because it is racist. Furthermore, denouncing individual racism is a way for the state to perpetuate state-sponsored racism. Ahmad writes, "By condemning the racism of others, and of private actors in particular, the government implicitly seizes the mantle of equality. As the arbiter of racism, it lays claim to being free of racism itself. If it were not, the government's very ability to adjudicate the racism of others would be thrown into question. Thus, the condemnation of the most extreme racist acts of others obscures and normalizes the government's own racism."[137]

What can we learn about racial gaslighting when we think about a spectrum of denials? How might we think about denying Muslims and transgender youth murders a hate crime designation and denying Black Americans recognition of persistent systemic racism in the cases of police brutality as interrelated operations of racial gaslighting? Feminist sociologist Sherene Razack argues that racial terror is at the heart of settler colonialism given the history of slavery and violence against Indigenous people and people of color, that the state continuously consolidates itself through racial violence. I would add that ensuring that "justice is served" in cases of extralegal or vigilante violence only serves to further consolidate the state's power and monopoly on violence, especially racial violence.[138] The system works by showcasing justice for Muslims in the form of multiple life sentences in these cases (while denying that they are hate crimes), and at the same time protecting police officers (as state actors) from any consequence for shooting unarmed Black people. The system also works by giving this form of justice to Muslims (death penalty for civilians who murder them) while continuing surveillance, drone strikes, and other forms of violence against Muslims domestically and globally. Denial of the persistence of racism and other forms of discrimination relies on cases in which "justice is served," in the law-and-order sense of the term. Such cases operate to project a seemingly just system in which the state prosecutes perpetrators of racial violence but deems irrelevant the designation of racial violence. In other words, the violence that is prosecuted is approached as "equal opportunity" violence and thus the persistence of racism is gaslighted.

Scholars of hate crime law such as James A. Tyner, Doug Meyer, and Dean Spade caution against too great of a focus on hate crime laws. Tyner writes that "the post-racial project of neoliberalism renders racism as a manifestation of individual prejudicial behaviour; in so doing, post-racial conceptualizations of racial violence deflect attention from a more deeply entrenched white supremacy. [. . .] Consequently, an uncritical engagement with hate-crimes as actions of racist, bigoted persons may reify white supremacy through a silencing of more subtle but decriminalized forms of racism."[139] In other words, the focus on hate crime laws renders invisible other forms of violence, such as state violence, and creates the impression that the social order is otherwise equal and just.[140] The state is absolved from any wrongdoing or responsibility.

The centering of both the history and ongoing legacy of white supremacy in the US and the project of US empire that provides justification for endless wars and murder in predominantly Muslim countries offers an important analytical opening to this problematic of hate crimes. Anti-Muslim racism (like other, connected forms of racism) is often conceptualized as whites inflicting racist harm, overlooking how all people and communities are implicated in what Rana terms "racial infrastructure." Racial infrastructure refers to the ways in which racial systems make up the social, economic, and political organization of society; just as roads, bridges, water supplies, electrical systems, and Internet connectivity create a foundation for our lifestyle, so too does race.[141] What makes racism so powerful is that we are all interpellated[142] in some way and can reproduce those same discriminatory logics in relation to other marginalized communities. Nabra Hassanen's killer was an undocumented El Salvadoran immigrant. During the COVID-19 pandemic, a twenty-three-year-old Yemeni man stabbed a Chinese man in New

York City in yet another racially motivated crime that was dubbed "not a hate crime" by law enforcement.[143] Many Black Americans and Latinx people supported the racial profiling of Arab, Muslim, and South Asian communities after 9/11.[144] Arab and South Asian taxi drivers in New York supported and perpetuated racial profiling by not picking up Black passengers. Historian Natalia Molina proposes the term "racial scripts" to think about how different groups are racialized (in similar and different ways) and thus are connected through the process of racialization. She writes that "we can see different racial projects operating at the same time, affecting different groups simultaneously."[145] Driving while Black and flying while brown are similar racial projects. Police violence against Black American communities and military violence against Arab communities are similar racial projects. While Arabs receive crime and punishment acknowledgement, it comes with gaslighting of their racial experience. While Black Americans' racial experiences are also gaslighted, they do not get the crime and punishment acknowledgement. And while Arabs can be lulled into feeling that the state cares about them and seeks to protect them, the state is also responsible for unimaginable murder in their homelands such as Iraq, Palestine, and Yemen. More importantly, recognizing the impacts of white supremacy on multiple communities and drawing such connections has created important opportunities to form coalitions and to broaden the analysis.

The criminal justice system is one arm of the larger national security state that subjects Muslims to surveillance, detention, deportation, torture, drone strikes, and death. In the name of national security, the US government issues policies that construct Muslims as a "terrorist threat" and destroy Muslim lives and livelihoods. Given that the criminal justice system in the US is part of perpetuating the problem of anti-Muslim racism, incarcerating individual perpetrators of hate crimes like Craig Hicks and Darwyn Torres cannot resolve the problem of anti-Muslim racism. In other words, while criminal punishment for perpetrators of hate crimes and the possibility of state recognition of hate crimes might appear to be gains, such an approach actually delimits what is possible as a transformative politic. Ensuring that justice is served in these cases by issuing life sentences to the perpetrators of murders considered to be "not hate crimes" further consolidates state power by projecting the state as just, even as it advances of war and racial violence.

Ethnic studies scholar Chandan Reddy points out that the 2009 Matthew Shepard and James Byrd, Jr., Hate Crimes Prevention Act was attached to the National Defense Authorization Act of 2010, in which Obama approved $690 billion for the Department of Defense. It included sending ten thousand more troops to Afghanistan and the continued use of unmanned drone strikes in countries, such as Pakistan and Yemen, with whom the US was not at war. Reddy thus proposes that we see hate crime laws as attached to sanctioned state violence abroad, that we see "freedom with violence."[146] In other words, discussions about hate and discrimination are framed as involving the state protecting marginalized groups from attacks from individuals, not from attacks by the state or even attacks influenced by the state. To be clear, I am not stating that Muslims should stop seeking recognition from the state. Rather, I am asking, what would it look like if conversations about hate crimes extended beyond recognition from the state to include in the same frame state violence and how these forms of violence are interrelated? Racial gaslighting operates by distancing hate crime violence, that is, violence perpetrated by individuals, from state violence and approaching the state as if it is an arbiter of safety and security, of protection and justice. Furthermore, moments of "justice" for one group create the illusion of a just system and provide fuel for gaslighting injustice experienced by other groups.

To recap, the three strands I have highlighted are as follows: first, the problem revealed by examining the narrow definition of a hate crime is that by refusing to classify certain murders as hate crimes, racism becomes further exceptionalized and Muslims' experiences of racism become gaslighted or denied. Second, the problem with the tough-on-crime approach is that "justice" is based in punishment over social justice and, consequently, the persistence of anti-Muslim racism is gaslighted. And third, Muslims' efforts to seek recognition from the state expose a dilemma since the state itself perpetuates violence against Muslim communities domestically and globally and inspires hate crimes. These three problematics work together in configuring racial gaslighting in the case of US Muslims. The next chapter extends the examination of responses to the crisis of anti-Muslim racism, but the focus shifts from law enforcement to corporations, particularly how corporations fire public figures for anti-Muslim speech.

4

Racial Purging

On December 18, 2015, Destiny Vélez, then Miss Puerto Rico, did something not generally associated with women's pageant winners: she got political. Even worse, she did so on that most unforgiving forum of social media, Twitter, where her posted views quickly went viral. Vélez's comments responded to a series of precipitating events. On December 2, 2015, a married Muslim couple, Syed Rizwan Farook and Tashfeen Malik, killed fourteen people and injured twenty-two others at a Department of Public Health Christmas party in San Bernardino, California, where Farook was employed.[1] In response to this mass shooting (which was dubbed a terrorist attack by the media and government officials),[2] Republican presidential candidate Donald Trump proposed legislation banning Muslims from entering the United States as part of his prospective presidential platform: "Donald J. Trump is calling for a total and complete shutdown of Muslims entering the United States until our country's representatives can figure out what is going on."[3]

Documentary filmmaker Michael Moore responded to Trump's statement by standing outside of Trump Tower in New York City with a sign that read "WE ARE ALL MUSLIM."[4] The photo of Moore's protest went viral and he explained his position in an online letter to Trump: "So, in desperation and insanity, you call for a ban on all Muslims entering this country. I was raised to believe that we are all each other's brother and sister, regardless of race, creed or color. That means if you want to ban Muslims, you are first going to have to ban me. And everyone else. We are all Muslim"[5] (see figure 4.1). Responding, in turn, to Michael Moore's statement, Miss Puerto Rico 2015, Destiny Vélez, tweeted:

- All what Muslims have done is provided oil and terrorize this country and many others!!!!!!
- Many pull out the card of Muslims serving in our military. Are they in the military cuz they love our nation or to acquire benefits

Figure 4.1. Documentary filmmaker Michael Moore protests presidential candidate Donald Trump's proposal to ban Muslims from entering the United States, December 17, 2015, from Michael Moore's archived website.

- Why do ppl want to separate Muslims from Isis when ISIS is group of Muslim Animals
- Islamic God is not the same God as Christians & Jews.
- All they do is build their mosques, feel offended by American values and terrorize innocent Americans and plant gas stations . . . and get guns and kills innocent ppl and destroy precious artifacts.
- There's NO comparison between Jews, Christians and Muslims. Jews nor Christians have terrorizing agendas in their sacred books.
- If we are all the same then Muslims need to take off their napkins off of their heads cuz I feel offended by it.[6]

Pageant winners are usually encouraged to avoid politics at all costs, unless of a generic "world peace" variety. Vélez made it very clear that she was not advocating for world peace and that not all were welcome in the US. The Miss Puerto Rico organization indefinitely suspended Vélez for her anti-Muslim tweets. The organization issued a statement to their Facebook page the day after the tweets went viral stating that Vélez's words "do not represent the integrity and esteem of our program, nor that of our board members, our sponsors and partners, or the National Organization. Miss Vélez's actions were in contradiction to the organization, and therefore as a consequence of her actions, she has been suspended indefinitely. The Miss Puerto Rico Organization will not tolerate any actions or behavior contrary to the Miss Puerto Rico Organization."[7] Vélez issued an apology: "I apologize to the people I have offended with my words. I am first and foremost an #UpStander and as such I stand up against bullying." Being an UpStander was her platform when she ran for Miss Puerto Rico, an anti-bullying campaign that advocated for being proactive in preventing bullying as an "upstander" as opposed to a "bystander."[8] The case of Destiny Vélez is one of many cases in which a public figure faced professional consequences for racist or discriminatory speech.

After centuries of marginalization and demonization it is vindicating for those on the margins to experience some kind of justice. Such scandals, beginning in the 1980s and increasing in frequency over time, have ranged from anti-Black racist speech, with N-word scandals occupying a special place of their own, to antisemitic, sexist, anti-LGBTQ+, ableist, and xenophobic speech. Vélez's case reflects many of the common elements in a speech scandal: a racist statement that is highlighted as controversial by the media; followed by an organization's or corporation's response that involves distancing itself from the offender and punishing them for their speech; followed by an apology or defense of one's statements; followed by a public debate that spans from outrage at the racist statement and praise for the organization's response to criticism of the organization for violating free speech and taking political correctness too far. Some public figures caught up in a speech scandal face permanent damage to their public image and thus to their career, while others continue relatively unscathed, sometimes repositioning themselves after being hired or endorsed in some way by a conservative organization or corporation in the name of free speech.

Speech scandals have become one of the primary mechanisms through which racism and discrimination are talked about and understood in the United States today. How do corporations shape racial politics when they fire high-profile figures for anti-Muslim (and other kinds of discriminatory) speech? And do such penalties produce effective social change or have more problematic effects? This chapter examines two cases in which media corporations fired public figures for anti-Muslim speech. The first case is that of National Public Radio's (NPR) firing of journalist Juan Williams in 2010 after he stated on Fox News that he felt nervous whenever someone in Muslim garb was on the same airplane. The second case occurred when the Entertainment and Sports Programming Network (ESPN) suspended sports analyst and former Major League Baseball (MLB) player Curt Schilling in 2015 after he retweeted an anti-Muslim meme. Shortly thereafter, he was fired when he reposted an anti-transgender graphic on Facebook.

Muslims became included in conceptions of diversity and social justice through a series of crises, such as 9/11, the 2010 "ground zero mosque" controversy, the establishment of the Islamophobia Industry, and Donald Trump's 2015 announcement of a Muslim ban. These moments led to widespread recognition that Muslims are demonized and targets of individual hate and repressive state policies. As this recognition has evolved, it has included cases in which people are fired for anti-Muslim speech. This chapter examines the cases of anti-Muslim speech that garnered the most media attention (aside from Donald Trump's pronouncements). Juan Williams's firing was in 2010, a moment when Islamophobia was entering the US lexicon and during the "ground zero mosque" controversy, a crisis moment in the development of anti-Muslim racism in the US. Curt Schilling was fired by ESPN in 2016. His anti-Muslim tweet occurred in August 2015, just months before Trump announced the idea for a Muslim travel ban. Firing people for anti-Muslim speech is not something that would have happened before 9/11, when such speech was not only acceptable but Muslims (as well as Arabs and others from Southwest Asia and North Africa) were not understood as racialized or marginalized groups.

Not all speech scandals involve public figures. Government workers, teachers, and employees at a variety of organizations and corporations are fired or asked to resign for racist and other discriminatory violations. A Minnesota Republican politician, Jack Whitley, resigned from his post in 2014 after controversy ensued when he said that Muslims are "parasites," "terrorists," and should be bombed.[9] Also in 2014, Virginia Republican politician Bob FitzSimmonds resigned after ridiculing President Obama's comments recognizing Muslims for their contributions to the US; FitzSimmonds called Obama's commendation "utter nonsense" in a Facebook post.[10] And in 2016, Gladys Gryskiewicz, a school board member in New Jersey, resigned after stating on Facebook that Muslims should stay in their deserts and that the US needed to be rid of them.[11]

To be sure, there are many more cases of racist and other kinds of discriminatory speech that never receive public attention, let alone face any consequences. Nonetheless, firing people for racist speech has become such a popular approach to combating racism and discrimination that the Council on American-Islamic Relations, American-Arab Anti-Discrimination Committee, and other civil right groups call for people to be fired regularly.[12] While firing people to regulate racism and other forms of discrimination has become commonplace, there are actually a range of ways in which corporations respond to racist incidents and statements. After a Starbucks employee called the police in Philadelphia because two Black men sat at a table for a few minutes without having ordered anything, leading to their subsequent arrest and public outrage, Starbucks closed all of their approximately eight thousand US stores for one day in 2018 to conduct a "racial bias education day."[13] After the Atlanta Hawks leadership made racist statements, they hired a chief diversity and inclusion officer in 2014, the first such position created by an NBA team, and some team members rode on a float in the Atlanta Pride Festival to show their support of the LGBTQ+ community.[14] This chapter examines the trend of firing (and hiring) public figures for racist speech. Such speech scandals—from the initial statements to the public's response, the media frenzy that creates a scandal, the corporate firing, and again the public's response—constitute a form of racial purging. Racial purging is a cathartic release of racism from society that takes place when the media seizes upon racist speech and highlights it as a scandal; the relevant entity (corporation or organization) responds by firing the individual responsible, and those that publicly support the firing participate in a form of collective outrage that restores society to a perceived semblance of racial equality.

On the surface, corporations firing individuals for discriminatory speech appears to be evidence that racism and other forms of discrimination are no longer tolerated in the United States. Laws and policies might not protect racialized and LGBTQ+ people from harassment and marginalization, but a Twitter scandal coupled with a corporate firing might send a clear message that such behavior will not be tolerated and will be met with significant consequences. However, the focus on purging individual speech offenders from the social order individualizes racism and thus reinforces the myth that the US is an equal society with the exception of a few aberrant individuals. Racism thus conceived is an individual-level problem appropriately dealt with via individual-level solutions, implemented by corporations and institutions that demonstrate their benevolence in the process. Corporations approach the offending individuals as "bad apples" who are purged from the corporation as if individuals are not shaped by institutions and vice versa, and as if corporations are the arbiters of justice. As long as the offending individuals are shamed, punished, and expelled, the narrative suggests, the social order (otherwise assumed to be equal at all times) will be restored. What is notable is not only that marginalized individuals can have power online, but that corporate participation raises the stakes. However, despite the firing of offending individuals signaling a shift in social norms, corporate power remains intact.[15]

The very framing of these events as "scandals" reinforces their interpretation as anomalous, crises that flare up and capture the public's attention for an intense period of time, but are eventually resolved and forgotten. Often, commentary presents both the offending speech and speaker as anachronistic relics of the past that have no place in today's multicultural modernity. Members of the public, given an unprecedented platform through social media, can participate in the scandal and the subsequent purging, rather than simply watching it unfold on the news. Indeed, an important dimension of a successful purge is the extent to which it enables the expression of public outrage, taking negative opinions and feelings and directing them toward individuals rather than the larger entities in which they operate. This purification ritual reinforces the belief that racism and other forms of discrimination are aberrations that, when dealt with swiftly, can simply be excised from the social order.

The corporate firing of public figures for discriminatory speech reveals much about how racial politics have been privatized and corporatized. These cases offer a template for how racism and discrimination are now dealt with by organizations and corporations. According to this increasingly universal formula, the process of purging offending individuals is no longer limited to simply apologizing and/or saving face on the part of the institution. Done correctly, a successful purge can instead become a powerful opportunity to articulate an organization's values or a corporation's brand. Taking a stance on racial politics has become good for business, useful for branding, and central to articulating diversity and anti-discrimination as important corporate and social values. In this sense, racial purging is an anti-discrimination practice reflective of neoliberal multiculturalism—it not only presents some corporations as being against racism and for equality, but also shapes and delimits racial politics in important ways.[16] Neoliberal governance refers to the increased privatization of both social and economic life that results when more and more domains previously regulated by the state become the jurisdiction of corporations and the responsibility of individuals. Tracking the seemingly virtuous ways in which corporations now participate in racial politics shows how questions of racial equality and social justice have become increasingly recoded and contained through this form of governance.

In what follows, I briefly review the history of organizations and corporations firing public figures for offending speech and such cases becoming controversial media scandals. I then examine the cases of Juan Williams and Curt Schilling through a discourse analysis of corporate statements on firing and hiring, statements made by the offending individuals when faced with being "cancelled," and the wider debates on social media and in op-eds. My analysis of the cultural politics revealed by these cases focuses particularly on how corporations are shaping racial politics today. Firing sends an important message: we do not tolerate racism or discrimination at the individual level. Our task, I counter, is to question that message. We must look beyond where our attention is being directed and ask instead who and what benefits from such an individualized, episodic approach. Is racial purging an effective solution to racism—or just the latest way of obscuring its broader continuation?

A Brief Cultural History of Firing Public Figures for Racist and Discriminatory Speech

The trend of corporations firing individuals for racist, sexist, anti-LGBTQ+, antisemitic, anti-Muslim, ableist, and other kinds of discriminatory speech after the media highlights such incidents began in the 1980s. In 1987, Rachel Robinson, widow of Jackie Robinson, the first Black athlete to play in MLB (1947–1956), commented on the lack of racial diversity in baseball since her late husband's involvement. She stated, "It's not coincidental that baseball in the forty-year period has not been able to integrate at any other level other than the players' level, we have a long way to go."[17] On a nationally televised interview on ABC's *Nightline*, news anchor Ted Koppel asked Los Angeles Dodgers vice president Al Campanis to reflect on Robinson's statement, asking why there were no Black managers or owners in professional baseball. Campanis replied that it was not the result of prejudice, but that "they may not have some of the necessities to be, let's say, a field manager, or perhaps a general manager."[18] His comments sparked national controversy, with some calling for Campanis's firing and others for an apology. Campanis issued an apology stating that he did not in fact believe that African Americans do not have the capacity to hold managerial positions. Nonetheless, Dodgers owner Peter O'Malley asked Campanis to resign, stating: "The comments Al made Monday night . . . were so far removed and so distant from what I believe and what the organization believes that it was impossible for Al to continue the responsibilities that he's had with us."[19]

Less than a year later, in 1988, CBS asked sports commentator Jimmy "The Greek" Snyder to resign after he stated in an interview that, if African Americans continued making progress in sports and getting coaching jobs, there would be nothing left for white people. He also stated that African Americans were better athletes than whites because of traits developed during slavery.[20] Snyder apologized for his comments but refused to resign. He stated, "One bad interview, with my making some foolish statements, could to some people ruin twelve years of good work for the network."[21] As a result, CBS fired him.

In 1996, CBS golf analyst Ben Wright was fired after making sexist and homophobic remarks about women golf athletes in an interview: "Let's face facts here. Lesbians in the sport hurt women's golf." He also said, "They're going to a butch game, and that furthers the bad image of the game. [. . .] Women are handicapped by big boobs. It's not easy for them to keep the left arm straight and that's one of the tenets of the game. Their boobs get in the way."[22] CBS Sports President David Kenin released a statement acknowledging the "continuing controversy" and stating that "CBS believes [Wright's] association with the network has detracted from its golf coverage" and "there are no plans for Wright's return to CBS Sports."[23]

As these examples show, there were cases in the 1980s and 1990s of companies firing public figures for racist, sexist, and anti-LGBTQ+ speech, but it was still relatively unusual. That such firings happened at all was the result of the civil rights, women's, LGBTQ+, and multicultural movements slowly shifting social norms. Many early cases involved sports; this could be because sports are figured as an unassailable national and masculine space that becomes easily disrupted when a speech scandal occurs. Today, speech scandals have become increasingly common, suggesting that disparaging remarks toward historically marginalized groups, at least in public, have finally become socially unacceptable. The contrast is clear when comparing the following examples side by side. In 1981, when tennis player Billie Jean King was outed as a lesbian by an ex-girlfriend, she lost all of her endorsements (except for one, NBC Sports). Being outed as a lesbian was clearly detrimental to her career. Thirty-four years later, in 2015, boxer Manny Pacquiao lost an extremely lucrative endorsement with Nike when he stated that gay people are worse than animals. This time, expressing anti-LGBTQ+ perspectives was detrimental to an athlete's career. Many would point to these examples as evidence of the progress that has been made, and they would not be wrong. The question, however, is whether they prove that discrimination is no longer a problem in our society and whether firing people is an effective solution for discrimination.

The increase in the number of speech controversies can be partly traced to the popularization of cell phone technologies with audio and visual recording capabilities, which became available to US consumers in 2006. Suddenly, witnesses equipped with nothing more than their personal phone were able to capture racially charged incidents, among others, and share them on the Internet. In contrast, consider how in 1991, when Rodney King was brutalized by Los Angeles Police Department officers, it was unusual for such incidents to be recorded because it was unusual for someone to have a video camera on them.[24] The first of such speech scandals, in 2006, involved stand-up comedian Michael Richards (best known for his role as Kramer on the sitcom *Seinfeld*), who went on an N-word tirade during one of his shows after an audience member heckled him. The incident was video-recorded on an audience member's cell phone, circulated on the Internet, and then broadcast by network news stations. Similarly, in 2014, the girlfriend/mistress of

Donald Sterling, owner of the Los Angeles Clippers basketball team, secretly audio-recorded him while he made anti-Black statements. The recording was then shared with the media and broadcast internationally, leading to a media scandal and the National Basketball Association (NBA) banning Donald Sterling for life and fining him $2.5 million.

Speech scandals have intensified because of social media. The popularization of Facebook, Twitter, and Instagram has increased the visibility of discriminatory speech and public shaming. The Miss Puerto Rico organization suspended Destiny Vélez after her comments on Twitter went viral. ESPN's firing of Curt Schilling was in response to his offensive social media posts. Together, these technological developments have had a profound effect on how racist incidents enter and are debated within the public sphere. Cell phone technologies have provided opportunities for individuals to participate in the surveillance of each other's speech, and social media has provided a platform (for better or worse) for public figures to express their unfiltered opinions to the masses and for the public to respond. The blurring of the public and private spheres is the key logic of social media.

Media scandals, however, are not exclusive to new technologies. Such scandals continue to persist in the "old-fashioned way," with public figures making statements on television or radio programs that are broadcast nationwide, or even spread by word of mouth. In 2006, actor Mel Gibson was arrested for drunk driving, and the arresting police officer reported that he unleashed a barrage of antisemitic remarks about Jews being responsible for all of the wars in the world.[25] His antisemitic remarks were followed by anti-LGBTQ+ and racist remarks; his career suffered for a few years and then bounced back. In 2007, shock jock Don Imus was suspended from his nationally syndicated morning radio show, *Imus in the Morning*, after referring to Rutgers University's women's basketball team as "nappy-headed hoes" on air. In 2010, Dr. Laura Schlessinger resigned from her nationally syndicated radio talk show, *The Dr. Laura Program*, after an on-air N-word tirade, and moved to SiriusXM satellite radio. Since the culture wars of the 1980s and 1990s, a heated debate has erupted over "politically correct" speech and whether sensitivity to historically marginalized identities is the mark of a more inclusive society or a dangerous trend of policing unpopular thought and expression. From celebrity chef Paula Deen losing her cooking shows on the Food Network and most of her endorsements after admitting to using the N-word, to CNN firing news anchor Rick Sanchez when he stated in an interview on satellite radio that, far from being an oppressed minority, Jews run the media networks,[26] such shocking cases have become simultaneously unsurprising, generating a national controversy over what constitutes an appropriate response to racist speech.

Scandals signal a breach in social norms, and these cases in particular reveal that norms around acceptable public speech have shifted since the 1980s. Communication studies professors James Lull and Stephen Hinerman write that scandals are the symbolic terrain upon which the terms of public morality are negotiated.[27] Furthermore, they add that "violation of the norms leads to sanctions, which promote outrage that threatens to expel the scandalizer from the community."[28] Sociologist Ari Adut importantly identifies three elements of scandal: "a transgression, someone who will publicize this transgression, and an interested public."[29] The cases are controversial not only because the media turns them into scandals, but also because the public opinion surrounding them is vast and conflicting. Some applaud corporate decisions to fire the offending individuals or to revoke their endorsements, believing that discrimination should not be tolerated in any form. But others believe the punishment is too harsh for an offense often excused as an accident, not something that should result in the offender losing their job and being forever stigmatized as racist or prejudiced. Still others see such decisions as evidence of political correctness run amok and criticize liberals for compromising freedom of speech, seeing such cases as involving liberals preaching tolerance while practicing intolerance through overzealous "witch hunts." As cultural critic Laura Kipnis insightfully summarizes, scandals are "the preeminent delivery system for knowledge about the moral and political contradictions of our time."[30]

What is particularly interesting with these cases is the role of the corporation. Given that racist speech is protected as free speech under the First Amendment, the legal system does not deal with such incidents as a matter of law. Fired employees can sue for wrongful termination, but fired public figures cannot be sued for hate speech. Many European countries have hate speech laws that identify such speech as interfering with another value deemed essential to democratic governance: the right to human dignity.[31] In contrast, in the US, despite the lack of legal recourse for the targets of hate speech, those who commit speech violations increasingly face repercussions to their reputations and careers. While the legal arena has been and continues to be a crucial space where matters of discrimination are handled (for better or worse), the "court of public opinion" has become ever more powerful in influencing corporate decisions and national debates.

Because public opinion is polarized, there are still a range of different corporate and voter responses to racist speech scandals. Donald Trump lost his show *The Apprentice* and multiple endorsements—from Macy's and Perfumania, for example—after declaring on the presidential campaign trail in 2016 that Mexicans are criminals and rapists. He stated: "When Mexico sends its people, they're not sending their best. They're not sending you. They're not sending you. They're sending people that have lots of problems, and they're bringing those problems with us. They're bringing drugs. They're bringing crime. They're rapists. And some, I assume, are good people."[32] In this case, corporate penalties were insufficient to sway voters from electing Trump to the highest office in the nation. Similarly, Juan Williams's unemployment after being fired by NPR was short-lived, as Fox News quickly offered him a multimillion-dollar contract. When ESPN fired Curt Schilling, the far-right news outlet Breitbart News hired him. And when Dr. Laura Schlessinger resigned from her nationally syndicated radio show, she simply shifted to SiriusXM. In these cases and others, public figures fired for their racist speech from one platform are seemingly rewarded for such speech on opposing platforms, all in the name of free speech. As a result, the issue of racist speech becomes polarized and interpreted as emblematic of one's political position as liberal or conservative in a binarized culture war. Free speech and combatting discrimination are framed as antagonistic values.

There are a few noteworthy trends in the unfolding of these media scandals, such as the central role of the apology and the moralizing emphasis on individual culpability. Those who refuse to apologize provoke debates about free speech as a cornerstone of democracy and the target of undue political correctness. Conversely, those who do apologize explain that they made a mistake and insist they are not racist in their essence, thus seeking to make a distinction between a racist person and a racist statement or human error. This then leads to a moralized conversation about whether or not the accused is a good (not racist, just made a human mistake) or bad (racist in their worldviews and behavior) person. This particular framing of the scandals reveals a paradox: while highlighting racist incidents, it simultaneously gives the impression that racism is no longer tolerated in the US. The individual offender is portrayed as an aberration, a relic of the past who must be purged from the present. The logic is that the erring individuals who holds racist perspectives face serious consequences and are socially shamed and ostracized. By reducing the matter to good and bad persons, this individualizing thrust generally eschews discussion of institutionalized racism.

By institutionalized racism, I am referring to three levels of persistent inequality: government policies, institutional practices, and institutional leadership structures. On the policy level, inequality persists, for example, through the Muslim ban, the USA PATRIOT Act, and Countering Violent Extremism. Institutional practices include, for example, stop-and-frisk police practices and police brutality against Black communities for which individual police officers are rarely convicted. There are wide racial disparities in education, health care, and wealth. At the institutional leadership level, inequality persists, for example, in the fact that the majority of owners and coaches of the NFL, MLB, and NBA are white men.[33] Ninety-six percent of Hollywood executives are white and 87 percent are men.[34] Among Fortune 500 CEOs, 72 percent are white men.[35] Sixty-six percent of Fortune 500 board seats are composed of white men, who also make up 91 percent of chairmanships of these boards.[36] This is not to say that there has not been progress in diversifying corporate leadership over the last decade.[37] Twenty-four Fortune 500 CEOs are women, three are Black, and one is openly gay.[38] Out of the thirty-two NFL teams, twenty-two are owned by white men, seven by white women, one by a Pakistani man, and one by a South Korean woman (co-owner).[39] In the NFL, three out of thirty-two head coaches are Black in a sport with 70 percent Black players.[40] The way in which racism becomes a matter of punishing the individual for speech violations gives the impression that racism and other forms of discrimination exist in the individual and that if such individuals are shamed, punished, and expelled, then the US will be free of racism and inequality. When racism is discussed in terms of a scandal, a debate ensues about political correctness and censorship, not about racism and other forms of discrimination, nor about institutionalized racism and its enduring impacts. Organizations and corporations emerge as heroes who stand against racism or as champions of free speech.

Recently, speech scandals have become part of "cancel culture." According to Ligaya Mishan, writing for the *New York Times*, cancel culture refers to incidents that occur online and off "that range from vigilante justice to hostile debate to stalking, intimidation and harassment."[41] Aja Romano of *Vox* defines it as when a person is "culturally blocked from having a prominent public platform or career."[42] It is part of a long tradition of individuals deciding to boycott a person or organization they disagree with that has expanded with the popularization of social media. The use of "cancelled" as the operating term to describe this phenomenon was appropriated from Black culture.[43] It has become a politically divisive issue, with political conservatives accusing political liberals of creating online mobs to prevent free speech.[44] Conservatives see it as a form of tyranny perpetrated by liberals who, they claim, lack tolerance for perspectives other than their own. Republicans have described cancel culture as advocating the "erasing of history, encouraging lawlessness, muting citizens, and violating free exchange of ideas, thoughts, and speech."[45] While most conservatives see it as a form of bullying or fearmongering, most liberals see it as a form of accountability for abuses of power not afforded by the state.[46] The two cases examined in this chapter took place before the popularization of the term "cancel culture" and shed some light on the early development of the phenomenon's contemporary iteration.

NPR Fires Juan Williams

In 2010, NPR fired journalist and political analyst Juan Williams after he stated on *The O'Reilly Factor* on Fox News that he gets nervous when on an airplane with a Muslim. Williams, who is Panamanian American, read as Black, and identifies as a centrist-liberal, had worked for NPR for ten years as a host of the talk show *Talk of the Nation* and as a senior national correspondent. He had also served as a Fox News contributor since 1997 and therefore frequently appeared on Fox News programs as a commentator. According to NPR, Williams was not fired based on one comment. Rather, a year earlier NPR's CEO requested that Fox News stop identifying Williams as affiliated with NPR after receiving hundreds of emails from NPR listeners stating that he dishonored NPR with some of the statements he made on Fox News.[47] In January 2009, Williams made controversial comments about First Lady Michelle Obama that many saw as describing her as an angry, militant Black nationalist with a victim narrative. In describing her as a potential liability to President Obama, he stated: "Michelle Obama, you know, she's got this Stokely Carmichael in a designer dress thing going. If she starts talking [. . .] her instinct is to start with this blame America, you know, I'm the victim. If that stuff starts coming out, people will go bananas and she'll go from being the new Jackie O to being something of an albatross."[48] NPR concluded that Williams spoke one way when on NPR and another on Fox News.[49]

The specific incident that preceded William's firing involved a conversation about controversial statements that Fox News anchor Bill O'Reilly made on the ABC talk show *The View*, prompting co-hosts Whoopi Goldberg and Joy Behar to walk off in protest. While discussing his opposition to the construction of the Park 51 Muslim community center two blocks from "ground zero," the site of the former Twin Towers and 9/11 terrorist attacks in New York City, O'Reilly stated, "Muslims killed us on 9/11." When Goldberg and Behar walked off, O'Reilly apologized and clarified that he did not intend to overgeneralize, stating: "If anybody felt that I meant all Muslims, I apologize."[50] However, once back on his own show, O'Reilly defended his comments, stating, "There's no question there is a Muslim problem in the world." He then turned to Juan Williams, a guest on the show that day, and asked if he was wrong.[51] Williams stated:

> Well, actually, I hate to say this to you because I don't want to get your ego going. But I think you're right. I think, look, political correctness can lead to some kind of paralysis where you don't address reality. I mean, look, Bill, I'm not a bigot. You know the kind of books I've written about the civil rights movement in this country. But when I get on the plane, I got to tell you, if I see people who are in Muslim garb and I think, you know, they are identifying themselves first and foremost as Muslims, I get worried. I get nervous. I remember also that when the Times Square bomber was at court, I think was just last week, he said

the war with Muslims, America's war is just beginning, first drop of blood. I don't think there's any way to get away from these facts.

What is notable about Williams's statement is that, to many people, he was simply stating what many Americans were thinking: that they were fearful when on an airplane with someone visibly Muslim given that the 9/11 hijackers were Muslim. But it also reveals the extent to which Muslim religiosity has come to be associated with the potential for terrorism and that identifying and appearing as Muslim overshadows one's humanity. That such a seemingly mild statement has such a dehumanizing effect also reveals the extent to which the linkage of Islam with terrorism has become an unquestioned assumption.

In keeping with the frequent pattern of events in a speech scandal, Williams did not apologize, but rather stated that his comments were taken out of context. Less than a year later, he published a book about the experience, *Muzzled: The Assault on Honest Debate*, in which he vehemently critiqued political correctness.[52] Offering his side of the story, Williams stated that he joined Fox News in 1997 as a centrist-liberal who would debate conservative talk show host Bill O'Reilly and his conservative guests. He later joined NPR, but argued that once Ellen Weiss became NPR's vice president for news, she sought to reduce Williams's role at NPR because of his relationship with Fox News. Williams claims that Weiss was waiting for an opportunity to fire him because she saw his role on a conservative news outlet as compromising his integrity on NPR, a liberal news outlet.

Looking more closely at the statement that led to Williams's firing, there are three notable utterances. First, there is the disclaimer that he is not a bigot: "look, Bill, I'm not a bigot." This is a key feature of speech scandals. The person accused of racism seeks to manage the social stigma of the label by insisting that that they are not racist or prejudiced; more often than not, they give examples to purportedly prove their point. Williams cited his authorship of books on the civil rights movement as proof that he could not possibly perpetuate racist ideas. Just like Bill Maher (chapter 1) uses his liberal credentials to argue that he could not possibly perpetuate Islamophobia, Juan Williams uses his race credentials and civil rights credentials for the same purpose, given that he has written about the challenges Black people still faced in the pursuit of equality after the civil rights movement.[53] Michael Richards said: "I'm not a racist, that's what's so insane about this."[54] When asked directly by Matt Lauer on the *Today Show* whether she was a racist, Paula Deen insisted, "No, I'm not."[55] Laura Schlessinger on the *Today Show* criticized CNN for suggesting that she is racist: "to call me a racist? That was absurd."[56] And when Don Lemon on CNN asked Trump whether he was racist, the latter replied: "I am the least racist person that you have ever met."[57]

Philosopher Kenneth Stikkers notes this pattern of "beginning appallingly and blatantly racist rants with 'I'm not racist, but,' or concluding such rants with 'but I'm not racist,' as if such disclaimers somehow nullify the clearly racist content of their rants," and argues that "what counts as 'racist' seems to be so absurdly high that scantly any white person clears it."[58] Williams is not white, yet he likewise subscribes to this high bar for defining racism. Importantly, when racism and other forms of discrimination manifest at the individual level, they are far from the exclusive domain of white people. Instead, as cases like those of Williams and Destiny Vélez reveal, racism and other forms of discrimination are so embedded in our society that anyone can be interpellated into discriminatory logics that they, in turn, help to perpetuate.[59]

In his book, Williams characterizes his statement that he worries when on an airplane with people in Muslim garb as an admission about his feelings, not a bigoted statement: "This was not a bigoted statement or a policy position. It was not reasoned opinion. It was simply an honest statement of my fears after the terrorist attacks of 9/11 by radical Muslims who professed that killing Americans was part of their religious duty and would earn them the company of virgins in heaven. Anyone who has lived through the last few years of attacks and attempted attacks knows that radical Islam continues to pose a threat to the United States and to much of the world."[60] Williams goes on to say that his statement was taken out of context and ignored, especially given that, in the same interview with O'Reilly, he cautioned the latter against stereotyping Muslims. He writes that he urged O'Reilly

> to choose his words carefully when he talks about the 9/11 attacks, so as not to provoke bigotry against all Muslims, the vast majority of whom are peaceful people with no connection to terrorism. I pointed out that Timothy McVeigh—along with the Atlanta Olympic Park bomber and

the people who protest against gay rights at military funerals—are Christians, but we journalists rarely identify them by their religion. I made it clear that all Americans have to be careful not to let fears—such as my own when I see people in Muslim clothes getting on a plane—color our judgment or lead to the violation of another person's constitutional rights, whether to fly on a plane, to build a mosque, to carry the Koran, or to drive a New York cab without the fear of having their throat slashed— what had happened earlier in 2010.[61]

He defends his statements and character by concluding that in the controversial segment that led to his termination "there was no bigotry expressed, no crude provocation, and no support for anti-Muslim sentiments of any kind. Just the opposite was true. I left the studio thinking I'd helped to dispel some of the prejudice towards Muslims and moved an important national conversation forward in some modest way."[62] Williams justifies his comment by characterizing it as fear as opposed to bigotry and also by characterizing it as anti-racist when considered in the full context of his statements. His speech is notable because it shows how the individual can disavow racism while perpetuating it and, in doing so, set a high bar for speech to qualify as racist.

The second notable utterance in Williams's controversial statement is his description of the Times Square bomber as saying that America is at war with "Muslims." Williams's explanation of the fuller context of his remarks and his attempt to distinguish fear from bigotry is useful in understanding what transpired. However, his book *Muzzled* only further solidifies his own association of the figure of the Muslim with terrorism. In other words, while he seeks to clarify that the speech that led to his firing was wrongfully taken out of context, the context of his book illustrates that the offending speech is consistent with his view of Islam:

It is censorship to discourage talk about the fact that terrorism in the world today is coming largely from Muslim countries and the people embracing it claim to be serving their Muslim faith by engaging in what they call jihad. It does not make you a bigot to recognize that that the major terrorist threat in our time to stable governments and civil societies around the globe is rooted in Islam. It does not make us bigots if we dare to speak the truth: Islamic extremism is a grave threat to U.S. national security.[63]

Williams's approach to Islam fits the larger trend of explaining complex political events through religion or culture.[64] He argues that "Americans must call Muslim terrorism by its name, identify it for what it is. In order for change to take place, reformers have to be empowered to take on the extremists who threaten us all."[65] This sentiment that Muslim reformers are the solution to the problem of terrorism echoes Bill Maher and Sam Harris's approach to Islam, as delineated in chapter 1, that the nominal Muslim should be propped up by the West to reform the faith. Similarly, Williams's approach to the issue is uninformed, reductionist, and therefore dangerous. In 2016, the Center for Disease Control and Prevention published a study indicating that for every American killed by terrorism—through acts perpetrated by a variety of groups, not only Muslims—one thousand have been killed by gun violence including homicides, accidents, and suicides.[66] Williams, however, perpetuates the idea that terrorism is the primary threat to national security and that Islam writ large is to blame.

His impoverished understanding of political violence is more evident when he turns to CNN's firing of Senior Editor of Mideast Affairs Octavia Nasr for tweeting: "Sad to hear of the passing of Sayyed Mohammed Hussein Fadlallah . . . one of Hezbollah's giants I respect a lot." She was fired for stating support for someone regarded in the US as a terrorist. A spokesperson for CNN released a statement explaining the network's decision to fire Nasr: "We believe that her credibility in her position as senior editor for Middle Eastern affairs has been compromised going forward."[67] Nasr apologized and tried to explain that she does not support Fadlallah's life work, given that he praised violence against the US and Israel, but that she respected him for his advocacy of women's rights.[68] Williams adds his perspective on her firing:

> Fadlallah served as a spiritual leader for Islamic Jihad, a forerunner to Hezbollah, the group that bombed the U.S. Marine barracks in Lebanon, killing 229 people. The problem is not that one journalist praised this violent Muslim cleric. The larger issue is that she was speaking for millions of people in the Muslim world who have a favorable view of Muslim terrorists and their organizations. Only by confronting the varying perceptions that really do exist can Americans and Western leaders hope to defeat terrorism.[69]

Williams characterizes Nasr's tweet as representing millions of Muslims and as unqualified support of terrorism. He portrays the US and the West more broadly as united in a fight against evil and the US in particular as an innocent victim of senseless violence. Not only does this overlook the role of the US in the politicization of Islam during the Cold War, but it obscures, for example, how praise for the US military, which is responsible for countless civilian deaths in the Middle East, could be perceived as terrorism by people in the Middle East.[70]

The third notable utterance in Williams's controversial statement is that political correctness gets in the way of addressing pressing social and political problems. The conclusion Williams makes in his book about his experience of being fired is that the "political left" (which gets conflated with political liberals) is becoming intolerant:

> it was painfully clear to me that the left wing, represented by NPR and liberal lobbying groups, had become [. . .] intolerant of people who did not agree with them. In demonizing Fox News and the right wing as a powerful conspiracy of wealthy, militaristic bigots—antiblack, antifeminist, and antigay—they hid their own prejudice against different points of view. They do not believe in tolerance. They do not care about open-minded debate. They care first and foremost about liberal orthodoxy. If you dare to challenge it or deviate from it even slightly, you will be punished.[71]

Thus, the goal of his book is "to look more deeply at the problems of censorship and political correctness in our society and show how they are undermining our ability to have meaningful discussions about important issues."[72]

Williams's argument reflects a larger trend among conservatives to appropriate the language of liberals in order to negate claims that racism and other forms of discrimination persist. For example, Ward Connerly, the Republican anti–affirmative action activist, appropriated the language of civil rights in his effort to end affirmative action in several states by naming his anti–affirmative action bill the "Civil Rights Initiative." Similarly, in Williams's case a political conservative is appropriating the language of tolerance. Conservatives claim that there is a new kind of prejudice promoted by liberals—intolerance that threatens freedom of speech. Williams, like many politically conservative critics of political liberals, claims that liberals are dogmatic about racism and discrimination to an extent that prevents free speech and dialogue. Liberals use tolerance to signal that people of different backgrounds, particularly those who have been historically marginalized as the result of their race, ethnicity, gender, sexuality, gender identity, religion, etc., should be "tolerated" in order to foster a multicultural society. Political theorist Wendy Brown offers a necessary criticism of discourses of tolerance, pointing out that it reproduces the position of the Other, creating a power imbalance between those tolerating and those tolerated.[73] In contrast, conservatives use tolerance to make the claim that they are being excluded for their narrow or offensive perspective, as if liberals must prove that they are tolerant by tolerating racist, sexist, anti-LGBTQ+, and other discriminatory perspectives. To many who agreed with NPR's firing of Williams, not reacting to his comments would have further normalized anti-Muslim racism. Those who are against NPR's decision point to liberal ideology as hypocritical for its intolerance and as exemplifying the tyranny of political correctness.

Writing about the #MeToo movement, professor of media and communications Sarah Banet-Weiser argues that "the discourse of victimhood is appropriated not by those who have historically suffered but by those in positions of patriarchal power."[74] Examining statements made by men like Harvey Weinstein and Matt Lauer, she highlights how they mobilized the notion that they are heroic truthtellers and victims of women who want to ruin their lives. She importantly notes, "since the neoliberal context does not challenge the structural logics of inequities, it becomes possible for those in positions of privilege to use the same rhetoric of discrimination and equality and apply it to themselves."[75] These men draw on their privilege or authority to make claims that they in fact are the victims in the scenario, a process in which they seek to secure white masculine hegemony.[76] In the cases of racist speech, Juan Williams and Curt Schilling claim that they are victims of political correctness. This reversal, a form of gaslighting, is made possible in an era of neoliberal diversity that is not about restorative justice. Furthermore, "the focus on the individualism of the men accused detracts attention from structural issues."[77] In the case of anti-Muslim speech, the focus on free speech detracts from addressing the larger problem of anti-Muslim racism.

The public response to Williams's firing was polarized. Those who were opposed to it blamed liberals for their intolerance and some defended Islamophobia. Posting to a forum at the *Washington Post*, one person wrote: "NPR was absolutely wrong. Add Juan Williams to an ever-growing list of commentators fired by liberal media for having the 'wrong' view."[78] Another posted, "Juan does not have 'Islamophobia.' The term is not meaningful, because it implies a fear of Islam that is irrational. There are plenty of rational reasons to fear Islam."[79] In contrast, those who supported NPR's decision praised the organization for having integrity. One poster wrote, "Juan Williams violated NPR's standards and deserved his firing. This is not a First Amendment issue. [. . .] NPR is one of the best things out there, and I'm grateful that they still have integrity."[80] Another posted, "Juan Williams deserved to be fired. I guess he thinks his opinions and fears are of interest to everyone . . . and so important that he can ignore standards of good journalism."[81] Public outrage is a central feature of the racial purge. Those who support NPR's decision to fire Williams see it as an act of integrity, professional standards, and quality journalism. The decision and debate become part of NPR's brand as the firing controversy unfolds. NPR and Fox News come to be known for their opposing values. But Fox News's hiring of Juan Williams halts the racial purge, maintaining and protecting racist speech in the name of free speech and denying the persistence of racial inequality.

I am not seeking to defend Williams or NPR, but rather to examine how this larger phenomenon of firing individuals for offensive speech is shaping racial politics today. Williams's firing highlights how upholding freedom of speech and seeking to restrict racist speech have come to be positioned in public discourse as opposing values. It also raises important questions around what an appropriate response is to racist speech and what impact the kind of public firings described here have on how racism is understood in US culture. In this case, NPR took a stance and punished Williams for contradicting NPR's values on more than one occasion. They decided to remove his platform and disassociate their organization from his comments. However, what happened next is that Fox News stepped in, providing Williams with a continued platform in the name of free speech and as a stance against political correctness. Shortly after NPR fired Williams, Fox News offered him a three-year,

$2 million contract,[82] and the corporation's president, Roger Ailes, explicitly framed the offer as protecting Williams's freedom of speech. In sum, such debates are often framed as ones between free speech and political correctness, as opposed to ones about the extent to which racism and other forms of discrimination persist and shape our lives. The focus on and criticism of political correctness glosses over and minimizes the persistence of racist logics and their impacts.

Many prominent conservatives (including Bill O'Reilly and Newt Gingrich) called for Congress to investigate NPR and cut its government funding after Williams was fired. O'Reilly called NPR a "left-wing outfit that wants one opinion" and said that would be fine if it wasn't a government-sponsored platform.[83] Republican politician and former governor of Alaska Sarah Palin echoed O'Reilly on her Facebook page, writing: "If NPR is unable to tolerate an honest debate about an issue as important as Islamic terrorism, then it's time for 'National Public Radio' to become 'National Private Radio.' "[84] Republican politician and former governor of Arkansas Mike Huckabee used Fox News to release his commentary on the matter:

> NPR has discredited itself as a forum for free speech and a protection of the First Amendment rights of all and has solidified itself as the purveyor of politically correct pabulum and protector of views that lean left. While I have often enjoyed appearing on NPR programs and have been treated fairly and objectively, I will no longer accept interview requests from NPR as long as they are going to practice a form of censorship, and since NPR is funded with public funds, it IS a form of censorship. It is time for the taxpayers to start making cuts to federal spending, and I encourage the new Congress to start with NPR.[85]

For her part, Vivian Schiller, president and CEO of NPR, released a statement explaining why Williams was fired: "News analysts may not take personal public positions on controversial issues; doing so undermines their credibility as analysts" and "NPR journalists should not express views they would not air in their role as an NPR journalist."[86] In short, NPR said that Williams violated the organization's stated values and expectations.

A key feature of neoliberalism is a focus on individual value. As Brown put it, neoliberalism both assumes and produces *homo oeconomicus*, an individual whose value is based on their ability to turn themselves into a unit of human capital.[87] In the case of speech scandals, the economic value of the individual increases and decreases through these scandals; public figures literally lose their jobs, with some suffering more permanent disgrace, while others are rewarded with an even more lucrative job. Thus, the public figure who has uttered racist speech, whose speech has become a media scandal, and who has been fired by an organization or corporation loses their value; their social and economic value decreases. Firing the individual lowers the offending individual's value—both figuratively in society and literally in terms of their losing income. When another corporation responds to the controversial firing by hiring the offending individual, competing "market forces" promote different social values and simultaneously link them with economic value. The competing social value is that of free speech, a value entwined with the denial of the persistence of racism. Yet hiring the offending individual increases their value. In these cases that individualize racism there is also a convergence of individual value with economic value.

Not all people involved in a speech scandal face the same consequences. Not all people have a platform to talk about how their free speech has been infringed. Not all people get hired by Fox News on a multimillion-dollar contract like Williams or become the president of the United States like Trump after being cancelled. Similarly, while Bill Maher's ABC show, *Politically Incorrect*, was cancelled following 9/11 after he said that the terrorists were not cowards, his subsequent HBO show, *Real Time with Bill Maher*, was not cancelled for his repeated anti-Muslim remarks.[88] Such examples illustrate the phenomenon of "cancelling up"—those who have been cancelled and then hired by another corporation or promoted in some way as a result of the controversy. As Romano points out, few powerful public figures have truly been cancelled unless they face criminal charges (e.g., Harvey Weinstein, Bill Cosby, Kevin Spacey), but even then it is not guaranteed.[89] Banet-Weiser writes that some people who have been cancelled have a chance at redemption or a comeback story.[90] Writing about the #MeToo movement, she points out that perpetrators of sexual harassment and assault like

Mario Batali, Louis C.K., and Charlie Rose have publicists to work on rehabilitating their image while the women who have been victimized do not. Romano writes, "In many cases, instead of costing someone their career, the allegation of having been 'canceled' instead bolsters sympathy for the offender, summoning a host of support from both right-wing media and the public."[91] When celebrity chef Paula Deen lost her cooking shows on the Food Network and most of her endorsements after admitting to having used the N-word in a deposition, there was a decrease in her value or human capital. In contrast, when Donald Trump lost his TV show, *The Apprentice*, and several significant endorsements for stating that Mexicans are rapists, competing market forces factored into his subsequent election as president of the United States. When NPR fired Williams, his social and economic value decreased, but when Fox News hired him, his social and economic value increased, exposing the polarized political environment. Firing public figures for discriminatory speech, rather than rectifying power imbalances, has been weaponized by the most privileged.[92]

Of course, not everyone agrees with firing individuals for their racist or otherwise offensive speech. Those who disagree deflect the topic from the enduring racism and discrimination to free speech, the tyranny of political correctness, and argue that there is a new form of discrimination against those that promote discriminatory perspectives. While the political liberals deflect the issue by focusing on scandalous individual speech at the expense of institutional forms of discrimination that do not undergo an equivalent societal purge, political conservatives deflect the issue by accusing liberals of intolerance. The purge is complete and successful when the individual is fired, not rehired, and faces severe career consequences, as in the case of Destiny Vélez, Paula Deen, and Michael Richards. However, when the individual is rehired and their career salvaged, then one could argue that it is the competing value that has won—free speech trumps hate speech, as in the cases of Juan Williams and Curt Schilling.

By expressing their values through firing and hiring offending individuals, organizations and corporations are actively participating in the culture wars through branding, a neoliberal process through which racial politics get articulated and contested. Polarized racial politics are co-opted in the service of branding and profit. Professor of mass communication Christopher P. Campbell writes, "what I've noticed in many commercials directed at millennials is that the advertisers themselves seem to be encoding politically loaded messages as a means to sell products. Antiwhite supremacy? Have some Cheerios. Pro #MeToo? Use Always hygiene products. Support the Dreamers? This Bud's for you. The millennial era seems to be one in which marketers believe they can tap into the Resistance—the progressive, anti-Trump political movement that embraces racial, gender and environmental activism—to sell products."[93] While Campbell characterizes the co-optation of racial politics with millennials, I would characterize it as reflective of neoliberal governance in which corporations play an increased role in mediating racial politics. Speech scandals are appropriated for the purpose of branding: the convergence of social value with economic value means that politics get reshaped into economic terms. Some brands become known for their commitment to diversity or even racial justice and others become known for their commitment to free speech and disavowal of the idea that racism continues to be a social problem. By using racial politics to develop their brand, corporations sell culture, affect, and politics.[94] Decisions to fire and hire reflect the convergence of social values and profit and therefore become a key component of branding. Branding and commodity activism are not new, as demonstrated by "wokevertising."[95] However, what is being bought and sold with Williams is media branding. NPR and Fox News are each holding onto and reinforcing their brands. The speech scandal turned network media branding then becomes a debate about free speech versus political correctness. The figure of the Muslim becomes used as currency in this tense exchange between media companies, and in the process, the issue at hand—anti-Muslim racism—gets flattened out.

NPR and Fox News are known for their opposing values. NPR is a nonprofit news media organization that attracts predominantly Democratic listeners.[96] Fox News is a for-profit news channel that attracts a conservative Republican audience. By taking a clear position on Williams's statement, they clarify their values and subsequently their respective brand, leading to a different audience for each media outlet. The different audience is also reflective of the divisiveness of the issue. NPR's act of firing is a racial purge that conveys that the organization will not tolerate racist speech. Fox News's hiring articulates that they stand for free speech and against political correctness in the culture wars. Fox's hiring of Williams subsequently represents, under the guise of free speech, the protection of racist speech and a denial of the persistence of racism and other forms of discrimination. Firing and then hiring, or cancelling and then cancelling up, reflect two different customer bases with different political ideologies and notions of morality. Firing relies on the political liberal's sense of morality, in particular the belief that discrimination is wrong and must be stopped. Corporations decide to fire someone at the point when an individual who is making money for them jeopardizes the customer base and thus a corporation's image. Firing becomes an act of branding, of taking a side, and claiming a particular customer base. In contrast, those who have been fired who are then hired by a different corporation with a different customer base—political conservatives who value free speech over social equality—use the hiring to similarly brand themselves and secure their customer base.

Are corporate decisions to fire or hire individuals embroiled in speech controversies based on a certain set of corporate values, profit, or a convergence of the two? Professor of business Archie B. Carroll says that it is difficult to determine what corporations are doing for business reasons and for social reasons.[97] The concept of corporate social responsibility (CSR) has been developing since the 1950s, from corporations engaging in philanthropy to community affairs and social problems.[98] Carroll writes that "it is clear from CSR trends and practices that social responsibility has both an ethical or moral component as well as a business component. In today's world of intense global competition, it is clear that CSR can be sustainable only so long as it continues to add value to corporate success. It must be observed, however, that it is society, or the public, that plays an increasing role in what constitutes business success, not just business executives alone."[99] Banet-Weiser writes that the logic of corporate social responsibility is for a corporation to engage in social issues in order to build their brand and increase profits.[100] She writes that "brands are about *culture* as much as they are about economics" and that branding "entails the making and selling of immaterial things—feelings and affects, personalities and values—rather than actual goods."[101] Corporations that fire individuals for offensive speech often state that it conflicts with their values as a corporation. Banet-Weiser argues that "the emergence of brand culture in the contemporary moment means that realms of culture and society once considered out-side the official economy—like politics—are harnessed, reshaped, and made legible in economic terms."[102]

If politics gets reshaped into economic terms, or social causes into business logic, then in the case of speech controversies, racist and other kinds of discriminatory speech becomes profitable. While speech controversies do not reimagine corporate power, the social issue gets co-opted into the brand.[103] Given that speech controversies are politically divisive, corporations take a risk in alienating some consumers. But at the same time, they earn a consumer who identifies with not just their product, but their position or values as well. When Nike used Colin Kaepernick in a 2018 advertising campaign, some people burned their Nike apparel on social media in protest.[104] During the 2016 NFL season, Kaepernick, a quarterback with the San Francisco 49ers, had protested police brutality against unarmed Black people by kneeling during the playing of the national anthem. Critics, including President Trump, called him unpatriotic and disrespectful of the flag.[105] Kaepernick explained his protest as follows: "I am not going to stand up to show pride in a flag for a country that oppresses black people and people of color. To me this is bigger than football and it would be selfish on my part to look the other way. There are bodies in the street and people getting paid leave and getting away with murder."[106] When Kaepernick became a free agent in 2017, no team hired him.[107] He became unhirable because of his protest for racial justice, and his economic value decreased. Nike was well aware of this controversy when they decided to capitalize on it and take a position for racial justice.[108] The day after Nike released the ad, their stock decreased by 3.2 percent.[109] However, Nike sales increased by 33 percent in the days after the ad was released, the company's stock price soared, and the ad even won an Emmy award.[110] Kaepernick's economic value also then increased with the Nike ad.

Banet-Weiser writes, "In the contemporary US, building a brand is about building an affective authentic *relationship* with a consumer. [. . .] It is through these affective relationships that our very selves are created, expressed, and validated. Far more than an economic strategy of capitalism, brands are the cultural spaces in which individuals feel safe, secure, relevant, and authentic."[111] NPR's firing of Williams furthered an affective relationship with their audience. It made those who identify with the NPR brand feel identification with NPR's values. It created a cultural space in which NPR's audience could participate in the purging of racism from society. Similarly, Fox News's hiring of Williams also created an authentic affective relationship with their audience to protest the racial purging and uphold free speech as a value. One consequence of the racial purge is that it activates a counter-response in which other corporations brand themselves as defenders of freedom of speech, regardless of how vile the speech, and thus uphold the racist speech as part of their brand and as part of their social value.

ESPN Fires Curt Schilling

In August 2015, ESPN sports analyst (and former Major League Baseball player) Curt Schilling reposted an Internet meme on Twitter with an image of Adolph Hitler that stated: "only 5–10% of Muslims are extremists. In 1940, only 7% of Germans were Nazis. How'd that go?" Schilling then added: "The math is staggering when you get to true #'s."[112] What is staggering is how these stated figures compare to existing statistics. Charles Kurzman's research has shown that the fear of terrorism committed by people who identify as Muslim is vastly out of proportion: "For each of the last four years, Americans have been more likely to be killed by an extremist for being Muslim (a rate of 1 in 3 million in 2017) than to be killed by a Muslim extremist (a rate of 1 in 19 million in 2017)."[113] ESPN suspended Schilling and explained in a statement: "Curt's tweet was completely unacceptable, and in no way represents our company's perspective."[114] In response, Schilling tweeted: "I understand and accept my suspension. 100% my fault. Bad choices have bad consequences and this was a bad decision in every way on my part."[115] He also deleted the offensive tweet.

Similar to the case of Juan Williams, Schilling was fired after a repeated offense and not based on a single speech violation. The similarities between Schilling's first and second offenses reveal how discriminatory logics are interconnected and racial meanings and hierarchies are coproduced.[116] In April 2016, ESPN fired Schilling after he reposted an antitransgender graphic on Facebook.[117] The image depicts a man wearing a wig of long blond hair, a black cropped top with cut outs in the chest, ripped shorts that expose the stomach, black stockings, and high heels. The accompanying caption reads: "Let him in! To the restroom with

Figure 4.2. Curt Schilling's tweet that led to
ESPN suspending him, August 25, 2015.

Figure 4.3. Curt Schilling's Facebook post that led to
ESPN firing him, April 19, 2016.

your daughter or else you're a narrow minded, judgmental, unloving, racist bigot who needs to die!!!" Schilling posted commentary: "A man is a man no matter what they call themselves. I don't care what they are, who they sleep with, men's room was designed for the penis, women's not so much. Now you need laws telling us differently? Pathetic." The post was Schilling's response to the passing of controversial legislation in North Carolina in 2016, House Bill 2, which requires transgender people to use public bathrooms that correspond to their biological sex rather than the gender with which they identify.[118] The bill provoked condemnation by some musicians, businesses, and sports teams. PayPal and Adidas backed out of projects, Bruce Springsteen and the NBA All-Star Game cancelled their events, and the NAACP initiated a boycott of the state.[119] The image frames transgender identity as an impossibility, a failure, a monstrosity, and a threat. It highlights perversity through the imagined threat of daughters being assaulted in bathrooms. Taken together, Schilling's anti-Muslim and anti-transgender social media posts articulate what Jasbir K. Puar and Amit S. Rai have pointed to as hierarchies of monstrosity,[120] the figure of the Muslim and the transgender person.

ESPN released a very brief statement: "ESPN is an inclusive company. Curt Schilling has been advised that his conduct was unacceptable and his employment with ESPN has been terminated."[121] This time, Schilling was unapologetic. He defended himself in a blog post:

> The latest brew ha ha is beyond hilarious. I didn't post that ugly looking picture. I made a comment about the basic functionality of mens and womens restrooms, period. [. . .] I do NOT care what color you are, what race, what sex, who you sleep with, what you wear. I don't care and never have. I have opinions, but they're just that, opinions. [. . .] You frauds out there ranting and screaming about my 'opinions' (even if it isn't) and comments are screaming for "tolerance" and "acceptance" while you refuse to do and be either.[122]

Schilling's self-defense is in line with the criticism of political correctness explored above, whereby political conservatives claim to be ideologically marginalized. Schilling takes issue with being perceived as bigoted and narrow-minded and instead claims that it is liberals who are being bigoted and narrow-minded in their interactions with conservatives. Also typical of how these controversies unfold is Schilling's defense of himself: stating that he is not racist or anti-LGBTQ+, despite implying that transgender identity is an impossibility and that Muslims are a sleeper cell threat to the US. Shortly after ESPN fired Schilling, he was cancelled up when the notorious conservative online magazine Breitbart News hired him to host an online radio show.[123]

One way the offending individual who has lost their value seeks to recuperate it is through the public apology or defense of their speech. Destiny Vélez apologized. Williams defended his speech and even wrote a book to recuperate his public image. Schilling apologized after the anti-Muslim incident. But after the anti–transgender rights incident he defended himself and criticized those who were criticizing him. The apology is central to the discriminatory speech scandal. Public figures either apologize in an attempt to salvage their public image and career or refuse to apologize, making statements about free speech. Whether one apologizes or not, statements from the offending individual are efforts to manage the scandal and defend oneself; they are vital pieces in how racism gets defined and contested through these scandals

Professors of communication Michelle A. Holling, Dreama G. Moon, and Alexandra Jackson Nevis refer to the apology as "racializing apologia," stating that it is as important as the offense itself and often involves continuing to offend. They write:

> a racist violation expresses racism via microaggressions, supports various ideologies, such as beliefs in white superiority or adherence to colorblind ideology, and acts to maintain systems of white supremacy. [. . .] In contrast, "racializing apologia" are public statements by individuals (or, violators) who are called on their perceived racist comments and seek to redress and apologize. In doing so, however, violators continue to offend consequently, the apologia exacerbates the racialization process that surfaced in a violation.[124]

Professor of anthropology John Hartigan Jr. says that the apology limits the potential national conversation about race.[125] He writes that "the point of the apology is to end the discussion and establish immediate closure over a queasy-making, disturbing rupture of social conventions designed to keep race from 'coming up' in public discourse."[126] In contrast, English professor Adam Ellwanger states that public apologies operate as ritualistic punishment and humiliation, that the offending individual must perform radical existential change to resolve the offense.[127] Thus, for the offending individual, the point of the apology is to end the matter; however, for the spectator-citizen, the apology becomes a ritualistic aspect of the purge.

As expected, opinions varied on ESPN's firing of Schilling. Christine Brennan, writing for *USA Today*, was in favor of ESPN's decision to fire:

> A member of the sports media should cover and comment on sports news, not actively try to make news. [. . .] It's called professionalism. Why would a cable TV baseball analyst think anyone wanted to hear anything he had to say beyond what's up with someone's slider? Because he had no filter. Or, for that matter, good judgment. Schilling was a loose cannon, a detriment to his employer. [. . .] [T]he man who cannot stop himself from sharing his most recent repulsive opinion and the gift of a vast technological receptacle that can gather his thoughts and disseminate them to every single one of us? Had Schilling been born 30 years earlier, he would have been relegated to rants over his cereal bowl at the breakfast table, his only audience the few people on Earth who share his last name. Lucky for them, they could get up and leave for school or work. ESPN finally got up and left Schilling on Wednesday night. We're all the better for it.[128]

Roxanne Jones, a founding editor of *ESPN The Magazine*, agreed that Schilling deserved to be fired. She made a similar argument: Schilling is paid for his expertise in sports, not to voice his uninformed opinions on political issues. She wrote, "while the public may care very much about his expert baseball insights and opinions, his uninformed, biased opinions on everything from Muslims to Nazis to Hillary Clinton and her emails, and now transgender communities, have added nothing intelligent to any conversation, sports or otherwise."[129] Interestingly, even though Juan Williams was similarly deeply misinformed, he was not criticized for sharing uninformed opinions, given his profession as a journalist and political analyst.

Both those who agreed and disagreed with ESPN's firing of Schilling pointed to how social media provides a platform for making controversial opinions public. Sports journalist for Fox Sports Radio Clay Travis made a point similar to Brennan's about how social media has led to publicizing one's personal views, but unlike Brennan, he did not believe that the consequences were justified. He wrote that, although he disagreed with Schilling's political opinions, he also disagreed with corporations firing employees for their opinions and argued that it proved certain opinions were acceptable while others were not:

> That's the standard operating behavior in stories like these. My contention is this policy is lazy and actually harmful to our public discourse. [. . .] [I]t's important to keep in mind that with the rise of social media our public and private lives have become inextricably intertwined. It used to be that most of us had well defined public and private lives. If, for instance, Curt Schilling had strong conservative political views in 1985, it would have been hard for most people to know that. Absent running for political office, writing a book, or paying millions to distribute fliers, it was hard for regular people to share their political beliefs to millions with ease. That's no longer the case. Whether you're a famous public figure or a mom posting on Facebook, the line between public and private has become nonexistent. And we're still grappling with what that means.[130]

While Travis argued that we need to contend with the ways in which social media blurs the boundary between public and private, Todd Starnes of Fox News opposed ESPN's firing and invoked the notion of "traditional values," writing:

> Curt Schilling joins a growing list of Americans who have been punished for rejecting the basic tenets of the gender revolution. From bakers in Oregon to a florist in Washington State—there is a nefarious movement afoot to silence anyone who dares oppose the LGBT agenda. [. . .] Again, those who preach tolerance have demonstrated time and time again— that they are the least tolerant. [. . .] It's a very unusual time to be an American, folks. We've reached a point where choosing a bathroom based on your God-given plumbing makes you a transphobic bigot. Traditional values just got double-flushed. Schilling has learned a very important

lesson—free speech comes with a price. And those who dare defend traditional values—will be silenced.

In addition to the now common argument that liberals preach tolerance but are intolerant, Starnes adds another layer to arguments against
firing individuals for racist speech through his defense of traditional
values. "Tradition" becomes code for being against social change that
would lead to a more equal society; it is an argument for white supremacy and all of its discontents—racism, sexism, anti-LGBTQ+ discrimination. It advocates reestablishing the white cisgendered heterosexual
able-bodied Christian man as the normative identity and marginalizing
other identities. The argument that liberals are intolerant suggests that
liberals should tolerate racist, sexist, anti-LGBTQ+, anti-immigrant,
antisemitic, anti-Muslim, and anti-disabled sentiments and practices to
prove that they are practicing the tolerance that they preach. Such arguments for "traditional values" normalize the perpetuation of inequality.

Punishing the Individual, Absolving the Institution

Firing public figures for racist speech gives the impression that racism
begins and ends with the individual. It does not lead to a conversation
about the legacy of enduring racism in the US, but rather to conversation about the incident, whether the firing was justified, and whether or
not it is a matter of free speech. Corporate firing practices, while articulating a strong anti-discrimination message, do not prevent people from
saying offensive things and do little to shed light on enduring inequality in the US. The focus on individuals as the problem distracts from
institutionalized forms of discrimination that persist at the policy and
institutional levels. When corporations fire employees caught in speech
scandals, they seek to publicly position themselves as not only opposed
to racism, but also innocent of it in their own practices and policies.
Professor of discourse studies Teun van Dijk notes that:

> since discrimination and racism are legally and morally prohibited, most
> western countries share the official belief that *therefore* discrimination
> and racism no longer exist as a structural characteristic of society or the
> state. If discrimination or prejudice still exist, it is treated as an incident,

as a deviation, as something that should be attributed to, and punished at the individual level. In other words, institutional or systemic racism is denied.[131]

In short, the ongoing pattern of individualizing racism absolves institutions of racism. Put even more briefly, where the individual fails, the corporation succeeds.

Similar to how Hollywood cast itself as heroic during the Trump era's resurgence of overt white supremacy (as explored in chapter 2), corporations appear heroic when they fire people who utter racist, sexist, anti-LGBTQ+ speech. The individual contaminant is removed, but without interrogating how the corporate world has enabled racism to exist as part of its logic since its inception. Organizations and corporations that fire individuals for their racist speech approach the individual as "one bad apple" that must be expelled to maintain the fiction of an equal social order and, at the same time, the power of the organization, corporation, or institution. As feminist scholar Sara Ahmed aptly puts it:

Racism should not be seen as about individuals with bad attitudes (the "bad apple model"), not because such individuals do not exist (they do) but because such a way of thinking underestimates the scope and scale of racism, thus leaving us without an account of how racism *gets reproduced*. The argument can be made in even stronger terms: the very identification of racism *with* individuals becomes a technology for the reproduction of racism *of* institutions. So eliminating the racist individual would preserve the racism of the institution in part by creating an illusion that we are eliminating racism. Institutions can "keep their racism" by eliminating those whom they identify as racists.[132]

Media companies transform their employees into media content, and when they exceed that instrumentalization, then the company removes the content as if they are excising racism.

The #MeToo movement follows a similar logic. Men in positions of power who have sexually harassed or assaulted women are outed and shamed. In some cases, the courts get involved and the men are charged and go to trial. Some go to prison. The media reporting of it creates a scandal and the public participates in the outrage machine. It appears that society has purged these sexist monsters with the help of corporations that formerly normalized and upheld their behavior. It appears that there is some justice. Professor of American literature and culture Eva Cherniavsky, however, points out that the #MeToo movement traffics in a political fantasy that women can dismantle an entire system of male privilege by using Twitter. The politics of #MeToo, she argues, remain too narrowly focused on publicity (aka the media scandal)—this form of politics is "powerfully performative and dangerously limited."[133] A similar argument can be made about the anti-Muslim speech scandals considered here. The responses to them promote a political fantasy that anti-Muslim racism is unacceptable and that US society will do away with racism and other forms of discrimination once and for all given that corporations are firing the offending individuals and the public is collectively participating in their purging from society. It is powerfully performative given the anatomy of a speech scandal—the controversial utterance, the media scandal, the corporation's firing, the public's outrage, the offender's apology or defense of free speech, and the possibility of cancelling up. It is also dangerously limited. Institutions appear to use their power for good and to promote diversity and equality as a social value. But, as Ahmed says, we are left without an account of how racism, sexism, or other forms of power and inequality get reproduced and institutions get to keep their racism.[134]

Professor of Afro-American literature and culture Michael Awkward, writing about the firing of Don Imus from CBS for referring to the Rutgers University women's basketball team as "nappy-headed hoes," states that firing operates as a kind of national atonement for past wrongs like slavery. He writes, "Put simply, Imus was made to stand in for millions of well-know and faceless whites whom blacks (and liberal and progressive whites) want desperately to identify, put on trial, and excoriate because of incontrovertible—but to this point often easily dismissed—'evidence' of centuries of racially motivated sins."[135] Similarly, the individual offender overcompensates for the nation's enduring inequality; the corporation is absolved of racism and becomes a hero in the fight for racial justice and equality; and institutional racism remains unchanged. I agree with Awkward that the individual is made to overcompensate for the nation's past and present inequalities. To be clear, my critique about the tendency to individualize racism and other forms of discrimination is not intended to suggest that the individual does not matter when it comes to rectifying racism. Rather, my position is that the individual is but one component in a multidimensional "racial infrastructure"[136] and our focus on punishing the individual comes at the expense of addressing the institutional, corporate, and policy levels that remain unpurged. Granted, individuals make up institutions and collectively create policies and thus are an important component in challenging racism. Individuals are interpellated into logics that legitimize inequality. But getting rid of individuals and leaving our institutions intact as heroes in the fight against racism produces questionable social change.

Racial purging is reflective of the privatization and corporatization of racial politics as is the way in which corporations take political stances to further their brands. Through this process, racial purging is embraced by some as a viable solution to racism and fiercely contested by others. Those who contest it by arguing for freedom of speech tend to co-opt the language of inequality to argue for their own marginalization and in doing so completely overlook and negate the history of white supremacy and inequality in the US. While liberals seeks to combat racial injustice through the firing of offending individuals, conservatives defend a perceived injustice in the violation of free speech. Whether for or against the racial purge, systemic inequality remains intact.

What are the alternatives to purging individuals from the social order? Social justice movements have long practiced "calling out," which involves interpersonal confrontation in person or through social media to let someone know they did or said something wrong. Whether call-out culture is an effective tool for learning and growth has been debated, because it also involves shame, embarrassment, and social consequences.[137] Some have advocated for an alternative, "calling in," which is the same as calling out except it is done with love, respect, and the possibility for growth and forgiveness instead of shame and judgment.[138] While a call-in model holds more potential for productive dialogue and transformation, to be sure, even if a call-in model were to be adopted as an approach to speech scandals, some will continue to gaslight inequality in the name of free speech and refuse the opportunity to learn. Regardless, the goal should be to galvanize such incidents into productive conversations that raise awareness about enduring inequality and how individuals and institutions perpetuate logics and practices that justify inequality. While individuals should be held accountable for their speech, we also need to challenge the illusion that racism is located only in individuals and if we purge them from the social order then institutions can continue their role as purveyors of social justice.

5

Flexible Diversity

It is not possible to understand Muslim and Middle Eastern/North African (MENA) students' inclusion on college campuses without considering how they are targeted and marginalized by Zionist organizations for their Palestinian rights activism. In the institutional context of the university, crisis-driven responses have created both challenges and opportunities for Muslim and MENA students. As a faculty member at the University of Michigan (UM) from 2005 through 2018, I witnessed (and at times participated in) changes made by the administration to meet the needs of these students. In 2007, the university's Office of Multiethnic Student Affairs supported students in organizing an Arab Student Summit and a Muslim Student Summit, which offered opportunities for students of these identities to gather over a weekend and attend workshops, engage in difficult but productive dialogues about common divisions within each community, and build connections. In addition, UM has sought to incorporate Arab American students into existing models of inclusion. Multiethnic Student Affairs began honoring Arab Heritage Month in 2014 with programming to parallel that for Black History Month and Women's History Month. The Office of Multicultural Academic Initiatives created an Arab Graduation ceremony in 2015 to parallel Black Graduation, Latinx Graduation, and Lavender (LGBTQ+) Graduation. In response to student demand for a multicultural lounge in honor of an Arab American to follow in the tradition of other multicultural lounges named after Angela Davis, Audre Lorde, Cesar Chavez, Mahatma Gandhi, Grace Lee Boggs, Rosa Parks, and Martin Luther King Jr., an Edward Said Lounge was inaugurated in 2015, named after the influential Palestinian American scholar who wrote the book *Orientalism* in 1978.[1] Meanwhile, University Housing sought to figure out how best to accommodate Muslim students who fast during Ramadan and University Facilities increased the number of reflection spaces on campus to facilitate daily prayer practices of religious Muslim students.

Such efforts, which came to fruition in response to a combination of anti-Muslim racist incidents and student demands for recognition, signal the inclusion of both Muslim and Middle Eastern and North African students in university diversity approaches. Crisis diversity has facilitated the recognition and inclusion of Muslims and MENA people in conceptions of diversity.

Yet while the administration took actions to include Muslim and MENA students in response to various crisis moments in anti-Muslim racism, these very same students contend with being accused of anti-semitism[2] and supporting terrorism because of their involvement in activism for Palestinian self-determination and criticism of Israeli state violence. In January 2014, for example, Yazan Kherallah, an Arab American student at UM, posted to his Facebook page a photo of himself wearing a face-covering keffiyeh and holding a knife to a pineapple with the caption, "It's on."[3] It was a joke to his friends who played on a basketball team called Ananas ("pineapple" in Arabic) whom he would be competing against. Two months later, while he was engaged with other student activists for Palestinian rights to pass a divestment resolution with Central Student Government, Adam Kredo, writing for the politically conservative *Washington Free Beacon* website, reposted the photo, speculating that Kherallah was threatening pro-Israel students, that the pineapple was symbolic of Israel and the Jewish people, and that the photo "could contribute to the culture of fear within the University of Michigan's pro-Israel community."[4] The article's larger context was that pro-Israel students were facing death threats and racist epithets from students who were advocating for the Boycott, Divestment, Sanctions movement. When the University of Michigan asked the *Washington Free Beacon* to remove the photo of the student, the photo was not taken down, and instead articles on the website continued to condemn Kherallah and other activists for Palestinian rights.[5] Kredo claimed that "campus insiders said the Michigan incident is just the latest heavy-handed campaign by anti-Israel activists bent on using U.S. college campuses as a means to foment hate for the Jewish state" and characterized students who advocate for Palestinian rights as threatening the civil rights of Jewish students and associating with "anti-Israel extremists."[6] Kherallah stated that he and his peers were "falsely accused of using racial epithets against opponents of the resolution in an attempt to distract from our real message—that complicity in Israel's human rights violations has to stop—and paint us as motivated by anti-Semitism."[7] He clarified that the photo was intended to be a satire of Arab stereotypes, but was deliberately misinterpreted and used against him. As the result of Kredo's articles, Kherallah received hate messages on social media calling him a "jihadist" and "infidel slayer." The incident caused Kherallah a great deal of distress as he was blacklisted on the website Canary Mission and Google searches of his name yielded multiple articles portraying him as a violent threat to Jewish students, potentially impacting his future career prospects.

It has become a common occurrence on college campuses across the US for students advocating for Palestinian self-determination to be accused of promoting antisemitism. Palestine Legal, a nonprofit legal and advocacy organization, identifies the following eighteen organizations as driving efforts to suppress speech advocating for Palestinian rights: Louis D. Brandeis Center for Human Rights Under Law, the Zionist Organization of America, the AMCHA Initiative, Hillel International, Shurat HaDin Israel Law Center, StandWithUs, the Anti-Defamation League, the American Israel Public Affairs Committee, the Jewish Federations of North America, the Jewish Council for Public Affairs, Scholars for Peace in the Middle East, the American Jewish Committee, the Committee for Accuracy in Middle East Reporting in America, Divestment Watch, the Israel on Campus Coalition, Campus Watch, the David Project, and the David Horowitz Freedom Center.[8] While each organization has a distinct approach, they tend to frame their activities as challenging the "delegitimization" of Israel.[9] Some of these organizations (e.g., Hillel) have an established presence on college campuses, while others (e.g., Canary Mission, AMCHA Initiative, Israel on Campus Coalition) insert themselves into campus politics and heavily impact the experiences of student activists for Palestinian rights.

Such Zionist organizations frame instances of this activism as racist incidents that require immediate remediation and punishment. Advocates of Palestinian self-determination are marked as antisemites, those who are Jewish as self-hating Jews, and those who are MENA or Muslim as terrorists or supporters of terrorism. These organizations strategically mobilize anti-Arab/anti-Muslim tropes—violent, jihadist, threatening the safety of Jewish students—to smear and discredit supporters of Palestinian rights in the face of the Israeli government's illegal military occupation and violent dispossession of Palestinians. Such accusations of antisemitism create a crisis that undermines the university's efforts to include MENA and Muslim students in diversity, equity, and inclusion (DEI) initiatives, creating a paradox for students who are included in one moment and slandered the next.

Since MENA and Muslim identities are conflated, DEI initiatives often address both communities as one and the same, or if one is addressed, both benefit (or are adversely impacted) because of how these identities have been co-produced. When I talk about DEI, I refer to MENA and Muslim students who are being including in DEI initiatives as such. These same students and a wider constituency of allies participate in Palestinian rights advocacy. I do not use MENA and Muslim to refer to this latter, overlapping group of students to avoid the false impression that the conflict is between "Muslims" and "Jews" or the false notion that what is happening in Israel and Palestine is a "religious" conflict. Therefore, I refer to student advocates for Palestinian self-determination as such and to students with an opposing position as political Zionists. Student activists for Palestinian rights are Arab, MENA, South Asian, and/or Muslim; in addition, the broader coalition includes a range of students of color—Black, Latinx, Native, Asian American—as well as Jewish students and white students. The politics of Palestinian advocacy on campuses impacts all involved, but uniquely racializes Arab, South Asian, MENA, and Muslim students as terrorists and terrorist supporters.

The interaction of DEI with Zionism on college campuses gives rise to a range of responses. UC Irvine and Fordham University have penalized student activists for Palestinian rights. The University of Michigan administration, in contrast, has sought to appease all constituents through what I call "flexible diversity," an all-inclusive approach to diversity. Flexible diversity happens when the UM administration seeks to include all students equally, without attention to the power dynamics that sustain inequality; it happens when university administrations redraw the lines of inclusion seemingly to include (and appease) everyone, but in setting aside power dynamics, render the project of DEI meaningless. Flexible diversity reflects a larger neoliberal trend that involves reimagining diversity as a beneficial resource to which all may lay equal claim and is dangerously unmoored from unequal distributions of power. Replacing social justice with diversity changes the approach from rectifying the persistence of a legacy of inequality and racial violence to ensuring that everyone is included as if everyone is equally marginalized. When the university employs flexible diversity, the project of diversity gets watered down and loses its meaning.

Flexible diversity describes UM's strategy for dealing with the intersection of DEI with Zionism when it comes to undergraduate student activism from roughly 2014 to 2018. Accusations of antisemitism lead to UM administrators making statements that Jewish students are included and matter and that students advocating for Palestinian self-determination have the right to free speech. On the surface, this all-inclusive approach is meaningful as it does not deliberately exclude anyone. However, the university is unable to achieve meaningful inclusion because it sets up DEI in a neoliberal, individualizing, even-playing-field way and because students advocating for Palestinian self-determination are left vulnerable to threats with little to no support behind them. Therefore, in the case of Muslim and MENA students, university administrators include them in DEI initiatives, but when political Zionism enters the conversation, they are smeared as "terrorists" and "jihadists" and thus marginalized. When Zionism intersects with DEI on college campuses, it perpetuates anti-Arab and anti-Muslim racism and undermines the inclusion of MENA and Muslim students.

In considering how Muslims get included at universities, this has taken place in the "age of Islamophobia" through DEI initiatives that have benefitted Muslim students who have gained reflection spaces and dining hall accommodations during Ramadan, as well as through the recognition that MENA students' identities are racialized and hence marginalized. While UM has sought to be inclusive of Muslim and MENA students, such efforts are challenged when these students are involved in Palestinian rights activism; they backfire because a powerful network of Zionist organizations claim that these students are promoting antisemitism, generating a range of serious consequences to their present lives and future careers. Student activists for Palestinian rights deal with severe psychological distress as they face character defamation and threats to their career prospects. While Zionist organizations are responsible for the crisis student activists for Palestinian rights experience, the way in which the university manages and mediates this crisis impacts the extent to which these students experience that they matter or are included at the university.

Of course, UM's approach is not representative of all college and university approaches to diversity. UM is a public research university with a critical mass of Muslim and MENA students. For the purposes of this chapter, I focus on the academic institution I know best, and in doing so it is important to acknowledge that an examination of other public, private, research, liberal arts, and/or community college approaches might yield different results. Public universities have a very different relationship to the First Amendment and free speech debates compared to private universities. The First Amendment must be upheld by all government/state spaces, which means that public universities are subject to the rule. In contrast, private universities do not have to follow it, since they do not represent the state. While the government and public universities cannot favor one kind of speech over another, the consequences faced by Palestinian rights activists results in what Palestine Legal calls the "Palestine exception to free speech."[10] When Zionism intersects with DEI on college campuses, the distinction between DEI and free speech becomes blurred. Criticizing Israeli state policies, or any government's policies for that matter, is protected as free speech, but when it is classified as antisemitic, it becomes a DEI issue.

At the University of Michigan, a notable shift took place from the language of "diversity" to that of "diversity, equity, and inclusion" in 2014. A January 16, 2014, email to "Members of the University Community" from Provost Martha E. Pollack, titled "Message on Diversity and Inclusion," affirmed the campus's commitment "to advancing diversity and improving the climate of inclusion," and outlined two objectives: to hire a vice provost for educational equity and inclusion and to establish the Provost Committee on Diversity, Equity, and Inclusion. The email referenced #BBUM (Being Black at UM), a Twitter hashtag launched the prior semester by Black students at the University of Michigan to highlight their marginalization.[11] From 2006, when affirmative action became illegal in Michigan, to 2014, the number of Black students at UM declined from 8 percent to 4 percent.[12] The shift to DEI at the University of Michigan was partially a response to the crisis foregrounded by #BBUM. Through DEI initiatives, some universities are grappling with the demise of affirmative action and figuring out other ways to recruit and retain members of groups that have been historically underrepresented and those who are marginalized and underrepresented today. What is also notable is that DEI came on the heels of a statement by the University of Michigan president and provost opposing an academic boycott of Israel[13] in response to the American Studies Association's endorsement of boycotting Israeli universities.[14] The fact that institutionalizing DEI and condemning the academic boycott of Israel were happening simultaneously at the University of Michigan provides important context for the scenarios explored below in which Muslim and MENA students are included in DEI initiatives but are vilified when it comes to their Palestinian rights activism.

Including MENA and Muslim Students in DEI

The terrorist attacks in Paris on November 13, 2015, presented yet another crisis and a turning point on campus. It was a Friday night in Paris when ISIS coordinated six shootings and a suicide bombing at a stadium during a soccer match, a concert hall, and several restaurants that killed 130 people and injured almost 500.[15] Following these attacks, there was concern about potential backlash against Muslims around the globe, including at college campuses in the US. The dean of students at the University of Michigan sent an email communication to students that expressed support for "our French students studying in Ann Arbor, for others directly affected by this situation and all international students."[16] Muslim students felt the message revealed the administration's prioritization of certain students over others and that the administration had avoided taking a stance to protect Muslims during a time of increased anti-Muslim sentiment across the country.

An undergraduate student at the University of Michigan sent an email to UM's president, provost, two vice provosts, and me (in my role as director of the Arab and Muslim American Studies program), expressing concern about an increase in microaggressions against Muslim students. He wrote:

Early Monday morning, the University of Michigan's Instagram account posted a picture of the Yemeni Student Association's first mass meeting. In the comment section, a Michigan student decided to express their views about this post: "SEND THEM BACK OMG ISIS ISIS OMG NOOOOOOOOOOO." About an hour later, fortunately, the University of Michigan account deleted the student's comment. [. . .] Arabs and Muslims are under attack from all sides—from the vile groups that have stolen our identities and from the people who believe the thieves. Many Arab students already feel unwelcomed and stripped of their identity due to the fact that there is no identifying box for them—they must check White or Other.

The attacks in Paris and the fears of an increase in anti-Muslim hate, along with this brave email from an undergraduate student to university leadership concerned that ISIS was succeeding in representing all Arabs and Muslims, sparked a flurry of institutional activity. I was thrust into a series of meetings with the provost, lead council to the president, and assistant vice provost for academic affairs, as well as numerous students, all asking me for advice. I quickly emphasized that I could not become the sole spokesperson on campus for all Muslim and MENA faculty, staff, and students. Along with a long-time staff member at the University of Michigan, the assistant dean for undergraduate education, and several undergraduate students, we collectively formed the Islamophobia Working Group (IWG). Our objective was to respond to the most recent events, but also more broadly to advise the administration on how to include Muslim and MENA students in DEI conversations and plans.

DEI plans at colleges and universities do not usually account for the needs of Arab, Middle Eastern, North African, and/or Muslim students, staff, and faculty. Since the US Census classifies people from the Middle East and North African region as "white," these populations do not figure into how "diversity" is commonly conceptualized. Furthermore, religion is not a category that is tracked and used in diversity efforts and therefore it is difficult to speak of "Muslim" inclusion. Nonetheless, conversations about the inclusion of Muslim and MENA identities have been made possible by the students, staff, and faculty who have mobilized for inclusion in diversity efforts, coupled with a crisis that prompts some university administrators to be open to new initiatives. Given that there is a relatively large Arab Muslim student population at

UM—partly due to its proximity to Dearborn, Michigan, an area that boasts the largest concentration of Arabs in the US—this critical mass also contributed to the increasing recognition of Muslim and MENA students and their needs.

The IWG consisted of one hundred faculty, staff, and students from across the campus with an average of twenty-five to thirty members attending each meeting, starting on February 5, 2016.[17] We immediately set about doing two things: first, we created a resource list for victims of anti-Muslim racism. The list included information on the Department of Public Safety, the Bias Response Team, and counseling services on campus. Our long-time staff member researched which therapists Muslim students could trust to not retraumatize them by asking Islamophobic questions about their family life, a frequent complaint from Muslim students. One Muslim therapist from Counseling and Psychological Services joined the Islamophobia Working Group. Second, we drafted a report for inclusion in the university's DEI plan.[18] The School of Literature, Science, and Arts was drafting a DEI plan and the deadline for inclusion in its report was fast approaching. We worked feverishly over a two week period to write a report. The report's overview states:

> The national climate of Islamophobia and anti-Arab racism impacts students, faculty, and staff at the University of Michigan. Students have reported hostility from faculty and other students; verbal assaults on the streets; the receipt of hate mail; hostility toward activists organizing around MENA-related issues, especially the Israeli-Palestinian conflict; and a reluctance to call the police or to report bias incidents. [. . .] This report's objective is to identify the experiences of Arab, Muslim, and MENA (Middle Eastern and North African) students and faculty and to suggest ways for the administration to build upon the initiatives that it has already implemented to create a more diverse, equitable, and inclusive campus environment for Arab, Muslim, and MENA students. We offer some suggestions [. . .] around three categories: resource building, crisis support, and education.[19]

The report highlighted what the university had already done well (as mentioned above, creating an Edward Said Lounge, Arab Heritage Month, and Arab Graduation), acknowledging that there was a history of the administration responding to the needs of Muslim and MENA students. In addition to hiring more Arab, Muslim, and MENA-identified faculty and staff and increasing support for ethnic studies programs to educate the campus on crucial issues of social justice, the suggestions we made included (a) adding a MENA box on the under-graduate application and on pool reports when faculty and staff are hired in order to collect data and assess needs; (b) improving the bias reporting system because some students felt that reporting under the current system would not help them; and (c) educating the police and other bias responders on Islamophobia and the Israeli-Palestinian conflict so that they understand the issues involved.

The IWG's report was included in the appendix to the College of Literature, Science, and the Arts five-year diversity, equity, and inclusion plan, which we celebrated as a win. Our issues were now part of the official record. Our efforts were recognized by speeches made by the president of the university at Arab Graduation and became part of the university's metrics to show the kind of progressive and effective DEI work they were doing. Regarding creating documents like a DEI report, feminist scholar Sara Ahmed states that diversity at universities often becomes a matter of documents that provide an action plan and metrics to assess progress.[20] As Ahmed points out, such bureaucratization has mixed results; the focus on audits and monitoring can lead to a matter of checking boxes rather than challenging inequalities. The IWG's work and concerns were recognized by the leaders of the university, and the administration's recognition of a global crisis in Islamophobia created opportunities. At the same time, being part of the official DEI plan also meant that our work came to reflect and represent the concerns of the university. On the one hand, it gave us legitimacy. On the other hand, continued vigilance was required to ensure the administration actually implemented our recommendations.

Studies have shown that most campuses do not accommodate the need of religious Muslim students to pray five times per day.[21] Muslim students report having to defend their religious values to their peers and dealing with faculty who perpetuate stereotypes about Islam in the classroom.[22] In addition, many report that they do not feel like their experiences of marginalization are addressed by their campus administration but rather that they are treated like a problem.[23] Students at the University of Michigan have reported experiences that concur with these studies. However, unlike other campuses, given its critical mass of Muslim and MENA students, UM has a track record of being responsive to the needs of these students. The IWG's emergence at the intersection of the recognition of a global crisis in anti-Muslim racism and the university's expressed commitment to DEI created a unique opportunity to make institutional changes to improve the experiences of students impacted by anti-Muslim racism.

Now that our issues were documented, we set about identifying a few specific matters to pursue with the administration. Student members of the IWG identified three areas in which to begin our work together. First, we sought to increase the number of reflection spaces on campus to facilitate prayer for those Muslim students who pray five times per day. Muslim students who follow this schedule reported sometimes having to walk twenty minutes to a building with a reflection space to pray. A student and the assistant dean worked with Facilities to increase the number of reflection rooms on campus, spaces that can be used for multiple purposes such as meditation, prayer, or breast feeding.[24] The administration was responsive, adding several reflection rooms in buildings across campus; the change had a tangible impact on the lives of observant Muslim students on campus.

Second, we advocated changing the Arabic language textbook used at UM, *al-Kitaab* (the Book).[25] This textbook is internationally recognized as the standard in Arabic language instruction. However, students at the University of Michigan, Stanford University, Tufts University, and other campuses have noted that it primarily prepares students to work for the US State Department and, as such, makes the teaching of Arabic distinct from that of other languages.[26] Students report that they learn terms like "terrorism," "army," and "United Nations" long before they learn the words for basic colors. The textbook has been criticized for politicizing Arab culture and portraying it as exotic and violent, as well as promoting Orientalism and militaristic approaches to the Middle East. As a result, a few UM students and Near Eastern Studies faculty began raising awareness about the textbook's flaws and calling for its replacement. In the fall 2017 semester, Near Eastern Studies created a task force to discuss the textbook and the IWG received funding from the National Council for Institutional Diversity to send the two students who were spearheading the initiative to the Middle East Studies Association convention in Washington, DC, to present on the issue.

Third, the IWG advocated for a Middle Eastern/North African category on undergraduate student applications and other data collection forms at the university. Such metrics are crucial to determine how many MENA students, staff, and faculty are on campus and thus better serve their needs.[27] Since the 1990s, Arab American civil right organizations like the Arab American Institute and the American-Arab Anti-Discrimination Committee have been lobbying for a MENA box on the US Census with no success.[28] People of Middle Eastern and North African descent are expected to check the "white" box even though many do not experience themselves or identify as white in the US in light of their racialization by the US security state.[29]

There is much debate over which term to use to refer to people who come from Southwest Asia and North Africa. The term "Middle East" is a colonial and Eurocentric term because it refers to the middle of the East if one is in Europe.[30] Nonetheless, MENA has come to be used in order to be more inclusive of those who do not identify as Arab in the region, such as Iraqi Chaldeans, Egyptian Copts, and Kurds, and also to be inclusive of non-Arab nations and identities, such as Iranians, Turks, and Armenians. While people from the MENA region do not identify as "MENA" but rather as "Arab," "Egyptian," "Persian," "Chaldean," etc., this regional term has been increasingly and deliberately used to be inclusive of a range of identities. It is important to note that students within the University of California system lobbied and achieved a Southwest Asian and North African (SWANA) identity box. They chose SWANA over MENA to avoid reproducing the normalization of a colonial perspective that comes with MENA. Students at the University of Michigan chose MENA to be consistent with the expectation that the US Census Bureau would include a MENA box in 2020 (it did not). Various student governments on campus passed resolutions to support a MENA box, faculty and staff signed a petition of support, we had meetings with the provost and president, and presented on the MENA box to the regents. There was widespread support for the MENA box. The students' campaign for a MENA box was called We Exist, highlighting their experience of racial invisibility. Obtaining a MENA box would not only rectify institutional invisibility, but it would also solidify the inclusion of MENA students, staff, and faculty in DEI initiatives since it would provide the opportunity to collect data and assess diversity projects, such as those concerning recruitment and retention.

I accompanied students to many meetings with the UM president, provost, and various deans. Everyone was supportive but stated that adding a MENA box was not a simple fix; as a public institution, the school had to comply with the US Census and also ensure that the collection of data did not breach privacy. As Kedra Ishop, vice provost for enrollment management, explained: "It is important to understand that we remain subject to reporting requirements of the federal government, the state of Michigan, etc. that require our use of and alignment to the US Census race and ethnicity categories for reports to them."[31] After many meetings over a two-year period, the administration's research uncovered, to everyone's surprise, that there was already a MENA box on UM undergraduate applications for admissions. No one was aware of this and it came as an odd discovery after so many meetings and advocacy for this identity box. The University of Michigan accepts two kinds of undergraduate applications—the Common application and the Coalition application that enable prospective students to apply to multiple universities. Apparently, both applications offer a MENA box—*but*, to even see this option, one had to first select the "white" box. This, of course, fails to resolve the problem that many people of MENA descent do not identify as white and that several years of MENA data are thus questionably aggregated under the "white" checkbox. But it also meant that the university could access the data and make it available and would not be in violation of census standards. The graduate school followed suit and added a MENA box under the "white" category. A mechanism was not yet in place to collect data on staff or faculty.

The advocacy of the IWG revealed a responsiveness on the part of the administration that was made possible by a crisis in anti-Muslim racism. The process was unsurprisingly bureaucratic; some issues were easily addressed and quickly resolved (reflection rooms), while others involved starting a longer conversation (changing the Arabic-language textbook) with no definitive end or outcome. Yet other issues were unexpectedly and unsatisfactorily resolved (the MENA box). Reflecting the diversity compromise explored in chapter 2, people who identify as MENA can finally identify as such but locating the option in the white category reflects an unwelcome compromise for many. MENA people are prevented from identifying as *non*-white, an important distinction because existing mechanisms for inclusion are organized around civil rights categories, which have historically been associated primarily with African Americans, Native Americans, Latinxs, and Asian Americans. Furthermore, categorizing MENA people as white erases Black people from the MENA region as well as those who are not only racialized by the security state but whose brown skin further impacts their experience of racialization. "Diversity, equity, and inclusion" has led to the inclusion of Muslim and MENA students in ways not possible before, but that inclusion is effected through means with problematic implications.

What does it say about the parameters of DEI when the same students who are included for one type of activism (challenging anti-Muslim racism) are smeared for another (Palestinian rights)? Below, I explore this paradox further.

How Zionism Fuels Anti-Muslim Racism

Zionism might seem like an issue tangential to Islamophobia or anti-Muslim racism, but it is central to its formation.[32] The Muslim Law Students Association makes this link clear in a 2021 letter denouncing the retaliation faced by Muslim law students and professionals who work on the Israeli military's human rights abuses of Palestinians. They write, "Professional retaliation for Palestine related work is not a Muslim-specific issue, however, it impacts the Muslim community in disparate ways. [. . .] The shared trauma Muslims experience by witnessing the destruction of Palestinian communities, the desecration of revered Islamic holy sites, and the Islamophobic language often surrounding the issue is undeniable."[33] The stereotype of the Arab/Muslim terrorist developed out of the establishment of the state of Israel in 1948 and the subsequent Arab-Israeli War in 1967. It emerged out of Israel's ability to set the terms of perception: that violence perpetrated by Palestinians is unjustifiable terrorism and violence perpetrated by Israelis is justifiable self-defense. The US government has supported this perception, which has been central to the formation of anti-Arab and anti-Muslim racism.[34] In 1987, the deputy director of the Arab American Institute, Helen Samhan, wrote about "political racism" rooted in the Palestinian struggle that resulted in civil rights abuses, violence, and harassment against Arab Americans.[35] In 2011, the Center for American Progress identified a small networked group with more than $42 million in funding who spread misinformation about Islam, constituting the Islamophobia Industry.[36] They name Brigette Gabriel's ACT! for America, Pamela Geller's Stop the Islamization of America, and David Horowitz's Freedom Center as organizations that not only spread the fear of "creeping Sharia" law in the US but also promote the idea that Muslims, Arabs, and Palestinians are barbaric, in contrast to Israelis, who are civilized and peaceful. Similarly, Hatem Bazian, director of the Islamophobia Research and Documentation Project, has identified pro-Israel groups in the United States, such as the American Freedom Defense Initiative and the Clarion Fund, as the primary funders, producers, organizers, and distributors of Islamophobic content.[37] As Asian American studies scholar Sunaina Maira writes, "both Orientalism and Islamophobia acutely shape attempts to delegitimize Palestine solidarity activism in the US."[38]

Furthermore, it is not unusual for a Zionist organization to stand against Islamophobia but also condemn Muslim students for their Palestinian rights activism.[39] For example, it is not uncommon for Hillel on college campuses to host panels expressing opposition to Islamophobia.[40] The ADL issued multiple statements against Trump's Muslim ban.[41] Salam Al-Marayati, president of the Muslim Public Affairs Council, argues in an op-ed that the ADL cannot have it both ways; they cannot be against the Muslim ban and then perpetuate anti-Muslim racism by smearing critics of Israeli state policies as antisemitic. He writes, "Our organizations actively condemn acts of violence wrongfully committed in the name of Islam, including terrorism against Israelis. But I have yet to see the ADL condemn any act of violence against Palestinians committed by the State of Israel. [. . .] The ADL seems to want to have it both ways: it sends encouragement and messages of support after a tragedy, but it also participates in singling out Muslims as part of a larger existential threat to our society."[42] A central tactic in establishing Zionist legitimacy that involves justifying Israeli state violence against Palestinians is to take a stance against Islamophobia to appear to be against discrimination and to then perpetuate it by using anti-Muslim tropes about terrorism to slander critics of Israel.

Despite a powerful Israel lobby, public opinion in support of Israel is waning considering the Boycott, Divestment, Sanctions movement, solidarity activism, and reports published by reputable organizations that characterize Israel as instituting apartheid. The BDS movement began in 2005 when more than 170 Palestinian civil society groups called for boycotts of, divestment from, and sanctions against Israel. The movement seeks to "hold Israel accountable to international law and universal principles of human rights, in the pursuit of freedom, justice, self-determination, equality, and sustainable peace."[43] Maira likens it to other boycott movements, such as the Montgomery bus boycott and the South African apartheid boycott.[44] More specifically, it is a nonviolent campaign demanding that Israel end its occupation of Palestine, confer equal rights to the Palestinian citizens of Israel, and recognize the right of Palestinian refugees to return to their homes.[45]

The BDS movement has created an important avenue for solidarity activism over the last decade. In 2011, civil rights icon Angela Davis took a publicized trip to Palestine.[46] The popular singer and musician Lorde canceled her 2017 concert in Israel, saying, "I pride myself on being an informed young citizen . . . but I'm not proud to admit I didn't make the right call on this one."[47] Historian Robin Kelley attributes the shift in public opinion partially to the ways in which Israel's war on Gaza in 2014 overlapped with the highly publicized US police killings of Eric Garner, Michael Brown, and other Black people.[48] The comparison between the struggles in Ferguson and Gaza led to renewed Black-Palestinian solidarity.[49] Ironically, the BDS movement has been so successful in inspiring solidarity activism and increasing public support for Palestinian rights that, arguably, the clearest evidence of this success has been the powerful backlash against it.

Human Rights Watch's 2021 report categorizes Israeli government policies against Palestinians as "so severe that they amount to the crimes against humanity of apartheid and persecution."[50] Similarly, B'Tselem, the Israeli Information Center for Human Rights in the Occupied Territory, also released a report in 2021 stating that terms like "prolonged occupation" no longer adequately describe the situation and that apartheid is a more accurate descriptor in light of Israeli government policies "restricting migration by non-Jews and taking over Palestinian land to build Jewish-only communities, while relegating Palestinians to small enclaves [. . .] [and] draconian restrictions on the movement of non-citizen Palestinians and denial of their political rights."[51] The report states that it is not possible for Israel to be considered a democracy under the circumstances. Scholars of Palestine in American studies Loubna Qutami and Omar Zahzah write that the language used to talk about Zionist settler colonialism and Palestinian liberation reveals who has the power to define the terms of the debate. They argue that the language of liberation, movement, right of return, colonialism, and anti-Zionism has recently started to replace the terms that have long defined and delimited understandings of the situation—human rights, peace, dialogue, a conflict on both sides, and coexistence.[52]

Zionism, like other political ideologies, encompasses a spectrum of ideas.[53] Zionists are committed to Jewish nationalism and maintaining Israel as a Jewish state, but whether one identifies historically or presently as a political, labor, religious, revisionist, cultural, humanist, reform, Meretz, or liberal Zionist speaks to one's willingness to compromise with Palestinians on territory, acknowledge that Palestinians deserve rights and a homeland too, and recognize the unfathomable oppression of Palestinians under Israeli military occupation. Some who identify as Zionist no longer believe in a Jewish state because Israeli government policies have deprived Palestinians of rights and squandered the possibility of a two-state solution by encouraging Jewish settlements in Palestinian territories.[54] Jewish Voice for Peace identifies as anti-Zionist because they see Zionism as "a false and failed answer to the desperately real question many of our ancestors faced of how to protect Jewish lives from murderous antisemitism in Europe. While it had many strains historically, the Zionism that took hold and stands today is a settler-colonial movement, establishing an apartheid state where Jews have more rights than others."[55] When I refer to the pro-Israeli lobby or Zionist organizations, I am referring to a powerful collective of individuals and organizations that take a hardline stance to protect Israel from any and all criticism.

Anti-Semitizing Palestinian Rights Activism

Student activism for Palestinian rights on college campuses as well as efforts to marginalize or suppress it are hardly new.[56] In 1969, Gerald

Ford, a Michigan congressman at the time, characterized Arab students as radical agitators and potential terrorists, and the Anti-Defamation League (ADL) characterized their activism as "thinly veiled anti-Semitic propaganda."[57] The American Israel Public Affairs Committee (AIPAC) accused them of promoting Palestinian terrorist ideas and the FBI launched a surveillance campaign to detail the student group's interaction with Palestinian revolutionary groups and their funding sources.[58] What is new is how these dynamics get played out in light of diversity initiatives on campuses; the crisis presented when Palestinian rights activists are accused of antisemitism is now mediated through the language and values of diversity and inclusivity that blur the line between DEI and free speech. DEI has largely replaced affirmative action as an approach to rectifying historic inequality. As a result, the very notion of "diversity" has been largely emptied of its restorative-justice meaning and is often emphasized as applying to, and benefiting, everyone— including dominant groups. Consequently, for example, Republican students can now claim that they are being excluded and penalized for their beliefs and call for "intellectual diversity" to counter the "diversityspeak" that they argue liberal students and faculty use to silence more conservative voices. Such arguments completely erase the impacts of historic inequality and any kind of power dynamics, while co-opting diversity discourse to claim victim status for dominant groups.

To be sure, the way in which Zionist groups use diversity to claim victim status is more complicated given that Jewish people are, indisputably, a historically marginalized group and a minority in the Christian-dominant US. They are making claims to diversity and inclusivity at a time when antisemitism is indeed on the rise given the Unite the Right rally in Charlottesville, Virginia, in 2017 where white supremacists chillingly chanted, "Jews will not replace us," and the white supremacist who gunned down eleven Jewish people at the Tree of Life Synagogue in Pittsburgh in October 2018. However, Zionist organizations are claiming antisemitism to silence criticism of Israel, which is distinct from protecting Jewish students from antisemitism and including them within DEI plans. Communications and media studies scholar Sarah Banet-Weiser (writing about the men's rights movement's response to feminism) likens this to a funhouse mirror in which politics are distorted to make the dominant identity the victim when the marginalized identity engages in advocacy.[59] It creates a "dual dynamic of injury"[60]—Palestinian rights activists highlight the Israeli government's illegal military occupation, Israel's status as a settler colonial state, and state-sanctioned violence against Palestinians and in turn Zionists claim that they are ones injured by such speech. Postcolonial studies scholar Ella Shohat points out that Zionist narratives rely on Jewish victimization and as a result there is no space to acknowledge that Jewish nationalism which has sought to resolve a history of Jewish victimization has led to Palestinian victimization.[61] Subsequently, if MENA and Muslim students are blamed for antisemitism, their full inclusion in DEI initiatives on college campuses becomes impossible; the university must focus on rectifying claims of antisemitism and in the process MENA and Muslim students lose their newly recognized status as a marginalized group because they are now alleged perpetrators of discrimination.

Students who identify as Zionists and those who advocate for Palestinian rights are not equally supported or equally marginalized on college campuses. The power dynamics play out in terms of campus resources and support and extend to US policies that seek to demonize those who criticize Israeli policies. At the University of Michigan, students who identify as political Zionists have access to institutional support through the university's chapter of Hillel, supported by a $2 million budget and staff of fifteen people.[62] In addition, they have a vast network of organizational support that includes "an army of consultants, researchers, organizers, and other professionals, a network of on-and-off campus institutions and organizations that works to re-brand Israel's image, quash BDS, and suppress student activism for Palestinian rights."[63] As it states on their website, "Hillel promotes a continuum of experiences to engage students with Israel, educate their campus communities about Israel, and advocate for Israel's right to exist as a Jewish and democratic state in peace and security," and they refuse to partner with groups or speakers that "support boycott of, divestment from, or sanctions against the State of Israel."[64] Hillel is part of a larger project of the Israel lobby to align Jewish identity with the Israeli state to the point that any criticism of Israel is taken as a criticism of Jewish identity itself. The Israel on Campus Coalition, an affiliate of the Israeli Ministry of Strategic Affairs, helps students write speeches and learn how to strategically argue against BDS resolutions when they are proposed on college campuses.[65] Common talking points include arguing that critics apply a double standard to Israel, making demands of kinds that they do not make of other nations, implying that they are singling out Israel and thus have antisemitic motives. Other talking points include the idea that Palestinian "terrorism" is to blame for ruining the peace process and that criticism of Israel constitutes antisemitism because it (supposedly) implies that Jews do not deserve safety, as opposed to meaning that Palestinians deserve safety too. Former national campus coordinator for Jewish Voice for Peace Ben Lorber writes, "Opposition groups help students frame their support for Israel, not as a personal political preference, but as the collective will of the Jewish campus community, compelling administrators to treat their anti-BDS demands as they would the demands of any other group for gender-neutral bathrooms, diversity and inclusion, cultural studies departments, and the like."[66] In other words, by couching opposition to criticisms of Israeli policies as antisemitism, university administrators use the framework of DEI to navigate this terrain.

In contrast to Zionist students, who have the support of Hillel and other Zionist organizations, Palestinian and Palestinian-solidarity activists do not have institutional support beyond finding a supportive faculty or staff member to offer validation, which can place that faculty or staff member's career at risk. Some have found a larger network of support by attending the annual Students for Justice in Palestine conference. Students for Justice in Palestine (SJP), founded at UC Berkeley in 1993, has become the primary group organizing activism and education on college campuses. Jewish Voice for Peace, founded at UC Berkeley in 1996, has also been active on college campuses advocating for Palestinian rights. At the University of Michigan, the Palestinian rights student group is called Students Allied for Freedom and Equality (SAFE). None are supported by millions of dollars, nor do they have access to a well-paid staff of consultants.

Sociologist Tom Pessah challenges those who would characterize every criticism of Israeli government policies as antisemitic by describing that very effort as "anti-Semitizing."[67] To be sure, he acknowledges that some critics of Israel do promote antisemitism, but Pessah also points out that the leaders of the BDS movement are not promoting antisemitism but human rights.[68] Pessah cautions: "Anti-Semitizing comes at a serious price: it derails any serious conversation on Israel/Palestine, since opponents of the status quo can easily be dismissed as potential terrorists [. . .] it de-sensitizes people to genuine anti-Semitism, and it keeps much of the Jewish American community in a permanent sense of panic, as if a new Holocaust is imminent."[69] The needs of Jewish students are presented as being in crisis not because they are targeted for their identity but because Israeli government policies are criticized for violating human rights and international law. This argument reasons that any criticism of how Israeli policies violate Palestinian rights constitutes a lack of support for Jewish people living in safety and security in the one and only Jewish state in the world, which was created after the Holocaust and millennia of antisemitism. It silences the idea that creating a safe haven for Jewish people has been predicated on dispossessing Palestinian people. Such accusations of antisemitism distort the arguments of those who critique the Israeli government for demolishing Palestinian homes, building settlements on Palestinian land, upholding the military occupation of Palestinian territories in violation of international law, and instituting an apartheid system. Instead, such critiques are reframed as arguments that Jewish people are not deserving of safety, security, and a state. That the Palestinians likewise deserve safety, security, and a state in which they have full citizenship rights is not addressed, or to be more accurate, is deemed antisemitic.

This dynamic, which Arab American media studies scholar Umayyah Cable refers to as compulsory Zionism, the imposition of support for Israel in the US that enforces the privileging and normalization of a Zionist perspective,[70] is not unique to college campuses. US laws enable Israeli state violence against Palestinians because of the powerful influence of the Israel lobby, "a loose coalition of individuals and organizations that actively works to move US foreign policy in a pro-Israel direction."[71] Every US president since the creation of the state of Israel in 1948 has unequivocally supported Israel at the expense of Palestinian rights, and those who challenge the Israel lobby's platform risk their chance of becoming president.[72] As political scientists John J. Mearsheimer and Stephen Walt write, "America's generous and unconditional support for Israel is rarely questioned, because groups in the lobby use their power to make sure that public discourse echoes its strategic and moral arguments for the special relationship."[73] Nathan Thrall, writing for the *New*

York Times, notes that while public opinion is shifting on Israeli policies, the official position of the US remains unchanged: "year after year, Congress, citing 'shared values' and Israel's strategic importance, among other things, votes to give military aid to Israel, which is currently $3.8 billion per year: $500 million in missile defense and $3.3 billion in foreign military financing, more military financing than the United States provides to the rest of the world combined."[74] Arab American studies scholar Steven Salaita points out that Zionism has achieved normative status in the US and as a result is positioned as apolitical, while advocacy for Palestinian rights is positioned as political, the wrong kind of politics, and thus objectionable.[75]

After 9/11, the narrative that the US and Israel have "shared values" shifted to include the notion that both countries were also fighting the same enemy—namely, Arab Muslims—completely eliding the vast political and historical differences between the two contexts. The late American studies scholar Amy Kaplan details how, after 9/11, politicians said, "Now we are all Israelis," journalists compared 9/11 to attacks in Tel Aviv and Jerusalem, and Israeli TV shows like *Homeland* were remade for US audiences.[76] The identification of the US with Israel also came with the narrative that, like Israel, the US was hated for no other reason than its identity, not its actions.[77] The US government turned to the Israeli government for guidance on sacrificing civil liberties as part of counterterrorism training and partnered to create new homeland security technologies.[78] Identification with Israel became a means to explain a seemingly incomprehensible event to the public. In this process of domesticating Israel during the "War on Terror," the US and Israel were constructed as two peas in a pod. An already fraught political field became even more fraught, especially for MENA and Muslim students entering this arena.

The influence of political Zionism penetrates US culture. Advocates for Palestinian rights have been fired from their jobs or faced other forms of disciplining. In 2018, CNN terminated its contract with commentator Marc Lamont Hill, a professor at Temple University, after he issued comments that were deemed antisemitic. In a speech he delivered at the United Nations on the International Day of Solidarity with the Palestinian People, Lamont Hill remarked upon the irony that the Universal Declaration of Human Rights was passed after World War II, yet Palestinians are denied their rights by the Israeli government. He was deemed purportedly antisemitic because of the last six words of the speech that called for a free Palestine "from the river to the sea." Critics claimed that this was a call for the destruction of the state of Israel and thus promoted antisemitism.[79] As a result of his use of this phrase and the resulting controversy, CNN fired Lamont Hill as a political commentator, stating that his speech was inconsistent with the network's values.[80] Despite urging from Zionists, he did not lose his position as a professor at Temple University, but other professors have lost their academic jobs. In 2009, Professor Thomas Abowd resigned from Wayne State University after a backlash in response to his participation in organizing events on campus about Israel's illegal military occupation and its impact on Palestinian rights and livelihood.[81] In August 2014, Professor Steven Salaita, after being offered and accepting a faculty position at the University of Illinois Urbana-Champaign, was notified that the job offer was being "rescinded" because of his tweets criticizing the Israeli government during Israel's invasion of Gaza.[82]

Legislation has been written to support criminalizing support of the Boycott, Sanctions, Divestment movement in the US.[83] Two kinds of legislation have been pursued by Zionist organizations.[84] The first is anti-BDS legislation and the second redefines antisemitism on the federal and state levels to include criticisms of Israel. As of January 26, 2019, twenty-six states including New York and Texas had regulations to force companies to make a choice: participate in BDS or continue their business with the state.[85] State employees are told they must sign employment contracts that specify that any boycotting of Israel will result in their contract being revoked; likewise, companies are informed that they will not be eligible for a government contract if they boycott Israel. In 2018, speech pathologist Bahia Amawi refused to sign her contract renewal with the Pflugerville Independent School District in Texas when she noticed a new clause that required she not boycott Israel during the term of the contract; she refused to sign and as a result her contract was not renewed.[86] A federal bill co-authored by Republican senator Marco Rubio sought to legally protect states who take this political stance and encourage other states to follow suit. Democratic senators Bernie Sanders and Dianne Feinstein opposed the bill because of how it violates free speech by seeking to regulate and punish it.[87] Circuit courts in Arkansas and Arizona ultimately blocked the legislation.

The second kind of legislation involves redefining antisemitism to encompass criticisms of Israeli policy and targeting and criminalizing activism for Palestinian rights, particularly on college campuses.[88] In December 2019, Trump issued an Executive Order on Combating Anti-Semitism that purports to address a global increase in antisemitism, but focuses particularly on schools and colleges campuses.[89] The executive order states that the 1964 Civil Rights Act, which prohibits discrimination on the basis of race, color, and national origin, is being expanded to include religion and specifically that "discrimination against Jews may give rise to a Title VI violation when the discrimination is based on an individual's race, color, or national origin." Trump's executive order relies upon the International Holocaust Remembrance Alliance (IHRA) definition of antisemitism, which includes "Denying the Jewish people their right to self-determination, e.g., by claiming that the existence of a State of Israel is a racist endeavor."[90] Revealingly, the author of this definition of antisemitism, Kenneth S. Stern, opposes how it is being used by the US government because the definition was created for one purpose—data collectors' monitoring of antisemitism in Europe—but is being used for another—stifling free speech on college campuses.[91] The way that the IHRA definition has been weaponized by the US government and universities to suppress political speech by legitimizing the use of lawsuits to enforce it[92] has been condemned by many.[93]

In response to the controversial IHRA definition and its appropriation, a collective of academics and experts drafted a new definition of antisemitism, the "Jerusalem Declaration on Antisemitism." It offers a set of fifteen guidelines to recognize antisemitism. It clarifies that criticizing or opposing Zionism as a form of nationalism and supporting BDS are not in themselves antisemitic.[94] The Middle East Studies Association issued a statement criticizing the use of the IHRA definition and encouraging universities to refrain from adopting it in the interest of protecting the right to free political speech.[95] Nonetheless, some universities have banned Palestinian rights activism and others have adopted a definition of antisemitism that anti-Semitizes criticisms of Israeli state violence.[96] At UC Irvine in 2010, eleven Palestinian rights activists were arrested for protesting a speech by Michael Oren, the Israeli ambassador to the United States. Not only did the university administration punish the Muslim Student Union by suspending the student group for a quarter and requiring one hundred hours of community service before reinstatement, but the case also went to court and ten out of the eleven students were convicted of conspiring to disrupt a meeting and disrupting a meeting; they were sentenced to community service. While they did not face any jail time, the conviction resulted in a misdemeanor conviction on their records and three students were sentenced to informal probation. At Fordham University, the administration banned the Palestinian rights student group on campus.[97]

Kenneth Marcus, founder and former president of the Louis D. Brandeis Center for Human Rights Under Law, a pro-Israel lobby group, was nominated by Donald Trump to become assistant secretary for civil rights at the US Department of Education in 2018.[98] He has helped file Title VI discrimination complaints with the Department of Education against Palestinian and Palestinian-solidarity activists on a number of college campuses, such as UC Irvine, UC Santa Cruz, and Rutgers University. These complaints allege that Palestinian rights activists create a hostile educational environment for Jewish students. The Department of Education has dismissed most of these cases, citing the right to free speech. Marcus is known for advocating that Palestinian rights activism is not a free speech issue but a legal issue that should be dealt with by courts.[99] Admitting that fear and smear tactics are strategically used to suppress speech that sheds light on Israeli-sanctioned violence against Palestinians, he writes, "At many campuses, the prospect of litigation has made a difference. If a university shows a failure to treat initial complaints seriously, it hurts them with donors, faculty, political leaders and prospective students. No university wants to be accused of creating an abusive environment."[100] Furthermore, he writes, the option of filing a civil rights complaint serves as a strong disincentive for Palestinian rights student activists: "Needless to say, getting caught up in a civil rights complaint is not a good way to build a resume or impress a future employer."[101] Palestinian American journalist Ali Abunimah writes, "Students across the United States now face the perverse and dangerous situation where the most senior federal official entrusted with protecting their civil rights may use his position—in the interests of a foreign state—to press for their criminal prosecution merely for exercising their First Amendment rights."[102] Dima Khalidi, founder and director of Palestine Legal, states that the objective of such legislation is to make it too costly for students to engage in this type of activism.[103] Both of these legislative approaches stifle free speech and protest protected by the First Amendment.[104] Needless to say, lawfare, or using the law to combat criticism of Israel, is a very powerful tactic. Even if many of these cases are dismissed in court, the prospect of litigation creates a chilling effect on free speech. Palestine Legal published a report that stated that they worked on 152 incidents of "censorship, punishment, or other burdening of advocacy for Palestinian rights" in 2014 alone and received "68 additional requests for legal assistance in anticipation of such actions."[105] Of course, not everyone who faces repercussions for Palestinian rights activism seeks assistance from Palestine Legal, and there are likely many more who self-censor out of fear of the consequences.

Zionism and Palestinian Rights Activism Meet DEI at the University of Michigan

In addition to setting up mock checkpoints and distributing mock eviction notices in dormitories to raise awareness about life for Palestinians under Israeli military occupation, one of the key ways that student activists have sought to advocate for Palestinian rights is by proposing resolutions within student governments to request that the university divest from corporations that are complicit in the Israeli occupation of Palestine. This includes companies like Caterpillar, which makes bulldozers that are used to demolish Palestinian homes, and Boeing, Hewlett-Packard, and United Technologies, which supply weapons and other technologies that are used in Israeli military airstrikes and in the continued military occupation of Palestine.[106] In 2014, the University of Michigan's Central Student Government (CSG) voted to indefinitely postpone voting on a resolution proposing that the university form a committee to investigate how investments in certain companies affect Palestinian human rights in the West Bank and Gaza. CSG's indefinite postponement prompted approximately one hundred students to stage a sit-in at the Student Union building, demanding a vote on the bill. As in the case of Yazan Kherallah described above, many of these students advocating for Palestinian rights received hateful messages on email and Twitter that called them "jihadists" and "infidel slayers."[107] Students compiled some of the hate messages they received and posted the collection to a website. It includes the following:

> The Islamist cult [. . .] is now the most dangers and violent cult in the world. They have over 600 young jihadists living in the United States in and around university's to gain the trust of students. They incite them by crying about the Jews and in some cases Christians, about their inhumane treatment by the Jews. Unfortunately due to the young ages of the university students along with rebelling against their parents teachings, they are ripe to new ideas and they also know it would be shocking to their parents their actions and thoughts. Read the Koran on the web and you will understand this ungodly cult for what it is. This cult is the devil not the Jews. DO NOT BELIEVE ANYTHING A MUSLIM TELLS YOU ABOUT PERSECUTION BY JEWS. IT IS THE ISLAMIST WHO PERSECUTE NONBELIEVERS.

> This Jew Boy is going to be on campus on April 10th, maybe I will look you up and bitch slap your ass from one side of the campus to the other.

> FUCK OFF you pieces of shit!!! Go back to where you came from. GET OUT, NOW!!!!

> Get out, you Palestinian murderer.[108]

Perpetuating anti-Muslim and anti-Arab racism, such messages associate Palestinian rights activism with Islam framed as a violent cult, with murder, and with foreigners who do not belong in the US. Meanwhile, Jewish students expressed concern that antisemitism was not taken seriously on campus. One stated that SAFE students had targeted him with hate speech, that he had been called "disgusting, filthy, shameful, dirty Jew, kike" and that "these derogatory terms harken back to the 1930's and 40's in a time when the Jewish people were targeted for extermination, which was largely successful."[109] Student members of SAFE insisted that these claims were fabricated, and they were not even familiar with the term "kike."

Vice President for Student Life E. Royster Harper defended the students who were organizing for Palestinian rights and pushed back against their racialization as violent. She said: "I have been enormously impressed with the thoughtfulness, the clarity of thought, how respectful the students have been. (I have) just been a little surprised that people have been talking about this as a violent movement; it's just not the case. It has been just what you would expect from smart U of M students that are passionate about an important issue."[110] She also defended their right to request that the university investigate the impact of the school's investments on human rights, stating that the students have a right to question the university's values and asking the university how it spends its money. In an effort to include all students, Dean of Students Laura Blake Jones weighed in, saying, "The climate issues have impacted a wide range of groups of our students this week. Many people have been harmed and have felt fearful, and we have to address the climate issues and care about the concerns of all of our students."[111] "Climate issues" has become part of "diversityspeak" to signal a problem with the inclusivity of a particular group that needs to be redressed. Blake Jones's statement aims to recognize the experiences of not only Zionist students who feel that criticisms of Israel constitute antisemitism, but also Palestinian and Palestinian solidarity activists who are declared antisemites for their activism. In other words, the dean of students sought to redraw the lines around who is included in diversity in an effort to include all constituents.

When CSG agreed to proceed with a vote in 2014 after the sit-in, the resolution did not pass. However, in November 2017, the controversial resolution was once again presented and passed during an extended session that began on a Tuesday night and ended early Wednesday morning.[112] SAFE students and supporters were surprised that the resolution passed given that they had submitted a dozen proposals over a fifteen-year period, none of which had passed.[113] This success was the result of years of struggle and perseverance involving sit-ins, demonstrations, and educational campaigns. These students celebrated; they felt heard and included after being erased and excluded for so long, after being portrayed as supporters of suicide bombings and other forms of terrorism.

The language of diversity, equity, and inclusion was embraced by students and defined in multiple ways to explain the significance of recognizing and including Palestinians through the passing of this resolution. After the resolution passed, a student member of SAFE said: "We recognize that right now there are people that aren't necessarily happy that this resolution did pass and we really identify with that feeling and we understand how it feels. Reaching out to all of the people that have been invested in this resolution, whether pro or against, and ensuring that people feel comfortable, ensuring that people understand that their identities are still welcome on this campus and creating more of a conversation around that dialogue."[114] Another member of SAFE, Hafsa Tout, stated: "I understand the very deep connection many, many students have with Israel. [. . .] I want to emphasize over and over again that this resolution emphasizes the voices of Palestinian students . . . and to give this community a voice for the first time in CSG history is to not take away from any other community."[115] What is notable is that principles of inclusivity guided many students' comments regardless of their political position on this polarizing issue. Some made the point that even though this was a victory for SAFE students who are predominantly Arab and Muslim, it was not about marginalizing students with different political positions.

Most student activists on both sides of the issue were clear that excluding students from a sense of belonging on campus was not acceptable or a desired outcome. Where students diverged was in their interpretation of DEI—specifically, whether its objective was to include everyone or to focus on those who have been historically marginalized. The Egyptian Students Association issued a statement making it clear that DEI is about hearing the voices of those who are marginalized and not necessarily about everyone feeling comfortable: "ESA strongly supports SAFE's mission to divest from companies that profit off the violation of human rights of the Palestinian people. [. . .] ESA is part of a large campus coalition that stands with this movement. [. . .] This is what real DEI looks like—listening to marginalized and silenced voices on campus that are being amplified by communities of color. We urge CSG to listen to these communities and not to be complicit in this abuse."[116] This statement equated DEI with listening to the voices of those who have been marginalized. During the recognized, ongoing global crisis of Islamophobia, Arab Americans, others from the broader MENA region, and US Muslims have come to be understood and accepted to a large extent as "people of color," given how they have been racialized by the national security state. Furthermore, the BDS movement and its comparison of the Israeli state and its policies with police brutality against Black people in Ferguson and across the United States, as well as with apartheid South Africa, has led to an understanding of Palestinians as a community subject to racialized state violence.

Students Ashley Tjhung and Jason Rowland, who identify as allies of SAFE and understand Palestinian students as racialized and therefore within the parameters of DEI, wrote an article in 2018 for the *Michigan Daily*. In it, they expressed their concern with

> statements made by incoming Central Student Government President [. . .], a Public Policy Junior, that he "won't elevate another minority at the cost of another minority" [*sic*] at the debate hosted by The Michigan Daily. Anti-Semitism is a constant threat on campus and in this country, but simplifying both sides to "minorities" ignores the blatant power imbalance between the Israeli state and Palestinian population. The notion that divestment divides minorities is also concerning to us. The 2017 divestment proposal was supported by numerous organizations representing students of color on campus including La Casa, the Black Student Union, and United Asian-American Organizations. Divestment did not divide marginalized groups—it united us. Giving voice to a historically silenced community on campus does not take away that of another. [. . .] To pass the #UMDivest resolution is not an attack on Jewish students. Rather, it is a symbolic show of support for Palestinians of all faiths and backgrounds.[117]

While seeking to be inclusive by acknowledging the persistence of anti-semitism, Tjhung and Rowland also sought to clarify that Palestinians and Israelis are not equally disadvantaged in the context of Israel, given the latter's position of state power. Scholar of Hebrew literature Orian Zakai uses the term "power-blindness" to refer to the ways in which diversity and inclusivity discourses tend to veer away from considerations of how systems of power shape social relations to a focus instead on hurt or uncomfortable feelings that get mapped onto a minority identity category.[118] The *Michigan Daily* piece pushed back against this tendency and insisted that DEI be understood as addressing and rectifying marginalization resulting from historic and current structures of power.

Some Zionist students also embraced principles of inclusivity and sought not to marginalize SAFE students for their victory. At the same time, some also expressed that they experienced antisemitism in the form of microaggressions and therefore that there was a DEI issue at stake. A student member of Hillel stated:

> I am happy that members of SAFE, Palestinian students and allies were given a platform for their concerns to be heard. However, I am deeply upset that the address of these concerns meant that Jewish students' sentiments about feeling marginalized were pushed aside. It is so upsetting to me that last night, people were pitted against each other and that the vote was framed as a win or a loss. [. . .] I worry that because CSG leaders were unable to see the subtle yet crucial forms of antisemitism lying in this resolution and the broader BDS movement it represents, people will feel emboldened to let these types of subtle antisemitic comments run rampant. [. . .] We have so much work to do to address hate in all forms, and I hope we can work toward doing this in a way that does not cast any group aside.[119]

This student recognizes that the resolution was meaningful to SAFE and the group's allies but notes that antisemitic microaggressions were promoted in the process of criticizing Israeli state policies. The student chair and several other members of Hillel's governing board issued a similar statement:

> While there is a diversity of thought toward Israel within our community, many students were united in feeling hurt by the rhetoric used to address the one Jewish State and our community. [. . .] Anti-Semitism manifests itself in many different ways. Some forms of anti-Semitism are more obvious such as Nazi marches, painted swastikas, and alt-Right chants. Contemporary anti-Semitism takes the form of subtle remarks, micro-aggressions, and reinforcing negative stereotypes of the Jewish community. We saw many of these injustices in Tuesday night's meeting.[120]

Through such arguments, Zionist political advocates on college campuses characterize critiques of Israel as racist microaggressions in the age of DEI. "Racist microaggressions" are subtle or covert and often unconscious or unintended forms of racism that persist in daily verbal interactions or environmental hostilities that convey negative racial slights or insults.[121] This term has been used to point to the ways in which racism is not always overt but embedded in everyday interactions and often unconscious and unintended. Classifying criticism of Israel as a microaggression offers the perpetrator the benefit of the doubt that their racism is unintentional and can be corrected through awareness or education. The logic is that while activists might believe that they are simply criticizing the policies of a government, they are overlooking that Israel is the one and only Jewish state, that it represents the only safe haven for Jews, and thus criticizing Israel is inadvertently and unconsciously denying that Jews deserve safety and, ultimately, furthering antisemitism. As a result, terms like "settler colonialism," "apartheid," "occupation," and "racist state" are coded as microaggressions.

Hillel, calling for deeper ties with Israel without any acknowledgement of Israeli state violence against Palestinians as if it is irrelevant, requested that the administration condemn the resolution: "We trust that the Board of Regents will speak out against this one-sided resolution, as they have in (the) past, and remind the campus community that they have already rejected this resolution when it passed at University of Michigan-Dearborn last winter. We also hope that the University will expand its partnerships with Israel, develop new avenues for students to study in Israel, and encourage faculty to deepen their research ties with Israeli institutions."[122] The university, seeking to be politically neutral and focus on financial investments, issued a statement in response to the resolution affirming that investments are not determined based on politics but on the generation of the greatest possible return to support the mission of the university. It stated:

> It is important that the university maintain an investment portfolio diversified across a full range of legally recognized entities. To do otherwise would be to increase our investment risk and decrease our investment returns. For this reason, the university's longstanding policy is to shield the endowment from political pressures and to base our investment decisions solely on financial factors such as risk and return. This approach has been underscored consistently by university leaders, including the

Board of Regents, most recently in December 2015. We do not anticipate a change in this approach or the creation of a committee.[123]

The university tried to be politically neutral by focusing on the funding needed for its operations while also seeking to avoid alienating students by taking a political position. However, students pointed out that there had been two occasions in the university's history when it did divest from companies profiting from social or physical harm: in 1978, from companies profiting from apartheid in South Africa, and in 2000, from the tobacco industry.[124] In addition, in 2017, CSG requested that a committee be formed to consider fossil fuel divestment as a way to reduce environmental harm, and the university's Senate Assembly endorsed the proposal.[125] In this latter case, President Mark Schlissel encouraged students to lobby the Michigan state legislature, reasoning that, if the university were to divest from fossil fuels, it would be mostly symbolic and would not have an actual impact on the environment. Holding a consistent viewpoint about keeping politics and social issues out of investment strategies, he cautioned that divesting from fossil fuels could negatively impact the performance of the university's endowment and thus the university itself.[126]

Several members of the University of Michigan Board of Regents published a statement which echoed that the university's endowment should not be swayed by politics, but also went further and explicitly opposed BDS. It stated that the members of the board

> strongly oppose any action involving the boycott, divestment or sanction of Israel. [. . .] Most importantly, our university has long been a community that seeks to study and improve the human condition through our research and scholarship. We work together to better understand the most complex challenges we face on campus and beyond. We do this work through active engagement in the world around us. To boycott, divest or sanction Israel offends these bedrock values of our great university.[127]

Thus, while the university administration sought to not take a political stance, the regents took a side and in doing so rendered irrelevant Israeli state sanctioned violence against Palestinians and marginalized Palestinian rights student activists. In this context, stating that one of the objectives of the university is to improve the human condition excludes Palestinians from the human condition. SAFE and their allies embraced DEI as a social justice project that aims to empower groups that have long been marginalized. They made it clear that power differentials must be at the center of the DEI project and that justice for one community is not about marginalizing another. Some Zionist students embraced DEI by recognizing that SAFE's victory is meaningful but also by saying that they feel marginalized by criticisms of Israel. The university adminis-tration, in contrast, attempts political neutrality, and the most power-ful group, the regents, take a side that marginalizes student activists for Palestinian rights by stating that a divestment resolution is unacceptable and goes against the values of the university.

Flexible Diversity and the Defamation of Palestinian Rights Activists

How flexible diversity operates becomes clear when examining a form letter drafted on November 17, 2017, by the University of Michigan administration to Zionist constituents who expressed concern about CSG's resolution regarding divestment. While some administration statements are made publicly to appease donors and other constituents, other statements are done privately in meetings and letters. The letter makes four important points. First, the university assures the constitu-ents that Central Student Government does not represent the university and that "resolutions of this type are in no way binding on the univer-sity."[128] In other words, these particular concerned constituents need not worry that the university will investigate how their financial investments impact Palestinian rights and thus potentially condemn Israel's treat-ment of Palestinians; CSG's resolutions have no power or sway and are thus irrelevant and not worth the concern. Second, along similar lines, the letter also expresses that the university's approach to investments aims "to shield the endowment from political pressures and to base our investment solely on financial factors." The administration's stance is that it does not take political positions. Yet by refusing to investigate the mat-ter, the school is taking a political position that normalizes Israeli state violence against Palestinians, a stance that appeases concerned Zion-ist constituents. Third, the letter assures that "our campus has a large, strong and resilient Jewish community. Our Hillel chapter and Chabad House have great leadership and provide a 'home away from home' for many students." The university clearly states that Jewish students are welcome and that there are substantial resources available on campus to ensure that their needs are met—they are included. Fourth, the letter states that students have a right to protected free speech: "The Israeli-Palestinian conflict is just one of many issues across our campus, and society, around which there is passionate disagreement. We encourage students with divergent points of view to discuss these with one another in order to learn and achieve greater levels of mutual respect and understanding. Our students enjoy the same speech rights as all members in our community and our campus leaders have great respect for those rights." This fourth point protects Palestinian and Palestinian-solidarity activists' right to free speech. It importantly rejects the equation of criticisms of Israeli policies with antisemitism. Thus, the letter effectively redraws the lines of diversity, equity, and inclusion. It includes Jewish students as part of a diverse and inclusive campus, but more importantly defends activism and speech rights.

UM's approach is distinct from some other universities' approaches in seeking to include all students, even those advocating for Palestinian rights, while other universities have banned Palestinian rights activism and facilitated lawfare. UM tries to walk a fine line to appease all constituents when undergraduate students are involved. The university administration appeases its concerned Zionist constituents by clearly stating that students do not determine university policies and that the school's investments are based on financial decisions, not political ones, and furthermore that Jewish students have a home on campus. In other words, they need not concern themselves with CSG's resolutions, which have no bearing on university governance. At the same time, the administration also affirms that it stands by students' right to free speech and therefore that activism for Palestinian self-determination can proceed (even if it will not be taken seriously). The UM administration mediates this political terrain by enacting an all-inclusive of flexible approach to diversity.

However, student activists for Palestinian rights nonetheless experience marginalization in several ways. First, while certain high-level administrators protect their right to speech, their speech is rendered irrelevant. To be sure, not every student activist demand will be addressed by the university administration, but the politics around this issue are so fraught that, even while the university seeks to satisfy all parties, the lack of recognition of the illegal military occupation and violent violation of Palestinian rights perpetuates the normalization of a perspective that protects Israeli government policies at all costs. Thus, student activists for Palestinian rights are not condemned but neutralized; the content of their speech is rendered irrelevant. Ethnic, gender, and sexuality studies scholar Roderick Ferguson argues that radical epistemologies that challenge the normalization of power structures—imperialism, colonialism, capitalism—are blocked by universities, and that neoliberal diversity is designed to thwart activists who demand justice and criticize the status quo.[129]

Second, these students are smeared as antisemitic, subjected to hate via social media, blacklisted by various Zionist organizations, and left to deal with the repercussions on their own. Canary Mission and the AMCHA Initiative, founded respectively in 2012 and 2015, use blacklists as a tactic to halt criticism of Israeli policies, publicly posting lists of professors and students who support the BDS movement or advocate for Palestinian rights. Their intention is to harm students' educational and job prospects.[130] Both organizations list thousands of people and have been criticized for operating McCarthy-style blacklists. Canary Mission has caused many student activists extreme anxiety at the thought that being on this list will negatively impact their job prospects. The *Intercept* reports that "the blacklist has taken a remarkable toll on activists' mental health and ability to engage in free speech and public advocacy on Palestine. A survey of over sixty people profiled on Canary Mission, conducted by the group Against Canary Mission, found that 43 percent of respondents said they toned down their activism because of the blacklist, while 42 percent said they suffered acute anxiety from being placed on the website."[131] While Canary Mission and AMCHA claim to be highlighting and challenging antisemitism on college campuses, their objective has been to intimidate student activists for Palestinian rights into ceasing their activism and speech.[132] Liz Jackson, an attorney with Palestine Legal, says that "targets of Canary Mission have been denied entry to Palestine, fired from jobs, interrogated by employers and university administrators, and targeted with death threats and racial, homophobic misogynist harassment from Canary Mission followers."[133]

SAFE's Facebook and email accounts have received hate messages from the public, including death threats. Students at the University of Michigan, like those at other universities, were anxious and concerned about their graduate school and future employment prospects being negatively affected because a Google search of a student's name would lead to the Canary Mission website, where photos and social media posts are displayed to "prove" a student's desire for the destruction of the state of Israel. One student quoted in the *Michigan Daily* related: "I know specifically a Palestinian student who was at the frontline of this issue, she literally attended therapy sessions because she was put on a blacklist for voicing her concerns about the violations of human rights of the people in her country. [. . .] When you're sitting there studying and then you get a tweet from a blacklist or a tweet that literally says we're watching you, obviously that's going to take away from your focus."[134] A student activist with SAFE, the pseudonymous Z. Zidan, said: "I do not want my name associated with these false allegations at all, especially in print, or beyond campus circles. I fear prospective graduate schools or employers looking at this information and dismissing me—even if it isn't true. [. . .] I also worried that there would be backlash because of the powerful networks [. . .] that would come after me or target me."[135] Student Reem Al-Khatib explained student concerns about being listed on Canary Mission's website: "Education is really important to us because, in my case, the reason my parents came is so that I could get a better education and I could thrive with the resources in America, following the American Dream. [. . .] Canary Mission threatens that for us. I think that's a very real fear that first-generation Americans have. It's the most important thing for us to achieve our education. So a lot of people are immediately turned off. They're like, 'It's better to stay quiet, not make a sound, make it through my education,' because we don't have the privilege of being able to express our political opinions without having any consequences that affect not only us, but our families."[136] This student points out that first-generation college students who are Arab or Muslim come to understand that the cost of expressing their political opinions is too high and that they are not thus entitled to free speech even if their school indicates otherwise.

Although UM did not penalize Palestinian rights activists, these students felt abandoned by the university. Indeed, not penalizing is very different from providing support. Z. Zidan writes about their perspective on the university after facing defamation for their activism: "I and others have been targeted and slandered in grossly personal and unethical ways. I have quietly endured this abuse thinking that if I worked with the system, if I just followed procedure, then as a student, the University would protect me and help put such inflammatory behavior to rest. But I am not white, male, or part of some strong fraternity network. In other words, I am fair game."[137] Even in the rare instance when the university attempts to protect students who have been maligned by Zionist organizations, as when a school official asked the *Washington Free Beacon* to remove the article that smeared student Yazan Kherallah, it had no impact. Students were on their own to deal with the fallout. Lorber writes, "Beyond their encounters with explicit hate speech or implicit stigmatization, Palestinian, Arab, and Muslim students face structural discrimination in their daily struggle to make their voices heard. The bureaucratic roadblocks, sanctions, and other concrete repression disproportionately faced every day by SJP chapters constitute a full-frontal attack against what, on many campuses, is the sole or most prominent space for Palestinian, Arab, and Muslim students to gather and act politically."[138] While the university administration employs flexible diversity to ensure that everyone feels included and protects Palestinian rights advocates' right to free speech, the groups that defame Palestinian rights activists are so effective that the university does not succeed in protecting such students from receiving hate mail, being blacklisted, and facing intimidation and silencing. In addition to intimidation and threats, these students also face racialization as they are smeared as terrorists and terrorist supporters.

While UM did not punish SAFE students, it did punish Professor John Cheney-Lippold in 2018 by withholding a pay raise, canceling his sabbatical, and threatening to fire him from his tenured position for refusing to write a letter of recommendation for a student seeking to study abroad in Israel. Cheney-Lippold told the student that he supports the BDS movement and therefore would not write the letter, but that he would write letters of recommendation for other opportunities the student might seek.[139] A graduate student refused on the same grounds to write a letter of recommendation for a different student. While the university initiated a series of meetings with the graduate student and graduate student union in which the expectation that faculty and graduate students will write letters for students despite their political views were made clear, the school did not take explicit punitive actions against the graduate student. Rather, she was warned of possible dismissal from the graduate program if she repeated the offense.[140] The UM president and administration refused the anti-Semitizing of criticisms of Israel when it came to undergraduate students to ensure that all students feel included. Flexible diversity applies to undergraduate students who pay tuition, but not to faculty who are employees. Graduate students occupy a middle space; most who are pursuing a PhD do not pay tuition because they are funded by university fellowships and are employees of the university when they take on teaching assistantship positions. Regarding the professor, the administration was no longer politically neutral; the president and provost issued a statement in which they took a stance against the BDS movement, echoing the aforementioned statement issued by the provost in 2014: "As we have stated, U-M strongly opposes a boycott of Israeli academic institutions, and no school, college, department or unit at our university endorses such a boycott."[141] Regent board member Denise Illich went further, stating explicitly: "Let's call this what it really is: anti-Semitic."[142]

Power-denial, or racial gaslighting, is a central feature of the shift from institutions' seeking to rectify current and historic racism and inequality to their seeking to create an environment where everyone feels welcome as if there are no power differentials with which to contend. Power-denial is central to the Israel lobby's approach to Israeli state violence against Palestinians, and power-denial becomes the vehicle through which DEI addresses and resolves the supposed problem of Palestinian rights activism on college campuses. The neoliberal all-inclusive approach to diversity embraces a denial of power dynamics to appease everyone. Zakai writes, "In this framework the realities of Israel/Palestine and the realities of the occupation are relegated to the margins. The real face of unbalanced power in Israel/Palestine—movement restrictions, humiliations at checkpoints, land grabs, house demolitions, settlers abuse of Palestinians, daily arrests of children, violent suppression of protest, torture, administrative detention, the cheapening of Palestinian lives that makes possible mass killings of Palestinian civilians every few years—all of this is relegated to the margins of the debate, while Jewish American crisis of identity is centralized."[143] In the context of the university, power-denial gives the impression that everyone is equally marginalized and thus equally needs to be included. In the context of political Zionism, power-denial flips the power dynamic and positions Zionists as the victims and advocates for Palestinian rights as the aggressors.

Normalizing Power

Student activists for Palestinian rights felt heard for the first time when the CSG voted in favor of forming a committee to examine the impact of the school's investments on Palestinian rights. But their celebration was quickly halted when the university released a statement that no such committee would be formed and the regents released their statement taking an explicit stance against BDS. These statements made it clear that the activists' voices were irrelevant—particularly when compared with the demands of a much more powerful group. While the university administration protected the SAFE students' right to free speech and did not conflate their activism with antisemitism—which is more than many other universities have done—students were left on their own to deal with Zionist groups sending them hate mail, blacklisting them, and threatening to jeopardize their future careers in a deliberate and organized way. While Zionist students had Hillel on their side and the Israel on Campus Coalition supporting them and offering talking points, Palestinian rights activists had a few faculty and staff they could turn to for support. These students are therefore marginalized not only because they do not have the institutional support of an organization like Hillel backing them, but also because there is no acknowledgement of the power imbalance. In a 2021 open letter to the university administration, SAFE students express that the university administration has failed them:

> We know the current situation on campus and in Palestine has not
> gone unnoticed within the administration. We also know that the

administration has deliberately chosen not to properly respond and thus continues to maintain the status quo of silence in regards to Palestinian human rights and the experiences of Palestinian students and their allies across campus. [. . .] Your silence allows students to be harassed in their dorms, placed on blacklists, and selectively excluded from the broader campus mission of promoting Diversity, Equity, and Inclusion.[144]

The university works to be inclusive by issuing statements during times of crisis, by creating reflection rooms to accommodate religious Muslim students, and by defending a students' right to free speech. But moments of crisis also reveal which students are privileged and which are not in the calculus of the university's political and economic interests.

Through this process, the values of free speech and diversity become conflated and blurred. Sociologist James M. Thomas uses the term "condensation" to refer to "the process whereby a variety of seemingly unrelated phenomenon, or signifiers, are condensed under the sign 'diversity.'"[145] Condensation, for example, occurs when Republican students use the banner of diversity to argue for the inclusion of their political viewpoint, and therefore a variety of different issues are discussed "as if they all have equal bearing on a person's access to opportunities, resources, power and decision making."[146] As a result, the meaning of diversity becomes all-encompassing and divorced from race consciousness.[147] Flexible diversity operates by including those who express discontent, while failing to focus on the larger structural issues that make DEI a necessity on historically white college campuses and in a society founded upon white supremacy and settler colonialism. The important reference point or center of gravity is displaced in favor of including everyone. In these cases, diversity becomes relativist so that anyone can be a victim and claim exclusion that requires remediation. However, what is different when it comes to the intersection of Zionism with DEI is the way in which flexible diversity reveals a limit: for one, critiques of military occupation, settler colonialism, and US support of Israel are bracketed out of the conversation, putting them beyond question. When student activists are delegitimized for their presumed antisemitism, they are called racists and terrorists and undermined as much for their identities as their politics. This process of racialization as terrorists and antisemites changes how the free-speech debate plays out. What's more, these student activists are not only marginalized but smeared, blacklisted, attacked through hate mail, and their future careers threatened. Journalist Peter Beinart argues that anti-Palestinian bigotry needs to be named and defined in order to make it visible, and the conversation changed to highlight how normalized it has become to deny Palestinians equality and to cast advocacy for their equality as a form of bigotry.[148]

I am not arguing that students and other members of a campus community with a particular political perspective, for example Republicans or Zionists, should not be included in the campus community. I am arguing that doing so through the rubric of diversity, equity, and inclusion instead of free speech and academic freedom empties the meaning of "diversity." Universities can do better by not conflating antisemitism with criticisms of Israel, by protecting free speech, and by protecting student activists, especially when an organization like Canary Mission systematically targets them. They can do better by focusing on rectifying inequality instead of assuming that all have an equal playing field in which to thrive at the university unless a crisis emerges. Muslim and MENA students can have prayer rooms, multicultural lounges, and the possibility of recognition through a MENA checkbox, but acknowledging the power dynamics in the Israeli occupation of Palestine has proven to be off-limits. The Israeli military occupation of Palestine is normalized; criticisms of Israeli state violence are neutralized; and Muslim and MENA students are racialized and marginalized on campus.

Epilogue

Beyond Crisis Diversity

In addition to institutions—media, law and the criminal justice system, corporations, and universities—the US government has also diversified: Rashida Tlaib and Ilhan Omar are the first two Muslim women to serve in Congress, rising to prominence during the Trump administration. Somali refugee Ilhan Omar was elected to Minnesota's House of Representatives in 2016 and to the US House of Representatives in 2018, where she replaced Keith Ellison, the first African American elected to Congress from Minnesota and the first Muslim to serve in the House. Palestinian American Rashida Tlaib was elected to the Michigan House of Representatives in 2008 and to the US House of Representatives in 2018, making her the first Muslim woman to serve in the Michigan legislature and the first woman of Palestinian descent in Congress. Omar and Tlaib are part of what has come to be known as "The Squad," originally four women of color elected to the US House in 2018—Ayanna Pressley, Alexandria Ocasio-Cortez, Omar, and Tlaib—who are pushing Democrats to become more progressive.

Both Omar and Tlaib have faced a great deal of opposition and smearing as a result of their advocacy for the Boycott, Divestment, Sanctions movement, as well as their critique of Israeli state violence against Palestinians and of the US government and Democratic Party's unequivocal support of Israel. In February 2019, journalist and lawyer Glenn Greenwald commented on Republican politician Kevin McCarthy's efforts to penalize Omar and Tlaib for such criticism; Greenwald marveled at "how much time US political leaders spend defending a foreign nation even if it means attacking free speech rights of Americans."[1] In response, Omar tweeted, "It's all about the Benjamins baby," a line from a Puff Daddy song referencing $100 bills. Omar was subsequently criticized for perpetuating antisemitism. Some leaders from the Democratic

Figure 6.1. Representative Ilhan Omar's swearing-in ceremony on Capitol Hill, January 3, 2019. Her wearing the hijab required the removal of a 181-year-old rule that banned headwear on the floor. Omar, wearing a Somali dress, swears on her grandfather's Qur'an. Erik S. Lesser/European Pressphoto Agency.

Figure 6.2. Representative Rashida Tlaib's swearing-in ceremony on Capitol Hill, January 3, 2019. She wears a Palestinian *thobe* and swears on a Qur'an. AP Photo/Susan Walsh.

party, such as Nancy Pelosi, characterized Omar's comments as using "anti-Semitic tropes" and as "deeply offensive."[2] Another Democratic politician, Eliot Engel, said, "It's shocking to hear a Member of Congress invoke the anti-Semitic trope of 'Jewish money.'" President Trump and other Republicans called for her to resign. Omar apologized in a tweet for perpetuating antisemitic tropes, but she also defended her criticism of the Israel lobby's undue influence on US politics:

> Anti-Semitism is real and I am grateful for Jewish allies and colleagues who are educating me on the painful history of anti-Semitic tropes. My intention is never to offend my constituents or Jewish Americans as a whole. We have to always be willing to step back and think through criticism, just as I expect people to hear me when others attack me for my identity. This is why I unequivocally apologize. At the same time, I reaffirm the problematic role of lobbyists in our politics, whether it be AIPAC, the NRA or the fossil fuel industry. It's gone on too long and we must be willing to address it.[3]

In a bizarre but telling turn of events, Republicans proposed a resolution in the House to condemn antisemitism. While it did not identify Omar by name, it was in direct response to Omar's tweet and more broadly in opposition to Omar's (and Tlaib's) criticism of Israeli policies and the US government's support of them. Members of the Congressional Black Caucus and Congressional Progressive Caucus pointed out the irony of punishing Omar while Trump promoted white supremacy without consequence. Some brought up the anti-Muslim racism to which Omar has been subjected, such as a poster displayed at a Republican event in West Virginia that linked her to the terrorist attacks on 9/11, and death threats from people who do not want a Muslim in office.[4] Those supporting Omar insisted that any such resolution must be broadened to include other forms of discrimination. In response, Democrats revised the resolution to include Islamophobia in addition to antisemitism.[5]

As a result, a bill was passed "condemning anti-Semitism as hateful expressions of intolerance that are contradictory to the values and aspirations that define the people of the United States and condemning anti-Muslim discrimination and bigotry against minorities as hateful expressions of intolerance that are contrary to the values and aspirations of the United States."[6] Islamophobia is included as an add-on to a bill that purports to condemn antisemitism but is really condemning Omar and other critics of Israeli state violence and the US's complicity in it. Antisemitism is condemned by Republicans, most of whom supported Trump while he inspired an increase in white supremacy and consequent antisemitic speech and hate crimes during his presidency. Most notorious was the Unite the Right Rally in Charlottesville, Virginia, where Trump supporters chanted "Jews will not replace us"[7] and one of them deliberately drove his car into a crowd of peaceful counterprotesters, killing Heather Heyer, a white woman counterprotester. Trump defended his white supremacist supporters, saying that there were "very fine people on both sides."[8] The resolution connects condemnation of antisemitism to US support of Israel: "Be it resolved the House of Representatives rejects the perpetuation of anti-Semitic stereotypes in the United States and around the world, including the pernicious myth of dual loyalty and foreign allegiance, especially in the context of support for the United States-Israel alliance." Despite the layered contradictions in the development of this resolution, Omar, Tlaib, and Representative André Carson of Indiana released a statement marking the moment: "It's the first time we have voted on a resolution condemning anti-Muslim bigotry in our nation's history."[9]

This incident of the congressional resolution reveals the minefield in which Muslims have come to be included in the US. The first two Muslim women in the US government and the first legislative statement against anti-Muslim racism signal the inclusion of Muslims in the US polity. At the same time, this historical inclusion was, in many ways, made possible through a series of crises, accusations, and controversies—from Trump's election to the presidency and his promotion of white supremacist logics to Omar and Tlaib's taboo criticism of US government support for Israeli state violence against Palestinians and subsequent efforts to silence and penalize them for daring to cross this line. Omar and Tlaib are personally attacked as being antisemitic and a resolution against antisemitism is proposed to silence their criticism of the Israeli government. Eventually, condemnation of Islamophobia is added on to the resolution, a solution that seems to appease all. The resolution equates antisemitism and Islamophobia. On the surface, coupling these two forms of religious discrimination that have also been racialized seems like a productive move. However, given that Islamophobia was only added because of the backlash against Omar, it glosses over how accusations of antisemitism are used to promote anti-Muslim racism, specifically the notion that Muslims are a violent threat. These mental gymnastics illustrate the convoluted and contradictory ways that Muslims have been included in diversity politics today. It is a messy terrain marked by celebratory moments and profound disappointments.

Broken: The Failed Promise of Muslim Inclusion identifies certain tendencies in the "project" of diversity that defang its potential. Media representations expand to include more Muslims, but often as limited tropes that, paradoxically, remain tethered to the very stereotypes they are meant to counteract; the Muslim extremist, for example, meets their match in the nominal Muslim. In other instances, a more robust expansion of representations results, yet continues to be undercut by diversity compromises that get one thing right but not another—for example, finally casting Middle Eastern and North African actors to play MENA roles but still perpetuating Orientalist representations of an exotic East. Muslim victims of hate crimes receive "justice" when their attackers are charged and incarcerated, but the victims' very experiences are discounted and denied when hate crimes are not classified as such and when the role of the state in inspiring hate crimes by constructing Muslims as a national security threat is rendered irrelevant to the conversation or the solution. Meanwhile, in the corporate realm, by firing public figures who engage in anti-Muslim speech, corporations rebrand themselves as anti-racist (or, conversely, as defenders of free speech), audiences participate in purging racism from society, and systemic anti-Muslim racism remains intact because the scandal is framed as strictly limited to individuals, as opposed to any institutional or structural problem. As for universities, the same Muslim and MENA students now included in DEI initiatives are silenced and attacked when they speak out against Israeli state violence against Palestinians. High profile, example-setting institutions like the University of Michigan employ a form of flexible diversity that insists that all students be included but flattens out the vastly unequal power dynamics that ensure some students are protected, while others are marginalized.

And yet, despite these limitations, institutions can all too easily emerge as heroes in the age of diversity. Hollywood sticks it to Trump by finally including Muslims in roles that have nothing to do with terrorism, without acknowledging how the industry itself has demonized Muslims for over a century. Law enforcement offers justice to some Muslim families who have lost loved ones and emerge as heroes in the fight against anti-Muslim violence, yet resist naming hate crimes *as* hate crimes and downplay the role of government policies in inspiring them. Corporations performatively fire people who utter discriminatory speech, sending a clear message that racism will not be tolerated, without acknowledging the role of corporations in upholding racist and discriminatory practices. Universities are applauded for accommodating Muslim students in dining halls during Ramadan or creating reflection rooms that can be used for ritual prayer, but then allow accusations of antisemitism to be weaponized against those students who dare to advocate for Palestinian self-determination. By mapping these various situations in which anti-Muslim racism is simultaneously addressed in some forms and levels, but reinscribed in others, I highlight the ways that this new inclusivity can be exclusionary or limited. Stereotype-confined expansions, compromised diversity, racial gaslighting, racial purging, flexible diversity, and the tendency to deal with anti-Muslim racism as an individual problem as opposed to an institutional one are all common approaches that cloud our vision of the problem, and hence the solution.

"But what then *is* the solution?" After all, some progress *has* been made and Muslims are offered solutions that we want. We want to see ourselves represented in Hollywood. We want the criminal justice system to respond to the racialized violence inflicted on us. We want corporations to recognize the harm inflicted by racist ideas, speech, and actions and to not tolerate it. We want universities to include Muslim students in diversity plans. But all too often it seems that wanting such things requires a tacit agreement never to question whether and how they are delivered. We are asked: What on earth is it that Muslims expect if even these efforts to address anti-Muslim racism are criticized? US Muslims' continued critique of anti-Muslim racism can be distorted and framed as unreasonable—revealing, most disturbingly, an implicit expectation among some that we should be not only satisfied, but quietly grateful.

The point and the value of such continued critique of anti-Muslim racism and of measures proposed to address that racism is not simply to ensure that Muslims remain part of the diversity conversation. It is to use our relatively recent inclusion as an opportunity to investigate just who can make demands of diversity, how, when, and why. It is to identify the neoliberal logic by which diversity has come to be defined and to expose how this logic limits the promise of diversity for everyone. For in this late-capitalist moment, neoliberalism has become ingrained and naturalized not just in corporations but across institutional contexts, shaping how a social good like diversity is branded, strategized, packaged, and made more profitable for some than for others. Journalist Pamela Newkirk says that "it's impossible to understand diversity without exploring the big business of it, the tension between the rhetoric and expenditures, and the chronically disappointing results."[10] On the one hand, who cares if neoliberal logics are at work if we still get some progress? Can't positive change happen *despite* corporations making profit? And something's better than nothing, right? The problem with acquiescing to a neoliberal version of diversity is that it not only shapes *how* we go about "doing" diversity, but also *when*—specifically, only when crises arise.

Crisis diversity is about addressing a flare-up in racism or other forms of systemic discrimination—9/11, the Muslim ban, specific hate crimes—by quickly instituting diversity initiatives. Crisis diversity focuses our attention on only the most overt, public, and often seemingly sudden expressions of racism, obscuring its longevity and reach well beyond moments of crisis. In doing so, it obscures the enduring root causes of anti-Muslim racism: white supremacy and US global supremacy. Crisis diversity, as it plays out, conceals this contradiction; by defusing the problem, this paradox forms the core logic of diversity approaches. Aside from responding to crisis situations, the responses that become possible within neoliberal multiculturalism also neutralize political possibility.

Two major developments in 2020 and 2021 portend a promising turning point, a juncture where the United States is confronting both its history of white supremacy and its more recent history of "forever wars" in Muslim-majority countries: the police murder of George Floyd and the US withdrawal from Afghanistan.[11] On May 25, 2020, in Minneapolis, a security guard named George Floyd was arrested by police after a store clerk suspected him of using a counterfeit twenty-dollar bill. Police officer Derek Chauvin handcuffed and pinned Floyd to the ground, kneeling on his neck and back for eight minutes and forty-six seconds until Floyd died. A young bystander captured the arrest and murder on video, leading to nationwide protests that, according to scholars, count as the largest movement in US history.[12] George Floyd's murder was one of countless cases in which unarmed Black Americans have been murdered by the police.[13] But it was his death that led to national protests, thus producing a crisis that led to unprecedented recognition of anti-Black racism. Hundreds of corporations from Macy's to DoorDash issued pro–Black Lives Matter statements.[14] The US government declared Juneteenth, which commemorates the end of slavery, a national holiday. NASCAR finally banned the Confederate flag. State and city governments removed Confederate statues. Quaker Oats finally retired its brand based on the Aunt Jemima racial stereotype and donated $5 million to support the Black community.[15] Uncle Ben's, Mrs. Butterworth, Land O'Lakes, Eskimo Pie, and other food products initiated rebranding campaigns to ensure that they are not contributing to racism. Apple announced a $100 million initiative to dismantle racism and promote racial equality.[16] The football team the Washington Redskins was finally renamed the Washington Commanders after decades of refusing to change the name despite protests from American Indian communities. News outlets published readings lists and viewings lists to learn about Black history and how not to be racist. Lists of Black-owned businesses to support were circulated. Black activists, scholars, and citizens were called upon to speak, to educate, to comment, and to ride the wave with the hope for some social change. Dozens of state and local governments changed their laws about police behavior by setting limits on the use of force and mandating the use of cameras to make police officers accountable.[17]

Central to this racial awakening is education. In 2021, after a four-year process, the California Department of Education approved the Ethnic Studies Model Curriculum to institute the teaching of ethnic studies in K–12 schools. However, Arab Americans were cut out of the curriculum because Zionist advocacy groups objected to the inclusion of the Palestinian struggle, deeming it antisemitic.[18] Meanwhile, as more people are seeking out materials to learn about the history of racial politics in the US, state governments, such as Florida's, are banning critical race theory from being taught at public schools.[19] In what has become a typical reversal of reality or form of gaslighting, Governor Ron DeSantis of Florida claimed that critical race theory "teaches kids to hate our country and to hate each other" and constitutes state-sanctioned racism.

George Floyd's death and the historic protests for racial justice exhibits the features of crisis diversity. It inspired an urgent and unprecedented racial awakening and call to action to address a centuries-old problem, racial inequality. At the same time, the number of Black people killed by the police has not decreased.[20] This is why abolitionists call for defunding as opposed to reforming the police, because prison and punishment approaches produce more harm than good and reform does not solve the problem. Security approaches tend to feed a cycle of criminalization and violence with no end. Defunding would lead to a reallocation of resources toward education, childcare, housing, and healthcare to support people in living dignified lives as opposed to increased criminalization. As scholar of anti-Muslim racism Arun Kundnani explains, "an abolitionist framework entails understanding that genuine security does not result from the elimination of threats but from the presence of collective well-being."[21]

During the course of the Trump presidency, the news cycle focused less on violence perpetrated by Muslims and more on the resurgence of explicit white supremacy, the mass protests calling for racial justice, and an end to the state-sanctioned violence against Black people. Since 9/11, stories about Muslim-led violence have been a constant feature of news reporting reminding viewers of the necessity of the endless war on terror. A 2018 study out of the University of Alabama revealed that when a Muslim commits an act of violence it is reported on 357 percent more than violence committed by a white person.[22] However, toward the end of the Trump presidency, news reports focused more on the problem of white supremacy, the struggle for racial justice, examinations of enduring inequality in the US, and of course the COVID-19 pandemic. Muslims have been on the news as victims of violence and discrimination in Myanmar, India, and China more than as perpetrators. Furthermore, demonizing Muslims by proposing a Muslim ban was part of Trump's strategy to win the presidency but not part of his strategy for seeking reelection. This is not to say that the demonization of Muslims is on the decline. It is so engrained that it can be reactivated in an instant. Rather, it is to ask: Are the pandemic and white supremacy replacing the War on Terror as the organizing crises of the next decade?

In addition to the Black Lives Matter movement prompting individuals and institutions to reckon with racism, a second major development is Biden's withdrawal of the US military from Afghanistan in 2021. President Biden said that it is the longest war in the US history—twenty years, beginning right after 9/11—and that it should have ended a decade prior.[23] Just like the efforts to address racism are not ending racism, withdrawing from Afghanistan does not mean the end of war, surveillance technologies, drone strikes, or racializing Muslims as a threat to national security. Neither the US military withdrawal from Afghanistan nor the 2020 BLM protests constitute "progress" in themselves, but they are an opportunity to go beyond crisis diversity and to think about how US racial politics aren't separate from US war making. Kundnani applies abolitionism as a mode of political thinking to the national security state. Instead of making us safer, national security approaches, he argues, "exacerbate the insecurities they are ostensibly designed to minimize," resulting in pathological failure.[24] Therefore, in addition to defunding ICE and the police and investing those resources in structures of community care, the same vision should be applied to the War on Terror and the US imperative to dominate the globe by shrinking the US's military, intelligence, and border infrastructure.[25] When considering alternatives to a crisis diversity approach to addressing enduring inequality, what becomes clear is that we need to address the root causes if we want real change. I mention an abolitionist approach because it offers a transformational politics and a bold vision to imagine an alternative to racial inequality, white supremacy, and endless wars. It also provides a roadmap to prioritizing communities over corporations, an alternative to neoliberal diversity.

Donald Trump's explicitly divisive approach to the US presidency presented a crisis to many Americans and inspired action. While crisis-response diversity provides an opening and an important opportunity for change, it easily ushers in a weak diversity politics when it addresses only the crisis at hand, disconnected from longer histories. Diversity initiatives will be ineffective so long as we are not seeking to address the persistence of racism and other forms of structural inequality. Embracing diversity because it enhances the educational environment and makes us more marketable in a globalized economy is all well and good, but it does not solve the problem. Real change requires understanding and approaching the problem as one that is centuries old and not one that is constituted by a momentary temporal crisis. Furthermore, to adequately address social problems like racism, we must address the root causes. In the case of anti-Muslim racism, we need to deal with both the history of white supremacy in the US (as it impacts many different communities) and US-led wars in Muslim-majority countries that mark Muslims as the enemy. Lasting change requires addressing not only individual logics that perpetuate inequality but institutional logics, practices, and structures too. Anti-Muslim racism will not be resolved through a three- or four-point plan. It requires a paradigm shift in our understanding of the problem and its magnitude. Becoming aware of logics that legitimize inequality, their origins, and their enduring impacts will pave the way for all people to live with respect and dignity.

ACKNOWLEDGMENTS

Writing an academic book is a slog. I am grateful to the many people who supported me in countless ways throughout the years of writing this book. A generous and brilliant group of scholars participated in a manuscript workshop partially funded by the USC's Dornsife College Dean's Office and the Department of American Studies and Ethnicity. Sarah Banet-Weiser, Sarah Gualtieri, Alex Lubin, Natalia Molina, and Nadine Naber provided invaluable feedback on how to develop the theoretical frameworks, approach key contradictions, and make the manuscript more cohesive. I am indebted to all of them for their supportive and enthusiastic engagement with my manuscript.

After I published my first book with NYU Press, I knew that I would want to work with Eric Zinner again. He has played an important role building Arab American studies and US Muslim studies and understands the stakes in the debate. It was a pleasure to work with Furqan Sayeed at NYU Press, who brought both valuable editorial suggestions and insights into the subject matter. My thanks to production director Martin Coleman and copyeditor Dan Geist for their attentive work on my manuscript. I appreciate NYU Press's anonymous reviewers and the not-so-anonymous Moustafa Bayoumi for providing feedback on the whole manuscript and helping me clarify the objectives.

My thanks to those who offered feedback on parts of the manuscript: Carol Fadda, Mohammad Hassan Khalil, Zeynep Korkman, Radhika Parameswaran, and Sherene Razack. My sincere thanks to Eid Mohamad for inviting me to the Doha Institute for Graduate Studies, where I presented works-in-progress and received generative feedback from many, including Abdullah Al-Arian, Imed Ben Labidi, and Sami Hermez. A public forum with Melani McAlister at Brown University helped further my thinking. I benefitted from presenting works-in-progress at conferences and other forums where I received input from Sohail Daulatzai, Sondra Hale, Salah Hassan, Amira Jarmakani, Purnima Mankekar,

Minoo Moallem, Dana Olwan, Junaid Rana, and Linda Sayed. Editor extraordinaire Kim Greenwell read multiple versions of the manuscript over several years, offering patience and encouragement as well as incredible insight. At a crucial stage in the book's development, my dear friend and mentor Yeidy Rivero helped me figure out what the book is about and offered vital guidance in navigating the profession. Alex Stern also offered crucial support at an important stage of the process. Shazia Iftkhar helped me navigate pressing concerns as I finalized the manuscript. Mona El-Ghobashy provided insightful feedback every step of the way.

The research for this book was supported by a Luce/ACLS Fellowship in Religion, Journalism, and International Affairs from the American Council of Learned Societies, whose Valerie Popp and John Paul Christy pushed me to think about public engagement in new ways. I also benefited from other funding sources at the University of Michigan, including LSA's Associate Professor Support Fund, WOCAP's writing retreats, and ADVANCE's summer writing grants and write-ins.

I was fortunate to work with brilliant research assistants who collected materials and engaged with me in countless conversations about speech controversies and media representations: Belquis Elhadi, Mekarem Eljamal, Areeba Jibril, and Celia Shallal. In addition to dazzling me with her research skills, intellectual talents, comedic gifts, and a bond that is a source of sustenance, Belquis helped me prepare the manuscript for submission. My brilliant former students Haleemah Aqel, Zeinab Khalil, and Nicole Khamis helped me fill out the contours of one of the chapters.

Various writing groups provided intangible support, friendship, and fun. I thank my writing partner, friend, and mentor, Anan Ameri, whose allergy to injustice is inspiring. My co-conspirators Charlotte Karem Albrecht and Aliyah Khan are like having a personal advisory board on all things Arab and Muslim. Together, we were also part of the wonderful Arabish-Muslimish women's group that included Amal Fadlallah, Shazia Iftkhar, Mai Hassan, Yasmin Moll, Muniba Saleem, and Dalia Petrus. It was a celebratory feat when Nancy Khalil and Su'ad Abdul Khabeer joined us in Michigan right before my departure.

I wrote quite a bit of the book at the Huntington Library and then on Zoom during the pandemic with the encouragement and advice of my LA writing group: Natalia Molina, Neetu Khanna, and Kyla Wazana Tompkins. The cosmos gave me a gift by bringing the triple threat (teaching/research/service) that is Natalia and I together as we embarked upon our new lives in LA. I am grateful to Natalia for knowing how to approach everything, Neetu for her ability to be emotionally present, and Kyla for bringing the fierce and funny.

Much of this book was conceived during my fourteen years as a faculty member at the University of Michigan, where I developed the Arab and Muslim American Studies (AMAS) program and then the Islamophobia Working Group (IWG). I would like to acknowledge my colleagues in the Department of American Culture for their unwavering support of the AMAS program: Stephen Berrey, William Calvo-Quiros, Amy Carroll, Maria Cotera, Matthew Countryman, Greg Dowd, Julie Ellison, Anna Watkins Fisher, Jonathan Freedman, Mary Freiman, Judith Gray, Colin Gunckel, Sandra Gunning, Kristin Hass, Jesse Hoffnung-Garskof, Mary Kelley, Katelynn Klemm, Larry La Fountain-Stokes, the late Richard Meisler, Tiya Miles, Marlene Moore, Anthony Mora, Susan Najita, Silvia Pedraza, Tabitha Rohn, Amy Stillman, Penny Von Eschen, Alan Wald, Michael Witgen, Magda Zaborowska, and the late Tommy Hill. Special thanks to Phil Deloria for planting the seeds; to June Howard for cultivating them; to Nadine Naber for sharing the vision; to Charlotte Karem Albrecht for developing it with me; to Matt Stiffler for bringing so many students; and to John Cheney-Lippold, Manan Desai, and Lisa Nakamura for solidarity. A special shout-out to my amazing former students and collaborators: Haleemah Aqel, Silan Fadlallah, Nour Soubani, and Zeinab Khalil, who served at different times as the AMAS program assistant and/or the IWG coordinator.

The IWG inspired chapter 5. I would like to recognize those who formed the collective with me: Dalia Petrus, always seeking to uplift the underrepresented with so much heart; Marjorie Horton, my confidante and model of allyship; and the incomparable group of (former) students Ali Aboubih, Haleemah Aqel, Jad Elharake, Ryan Gilcrist, Nadine Jawad, and Ibtihal Makki. The work we did as a collective would not have been possible without Robbie Abdelhoq, Nadia Aggour, Samer Ali, Maryam Ahmed, Tina Alkhersan, Tahany Alsabahi, Carol Bardenstein, Riyah Basha, Ashley Bates, Nadia Bazzy, Abby Chien, Dilip Das, Silan Fadlallah, Yara Gayar, Alaa Hajeissa, Rima Hassouneh, Yahya Hafez, Sally

Howell, Daniel Hummel, Adam Mageed, Karla Mallette, Sammy Mansour, Hana Mattar, Lamees Mekkaoui, Alice Mishkin, Angelo Pitillo, Jessica Hill Riggs, Andrea Sahouri, Jumanah Saadeh, and others. I learned a lot about social justice education from the late Adrienne Dessel, who was part of the founding collective of the IWG and, before that, of the Israel-Palestine Working Group.

Those of us who are underrepresented know the experience of finding others who share our identity and sustain us with a greater sense of belonging. At UM, my classroom and office served this function for some. A magical synchronicity brought some very special and inspiring (former) students into my orbit who made it all worth it: Samantha Abdullah, Nour Abughoush, Tamer Abuhalawah, Zaineb Abdul-Nabi, Alyiah Al-Bonijim, Iman Ali, Anoud Allouzi, Sarah Alogaili, Noran Alsabahi, Tahany Alsabahi, Banen Al-Sheemary, Ryah Aqel, Devon Bathish, Gabrielle Borg, Iliria Camaj, Rama Chehouri, Fatima Chowdhury, Ghida Dagher, Sara Dagher, Tala Dahbour, Sena Duran, Nourelhoda Eidy, Mekarem Eljamal, Farah Erzouki, Bayan Founas, Kierra Gray, Omar Hassan, Noor Haydar, Mena Hermiz, Alicia Hirt, Mona Iskandarani, Jehan Jawad, Areeba Jibril, Madison Jones, Sally Kafelghazal, Ariel Kaplowitz, Diala Khalife, Nama Khalil, Nicole Khamis, Sarah Khan, Nadia Karizat, Samantha Kobbah, Kati Lebioda, Beatrix McBride, Nicole Miller, Mary Mikha, Noha Moustafa, Fadel Nabilsi, Mohamad Naim, Ali Nasrallah, Ramy Odeh, Ashley Ogwo, Hind Omar, Ebere Oparaeke, Simisola Oyeleye, Danielle Rabie, Samia Rahman, Fiona Ruddy, Jaber Saad, Barrie Schwartz, Sean Dajour Smith, Layla Zarkesh, Mohamad Zawahra, and others.

My former and current graduate students also inspire me: Yamil Avivi, Megan Awwad, Maryam Aziz, Noha Beydoun, Umayyah Cable, Kam Copeland, Dominic Garzonio, Sarah Gothie, Hannah Haynes, Rojeen Harsini, Meryem Kamil, Christina LaRose, Joo Young Lee, Rocío León, Waleed Mahdi, Michelle May-Curry, Deena Naime, Teraya Paramehta, Rachel Afi Quinn, Omar Baz Radwan, Mejdulene Shomali, Hanah Stiverson, Zaina Ujayli, Ida Yalzadeh, and Layla Zbinden.

For the last twenty years, I have been a part of a powerhouse growing cohort of scholars who are building the field by bringing conversations about Arabs and Muslims to ethnic studies. I am fortunate as I write to know that I am in such good company: Su'ad Abdul Khabeer,

Thomas Abowd, Moustafa Bayoumi, Umayyah Cable, Louise Cainkar, Sylvia Chan-Malik, Sohail Daulatzai, Thomas Dolan, Carol Fadda, Keith Feldman, Zareena Grewal, Sarah Gualtieri, Salah Hassan, Pauline Homsi Vinson, Charlotte Karem Albrecht, Nadeen Kharputly, Amira Jarmakani, Alex Lubin, Sunaina Maira, Waleed Mahdi, Nadine Naber, Therí Pickens, Junaid Rana, Steven Salaita, Mejdulene Shomali, Stan Thangaraj, and others.

Ella Shohat, my longtime mentor, has been influential in my thinking and approach to cultural politics. She has left a mark in everything I do. I am likewise grateful to Robert Stam for moral support over the years. Cherríe Moraga's imprint remains too. Dr. Jack Shaheen is no longer with us, but I think of him often as I do this work and am fortunate that Bernice Shaheen remains a tremendous support.

While writing this book, I started a new position at USC and joined a group of incredible colleagues: Nayan Shah, John Carlos Rowe, Alicia Chavez, Juan De Lara, Adrian De Leon, Chris Finley, Sonia Flores, Edwin Hill, Stanley Huey, Lanita Jacobs, Sarah Kessler, Dorinne Kondo, Oneka LaBennett, Kitty Lai, Shawn McDaniel, Lydie Moudileno, Viet Nguyen, Panivong Norindr, Jujuana Preston, George Sanchez, Karen Tongson, Jackie Wang, and Francille Wilson. It is a pleasure to collaborate with Sarah Gualtieri, a brilliant scholar, ethical human, and model for how to approach the profession with compassion and thoughtfulness.

My move to Los Angeles also led to some wonderful and unexpected collaborations that have allowed me to put my scholarship into practice. I am so grateful to conversations with Lorraine Ali, Azita Ghanizada, Khaula Malik, Farah Merani, Gillian Mueller, and Sue Obeidi that helped shape chapter 2. I am especially grateful to Sue for the opportunities to work with her on some projects through the Muslim Public Affairs Council's Hollywood Bureau and Azita through the MENA Arts Advocacy Coalition. Their unyielding commitment to changing the narrative is inspiring.

I am grateful to my fabulous LA Arab Women's Brunch Group: Abby Abdelkhalek, Stephanie Abraham, Deborah Al-Najjar, Lara Deeb, Jennifer Jajeh, Amira Jarmakani, Donia Jarrar, Randa Jarrar, Priscilla Wathington, Nina Zidani, and Sulafa Zidani. I am thankful to Stephanie for bringing us all together and for commiserating on our shared interests; to Deb for being my self-help guru; to Lara for her level-headed perspective and shared affinity for felines; to Amira for her ethical commitment to the field and to friendship; to Nina for bringing more life to my work-life balance; and to Sulafa for sorting through university politics with me.

Old and new friends have offered support throughout the process of writing this book: Magdalena Barrera, Moulouk Berry, Leila Buck, Christianne Cejas, Jennifer Chin, Amber Donnell, Reem Gibril, Heather Harris, Christina Hanhardt, Khaled Mattawa, Kelley McGarrigle-Putman, Nichole Diaz Mendoza, Marisol Negrón, Lavinia Pinto, Vanessa Primiani, Elizabeth Riley-Green, and Atef Said. Las Kwarentonaz- Mayte Green Mercado, Deirdre de la Cruz, and Shobita Parthasarathy—are a constant source of sisterhood and inspiration. Thanks to Shobita for working through hard stuff together; to Deirdre for bringing love and comic relief; and to Mayte for embodying resilience in the face of challenges. I am grateful to Victor Mendoza for support and solidarity; to Ruby Tapia, who gets me like no other; to Sheikha Rima Hassouneh for valuing friendship and time for life's pleasures; and to Jennifer Junkermeier and Osman Khan for feeling like family. To Nina Nabors, Tana Espino, and Jenna Torres, thank you for helping me find restorative pathways.

I am fortunate to have quite a few BFFs who have shared decades of life with me. My daily morning chats with Christine Burmeister mean everything; I am grateful to Christine for staying connected through it all and always seeing the best in me. One thousand and one thank yous to Mona El-Ghobashy for the extraordinary gift of getting into the minutiae with me—whether it is the minutiae of my writing and ideas or the minutiae of professional and personal experiences. My nurturing sisters are a true blessing: Mireille Abelin bears witness and reminds me how far I have come; Lauren Rosenthal supports through the ups and downs of life with shining strength; Elif Bali brings an eternally positive attitude and always finds the humor; and Nacisse Demeksa combines endless curiosity and dedication to continuous growth. Thanks to Ebony Coletu for her steadfast friendship and dazzling brilliance, and Nadine Naber, my longtime friend and collaborator, for her endless encouragement and sharing in personal growth.

I would like to acknowledge my supportive family. I thank Maggie Jimenez Alsultany, the mom who raised me, for her dedication since the beginning. I have been inspired by how she perseveres through life's challenges. Much gratitude to my brother, Fabian Alsultany, for always wanting to be together and for bragging about me to others; my sister-in-law, Eva Baboun Alsultany for cheering me on; my aunt Maria Jimenez for always being there; my cousin Fatima Chavez for meeting the challenges and making me proud; and my cousin Steven Cuevas for bringing a sense of humor. I am grateful to my in-laws Sara Ofosu-Benefo, Nana Ofosu-Benefo, and Osei Ofosu-Benefo for their constant support and encouragement. The new additions to the family, Gabito and Asha, bring much joy, while those who are no longer with us, Kamal Alsultany, Marta Rodriguez Alsultany, Raul Jimmy Chavez, Marta Jaramillo, and Kwadwo Ofosu-Benefo, will always be remembered. My extended family has offered fun diversions from work: Vivia Costalas, Stratos Costalas, Litsa Flores, Leonor Garcia, Barbara Alexander-Largie, Teresa Lawrence, Hussam Obaydi, Franchesca Rosario, George Smith, Brad Verebay, Gilda Rodriguez Zikria, Fernando Rodriguez, and the late Anita Garcia. My furry family members bring light to my life and obstruct my work at every opportunity: the late Zeeza, the late Meenu, the late Sage, Luna, Ama, and Petite.

I dedicate this book to my husband Benebo Ofosu Benelo, who has been in the trenches of life with me for twenty-five years, in conversation with me about changing racial politics, and has offered me a soft place to land.

NOTES

INTRODUCTION

1 The documents pertaining to the creation of the Arab and Muslim American Studies program have been archived at the Bentley Historical Library at the University of Michigan. The program was initially called Arab American Studies and was later renamed Arab and Muslim American Studies to account for the racialization of Islam and to meet the needs of Muslim students seeking Ethnic Studies courses who were not Arab.

2 Bridge Initiative Team, "Islamophobia in 2015: The Good, the Bad, and the Hopeful (United States)," Charter for Compassion, December 21, 2015, http://charterforcompassion.org.

3 Sociologists Steve Garner and Saher Selod use Google Scholar to chart the increase in the use of the term from 1980 to 2012, showing a gradual increase with a spike in 2011. Steve Garner and Saher Selod, "The Racialization of Muslims: Empirical Studies of Islamophobia," Critical Sociology 41.1 (2014): 9–19.

4 Bridge Initiative Team, "Islamophobia in 2015."

5 Sara Ahmed and Elaine Swan use the term "doing diversity." See "Doing Diversity," Policy Futures in Education 4:2 (2006): 96–100.

6 Toby S. Jenkins, "Committed to Diversity? Show Me the Money," Chronicle of Higher Education, September 18, 2016, www.chronicle.com.

7 INSIGHT Staff, "An INSIGHT Investigation: Accounting for Just 0.5% of Higher Education's Budgets, Even Minimal Diversity Funding Supports Their Bottom Line," INSIGHT into Diversity, October 16, 2019, www.insightintodiversity.com.

8 Lisa J. Disch and Jean M. O'Brien, "Innovation Is Overtime: An Ethical Analysis of 'Politically Committed' Academic Labor," in Feminist Waves, Feminist Generations: Life Stories from the Academy, ed. Hokulani K. Aikau, Karla. A. Erickson, and Jennifer L. Pierce (Minneapolis: University of Minnesota Press, 2007), 140–167; Patricia A. Matthew, "What Is Faculty Diversity Worth to a University?," Atlantic, November 23, 2016, www.theatlantic.com.

9 JoAnn Trejo, "The Burden of Service for Faculty of Color to Achieve Diversity and Inclusion: The Minority Tax," Molecular Biology of the Cell 31:25 (November 30, 2020): 2752–2754; Audrey Williams June, "The Invisible Labor of Minority Professors," Chronicle of Higher Education, November 8, 2015, www.chronicle.com.

10 Scholarship on "Islamophobia" is burgeoning, and many of these studies have been published since 2010. Some of these works include Khaled Beydoun,

American Islamophobia: Understanding the Roots and Rise of Fear (Berkeley: University of California Press, 2018); Saher Selod, *Forever Suspect: Racialized Surveillance of Muslim Americans in the War on Terror* (New Brunswick, NJ: Rutgers University Press, 2018); Erik Love, *Islamophobia and Racism in America* (New York: NYU Press, 2017); Christopher Bail, *Terrified: How Anti-Muslim Fringe Organizations Became Mainstream* (Princeton, NJ: Princeton University Press, 2015); Moustafa Bayoumi, *This Muslim American Life: Dispatches from the War on Terror* (New York: NYU Press, 2015); Arun Kundnani, *The Muslims are Coming!: Islamophobia, Extremism, and the Domestic War on Terror* (London: Verso, 2015); Todd Green, *The Fear of Islam: An Introduction to Islamophobia in the West* (Minneapolis: Fortress Press, 2015); Deepa Kumar, *Islamophobia and the Politics of Empire* (Chicago: Haymarket Books, 2014); Chris Allen, *Islamophobia* (Farnham, UK: Ashgate, 2013); Carl Ernst, ed., *Islamophobia in America: The Anatomy of Intolerance* (London: Palgrave Macmillan, 2013); Stephen Sheehi, *Islamophobia: The Ideological Campaign against Muslims* (Atlanta: Clarity Press, 2013); Nathan Lean, *The Islamophobia Industry: How the Right Manufactures Fear of Muslims* (New York: Pluto Press, 2012); John L. Esposito and Ibrahim Kalin, eds., *Islamophobia: The Challenge of Pluralism in the 21st Century* (Oxford: Oxford University Press, 2011); Andrew Shryock, ed., *Islamophobia/Islamophilia: Beyond the Politics of Enemy and Friend* (Bloomington: Indiana University Press, 2010); Peter Gottschalk and Gabriel Greenberg, *Islamophobia: Making Muslims in the Enemy* (Lanham, MD: Rowman & Littlefield, 2007); Kevin M. Dunn, Natascha Klocker, and Tanya Salabay, "Contemporary Racism and Islamophobia in Australia: Racializing Religion," *Ethnicities* 7 (2007): 564–589; Liz Fekete, "Anti-Muslim Racism and the European Security State," *Race & Class* 46:1 (July 2004): 3–29; Narzanin Massoumi, Tom Mills, and David Miller, eds., *What Is Islamophobia? Racism, Social Movements and the State* (London: Pluto Press, 2017); Erik Bleich, "Defining and Researching Islamophobia," *Review of Middle East Studies* 46:2 (Winter 2012): 180–189; Nasar Meer and Tariq Modood, "Refutations of racism in the 'Muslim question,'" *Patterns of Prejudice* 43:3–4 (2009): 335–354; Ramón Grosfoguel and Eric Mielants, "The Long-Durée Entanglement between Islamophobia and Racism in the Modern/Colonial Capitalist/Patriarchal World-System: An Introduction," *Human Architecture: Journal of the Sociology of Self—Knowledge* 5:1 (Fall 2006): 1–12.

11 Louise Cainkar, "Fluid Terror Threat: A Genealogy of the Racialization of Arab, Muslim, and South Asian Americans," *Amerasia Journal* 44:1 (2018): 27–59.

12 Nadine C. Naber, "So Our History Doesn't Become Your Future: The Local and Global Politics of Coalition Building Post September 11th," *Journal of Asian American Studies* 5:3 (2002): 217–242.

13 Tucker Carlson, "The 'Diversity' Delusion and the Destruction of the American Meritocracy," Fox News, December 1, 2020, www.foxnews.com.

14 Stephen Paul Foster, "'16 Tons' of Diversity & Racism," *Counter-Currents*, January 5, 2021, www.counter-currents.com.

15 Roderick A. Ferguson, *The Reorder of Things: The University and Its Pedagogy of Minority Difference* (Minneapolis: University of Minnesota Press, 2012), 27.

16 Cedric Herring and Loren Henderson, "From Affirmative Action to Diversity: Toward a Critical Diversity Perspective," *Critical Sociology* 38:5 (2011): 629–643. Also see Beth E. Schneider and Denise A. Segura, "From Affirmative Action to Diversity: Critical Reflections on Graduate Education in Sociology," *Sociology Compass* 8:2 (2014): 157–171; Ellen C. Berrey, "Why Diversity Became Orthodox in Higher Education, and How It Changed the Meaning of Race on Campus," *Critical Sociology* 37:5 (2011): 573–596.

17 Nadine Naber and Junaid Rana, "The 21st Century Problem of Anti-Muslim Racism," *Jadaliyya*, July 25, 2019, www.jadaliyya.com.

18 I use "enduring white supremacy" rather than "legacy of white supremacy" to caution against the implication that white supremacy is dormant. This is inspired by Ann Laura Stoler, who critiques the term "colonial legacy" and instead uses "durability of empire" to avoid the implication that imperial formations are dormant. See Ann Laura Stoler, *Duress: Imperial Durabilities in Our Times* (Durham, NC: Duke University Press, 2016), 352.

19 Andrea Smith, "Heteropatriarchy and the Three Pillars of White Supremacy: Rethinking Women of Color Organizing," *Color of Violence: The INCITE! Anthology*, ed. INCITE! Women of Color Against Violence (Durham, NC: Duke University Press, 2016), 66–73.

20 Melani McAlister, *Epic Encounters: Culture, Media, and U.S. Interests in the Middle East, 1945–2000* (Berkeley: University of California Press, 2001). Also see Nasar Meer, "Racialization and Religion: Race, Culture and Difference in the Study of Antisemitism and Islamophobia," *Ethnic and Racial Studies* 36:3 (2013): 385–398; Atiya Husain, "Retrieving the Religion in Racialization: A Critical Review," *Sociology Compass* 11:9 (2017).

21 Alex Lubin, *Never-Ending War on Terror* (Oakland: University of California Press, 2021), 5.

22 Ibid., 90–91.

23 Ibid., 102–103.

24 "Islamophobia: A Challenge for Us All" (London: Commission on British Muslims and Islamophobia, Runnymede Trust, 1997).

25 Wahajat Ali, Eli Clifton, Matthew Duss, Lee Fang, Scott Keyes, and Faiz Shakir, "Fear, Inc.: The Roots of the Islamophobia Network in America" (Washington, DC: Center for American Progress, August 2011), www.americanprogress.org.

26 See, for example, Sahar Aziz, *The Racial Muslim: When Racism Quashes Religious Freedom* (Oakland: University of California Press, 2021); Arun Kundnani, "Integrationism: The Politics of Anti-Muslim Racism," *Race & Class* 48:4 (2007): 24–44; Steven Salaita, "Beyond Orientalism and Islamophobia: 9/11, Anti-Arab Racism, and the Mythos of National Pride," *CR: The New Centennial Review* 6:2 (Fall 2006): 245–266; Javier Rosón Lorente, "Discrepancies around the Use of the Term 'Islamophobia,'" *Human Architecture: Journal of the Sociology of Self-Knowledge*

8:2 (Fall 2010): 115–128; Junaid Rana and Sohail Daulatzai, "Writing the Muslim Left: An Introduction to Throwing Stones," in *With Stones in Our Hands: Writings on Muslims, Racism, and Empire*, ed. Sohail Daulatzai and Junaid Rana (Minneapolis: University of Minnesota Press, 2018), ix–xxii.

27 For scholarship on the racialization of Arab Americans before 9/11, see Helen Samhan, "Not Quite White: Race Classification and the Arab-American Experience" in *Arabs in America; Building a New Future* (Philadelphia: Temple University Press, 1999), 209–226; Sarah Gualtieri, "Becoming 'White': Race, Religion and the Foundations of Syrian/Lebanese Ethnicity in the United States," *Journal of American Ethnic History* 20:4 (Summer 2001): 29–58; Nadine Naber, "Ambiguous Insiders: An Investigation of Arab American Invisibility," *Ethnic and Racial Studies* 23:1 (2000): 37–61; Therese Saliba, "Resisting Invisibility: Arab Americans in Academia and Activism," in *Arabs in America: Building A New Future*, ed. Michael W. Suleiman (Philadelphia: Temple University Press, 1999), 204–219; Soheir A. Morsy, "Beyond the Honorary 'White' Classification of Egyptians: Societal Identity in Historical Context," in *Race*, ed. Steven Gregory and Roger Sanjek (New Brunswick, NJ: Rutgers University Press, 1994), 175–198. For scholarship on the racialization of Arab Americans after 9/11, see, for example, Louise Cainkar, "No Longer Invisible: Arab and Muslim Exclusion after September 11," *Middle East Report* 224 (2002): 22–29; Steven Salaita, *Anti-Arab Racism in the USA* (London: Pluto Press, 2006); *Race and Arab Americans Before and After 9/11: From Invisible Citizens to Visible Subjects*, ed. Amaney Jamal and Nadine Naber (Syracuse, NY: Syracuse University Press, 2008); Salah Hassan, "Arabs, Race, and the Post-September 11 National Security State," *Middle East Report* 224 (2002); Hisham Aidi, "Jihadis in the Hood: Race, Urban Islam and the War on Terror," *Middle East Report* 224 (2002); Moustafa Bayoumi, "Racing Religion," *CR: The New Centennial Review* 6:2 (Fall 2006): 267–293.

28 Sherene Razack, "'A Catastrophically Damaged Gene Pool': Law, White Supremacy, and the Muslim Psyche," in Daulatzai and Rana, *With Stones in Our Hands*, 198.

29 Nadine Naber, "'Look, Mohammed the Terrorist Is Coming!': Cultural Racism, Nation-Based Racism and the Intersectionality of Oppressions after 9/11," in *Race and Arab Americans before and after 9/11*, 276–304; Cainkar, "Fluid Terror Threat."

30 "Radio Address by Mrs. Bush," Office of the First Lady, White House, November 17, 2001.

31 Nadine Naber, "Here We Go Again: Saving Muslim Women and Queers in the Age of Trump," *Jadaliyya*, April 22, 2019, www.jadaliyya.com. Also see Sherene Razack, *Casting Out: The Eviction of Muslims from Western Law and Politics* (Toronto: University of Toronto Press, 2007); Lila Abu-Lughod, *Do Muslim Women Need Saving?* (Cambridge, MA: Harvard University Press, 2013).

32 Jack Shaheen, *Reel Bad Arabs: How Hollywood Vilifies a People* (Northampton, MA: Olive Branch Press, 2001).

33 Ella Shohat, "Gender and the Culture of Empire: Toward a Feminist Ethnography of the Cinema," *Quarterly Review of Film and Video* 13:1–3 (1991): 45–84.

34 McAlister, *Epic Encounters*; Cainkar, "Fluid Terror Threat."

35 Carol Fadda, "Arab, Asian, and Muslim Feminist Dissent: Responding to the 'Global War on Terror' in Relational Frameworks," *Amerasia Journal* 44:1 (2018): 1–25, 8.

36 Ibid., 5.

37 Namira Islam, "Soft Islamophobia," *Religions* 9:9 (2018): 280.

38 Margari Aziza Hill, "What's In a Name?: Using 'Muslim' as a Cultural Category Erases and Stereotypes," *Margari Aziza* (blog), March 23, 2015, http://margari aziza.com.

39 Ella Shohat and Robert Stam, *Unthinking Eurocentrism: Multiculturalism and the Media* (London and New York: Routledge, 1994).

40 Shafik Mandhai, "Two in Five Americans Say Islam 'Is Incompatible with US Values,'" *Al Jazeera*, November 1, 2018, www.aljazeera.com.

41 Owais Arshad, Varun Setlur, Usaid Siddiqui, "Are Muslims Collectively Responsible?: A Sentiment Analysis of the New York Times," 416 Labs, 2015, http://416labs .com.

42 For more on the history of Islam in the US, see Kambiz GhaneaBassiri, *A History of Islam in America: From the New World to the New World Order* (New York: Cambridge University Press, 2010); Su'ad Abdul Khabeer, *Muslim Cool: Race, Religion, and Hip Hop in the United States* (New York: NYU Press, 2016); Zareena Grewal, *Islam Is a Foreign Country: American Muslims and the Global Crisis of Authority* (New York: NYU Press, 2013); Sally Howell, *Old Islam in Detroit: Rediscovering the Muslim American Past* (New York: Oxford University Press, 2014); Sylvia Chan-Malik, *Being Muslim: A Cultural History of Women of Color in American Islam* (New York: NYU Press, 2018).

43 Given that I argue against using the term "Islamophobia" to avoid conceptualizing this form of discrimination as a phobia, which obscures how state violence or institutionalized forms of racial profiling sustain it, it does make sense to then avoid terms like "homophobia" and "transphobia," which I do not take to be "phobias" either. Thus, I will be using "anti-LGBTQ+ discrimination" (or, here, "animus") when referring to homophobia and transphobia to be consistent.

44 Aysha Khan, "A Push to Deny Muslims Religious Freedom Gains Steam," *Religion & Politics* (blog), July 16, 2019, http://religionandpolitics.org.

45 Arun Kundnani, "Abolish National Security," Transnational Institute, Amsterdam, June 2021, 12.

46 Brian Levin and Kevin Grisham, *Special Status Report: Hate Crime in the United States* (San Bernardino: California State University Center for the Study of Hate and Extremism, 2016); Clare Foran, "Donald Trump and the Rise of Anti-Muslim Violence," *Atlantic*, September 22, 2016, www.theatlantic.com. Also see Engy Abdelkader, "When Islamophobia Turns Violent: The 2016 US Presidential

Elections," Bridge Initiative, Georgetown University, 2016, www.immigrationre
search.org.

47 Wenei Philimon, "Not Just George Floyd: Police Departments Have 400-Year History of Racism," *USA Today*, June 7, 2020, www.usatoday.com.

48 Sharon M. Collins, "Diversity in the Post Affirmative Action Labor Market: A
Proxy for Racial Progress?," *Critical Sociology* 37:5 (2011): 521–540, 523.

49 This 1998 Survey of Diversity Programs conducted by the Society for Human Resource Management (SHRM) is cited in Collins, "Diversity in the Labor Market,"
524.

50 Erin Kelly and Frank Dobbin, "How Affirmative Action Became Diversity Man-
agement: Employer Response to Antidiscrimination Law, 1961–1996," *American
Behavioral Scientist* 41:7 (1998): 960–984. This is cited in Collins, "Diversity in the
Labor Market," 524.

51 Rohini Anand and Mary-Frances Winters, "A Retrospective View of Corporate
Diversity Training from 1964 to the Present," *Academy of Management Learning &
Education* 7:3 (September 2008): 356–372, 356.

52 Scott Page, "Making the Difference: Applying a Logic of Diversity," *Academy of
Management Perspectives* 21:4 (2007): 6–20.

53 Anand and Winters, "Retrospective View," 362.

54 Robert Hayles, "History of Diversity and Inclusion," *The SAGE Encyclopedia of Intercultural Competence*, ed. Janet M. Bennett (Thousand Oaks, CA: SAGE, 2015),
385–390.

55 Liam Stack, "Halima Aden Will Be First Sports Illustrated Model in a Hijab and
Burkini," *New York Times*, April 29, 2019, www.nytimes.com.

56 Elizabeth Paton, "CoverGirl Signs Its First Ambassador in a Hijab," *New York
Times*, November 9, 2016, www.nytimes.com.

57 Rashmee Kumar, "Marketing the Muslim Woman: Hijabs and Modest Fashion
are the New Corporate Trend in the Trump Era," *Intercept*, December 29, 2018,
http://theintercept.com.

58 Sara Ahmed and Elaine Swan, "Doing Diversity," *Policy Futures in Education* 4:2
(2006): 96–100.

59 Sara Ahmed, *On Being Included: Racism and Diversity in Institutional Life* (Durham, NC: Duke University Press, 2012), 67.

60 Ibid., 66.

61 Ibid., 69.

62 Sara Ahmed, "Damage Limitation," *Feminist Killjoys*, February 15, 2019, www
.feministkilljoys.com.

63 Nancy Leong, "Fake Diversity and Racial Capitalism," *Medium*, November 23,
2014, www.medium.com.

64 Elizabeth A. Povinelli, *The Cunning of Recognition: Indigenous Alterities and the
Making of Australian Multiculturalism* (Durham, NC: Duke University Press,
2002), 7.

65 O'Connor, *Grutter v. Bollinger* (Opinion of the Court), 539 U.S. 306 (U.S. Supreme Court 2003).

66 Berrey, "Why Diversity Became Orthodox," 580.

67 Howard Winant, *Racial Conditions: Politics, Theory, Comparisons* (Minneapolis: University of Minnesota Press, 1994); Jodi Melamed, *Represent and Destroy: Rationalizing Violence in the New Racial Capitalism* (Minneapolis: University of Minnesota Press, 2011); Wendy Brown, *Undoing the Demos: Neoliberalism's Stealth Revolution* (New York: Zone Books, 2015).

68 Rabab Abdulhadi, Evelyn Alsultany, and Nadine Naber, "Arab and Arab American Feminisms: An Introduction," in *Arab and Arab American Feminism: Gender, Nation, and Belonging*, ed. Rabab Abdulhadi, Evelyn Alsultany, and Nadine Naber (Syracuse, NY: Syracuse University Press, 2011), xxxi.

CHAPTER 1. STEREOTYPE-CONFINED EXPANSIONS

1 Mahmood Mamdani, *Good Muslim, Bad Muslim: America, the Cold War, and the Roots of Terror* (New York: Three Leaves Press, 2004), 15.

2 Rosemary Corbett, *Making Moderate Islam: Sufism, Service, and the "Ground Zero Mosque" Controversy* (Stanford, CA: Stanford University Press, 2017).

3 Evelyn Alsultany, "Selling American Diversity and Muslim American Identity through Non-profit Advertising Post-9/11," *American Quarterly* 59 (September 2007): 593–622.

4 Mucahit Bilici, *Finding Mecca in America: How Islam Is Becoming an American Religion* (Chicago: University of Chicago Press, 2012), 201.

5 Khaled Beydoun, "Acting Muslim," *Harvard Civil Rights-Civil Liberties Law Review* 53 (2017): 1–64.

6 Inderpal Grewal, "Transnational America: Race, Gender, and Citizenship after 9/11," *Social Identities* 9 (2003): 535–561.

7 Evelyn Alsultany, *Arabs and Muslims in the Media: Race and Representation after 9/11* (New York: NYU Press, 2012).

8 24, FOX, 2001–2014.

9 Abdullah Al-Arian and Hafsa Kanjwal, "The Perils of American Muslim Politics," in *With Stones in Our Hands: Writings on Muslims, Racism, and Empire*, ed. Sohail Daulatzai and Junaid Rana (Minneapolis: University of Minnesota Press, 2018), 22. Also see Salah Hassan, "Muslim Presence: Anti-Muslim Politics in the United States and the Rise of Muslim American Culture," in *Muslims and US Politics Today*, 69–82.

10 Edward E. Curtis IV, "Blood Sacrifice and the Myth of the Fallen Muslim Soldier in the US Presidential Elections after 9/11," in *Muslims and U.S. Politics Today*, 48–66. Also see Edward Curtis, *Muslim Americans in the Military: Centuries of Service* (Bloomington: Indiana University Press, 2016), 6.

11 For example, see William Kilpatrick, "The Moderate Muslim Majority Myth," *Frontpage Magazine*, October 17, 2016, www.frontpagemag.com.

12 Ismat Sarah Mangla, "Hillary Clinton Has an Unfortunate Way of Talking about American Muslims," *Quartz*, October 20, 2016, www.qz.com.

13 On the Islamophobia Industry, see, for example, Nathan Lean, *The Islamophobia Industry: How the Right Manufactures Fear of Muslims* (New York: Pluto Press, 2012).

14 See, for example, Nicholas D. Kristof, "The Push to 'Otherize' Obama," *New York Times*, September 21, 2008, www.nytimes.com; Charles A. Radin, "False Alarms," *Jewish Advocate* 199:38 (September 19, 2008): 13; Fraser Sherman, "Beware! The Islamofascists Walk among Us!," *McClatchy-Tribune Business News*, May 31, 2008.

15 Debbie Schlussel, "Barack Hussein Obama: Once a Muslim, Always a Muslim," *Debbie Schlussel* (blog), December 18, 2006, www.debbieschlussel.com.

16 See the film's website: http://obsessionthemovie.com.

17 Moustafa Bayoumi, *This Muslim American Life: Dispatches from the War on Terror* (New York: NYU Press, 2015), 8.

18 Ibid., 7.

19 See, for example, Alex Seitz-Wald, "Texas Mosque and Educational Center Vandalized with Offensive Graffiti and Fire, Causing $20,000 in Damage," Think Progress, August 2, 2010, http://thinkprogress.org; Jana Shortal, "St. Cloud Graffiti May Be Investigated as Hate Crime," *KARE 11 News*, July 9, 2010, www.kare11.com; "Feces Smeared on Van Parked near Bellevue Mosque," *Seattle Times*, June 24, 2010, http://seattletimes.nwsource.com.

20 "Police: Cab Driver Stabbed by Passenger Who Asked 'Are You Muslim?,'" *NY1 News*, August 25, 2010, www.ny1.com.

21 "Islamic Center Defaced with Bacon Slices," Associated Press, October 12, 2010, www.cbsnews.com.

22 Michele McPhee, "Southwest Apologizes for Removing Muslim Passenger from Flight," *AOL Travel News*, March 16, 2011, http://news.travel.aol.com.

23 "Muslim Clerics Ordered Off Atlantic Southeast Airlines Flight," *WPIX 11*, May 8, 2011, www.wpix.com.

24 "Muslims Encouraged by Fox '24' Meeting," *U.S. Newswire*, January 13, 2005; Wayne Parry, "Muslims Protest '24' Terror Direction," *Toronto Star*, January 19, 2007, www.thestar.com.

25 Stuart Hall, "What Is This 'Black' in Black Popular Culture?," in *Black Popular Culture*, ed. Michele Wallace (Seattle: Bay Press, 1992), 24.

26 Nikhil Pal Singh, "Liberalism," in *Keywords for American Cultural Studies*, ed. Bruce Burgett and Glenn Hendler (New York: NYU Press, 2007), 139–140; Falguni Sheth, *Toward a Political Philosophy of Race* (Albany: SUNY Press, 2009).

27 Lisa Lowe, *The Intimacies of Four Continents* (Durham, NC: Duke University Press, 2015).

28 David Harvey, *A Brief History of Neoliberalism* (New York: Oxford University Press, 2005); Wendy Brown, *Undoing the Demos: Neoliberalism's Stealth Revolution* (New York: Zone Books, 2015).

29 Jodi Melamed, *Represent and Destroy: Rationalizing Violence in the New Racial Capital* (Minneapolis: University of Minnesota Press, 2011).

30 David Tusing, "Kim Kardashian Proud to Represent Middle Eastern Women," *Gulf News*, June 20, 2012, www.gulfnews.com.

31 *All American Muslim*, TLC, 2011–2012.

32 *Shahs of Sunset*, Bravo, 2012–2021.

33 Jack Shaheen, *Reel Bad Arabs: How Hollywood Vilifies a People* (Northampton, MA: Olive Branch Press, 2001).

34 Tim Brooks and Earle Marsh, eds., *The Complete Directory to Prime Time Network and Cable TV Shows, 1946–Present*, 8th ed. (New York: Ballantine Books, 2003), 777–778.

35 *Sister Wives*, TLC, 2010–2021.

36 Danielle Douglas, "Change or Die: Is TLC Reaching a Tipping Point with Its Reality Shows?," *Washington Post*, August 17, 2012, www.washingtonpost.com.

37 Danielle Douglas, "In TV's Increasingly Fractured Viewership, TLC Sticks to Reality," *Daily Herald*, August 27, 2012, www.heraldextra.com.

38 Razib Khan, "Discovery and TLC Viewers Lean Right?," *Discover Magazine*, April 14, 2010, http://blogs.discovermagazine.com.

39 Yvonne Villarreal, "Honey Boo Boo's Go-Go Rise," *Los Angeles Times*, August 29, 2012, www.latimes.com.

40 Kaylee Hultgren, "Q&A with TLC's Amy Winter," *Cablefax*, December 10, 2011, www.cablefax.com.

41 Lesley Goldberg, "TLC Cancels 'All-American Muslim,'" *Hollywood Reporter*, March 7, 2012, www.hollywoodreporter.com.

42 Lynette Rice, "TLC Cancels 'All-American Muslim,'" *Entertainment Weekly*, March 7, 2012, https://ew.com.

43 Leslie Bruce, "'Real Housewives': The Guiltiest Pleasure on Television," *Hollywood Reporter*, January 4, 2012, www.hollywoodreporter.com.

44 Erin Copple Smith, "'Affluencers' by Bravo: Defining an Audience through Cross-Promotion," *Popular Communication* (October 2012): 286–301.

45 Ibid., 292.

46 See Ann Becker, "Tracking Bravo's Rise: Bravo's Rise from Artsy Pay Channel to Network of the Hip and Smart," Broadcasting and Cable, September 30, 2006, www.broadcastingcable.com; "Bravo Media Marks Sixth Consecutive Best Year Ever Across All Key Demos, Digital Platforms, and Financial Metrics," Futon Critic, December 13, 2011, www.thefutoncritic.com.

47 Copple Smith, "'Affluencers' by Bravo."

48 Bruce, "'Real Housewives.'"

49 Melamed, *Represent and Destroy*, xvi.

50 Herman Gray, "Subject(ed) to Recognition," *American Quarterly* 65:4 (December 2013): 771–798, 784.

51 Ibid., 772.

52 Lisa Duggan, *The Twilight of Equality: Neoliberalism, Cultural Politics, and the Attack on Democracy* (New York: Beacon Press, 2003).

53 Comment by Ztlfire, IMDB, December 12, 2011, www.imdb.com.

54 Shaheen, *Reel Bad Arabs*.

55 Hussein Rashid, "Muslims Helped Legitimize Lowes' Decision to Pull Ads from All-American Muslim," *Religion Dispatches*, December 15, 2011, www.religiondispatches.org.

56 Jennifer Maher, "What Do Women Watch? Tuning In to the Compulsory Heterosexuality Channel," in *Reality TV: Remaking Television Culture*, ed. Susan Murray and Laurie Ouellette (New York: NYU Press, 2004), 197–213.

57 Brian Tashman, "Religious Right Groups Launch Fight against TLC Reality Show," *Right Wing Watch*, November 28, 2011, www.rightwingwatch.org.

58 Naomi Schaefer Riley, "Defining the 'All American Muslim,'" *Wall Street Journal*, March 22, 2012, www.wsj.com.

59 Comment by Chris Henry on Riley, "Defining the 'All American Muslim.'"

60 Comment by Stephen Spencer on Riley, "Defining the 'All American Muslim.'"

61 Comment by Barbara LeBey on Riley, "Defining the 'All American Muslim.'"

62 Alan Duke, "'All American Muslim' Sells Out, despite Lowe's Withdrawal," CNN, December 13, 2011, https://edition.cnn.com.

63 Alsultany, *Arabs and Muslims in the Media*, 21–22.

64 "The Fast and the Furious," *All-American Muslim*, TLC, season 1, episode 2, November 20, 2011.

65 "How to Marry a Muslim," *All-American Muslim*, TLC, season 1, episode 1, November 13, 2011.

66 Michael O'Connell, "TLC's 'All-American Muslim': Controversy Does Not Equal Ratings," *Hollywood Reporter*, December 14, 2011, www.hollywoodreporter.com.

67 "From the Old Country to Beverly Hills," *Shahs of Sunset*, Bravo, season 1 trailer, 2012.

68 "Image is Everything," *Shahs of Sunset*, Bravo, season 1, episode 1, March 11, 2012.

69 See Nellie Andreeva, "Bravo's 'Shahs of Sunset' Renewed for Second Season," *Deadline Hollywood*, April 17, 2012, https://deadline.com; Amanda Kondolay, "Tuesday Cable Ratings: 'Sons of Anarchy' Leads Night + 'Moonshiners,' 'Tosh.o,' 'Real Husbands of Hollywood' & More," TV by the Numbers, November 6, 2013, https://tvbythenumbers.zap2it.com; "Shahs of Sunset Season 2 Premiere Brings Huge Ratings; Plus, There's Only Room for One Persian Barbie!," Reality Tea, December 4, 2012, www.realitytea.com.

70 Mark Perigard, "Persian 'Jersey Shore' Is a Waste of TV Real Estate," *Boston Herald*, March 11, 2012, www.bostonherald.com.

71 Pete Vonder Haar, "Reality Bites: Shahs of Sunset," *Houston Press*, April 4, 2012, www.houstonpress.com.

72 Georgia Garvey, "Meet 'Shahs of Sunset's' Reza Farahan," *Chicago Tribune*, April 11, 2012, www.chicagotribune.com.

73 "Time for a Revolution?," *Economist*, April 21, 2012, www.economist.com.

74 "City Council Adopts a Resolution Condemning the Reality Television Program 'Shahs of Sunset,'" City of West Hollywood, March 22, 2012, www.weho.org.

75 See Herman Gray, *Cultural Moves: African Americans and the Politics of Representation* (Oakland, CA: University of California Press, 2005). Ella Shohat, *Israeli Cinema: East/West and the Politics of Representation* (Austin: University of Texas Press, 1989).

76 Michael J. Lee and Leigh Moscowitz, "The 'Rich Bitch': Class and Gender on *The Real Housewives of New York City*," *Feminist Media Studies* 13 (February 2012): 15.

77 Ibid.

78 "Persian Pride," *Shahs of Sunset*, Bravo, season 3, episode 6, December 8, 2013.

79 Inderpal Grewal, *Transnational America: Feminisms, Diasporas, Neoliberalisms* (Durham, NC: Duke University Press, 2005), 81; Ida Yalzadeh, "Solidarities and Solitude: Tracing the Racial Boundaries of the Iranian Diaspora" (dissertation, Brown University, 2020).

80 Grewal, *Transnational America*, 200.

81 Ibid., 206.

82 "Shahs of Sunset: Now, Here's a TV Show about Real 'All-American Muslims,'" Bare Naked Islam, March 8 and 12, 2012, www.barenakedislam.com.

83 Comment by Michelle on "Shahs of Sunset," Bare Naked Islam, March 8, 2012, www.barenakedislam.com.

84 Comment on "Shahs of Sunset," Bare Naked Islam, March 8, 2012, www.barenakedislam.com.

85 Slavoj Žižek, "Tolerance as an Ideological Category," *Critical Inquiry* (Autumn 2007), www.lacan.com.

86 Ibid.

87 "Return to the Homeland—Part 1," *Shahs of Sunset,* Bravo, season 3, episode 12, January 28, 2014; "Return to the Homeland—Part 2," *Shahs of Sunset*, Bravo, season 3, episode 13, February 4, 2014.

88 "Return to the Homeland—Part 1," *Shahs of Sunset*.

89 Ibid.

90 "Return to the Homeland—Part 2," *Shahs of Sunset*.

91 Ibid.

92 Jasbir Puar, "Rethinking Homonationalism," *International Journal of Middle East Studies* 45 (2013): 336–339.

93 Ali Behdad and Juliet A. Williams, "Neo-Orientalism," in *Globalizing American Studies*, ed. Dilip P. Gaonkar and Brian T. Edwards (Chicago and London: University of Chicago Press, 2010), 283–299.

94 "Is This 40?," *Shahs of Sunset*, Bravo, season 3, episode 14, February 11, 2014.

95 See "Hava Nagila, Hava Tequila," *Shahs of Sunset*, Bravo, season 6, episode 3, July 30, 2017; "Let My People Go," *Shahs of Sunset*, Bravo, season 6, episode 4, August 6, 2017; "Dreidels and Betrayals," *Shahs of Sunset*, Bravo, season 6, episode 5,

August 13, 2017; "Hooray for Holy Land!," *Shahs of Sunset*, Bravo, season 6, episode 6, August 20, 2017.

96   "Hava Nagila, Hava Tequila," *Shahs of Sunset.*

97   "Dreidels and Betrayals," *Shahs of Sunset.*

98   "The Day the World Changed," *All-American Muslim*, TLC, season 1, episode 7, January 1, 2012.

99   Raka Shome, "Mapping the Limits of Multiculturalism in the Context of Globalization," *International Journal of Communication* 6 (2012): 144-165, 153.

100 See Sara Ahmed, "Liberal Multiculturalism Is the Hegemony—Its [*sic*] an Empirical Fact—A response to Slavoj Žižek," *Darkmatter: In the Ruins of Imperial Culture*, February 19, 2008, www.darkmatter101.org; Slavoj Žižek, "Multiculturalism, the Reality of an Illusion," Lacan.com, January 2009, www.lacan.com.

101 "Hava Nagila, Hava Tequila," *Shahs of Sunset.*

102 "Sn 12 Ep 29: October 3, 2014," *Real Time with Bill Maher*, HBO, season 12, episode 29, October 3, 2014.

103 See Nicholas Kristof, "The Diversity of Islam," *New York Times*, October 8, 2014, www.nytimes.com; Robert Spencer, "The Diversity of Islam? Nicholas Kristof Allows His Fantasies about the 'Religion of Peace' to Obscure the Grim Reality," *Frontpage Magazine*, October 12, 2014, www.frontpagemag.com; Reza Aslan, "Bill Maher Isn't the Only One Who Misunderstands Religion," *New York Times*, October 8, 2014, www.nytimes.com; William Kilpatrick, "The Myth of Islam's Diversity," *Crisis Magazine*, November 11, 2014, www.crisismagazine.com.

104 "Reza Aslan: Bill Maher 'Not Very Sophisticated,'" CNN, September 29, 2014, www.youtube.com/watch?v=2pjxPR36qFU&t=3s.

105 Sam Harris and Maajid Nawaz, *Islam and the Future of Tolerance: A Dialogue* (Cambridge, MA: Harvard University Press, 2015), 16–17.

106 "Sn 12 Ep 29: October 3, 2014," *Real Time with Bill Maher.*

107 Sam Harris, *The End of Faith: Religion, Terror, and the Future of Reason* (New York: W. W. Norton, 2005), 15.

108 See Steven Salaita, *The Uncultured Wars* (New York: Zed Books, 2008); Alsultany, *Arabs and Muslims in the Media.*

109 For example, despite a major shift in public opinion regarding LGBT rights in the last two decades, a Gallup Poll shows that 40 percent of Americans still oppose gay marriage. See Justin McCarthy, "Americans' Support for Gay Marriage Remains High, at 61%," *Gallup*, May 19, 2016, https://news.gallup.com.

110 Many organizations have been created by Muslims to promote inclusion and rights for all, such as Muslims for Progressive Values, Feminist Islamic Trouble Makers of North America, the Al-Fatiha Foundation, Inclusive Mosque Initiative, and others.

111 Suad Joseph and Benjamin D'Harlingue, "The Wall Street Journal's Muslims," *Islamophobia Studies Journal* 1 (2012): 132–164. Also see Erik Bleich, Mira Chugh, Adrienne Goldstein, Yiyi Jin, Julien Souffrant, Emily Stabler, Maurits van der Veen,

and Varsha Vijayakumar, *Report on Media Portrayals: 2018 Newspaper Coverage of African Americans, Asian Americans, Latinos, Jews, and Muslims* (Middlebury, VT: Middlebury College Media Portrayals of Minorities Project, 2019).

112 Deepa Kumar, "The Persistence of Orientalist Myths," *Islamophobia and the Politics of Empire* (Chicago: Haymarket Books, 2012), 41–60.

113 Salaita, *The Uncultured Wars*.

114 Arun Kundnani, "Multiculturalism and Its Discontents: Left, Right and Liberal," *European Journal of Cultural Studies* 15 (2012): 155–166.

115 Harris, *End of Faith*, 30.

116 See Mamdani, *Good Muslim, Bad Muslim*; John Esposito and Dalia Mogahed, *Who Speaks for Islam?: What a Billion Muslims Really Think* (New York: Gallup Press, 2007).

117 Mohammad Hassan Khalil, *Jihad, Radicalism, and the New Atheism* (Cambridge, MA: Cambridge University Press, 2017), 101.

118 Sheth, *Political Philosophy of Race*, 14.

119 Ibid., 88.

120 Wendy Brown, *Regulating Aversion: Tolerance in the Age of Identity and Empire* (Princeton, NJ: Princeton University Press, 2008), 151.

121 Lowe, *Intimacies of Four Continents*, 2.

122 Sheth, *Political Philosophy of Race*, 14–15.

123 Mitra Rastegar, *Tolerance and Risk: Liberalism and the Racialization of Muslims* (Minneapolis: University of Minnesota Press, 2021).

124 For more on the film *Not Without My Daughter* and how Iran has been portrayed in the U.S., see Sylvia Chan-Malik, "Chadors, Feminists, Terror: The Racial Politics of US Media Representations of the 1979 Iranian Women's Movement," *Annals of the American Academy of Political and Social Science* 637 (2011): 112–140.

125 Evelyn Alsultany, "How Stereotypes Persist despite Innovations in Media Representations," in *With Stones in Our Hands*, 258–271.

126 Inderpal Grewal, *Saving the Security State: Exceptional Citizens in Twenty-First Century America* (Durham, NC: Duke University Press, 2016), 11.

127 See Nadia Marzouki, *Islam: An American Religion* (New York: Columbia University Press, 2017).

128 Edward Said, *Orientalism* (New York: Pantheon Books, 1978).

129 Joseph Massad, *Islam in Liberalism* (Chicago: University of Chicago Press, 2017), 3.

130 See Brown, *Regulating Aversion*.

131 See Dorothy Roberts, *Fatal Invention: How Science, Politics, and Big Business Recreate Race in the Twenty-first Century* (New York: New Press, 2011).

132 See Martha C. Nussbaum, *The New Religious Intolerance: Overcoming the Politics of Fear in an Anxious Age* (Cambridge, MA: Harvard University Press, 2013).

133 Pew Research Center's Forum on Religion and Public Life, "The World's Muslims: Religion, Politics, and Society," Pew Research Center, April 30, 2013, www.pewforum.org, 9–10.

134 Pew Research Center's Forum on Religion and Public Life, "US Muslims Concerned about Their Place in Society, but Continue to Believe in the American Dream: Findings from Pew Research Center's 2017 Survey of US Muslims," Pew Research Center, July 26, 2017, www.pewforum.org.

135 Bruce Drake, "How LGBT Adults See Society and How the Public Sees Them," Pew Research Center, June 25, 2013, www.pewforum.org.

136 Lauren Markoe, "Muslim Attitudes about LGBT Are Complex, Far from Universally Anti-gay," *USA Today*, June 17, 2016, www.usatoday.com; "Views about Same-Sex Marriage," Religious Landscape Study, Pew Research Center, May 12, 2015, www.pewforum.org.

137 Maher's problematic views on Muslims are not new. See Alsultany, "Regulating Sympathy for the Muslim Man," in *Arabs and Muslims in the Media*, 100–131.

138 Hassan, "Muslim Presence."

139 Evelyn Alsultany, "Argo Tries but Fails to Diffuse Stereotypes," *Islamic Monthly* 29 (2013): 104–107.

140 bell hooks, "Eating the Other: Desire and Resistance," in *Media and Cultural Studies: KeyWorks*, ed. Meenakshi Gigi Durham and Douglas M. Kellner (Malden, MA: Blackwell Publishing, 2001), 424–438.

CHAPTER 2. THE DIVERSITY COMPROMISE

1 Leila Fadel, "Muslims Are Having a Hollywood Moment," Morning Edition, NPR, October 30, 2018, www.npr.org.

2 Nico Lang, "Queer Muslims Are Still Rare on TV. One Writer Wants to Change That," *New York Times*, May 29, 2019, www.nytimes.com.

3 Jason Cohen, "Legends of Tomorrow: Muslim Hero's Inclusion Inspired by Trump," CBR.com, August 2, 2017, www.cbr.com.

4 Melena Ryzik, "Can Television Be Fair to Muslims?," *New York Times*, November 30, 2016, www.nytimes.com.

5 Donald J. Trump Statement on Preventing Muslim Immigration, December 7, 2015. See Christine Want, "Trump Website Takes Down Muslim Ban Statement after Reporters Grills Spicer in Briefing," CNBC, May 8, 2017.

6 Jeremy Diamond, "Donald Trump: Ban All Muslim Travel to U.S.," CNN, December 8, 2015, www.cnn.com.

7 Ibid.

8 Emily Stephenson and Mica Rosenberg, "Trump Signs Order to Keep Out Some Refugees, Prioritize Syrian Christians," Reuters, January 27, 2017, www.reuters.com.

9 THR Staff, "Hollywood Reacts with Outrage and Disgust over Trump's Immigration Ban," *Hollywood Reporter*, January 28, 2017, www.hollywoodreporter.com.

10 "SAG-AFTRA's Statement Regarding Executive Order on Immigration," SAG-AFTRA, February 2, 2017, www.sagaftra.org.

11 "DGA Statement Regarding the Executive Order on Immigration," Director's Guild of America, January 31, 2017, www.dga.org.

12 Marlon Wayans (@MarlonWayans), "To my Muslim people deeply sincerely apologize for this disgusting act of hate exhibited by our so called president. This is #unAmerican," Twitter, January 28, 2017, https://twitter.com/marlonwayans/status/825423377435201536?lang=en.

13 Rob Reiner (@robreiner), "Along with liar,racist,misogynist,fool,infantile,sick,narcissist-with the Muslim ban we can now add heartless & evil to DT's repertoire," Twitter, January 27, 2017, https://twitter.com/robreiner/status/825236068312109056?lang=en.

14 THR Staff, "Hollywood Reacts with Outrage."

15 "Muslim Actors Scoring More Roles in Hollywood . . . Take That, Prez Trump?," *TMZ*, March 21, 2017, www.tmz.com.

16 Sam Asi, "No Ban Here: Hollywood (Finally) Embraces Muslim and Middle Eastern Talent," Golden Globes, March 7, 2017, www.goldenglobes.com.

17 Maytha Alhassen, *Haqq and Hollywood: Illuminating 100 Years of Muslim Tropes and How to Transform Them* (New York: Pop Culture Collaborative Report, 2018), 32.

18 Mohammad Zaheer, "How Muslims Became the Good Guys on TV," BBC, June 21, 2019, www.bbc.com.

19 Devan Coggan, "Riz Ahmed Makes Oscar History as First Muslim Best Actor Nominee," *Entertainment Weekly*, March 15, 2021, http://ew.com.

20 Muniba Saleem, Sara Prot, Craig A. Anderson, and Anthony F. Lemieux, "Exposure to Muslims in Media and Support for Public Policies Harming Muslims," *Communication Research* 44 6 (August 201)). 841–69. Also see Nazita Lajevardi, "The Media Matters: Muslim American Portrayals and the Effects on Mass Attitudes," *Journal of Politics* 83:3 (July 1, 2021): 1060–79.

21 Chalabi, Mona. "Terror Attacks by Muslims Receive 357% More Press Attention, Study Finds," *Guardian*, July 20, 2018, www.theguardian.com.

22 Zaheer, "How Muslims Became the Good Guys."

23 Shea Vassar, "The 'Aila Test' Evaluates How Indigenous Women are Portrayed in Media," *Salt Lake Tribune*, May 24, 2020, www.sltrib.com.

24 Stories Matter, Walt Disney Company, https://storiesmatter.thewaltdisneycompany.com.

25 For more on Hollywood's exclusion of people of color, see Nancy Wang Yuen, *Reel Inequality: Hollywood Actors and Racism* (New Brunswick, NJ: Rutgers University Press, 2019).

26 Natalia Molina, "The Long Arc of Dispossesion: Racial Capitalism and Contested Notions of Citizenship in the U.S.-Mexico Borderlands in the Early Twentieth Century," *Western Historical Quarterly* 45 (Winter 2014): 431–447. Also see Cedric J. Robinson, *Black Marxism: The Making of the Black Radical Tradition* (Chapel Hill: University of North Carolina Press, 2000).

27 Jodi Melamed, "Racial Capitalism," *Critical Ethnic Studies* 1:1 (Spring 2015): 76–85, 77.

28 Sean Illing, "How Capitalism Reduced Diversity to a Brand," *Vox*, February 16, 2019, www.vox.com. Also see Nancy Leong, "Racial Capitalism," *Harvard Law Review* 126:8 (June 2013): 2151–2226.

29 Anamik Saha, *Race and the Cultural Industries* (Cambridge and Medford, MA: Polity Press, 2018).

30 Herman Gray, "Subject(ed) to Recognition," *American Quarterly* 65:4 (December 2013): 771–798; Saha, *Race and the Cultural Industries*.

31 Sarah Banet-Weiser, *Empowered: Popular Feminism and Popular Misogyny* (Durham, NC: Duke University Press, 2018), 23.

32 Ibid., 24.

33 Meeran Karim, "Orange Is the New Black's Commitment to Diversity Fell Short When Litchfield Added a Muslim Inmate," *Slate*, June 29, 2017, www.slate.com.

34 Ambereen Dadabhoy (@DrDadabhoy), "When you make an effort to include a Muslim character but can't be bothered to research how Muslims pray. Accurate representation matters @911LoneStar," Twitter, May 4, 2020, https://twitter.com /drdadabhoy/status/1257544680863969280?lang=en.

35 Leong, "Racial Capitalism," 2165.

36 "Peer Pressure," *7th Heaven*, WB, season 7, episode 8, November 11, 2002; "Getting to Know You," *7th Heaven*, WB, season 8, episode 7, November 3, 2003; "Isaac and Ishmael," *The West Wing*, NBC, season 3, episode 1, October 3, 2001.

37 Evelyn Alsultany, *Arabs and Muslims in the Media: Race and Representation after 9/11* (New York: NYU Press, 2012).

38 For more on #OscarsSoWhite, see Isabel Molina-Guzmán, "#OscarsSoWhite: How Stuart Hall Explains Why Nothing Changes in Hollywood and Everything Is Changing," *Critical Studies in Media Communication* 33:5 (2016): 438–454.

39 Brianna Holt, "To Make Change in Hollywood, Start with a Hashtag," *Quartz*, August 29, 2019, http://qz.com; Patrick Ryan, "#OscarsSoWhite Controversy: What You Need to Know," *USA Today*, February 2, 2016, www.usatoday.com.

40 See Caroline Framke, "John Oliver Explains the Long, Frustrating History of White Actors Playing Nonwhite Roles," *Vox*, February 22, 2016, www.vox.com; Alex Eichler, "Why Is a White Actor Playing 'Prince of Persia' Title Role?," *Atlantic*, May 26, 2010, www.theatlantic.com.

41 Nick Allen, "'I Can't Cast Mohammad So-and-So from Such-and-Such' Says Ridley Scott," *Telegraph*, November 28, 2014, www.telegraph.co.uk.

42 Peter T. Chattaway, "Box Office: *Exodus: Gods and Kings* Loses Its Audience Faster than Any Recent Bible Movie or Ridley Scott Film," *Patheos* (blog), December 21, 2014, www.patheos.com.

43 David Cox, "Did #OscarsSoWhite Work? Looking beyond Hollywood's Diversity Drought," *Guardian*, February 25, 2017, www.theguardian.com.

44 April Reign, "#OscarsSoWhite Is Still Relevant This Year," *Vanity Fair*, March 2, 2018, www.vanityfair.com.

45 Darnell Hunt, Ana-Christina Ramón, Michael Tran, Amberia Sargent, and Debanjan Roychoudhury, *Hollywood Diversity Report 2019: Five Years of Progress*

and Missed Opportunities (Los Angeles, CA: UCLA College of Social Sciences, 2019), 4.

46 Stacy L. Smith, Marc Choueiti, and Katherine Pieper, *Inclusion or Invisibility? Comprehensive Annenberg Report on Diversity in Entertainment* (Los Angeles: Media, Diversity, and Social Change Initiative, Institute for Diversity and Empowerment at Annenberg, USC Annenberg School for Communication and Journalism, 2016), 3.

47 Ibid., 4.

48 Ibid., 5.

49 Stacy L. Smith, Marc Choueiti, Katherine Pieper, Ariana Case, and Angel Choi, *Inequality in 1,100 Popular Films: Examining Portrayals of Gender, Race/Ethnicity, LGBT & Disability from 2007 to 2017* (Los Angeles: Media, Diversity, and Social Change Initiative, Institute for Diversity and Empowerment at Annenberg, USC Annenberg School for Communication and Journalism, July 2018), 2.

50 Al-Baab Khan, Dr. Katherine Pieper, Dr. Stacy L. Smith, Marc Choueiti, Kevin Yao, and Artur Tofan, *Missing & Maligned: The Reality of Muslims in Popular Global Movies* (Los Angeles: USC Annenberg Inclusion Initiative in partnership with the Ford Foundation, Pillars Fund, and Riz Ahmed/Left Handed Films, June 2021). For more on representations of Islam globally, see Kristian Petersen, ed. *New Approaches to Islam in Film* (New York: Routledge, 2021); Kristian Petersen, ed., *Muslims in the Movies: A Global Anthology* (Boston: Ilex Foundation, 2021)

51 Angelique Jackson, "Riz Ahmed, Pillars Fund, USC Annenberg & Ford Foundation Unveil the Blueprint for Muslim Inclusion," *Variety*, June 10, 2021, www variety.com

52 Alhassen, *Haqq and Hollywood*.

53 Nancy Wang Yuen, Christina Chin, Meera E. Deo, Faustina M. DuCros, Jenny Jong-Hwa Lee, and Noriko Milman, *Terrorists & Tyrants: Middle Eastern and North African (MENA) Actors in Prime Time and Streaming Television* (Los Angeles: MENA Arts Advocacy Coalition, 2018).

54 Vijay Eswaran, "The Business Case for Diversity in the Workplace Is Now Overwhelming," *World Economic Forum*, April 29, 2019, www.weforum.org. Also see Drew Harwell, "Diverse Movies Are a Huge Business. Why Doesn't Hollywood Make More?," *Washington Post*, December 15, 2015, www.washingtonpost.com.

55 Hunt et al., *Hollywood Diversity Report 2019*.

56 Zachary Burket and Marcy Kelly, "The Diversity Demand: Securing the Future of Moviegoing," White Paper, *MOVIO*, 2019, www.movio.co. Also see Evan Real, "Film Diversity Helps Drive Box Office Hits, Study Shows," *Hollywood Reporter*, October 24, 2019, www.hollywoodreporter.com.

57 Carl Rhodes, "Ethical Practice and the Business Case for LGBT Diversity: Political Insights from Judith Butler and Emmanuel Levinas," *Gender, Work, & Organization* 24:5 (September 2017): 533–546.

58 Author interview with Farah Merani, October 31, 2019.

59 Ibid.

60   Author interview with Azita Ghanizada, October 22, 2019.

61   Leong, "Racial Capitalism," 2188–2189.

62   See, for example, Nicole Martins and Kristen Harrison, "Racial and Gender Differences in the Relationship between Children's Television Use and Self-Esteem: A Longitudinal Panel Study," *Communication Research* 39:3 (2012): 338–357. Also see Sara Boboltz and Kimberly Yam, "Why On-Screen Representation Actually Matters," *Huffington Post*, February 24, 2017, www.huffpost.com.

63   Leong, "Racial Capitalism," 2169.

64   Alsultany, *Arabs and Muslims in the Media*.

65   Saha, *Race and the Cultural Industries*.

66   Ibid., 28

67   Ibid., 67.

68   Don Reisinger, "Why Disney Plus Has Added 'Outdated Cultural Depictions' Disclaimers to Some of Its Movies," *Inc.*, November 15, 2019, www.inc.com.

69   Sharareh Drury, "Disney+ 'Outdated Cultural Depictions' Disclaimer Raises Questions, Say Advocacy Groups," *Hollywood Reporter*, November 16, 2019, www.hollywoodreporter.com.

70   Ryan Lattanzio, "'Peter Pan,' 'Aristocrats' among Disney+ Titles Getting New Disclaimer for 'Negative Depictions' of Race," *IndieWire*, October 15, 2020, www.indiewire.com. Also see Bryan Pietsch, "Disney Adds Warnings for Racist Stereotypes to Some Older Films," *New York Times*, October 18, 2020, www.ny times.com; Stories Matter, https://storiesmatter.thewaltdisneycompany.com.

71   Ann-Derrick Gailliot, "Disney's Biggest Problem Isn't Casting, It's Racism," *Outline*, July 13, 2017, http://theoutline.com.

72   "Academy Establishes Representation and Inclusion Standards for Oscars Eligibility," Oscars, September 8, 2020, www.oscars.org; Guardian Staff and Agencies, "Oscars Reveal New Diversity Requirements for Best Picture Nominees," *Guardian*, September 8, 2020, www.theguardian.com.

73   Joellene Yap, "Oscars.So.Diverse," Business Careers in Entertainment Club, University of California at Berkeley, Instagram, November 27, 2020.

74   Su'ad Abdul Khabeer, "Representation as a Black Muslim Woman Is Good—and It's a Trap," Vice, March 27, 2019, www.vice.com.

75   Alison Bechdel, *Dykes to Watch Out For* (Ithaca, NY: Firebrand Books, 1986).

76   Monica Racic, "Do This Year's Best Picture Oscar Nominees Pass the Bechdel Test?," *New Yorker*, March 3, 2018, www.newyorker.com.

77   Anna Waletzko, "Why the Bechdel Test Fails Feminism," *Huffington Post*, April 27, 2015, www.huffpost.com; Alyssa Rosenberg, "In 2019, It's Time to Move beyond the Bechdel Test," *Washington Post*, December 21, 2018, www.washingtonpost.com.

78   Ben Child, "Ava DuVernay Backs 'DuVernay Test' to Monitor Racial Diversity in Hollywood," *Guardian*, February 1, 2016, www.theguardian.com; Manohla Dargis, "Sundance Fights Tide with Films Like 'The Birth of a Nation,'" *New York Times*, January 29, 2016, www.nytimes.com.

79   Dargis, "Sundance Fights Tide."

80 "The Vito Russo Test," GLAAD, 2014, www.glaad.org.

81 Vassar, "'Aila Test.'"

82 "The Riz Test: Measuring the Portrayal of Muslims on Film and TV," *Riz Test*, 2017, www.riztest.com.

83 Sue Obeidi and Evelyn Alsultany, "How Hollywood Can Better Represent Muslim Characters and Storylines," *Hollywood Reporter*, August 7, 2020, www.hollywood reporter.com.

84 Smith, et. al., *Inequality in 1,100 Popular Films*, 27–28.

85 Alhassen, *Haqq and Hollywood*, 8.

86 Sue Obeidi, "Four Ways the Entertainment Industry Can Counter Trump's Narrative of Muslims," *Variety*, February 2, 2017, http://variety.com.

87 Pillars Fund, *The Blueprint for Muslim Inclusion: Recommendations for Film Industry Professionals* (Los Angeles: Pillars Fund with Riz Ahmed/Left Handed Films, USC Annenberg Inclusion Initiative, and the Ford Foundation, June 2021).

88 Bobby Schuessler, "Nikohl Boosheri Plays a Queer Muslim Woman on TV—And Is Ready for More Representation," *Out*, June 12, 2018, www.out.com.

89 Su'ad Abdul Khabeer, "Aladdin 2.0: Hollywood Still Isn't Serious about Diversity," *Islamic Monthly*, May 28, 2019, www.theislamicmonthly.com.

90 "Conversations with Scholar of American Popular Culture: Su'ad Abdul Khabeer," *Americana: The Journal of American Popular Culture, 1900 to Present* 15:2 (Fall 2016).

91 Hussein Rashid, "Muslims in Film and Muslim Filmmaking in the United States," in *The Oxford Handbook of American Islam*, ed. Jane I. Smith and Yvonne Yazbeck Haddad (Oxford: Oxford University Press, 2015).

92 Alsultany, *Arabs and Muslims in the Media*, 23.

93 An earlier version of this section on Aladdin appeared as Evelyn Alsultany, "How the New 'Aladdin' Stacks Up against a Century of Hollywood Stereotyping," *Conversation*, May 26, 2019, http://theconversation.com.

94 Nancy Tartaglione, "'Aladdin' Passes 'Independence Day' as Will Smith's Biggest Box Office Hit," *Wrap*, June 30, 2019, www.thewrap.com.

95 Lyn Gardner, "Pure Genies," *Guardian*, July 16, 2003, www.theguardian.com.

96 A. O. Scott, "'Aladdin' Review: This Is Not What You Wished For," *New York Times*, May 22, 2019, www.nytimes.com.

97 Stina Chang, "Live-Action Remakes of 'Mulan' and 'The Little Mermaid' Continue to Push Diversity," *Study Breaks*, July 25, 2019, http://studybreaks.com.

98 Aisha Harris, "Rewriting the Past: The Shoehorned-In Progressive Messages Only Call More Attention to the Inherent Crassness," *National Post* (Ontario), May 29, 2019, B5.

99 Raina Hasan, "Disney's 'Aladdin': Diving into a Tale of American Orientalism," *Brown Girl Magazine*, June 17, 2019, www.browngirlmagazine.com.

100 جهانزیب / Jahanzeb/@Mastqalander, "The Problems with Aladdin: Orientalism, Casting, and Ramadan," *Medium* (blog), May 27, 2018, http://medium.com.

101 "'Salmon Fishing in the Yemen' and the Orientalist's Checklist," *Revolution Marginalia*, March 20, 2012, http://sohabayoumi.blogspot.com.

102 Andrea Gronvall, "Orientalism Is Alive and Well in Stephen Frears's *Victoria & Abdul*," *Chicago Reader*, October 2, 2017, www.chicagoreader.com.

103 Ella Shohat and Robert Stam, *Unthinking Eurocentrism: Multiculturalism and the Media*, (London and New York: Routledge, 1994).

104 McAlister, *Epic Encounters*.

105 Shaheen, *Reel Bad Arabs*, 9.

106 Fatima Zehra, "New Aladdin, Same Racism," *Kajal Magazine*, 2018, www.kajalmag.com; Maha Albadrawi, "How Does a Middle Eastern Critic Feel about Aladdin?," *Dazed Beauty Digital Spa* (blog), May 25, 2019, www.dazeddigital.com; Swara Ahmed, "Choose Wisely: My Very Complicated Feelings on the Live-Action 'Aladdin,'" *But Why Tho?* (podcast), October 12, 2018, http://butwhytho podcast.com; Hasan, "Disney's 'Aladdin.'"

107 John Evan Frook, "'Aladdin' Lyrics Altered," *Variety*, July 12, 1993, http://variety.com.

108 Joe Kadi, *Thinking Class: Sketches from a Cultural Worker* (Boston: South End Press, 1996), 132.

109 Jana Kasperkevic, "Poll: 30% GOP Voters Support Bombing Agrabah, the City from Aladdin," *Guardian*, December 18, 2015, www.theguardian.com.

110 Lorraine Ali, "From 'Aladdin' to Galaxy's Edge, How Hollywood Interprets Arab Culture," *Los Angeles Times*, June 14, 2019, www.latimes.com.

111 Kimberly Yam, "Disney Admits to Darkening White Actors' Skin For 'Aladdin,' Sparking Outrage," *Huffington Post*, January 9, 2018, www.huffpost.com.

112 Sima Shakeri, "Disney Criticized for Casting Naomi Scott as Princess Jasmine for 'Aladdin,'" *Huffington Post*, July 17, 2017, www.huffpost.com.

113 Piya Sinha-Roy, "How Disney Handled the Casting and Cultural Authenticity of Live-Action *Aladdin*," *Entertainment Weekly*, December 21, 2018, http://ew.com.

114 Khaled A. Beydoun, "It Doesn't Matter That an Arab Will Play Aladdin," *Al Jazeera*, July 19, 2017, www.aljazeera.com.

115 Gardner, "Pure Genies"; Shaina Oppenheimer, "1001 Lies: Everything You Know about Aladdin Is Wrong," *Haaretz*, May 19, 2019, www.haaretz.com.

116 Gardner, "Pure Genies"; Oppenheimer, "1001 Lies."

117 Oppenheimer, "1001 Lies."

118 Gardner, "Pure Genies."

119 Aditi Natasha Kini, "The Problem with 'Aladdin,'" *Bitch Media*, July 17, 2017, www.bitchmedia.org.

120 Lauren Michele Jackson, "The Racial Wonderland of Aladdin's Genie," *Vulture*, May 29, 2019, www.vulture.com. Also see Roxana Hadadi, "Review: Mena Massoud Is Perfect, but Count on Disney to Make 'Aladdin' More Orientalist than the Animated Classic Already Was," *Pajiba*, May 24, 2019, www.pajiba.com.

121 Oppenheimer, "1001 Lies."

122 Amira Jarmakani, *Imagining Arab Womanhood: The Cultural Mythology of Veils, Harems, and Belly Dancers in the US* (New York: Palgrave Macmillan, 2008), 106.

123 Ibid., 140.

124 Alsultany, *Arabs and Muslims in the Media*.

125 For more on how Jack Ryan reflects the new terrorism drama, hear an interview with me on Ahmed Ali Akbar, "Jack Ryan and Terrorism on TV," *Say Something See Something* (podcast), November 19, 2019, www.seesomethingpodcast.com.

126 "Pilot," *The Bold Type*, Freeform, season 1, episode 1, June 20, 2017.

127 "Before Tequila Sunrise," *The Bold Type*, Freeform, season 1, episode 9, August 29, 2017.

128 Alanna Bennett, "How 'The Bold Type' Finally Started to Address Kat's Blackness, One Step at a Time," BuzzFeed News, June 12, 2018, www.buzzfeednews.com.

129 "Why Adena's Story on The Bold Type Is So Important," *The Bold Type* News, Freeform, accessed September 29, 2020, https://freeform.go.com.

130 Meriam Meraay, "Why This Openly Lesbian Muslim Woman from 'The Bold Type' Is My Newest Obsession," *Muslim Girl*, July 2017, http://muslimgirl.com. For other articles that praised Adena and Kat's relationship, see Ariana Romero, "Why Summer TV Needs *The Bold Type*'s Kadena," *Refinery 29*, July 3, 2019, www.refinery29.com; Ryane DeFalco, "Nikohl Boosheri's Character on Living Life after a Breakup!," *Young Entertainment*, April 8, 2019, http://youngentertainmentmag.com; Schuessler, "Nikohl Boosheri."

131 Meraay, "My Newest Obsession."

132 NowThis (@nowthisnews), "This TV show introduced a queer, Muslim feminist, and she's badass," Twitter, July 29, 2017, https://twitter.com/nowthisnews/status/891433918108286976?lang=en.

133 Anna Silman, "8 Queer Muslim Women on the Power of 'The Bold Type," *Cut*, July 26, 2017, www.thecut.com.

134 Ibid.

135 Ibid.

136 "Pilot," *The Bold Type*.

137 Audrey Cleo Yap, "On 'The Bold Type,' Actress Nikohl Boosheri Plays a 'Confident, Empowered' Lesbian Muslim," NBC News, August 22, 2017, www.nbcnews.com.

138 "If You Can't Do It with Feeling," *The Bold Type*, Freeform, season 1, episode 4, July 25, 2017.

139 "No Feminism in the Champagne Room," *The Bold Type*, Freeform, season 1, episode 5, August 1, 2017.

140 NowThis (@nowthisnews), "This TV show."

141 Molly Alqarni (@MollyAlqarni), Sultana (@tall_girls_muse), and Elyaks O.B.E. (@realyakx), quoted in Mariam Nabbout, "Gay Muslim Character Featured in US TV Series Sparks Online Debate," Step Feed, August 1, 2017, http://stepfeed.com.

142 Blackmamba (@black2mamba), Twitter, July 30, 2017, replying to NowThis (@nowthisnews), "This TV show."

143 Derpybirdie (DerpyBirb), Twitter, July 31, 2017, replying to NowThis (@nowthisnews), "This TV show."

144 For more on sexuality in Muslim societies, see Kathryn Babayan and Afsaneh Najmbadi, *Islamicate Sexualities: Translations across Temporal Geographies of Desire*

(Cambridge, MA: Harvard University Press, 2008); Joseph A. Massad, *Desiring Arabs* (Chicago: University of Chicago Press, 2008).

145 "Messiah: Netflix Trailer 'Reveals Spoiler' to Muslim Viewers," BBC News, December 6, 2019, www.bbc.com/news.

146 CaptainSafi (@CAPTAINSAFI), Twitter, December 4, 2019, replying to Messiah (@MessiahNetflix), "Who do you think he is? Messiah begins streaming January 1, only on @netflix. #MessiahIsComing," Twitter, December 3, 2019, 7:00 a.m., https://twitter.com/CAPTAINSAFI/status/1202225180480655360.

147 Evelyn Alsultany, "Will Netflix's *Messiah* Spark Outrage at the Portrayal of Muslims?," *From the Square* (blog), NYU Press, January 10, 2020, www.fromthesquare.org.

148 "Rasha Zuabi," *LezWatch.TV*, http://lezwatchtv.com. Her character appears in episodes that aired across two seasons from January 6 to July 7, 2017.

149 Rhodes, "Ethical Practice," 534.

CHAPTER 3. RACIAL GASLIGHTING

1 Andy Campbell, "Craig Hicks Was Threat with 'Equal Opportunity Anger,' Neighbors Say," *Huffington Post*, February 13, 2017, www.huffpost.com.

2 Amanda Watts and Jason Hanna, "North Carolina Man Sentenced to Life after Pleading Guilty to the 2015 Murders of 3 Muslim College Students," CNN, June 12, 2019, www.cnn.com.

3 Diana Digangi, "Virginia Man Indicted for Rape, Murder of Muslim Teen near Mosque," CBS 6, October 16, 2017, www.ktvr.com.

4 Ibid.

5 Carol Kuruvilla, "Killer of Muslim Virginia Teen Nabra Hassanen Sentenced to Life in Prison," *Huffington Post*, April 1 2019, www.huffpost.com.

6 "Police: Nabra Hassanen Killed in 'Road Rage Incident,'" *Al Jazeera*, June 20, 2017, www.aljazeera.com.

7 Jessica Suerth, "Nabra Hassanen's Murder Highlights the Challenges of Designating a Crime a Hate Crime," CNN, June 21, 2017, www.cnn.com.

8 "CAIR Offers Condolences on Murder of Virginia Muslim Teen, Urges Probe of Possible Bias Motive," CAIR Press Release, June 19, 2017, www.cair.com.

9 Michael McGough, "Opinion: Not Every Hateful Crime Is a Hate Crime," *Los Angeles Times*, February 18, 2015, www.latimes.com.

10 Margaret Talbot, "The Story of a Hate Crime," *New Yorker*, June 22, 2015, www.newyorker.com.

11 Juliane Hammer, "Muslim Women, Anti-Muslim Hostility, and the State in the Age of Terror," in *Muslims and U.S. Politics Today: A Defining Moment*, ed. Mohammad Hassan Khalil (Cambridge, MA: Harvard University Press, 2019), 104–123.

12 Nadine Naber and Junaid Rana, "The 21st Century Problem of Anti-Muslim Racism," *Jadaliyya*, July 25, 2019, www.jadaliyya.com.

13 Khaled A. Beydoun, "Islamophobia: Toward a Legal Definition and Framework," *Columbia Law Review Online* 116.108 (2016), http://columbialawreview .org.

14 Nadine Naber, "'Look, Mohammed the Terrorist Is Coming!': Cultural Racism, Nation-Based Racism and the Intersectionality of Oppressions after 9/11," in *Race and Arab Americans Before and After 9/11: From Invisible Citizens to Visible Subjects*, ed. Amaney Jamal and Nadine Naber (Syracuse, NY: Syracuse University Press, 2008): 276–304.

15 Angela Y. Davis, *Are Prisons Obsolete?* (New York: Steven Stories Press, 2003); Ruth Wilson Gilmore, *Golden Gulag: Prisons, Surplus, Crisis, and Opposition in Globalizing California* (Berkeley: University of California Press, 2007); Mimi E. Kim, "From Carceral Feminism to Transformative Justice: Women-of-Color Feminism and Alternatives to Incarceration," *Journal of Ethnic & Cultural Diversity in Social Work* 27:3 (2018): 219–233.

16 Chris Hawley, "NYPD Monitored Muslim Students all over Northeast," Associated Press, February 18, 2012, www.ap.org.

17 Mahmood Mamdani, *Good Muslim, Bad Muslim: America, the Cold War, and the Roots of Terror* (New York: Pantheon Press, 2004).

18 Junaid Rana, "The Racial Infrastructure of the Terror-Industrial Complex," *Social Text* 34:4 (December 2016): 111–138, 114.

19 Minyvonne Burke and Shamar Walters, "4 Police Officers in San Jose Put on Leave over Racist, Anti-Muslim Facebook Posts," NBC News, June 16, 2020, www.nbcnews.com.

20 Tom my Swanson, "Controversial President of Chicago Police Union Faces Possible Firing over Inflammatory Posts on Social Media," *Chicago Tribune*, December 18, 2020, www.chicagotribune.com.

21 Will Carless and Michael Corey, "American Cops Have Openly Engaged in Islamophobia on Facebook, with No Penalties," *Reveal News*, June 2019, www .revealnews.org.

22 Ed Pilkington, "NYPD Settles Lawsuit after Illegally Spying on Muslims," *Guardian*, April 5, 2018, www.theguardian.com.

23 Caitlin Gibson, "What We Talk about When We talk about Donald Trump and Gaslighting,'" *Washington Post*, January 27, 2017, www.washingtonpost.com.

24 Rachel Bjerstedt, "Dear White America—Can We Please Stop Gaslighting Our Black Friends and Family??," *Medium* (blog), November 17, 2016, http://medium .com.

25 Greg Howard, "The Easiest Way to Get Rid of Racism? Just Redefine It," *New York Times Magazine*, August 16, 2016, www.nytimes.com.

26 Clara Lewis, *Tough on Hate?: The Cultural Politics of Hate Crimes* (New Brunswick, NJ: Rutgers University Press, 2013), 32.

27 *Ethnically Motivated Violence against Arab-Americans: Hearing Before the Subcommittee on Criminal Justice, Committee on the Judiciary, House of Representatives,*

99th Congress, Second Session (Washington, DC: US Government Printing Office, 1986).

28 Lewis, *Tough on Hate?*, 31.

29 Maxwell Leung, "Points of Departure: Re-examining the Discursive Formation of the Hate Crime Statistics Act of 1990," *Patterns of Prejudice* 52:1 (2018): 39–57.

30 Kai Wiggins and Maya Berry, "Underreported, Under Threat: Hate Crime in the United States and the Targeting of Arab Americans, 1991–2016," Arab American Institute Foundation, July 2018, http://decodehate.com. Also see David Shashwat, "A Critical Look at the FBI's Decision to Formally Start Tracking Hate Crimes against Sikhs, Arabs, and Hindus by the Year 2015," *Rutgers Race and the Law Review* 16:2 (2015): 263–288. Shashwat writes, "The categories listed on the Hate Crime Incident Report are based on race, ethnicity, sexual orientation, and/or national origin. Based on race, the FBI currently tracks hate crimes against Whites, African Americans, Native Americans, and Asians. People who do not fit into any of these race categories are categorized as 'Anti-other race.' Based on religion, the FBI tracks hate crimes against Jews, Catholics, Protestants, Muslims, and atheists. People who do not fit into these categories are labeled 'anti-other religion.' Based on ethnicity, the FBI only tracks hate crimes committed against Hispanics; the rest are categorized into anti-other ethnicity/national origin" (269).

31 Maxwell Leung, "The Politics of Arab and Muslim American Identity in a Time of Crisis: The 1986 House of Representatives Hearing on Ethnically Motivated Violence against Arab-Americans," *Islamophobia Studies Journal* 2:2 (Fall 2014): 94–113, 97.

32 *Ethnically Motivated Violence*, 1–2.

33 Leung, "Politics of Identity," 103.

34 Ibid., 110.

35 Ibid.

36 "Hate Crime Laws," US Department of Justice, March 7, 2019, http://justice.gov.

37 German Lopez, "Why It's So Hard to Prosecute a Hate Crime," *Vox*, May 23, 2017, www.vox.com.

38 "Hate Crimes," FBI, accessed October 6, 2017, http://fbi.gov.

39 Lopez, "Hard to Prosecute."

40 Heidi M. Hurd and Michael S. Moore, "Punishing Hatred and Prejudice," *Stanford Law Review* 56 (2004): 1081–1146.

41 James B. Jacobs and Kimberly Potter, *Hate Crimes: Criminal Law and Identity Politics* (Oxford: Oxford University Press, 2000).

42 Briana Alongi, "The Negative Ramifications of Hate Crime Legislation: It's Time to Reevaluate Whether Hate Crime Laws Are Beneficial to Society," *Pace Law Review* 37 (2016): 326.

43 See, for example, Michael Bronski, Ann Pellegrini, and Michael Amico, "Hate Crime Laws Don't Prevent Violence against LGBT People," *Nation*, October 2, 2013, http://thenation.com; Doug Meyer, "Resisting Hate Crime Discourse:

Queer and Intersectional Challenges to Neoliberal Hate Crime Laws," *Critical Criminology* 22 (2014): 113–125; Dean Spade, *Normal Life: Administrative Violence, Critical Trans Politics, and the Limits of Law* (Durham, NC: Duke University Press, 2015).

44 Leung, "Points of Departure," 40.

45 *Investigation of the Chicago Police Department* (Washington, DC: United States Department of Justice, Civil Rights Division and United States Attorney's Office, January 13, 2017), 141, http://justice.gov.

46 Lynn Langton, "Hate Crime Victimization, 2004–2015," Bureau of Justice Statistics, June 29, 2017, http://bjs.gov.

47 Ibid.

48 Bronski, Pellegrini, and Amico, "Hate Crime Laws."

49 Samantha Vicent, "November Trial Date Set for Tulsa Man Charged with Murder, Hate Crime," *Tulsa World*, March 22, 2017, www.tulsaworld.com. Also see Christopher Mathias, "The Killing of Khalid Jabara Is an American Tragedy," *Huffington Post*, August 23, 2016, www.huffpost.com; Mallory Simon, Sara Sidner, and Jason Morris, "After a Killing Driven by Hate, Family Wonders 'How Many Red Flags Does It Take?'" CNN, September 27, 2017.

50 Another more recent omission from official statistics is the case of Heather Heyer, a thirty-two-year-old white woman killed by a white supremacist at the Unite the Right Rally in Charlottesville, Virginia, on August 12, 2017 (exactly one year after Khalid Jabara was killed). Recognizing precisely this problem, the Khalid Jabara and Heather Heyer No Hate Act was passed on May 15, 2020, by the US House of Representatives, It will be considered by the US Senate to enhance the 1990 Hate Crimes Statistics Act by improving national hate crime reporting and data collection and helping hate crime victims receive support. See Susan Bro and Haifa Jabara, "Hate Crimes Are Slipping Through the Cracks," *New York Times*, August 12, 2019, www.nytimes.com; Mallory Simon and Sara Sidner, "Heather Heyer's Not on This FBI List. How Hate Crimes Become Invisible," CNN, August 12, 2019, www.cnn.com; Jabara-Heyer NO HATE Act of 2019–2020, S. 2043, 116th Cong. (2019), http://congress.gov.

51 Kai Wiggins and Maya Berry, "Underreported, Under Threat: Hate Crime in the United States and the Targeting of Arab Americans, 1991–2016," Arab American Institute Foundation, July 2018, http://decodehate.com.

52 Brian Levin, *Responses to the Increase in Religious Hate Crimes* (San Bernardino: California State University Center for the Study of Hate and Extremism; Washington, DC: United States Senate Committee on the Judiciary, Center for the Study of Hate and Extremism, May 2, 2017), www.csusb.edu.

53 German Lopez, "A New FBI Report Says Hate Crimes—Especially against Muslims—Went Up in 2016," *Vox*, November 13, 2017, www.vox.com. Also see Lynn Langton and Madeline Masucci, "Hate Crime Victimization, 2004–2015," Special Report, Hate Crime Series (Washington, DC: Bureau of Justice Statistics, June 29, 2017).

54 Ken Schwencke, "Why America Fails at Gathering Hate Crimes Statistics," *Pro-Publica*, December 4, 2017, http://propublica.org.

55 Maya Berry, "Charlottesville Won't Show Up in Federal Hate Crime Stats," *Washington Post*, September 21, 2018, www.washingtonpost.com.

56 See Mazin Sidahmed, "Family of Murdered New York Imam Demand Suspect to Be Tried for Hate Crime," *Guardian*, August 18, 2016, http://theguardian.com; Rick Rojas, Noah Remnick, and Emily Palmer, "First-Degree Murder Charge Added in Killing of Queens Imam and Aide," *New York Times*, August 16, 2016, www.nytimes.com; Georgett Roberts and Emily Saul, "Judge Denied Special Hearing for Alleged Imam Killer," *New York Post*, April 6, 2017, http://nypost.com.

57 Larry Celona, Tina Moore, and Shawn Cohen, "Man Charged in Murder of Imam, Assistant Felt 'Hatred' toward Muslims," *New York Post*, August 15, 2016, http://nypost.com.

58 Al Baker, "Imam's Killer Is Sentenced, but Motive Remains a Mystery," *New York Times*, June 6, 2018, www.nytimes.com.

59 Mila Madison, "Her Name was Ally Lee Steinfeld," *Transgender Universe*, September 27, 2017, http://transgenderuniverse.com; Jarrett Lyons, "Why Is the Brutal Murder of This Trans Teen Not a Hate Crime?," *Salon*, September 28, 2017, www.salon.com.

60 Sarah Friedmann, "Who Was Ally Lee Steinfeld? The Transgender Teen Was Allegedly Brutally Murdered," *Bustle*, September 27, 2017, www.bustle.com; Dakin Andone and Deanna Hackney, "Prosecutor: No Hate Crime Charges in Murder of Mutilated Transgender Teen," CNN, October 1, 2017, www.cnn.com.

61 Andone and Hackney, "Prosecutor: No Hate Crime Charges."

62 Ryan Roschke, "How Missouri's Hate Crime Legislation Is Failing Ally Lee Steinfeld," *Popsugar*, October 8, 2017, www.popsugar.com

63 Andone and Hackney, "Prosecutor: No Hate Crime Charges."

64 Monica Davey, "An Iowa Teenager Was Killed in an Alley, but Was It a Hate Crime?," *New York Times*, October 26, 2017, www.nytimes.com.

65 Monica Davey, "Guilty Verdict in the Death of a Gender-Fluid Iowa Teenager," *New York Times*, November 3, 2017, www.nytimes.com; Stephanie Gruber-Miller, "Second Defendant Is Found Guilty of Murdering Iowa Teenager Kedarie Johnson," *Des Moines Register*, October 5, 2018, www.desmoinesregister.com.

66 Naber, "'Look, Mohammed!'"

67 McGough, "Not Every Hateful Crime."

68 Andy Campbell, "Craig Hicks Was Threat with 'Equal Opportunity Anger,' Neighbors Say," *Huffington Post*, February 13, 2017, www.huffpost.com.

69 Talbot, "Story of a Hate Crime."

70 Jonathan Metzl, "NC Shooting: When a Parking Dispute Is Also a Crime of Hate," MSNBC, February 14, 2015, www.msnbc.com.

71 Ibid.

72 Spade, *Normal Life*, 42.

73 See, for example, Eduardo Bonilla-Silva, *Racism without Racists: Color-Blind Racism and the Persistence of Racism Inequality in America* (Lanham, MD: Rowman & Littlefield, 2003); Ian Haney López, *Dog Whistle Politics: How Coded Racial Appeals Have Reinvented Racism and Wrecked the Middle Class* (Oxford: Oxford University Press, 2014).

74 Nathan Lean, "The Chapel Hill Shooting Was Anything But a Dispute over Parking," ICNA Council for Social Justice, February 24, 2017, http://icnacsj.org.

75 Mohammad Abu-Salha and Farris Barakat, "Families of Chapel Hill Shooting Victims Speak Out on Anti-Muslim Hate," *Time*, February 10, 2016, http://time.com.

76 Rick Massim and Amanda Iacone, "Police: Road Rage Blamed for Killing of Va. Muslim Teen," WTOP, June 19, 2017, http://wtop.com.

77 Matthew Barakat, "Police: Road Rage Led to Bat Attack, Muslim Teen's Death," Associated Press, June 19, 2017, www.apnews.com.

78 FCPD Media Relations Bureau, "Road Rage Incident Leads to Murder of Reston Teenager: Evidence in Case Does Not Point to Hate Crime," Fairfax County Police Department News, June 19, 2017, http://fcpdnews.wordpress.com.

79 Ibid.

80 Christopher Brennan, "South Carolina Man Sets Fire to Memorial for Slain Virginia Teen Nabra Hassanen," *New York Daily News*, June 21, 2017, www.nydailynews.com.

81 Sarah Rankin, "Muslims: Was Girl's Killing a Hate Crime?," Associated Press, June 21, 2017, http://apnews.com.

82 Suerth, "Nabra Hassanen's Murder."

83 Antonia Blumberg "Police Call Teen's Beating Death 'Road Rage.' That Doesn't Sit Well with Muslim Americans," *Huffington Post*, June 20, 2017, www.huffpost.com.

84 Petula Dvorak, "Nabra Hassanen's Death May Not Legally Be a Hate Crime, but It Sure Feels Hateful," *Washington Post*, June 19, 2017, www.washingtonpost.com.

85 Azmia Magane, "Don't Tell Me Nabra Hassanen, the Muslim Girl Who Was Kidnapped outside a Mosque and Murdered, Was a Victim of Road Rage," *Independent*, June 21, 2017, www.independent.co.uk.

86 Mona Eltahawy, "Don't Tell Me Nabra Hassanen's Murder Wasn't a Hate Crime," *Cut*, June 19, 2017, www.thecut.com.

87 Yasmin Jilwani, *Discourses of Denial: Mediations of Race, Gender, and Violence* (Vancouver: University of British Columbia Press, 2006), 87.

88 See, for example, Phyllis B. Gerstenfeld, "Smile When You Call Me That!: The Problems with Punishing Hate Motivated Behavior," *Behavioral Sciences and the Law* 10 (1992): 259–285.

89 Lopez, "Hard to Prosecute."

90 Lewis, *Tough on Hate?*, 23–24.

91 Ibid., 39.

92 Meyer, "Resisting Hate Crime Discourse." 117.

93 Ibid., 118.

94 Massimo and Iacone, "Police: Road Rage Blamed."

95 Roschke, "Missouri's Hate Crime Legislation."

96 Daniel Greenfield, "Leftist Illegalophilia, Not Islamophobia, Killed a Muslim Teen," *Frontpage Magazine*, June 26, 2017, http://frontpagemag.com.

97 Ibid.

98 See responses to Ann Coulter (@AnnCoulter), "When a 'Dreamer' murders a Muslim, does the media report it?," Twitter, June 18, 2017, https://twitter.com /AnnCoulter/status/876614502892154880.

99 Greenfield, "Leftist Illegalophilia."

100 "UPDATE: No Evidence of Gang Affiliation for Nabra Hassanen Murder Suspect," *Fairfax County Police Department News*, June 28, 2017, http://fcpdnews.wordpress .com.

101 Catherine Douglas Moran, "Darwin Martinez-Torres Pleads Guilty to Murder of Nabra Hassanen," *Reston Now*, November 28, 2018, www.restonnow.com.

102 Armando Trull and Tamika Smith, "Update: Where Is the Investigation into Nabra Hassanen's Death?," WAMU, June 28, 2017, www.wamu.org.

103 Natalia Molina, *How Race Is Made in America: Immigration, Citizenship, and the Historical Power of Racial Scripts* (Berkeley: University of California Press, 2014).

104 Harriet Sinclair, "Who Is Darwin Martinez-Torres? Suspect in Murder of Muslim Teen Is Held by ICE," *Newsweek*, June 20, 2017, www.newsweek.com.

105 Metzl, "NC Shooting."

106 Lisa Sorg, "Why Did Craig Hicks Kill Three Muslim Students? Because He Lost His Humanity," *Indy Week*, February 13, 2015, www.indyweek.com.

107 Andrea Huncar, "Mustafa Mattan Shot Dead through Fort McMurray Apartment Door," CBC News, February 12, 2015, www.cbc.ca.

108 "Chapel Hill Shooting: Muslim Leaders Criticize Media Coverage," NBC News, February 17, 2015, www.nbcnews.com; Ali M. Latif, " 'Only Newsworthy When behind a Gun, Not in Front of It': On Media Coverage of #ChapelHillShooting," *Ceasefire*, February 14, 2015, www.ceasefiremagazine.co.uk.

109 BBC Trending, "How North Carolina Murders Sparked Global Outrage," BBC News, February 11, 2015, www.bbc.com.

110 Samira, @SSamiraSR, "The fact that the only info I am getting about the #ChapelHillshooting is via twitter showcases how permeating Islamophobia is in media," Twitter, February 10, 2015, https://twitter.com/SSamiraSR/status /565391967727910913.

111 Abdullah Azada Khenjani, Facebook post, February 11, 2015, www.facebook.com /abdullah.khenjani/posts/1037648879584422.

112 Greg Botelho and Ralph Ellis, "Chapel Hill Muslim Shooting Victim Said She Felt Blessed to Be an American," CNN, February 13, 2015, www.cnn.com.

113 Evelyn Alsultany, *Arabs and Muslims in the Media: Race and Representation after 9/11* (New York: NYU Press, 2012), 71–99.

114 Spade, *Normal Life*, 47.

115 Ibid., 14–15.

116 "Afghan Civilians," Cost of War, Watson Institute for International and Public Affairs, Brown University, January 2020, http://watson.brown.edu.

117 Iraq Body Count, www.iraqbodycount.org.

118 Muneer I. Ahmad, "A Rage Shared by Law: Post-September 11 Racial Violence as Crimes of Passion," *California Law Review* 92:5 (2004): 1259–1330.

119 Ibid., 1269, 1323.

120 All Dulles Area Muslim Society (ADAMS Center), www.adamscenter.org.

121 Botelho and Ellis, "Victim Said She Felt Blessed."

122 The letter to Attorney General Eric Holder regarding the Chapel Hill murders was signed by 150 organizations, February 13, 2015, http://muslimadvocates.org.

123 Erik Love, *Islamophobia and Racism in America* (New York: NYU Press, 2017).

124 Ibid., 23.

125 Dean Spade, "On Normal Life: Dean Spade, Interviewed by Natalie Oswin," *Society + Space*, January 15, 2014, www.societyandspace.org.

126 Nicole Nguyen, *Suspect Communities: Anti-Muslim Racism and the Domestic War on Terror* (Minneapolis: University of Minnesota Press, 2019), 10.

127 Moustafa Bayoumi, "Why Did Cup Foods Call the Cops on George Floyd?," *New York Times*, June 17, 2020, www.nytimes.com. The issue is not just a lack of engagement; Su'ad Abdul Khabeer shows how nonblack Muslims engage in Black expressions of Islam, "Muslim cool," to fashion themselves as authentically Muslim in the US. See Su'ad Abdul Khabeer, *Muslim Cool: Race, Religion, and Hip Hop in the United States* (New York: NYU Press, 2016).

128 Anas White, "A Black Muslim Response to #MuslimLivesMatter," *MuslimARC*, February 12, 2015, www.muslimarc.org.

129 Namira Islam, "I Caution All to Abstain from Using #MuslimLivesMatter," *MuslimARC*, Feburary 17, 2015, www.muslimarc.org.

130 Sabah, "Stop Using #MuslimLivesMatter," *Muslim Girl*, February 12, 2015, http://muslimgirl.com; Julie Walker, "#BlackLivesMatter Founders: Please Stop Co-opting Our Hashtag," *Root*, March 17, 2015, www.theroot.com; Bilal Mahmud, "Stop Using #MuslimLivesMatter," *Oppressed Peoples Online Word*, February 17, 2015, http://oppressedpeoplesonlineword.ning.com.

131 Khaled A. Beydoun and Margari Hill, "The Colour of Muslim Mourning: Why Didn't the Killing of a Black Muslim Inspire the Same Outrage as the Chapel Hill Shootings?," Al Jazeera, February 15, 2015, www.aljazeera.com.

132 "Virginia," The Arab American Institute Foundation, 2011, based on "2005–2009 American Community Survey Rolling 5-Year Average—U.S. Census Bureau."

133 Hannah Allam, "Muslims Mourn Teen Girl's Brutal Beating Death after Leaving Mosque in Virginia," BuzzFeed News, June 21, 2017, www.buzzfeed.com.

134 Sofia Arias, "Solidarity Is Not Co-optation," *Socialist Worker*, March 5, 2015, http://socialistworker.org.

135 Elizabeth A. Povinelli, *The Cunning of Recognition: Indigenous Alterities and the Making of Australian Multiculturalism* (Durham, NC: Duke University Press, 2002), 7.

136 Christina B. Hanhardt, *Safe Space: Gay Neighborhood History and the Politics of Violence* (Durham, NC: Duke University Press, 2013), 163.

137 Ahmad, "Rage Shared by Law," 1325.

138 Sherene Razack, "Settler Colonialism, Policing and Racial Terror: The Police Shooting of Loreal Tsingine," *Feminist Legal Studies* 28 (2020): 1–20.

139 James A. Tyner, "Hate-Crimes as Racial Violence: A Critique of the Exceptional," *Social & Cultural Geography* 17:8 (2016): 1063.

140 Ibid., 1071, 1073.

141 Rana, "Racial Infrastructure." Sherene Razack also uses the term "racial infrastructure" but specifically to analyze policing. See Razack, "Settler Colonialism."

142 Louis Althusser, "Ideology and Ideological State Apparatuses," in *Lenin and Philosophy and Other Essays* (New York: Verso Press, 1970).

143 Nicole Hong and Jonah E. Bromwich, "Asian-Americans Are Being Attacked. Why Are Hate Crime Charges So Rare?," *New York Times*, March 18, 2021, www.nytimes.com.

144 Muneer I. Ahmad, "Homeland Insecurities: Racial Violence the Day after 9/11," *Race/Ethnicity* 4:3 (Summer 2011): 337–350.

145 Molina, *How Race Is Made*, 21.

146 Chandan Reddy, *Freedom with Violence: Race, Sexuality, and the US State* (Durham, NC: Duke University Press, 2011), 13.

CHAPTER 4. RACIAL PURGING

1 Syed Rizwan Farook was Pakistani American and his wife, Tashfeen Malik, had recently moved to the US from Pakistan with a permanent resident visa. See, for example, Doug McIntyre, "A New Report on the San Bernardino Terrorist Attack Details the Shootout with Police," *San Bernardino Sun*, May 25, 2017, www.sbsun.com.

2 See, for example, Mark Berman, "One Year after the San Bernardino attack, Police Offer a Possible Motive as Questions Still Linger," *Washington Post*, December 2, 2016, www.washingtonpost.com.

3 Jeremy Diamond, "Donald Trump: Ban all Muslim Travel to U.S.," CNN, December 8, 2015, www.cnn.com.

4 Jessica Chasmar, "Michael Moore Holds 'We Are All Muslim' Sign in front of Trump Tower," *Washington Times*, December 17, 2015, www.washingtontimes.com.

5 Michael Moore, "We Are All Muslim," December 2015, http://michaelmoore.com.

6 Janel Saldana, "Miss Puerto Rico Destiny Velez Stands with Donald Trump on Muslim Ban," *Latin Times*, December 18, 2015, www.latintimes.com; Kaitlyn D'Onofrio, "Miss Puerto Rico Fired Off Anti-Muslim Rant," *DiversityInc*, December 22, 2015, www.diversityinc.com.

7 "A Message from the Miss Puerto Rico Organization," Miss Puerto Rico, Facebook, December 19, 2015, www.facebook.com.

8 Lee Moran, "Miss Puerto Rico Suspended for Anti-Muslim Comments on Twitter," *Huffington Post*, December 20, 2015, www.huffingtonpost.com.

9   "Big Stone GOP Chairman Steps Down after Anti-Muslim Remarks," *Star Tribune*, November 29, 2014, www.startribune.com.

10 Alex Lazar, "Virginia GOP Official Who Posted Anti-Muslim Facebook Comments Resigns," *Huffington Post*, August 7, 2015, www.huffpost.com.

11 "New Jersey School Board Member Quits over Anti-Muslim Comments," Reuters, April 22, 2016, www.reuters.com.

12 For example, see Ibrahim Hooper, "CAIR Calls for Firing of Anti-Muslim USAID Religious Freedom Advisor Mark Kevin Lloyd," Press Release, Council on American-Islamic Relations, May 27, 2020, www.cair.com.

13 Jennifer Calfas, "Starbucks Is Closing All Its U.S. Stores for Diversity Training Day. Experts Say That's Not Enough," *Time*, May 28, 2018, https://time.com. Also see Linda Dahlstrom, "Beyond May 29: Lessons from Starbucks Anti-bias Training—and What's Next," Starbucks Stories & News, July 2, 2018, http://stories.starbucks.com.

14 Marc J. Spears, "The Basketball Team, the Atlanta Hawks Make Inclusion a Priority after Embarrassing Episodes," *Undefeated*, October 7, 2016, https://theundefeated.com.

15 Ligaya Mishan, "The Long and Tortured History of Cancel Culture," *New York Times Style Magazine*, December 3, 2020, www.nytimes.com.

16 My use of "neoliberal multiculturalism" comes from Jodi Melamed, *Represent and Destroy: Rationalizing Violence in the New Racial Capitalism* (Minneapolis: University of Minnesota Press, 2011).

17 William Weinbaum, "The Legacy of Al Campanis," ESPN, April 1, 2012, www.espn.com.

18 Ibid.; Ian Casselberry, "Video: Al Campanis' Infamous Remarks on Minority Hiring in MLB, 25 Years Ago," *Bleacher Report*, April 13, 2012, http://bleacherreport.com.

19 Grahame L. Jones, "Dodgers Fire Campanis over Racial Remarks," *Los Angeles Times*, April 9, 1987, http://articles.latimes.com.

20 Jay Sharbutt, "Jimmy 'the Greek' Is Fired by CBS," *Los Angeles Times*, January 17, 1988, http://articles.latimes.com.

21 George Solomon, "'Jimmy the Greek' Fired by CBS for His Remarks," *Washington Post*, January 17, 1988, www.washingtonpost.com.

22 Leonard Shapiro, "Golf Analyst Dropped after Sexist Interview Verified," *Moscow Times*, January 11, 1996, http://old.themoscowtimes.com.

23 Richard Sandomir, "CBS Pulls Wright Off the Air," *New York Times*, January 9, 1996, www.nytimes.com.

24 See, for example, Azi Paybarah, "He Videotaped the Rodney King Beating. Now, He Is Auctioning the Camera," *New York Times*, July 29, 2020, www.nytimes.com. For more on Rodney King, see Robert Gooding-Williams, ed., *Reading Rodney King/Reading Racial Uprising* (New York: Routledge, 1993).

25 Audrey Gillan, "Mel Gibson Apologises for Anti-Semitic Abuse," *Guardian*, July 31, 2006, www.theguardian.com.

26 Brian Stelter, "CNN Fires Rick Sanchez for Remarks in Interview," *New York Times*, October 1, 2010, www.nytimes.com.

27 James Lull and Stephen Hinerman, "The Search for Scandal," in *Media Scandals*, ed. James Lull and Stephen Hinerman (New York: Columbia University Press, 1998), 1–33.

28 Ibid., 25.

29 Ari Adut, *On Scandal: Moral Disturbances in Society, Politics, and Art* (New York: Cambridge University Press, 2008), 12.

30 Laura Kipnis, *How to Become a Scandal: Adventures in Bad Behavior* (New York: Picador, 2011), xv.

31 Erik Bleich, *The Freedom to Be Racist?: How the United States and Europe Preserve Freedom and Combat Racism* (New York: Oxford University Press, 2011).

32 "On Mexican Immigrants: 'They're Bringing Drugs,' Crime and Are 'Rapists,'" *Newsday*, November 9, 2016, www.newsday.com.

33 Ahiza Garcia, "These Are the Only Two Owners of Color in the NFL," CNN, May 18, 2018, https://money.cnn.com.

34 Drew Harwell, "The Staggering Numbers That Prove Hollywood Has a Serious Race Problem," *Washington Post*, February 23, 2016, www.washingtonpost.com.

35 Stacy Jones, "White Men Account for 72% of Corporate Leadership at 16 of the Fortune 500 Companies," *Fortune*, June 9, 2017, https://fortune.com.

36 Jessica Baron, "We Know Diversity Is Good for Business, So Why Do Corporate Leaders Remain Predominantly White and Male?," *Diversity Jobs*, June 17, 2019, www.diversityjobs.com.

37 "Number of Fortune 500 Boards with Over 40 Percent Diversity Doubled in 2012," *Catalyst*, January 16, 2019, www.catalyst.org.

38 Miki Tsusaka, "Companies Have No Excuse for 'Diversity Fatigue,'" *World Economic Forum*, January 3, 2019, www.weforum.org.

39 Anthony De Bono, "LeBron James Called NFL Owners 'Old White Men,' but Is That Still Accurate?," *Global Sport Matters*, January 28, 2019, https://globalsport matters.com.

40 Ken Belson, "Only Three N.F.L. Head Coaches Are Black. 'It's Embarrassing,'" *New York Times*, December 31, 2019, www.nytimes.com; Ken Belson, "N.F.L. Owners Will Review Incentives to Boost Racial Diversity," *New York Times*, May 15, 2020, www.nytimes.com.

41 Mishan, "Long and Tortured History."

42 Aja Romano, "Is Cancel Culture a Mob Mentality, or a Long Overdue Way of Speaking Truth to Power?," *Vox*, August 25, 2020, www.vox.com.

43 Aja Romano, "The Second Wave of 'Cancel Culture,'" *Vox*, May 5, 2021, www.vox .com; Clyde McGrady, "The Strange Journey of 'Cancel.' From a Black-culture Punchline to a White-Grievance Watchword," *Washington Post*, April 2, 2021, www.washingtonpost.com.

44 Danielle Kurtzleben, "When Republicans Attack 'Cancel Culture,' What Does It Mean?," NPR, February 10, 2021, www.npr.org.

45 "Resolution Upholding the First Amendment to the Constitution of the United States of America in Response to the Coronavirus Pandemic and the Cancel Culture Movement," Republican National Committee, 2020, www.gop.com.

46 Mishan, "Long and Tortured History."

47 Alicia Shepard, "Juan Williams, NPR and Fox News," NPR, February 11, 2009, www.npr.org.

48 *The O'Reilly Factor*, Fox News, January 26, 2009.

49 Danny Shea, "NPR Tells Fox News: Please Don't Associate Juan Williams with Us," *Huffington Post*, March 15, 2009, www.huffpost.com.

50 "Williams Defends O'Reilly's 'Muslims Killed Us on 9/11' Remark: 'I Get Worried' with Them on Airplanes." *ThinkProgress*, October 19, 2010, http://archive.think progress.org.

51 Ibid.

52 Juan Williams, *Muzzled: The Assault on Honest Debate* (New York: Broadway Paperbacks, 2011).

53 For example, see Juan Williams, "Banish the Bling: A Culture of Failure Taints Black America," *Washington Post*, August 21, 2006, www.washingtonpost.com.

54 "'Kramer' Apologizes, Says He's Not Racist," CBS News, November 20, 2006, www.cbsnews.com.

55 Vidya Rao, "Paula Deen: I Would Not Have Fired Me," *Today*, June 23, 2013, www.today.com.

56 Rick Schindler, "Dr. Laura: Calling Me a Racist Is 'Absurd,'" *Today*, January 20, 2011, www.today.com.

57 Eugene Scott, "Donald Trump: I'm the Least Racist Person,'" CNN, September 15, 2016, www.cnn.com.

58 Kenneth W. Stikkers, "'. . . But I'm Not Racist': Toward a Pragmatic Conception of 'Racism,'" *Pluralist* 9:3 (2014): 1–17, 4.

59 My use of "interpellate" comes from Louis Althusser, "Ideology and Ideological State Apparatuses," in *Lenin and Philosophy and Other Essays* (New York: Verso Press, 1970).

60 Williams, *Muzzled*, 6.

61 Ibid., 7.

62 Ibid., 8.

63 Ibid., 94.

64 See, for example, Mahmood Mamdani on "culture talk," in *Good Muslim, Bad Muslim: America, the Cold War, and the Roots of Terror* (New York: Pantheon Press, 2004), and Sherene Razack on "culturalizing violence," in *Casting Out: The Eviction of Muslims from Western Law and Politics* (Toronto: University of Toronto Press, 2008).

65 Williams, *Muzzled*, 115.

66 Eve Bowler, "American Deaths in Terrorism vs. Gun Violence in One Graph," CNN, October 3, 2016, www.cnn.com.

67 Matea Gold, "CNN Mideast Affairs Editor Loses Post after Tweeting Her Respect for Militant Cleric," *Los Angeles Times*, July 7, 2010, http://latimesblogs.latimes.com.

68 Octavia Nasr, "Nasr Explains Controversial Tweet on Lebanese Cleric," CNN, July 6, 2010, http://news.blogs.cnn.com.

69 Williams, *Muzzled*, 116

70 See, for example, Rashid Khalidi, *Resurrecting Empire: Western Footprints and America's Perilous Path in the Middle East* (New York: Beacon Press, 2004); Mamdani, *Good Muslim, Bad Muslim*; Deepa Kumar, *Islamophobia and the Politics of Empire* (Chicago: Haymarket Books, 2012).

71 Williams, *Muzzled*, 27.

72 Ibid., 30.

73 Wendy Brown and Rainer Forst, "The Power of Tolerance: A Debate between Wendy Brown and Rainer Forst," in *The Power of Tolerance: A Debate*, ed. Luca Di Blasi and Christopher F. Holzhey (New York: Columbia University Press, 2014).

74 Sarah Banet-Weiser, "'Ruined' Lives: Mediated White Male Victimhood," *European Journal of Cultural Studies* 24:1 (2021): 60–80, 60.

75 Ibid., 67.

76 Ibid., 76.

77 Ibid., 72.

78 Posted by Kitchendragon50, October 22, 2010, in response to Andrew Caumont, "Post User Polls: Was NPR Right to Fire Juan Williams?," *Washington Post*, October 22, 2010, http://views.washingtonpost.com.

79 Posted by Jack29, October 22, 2010, in response to Caumont, "Post User Polls."

80 Posted by Bellsauf, October 22, 2010, in response to Caumont, "Post User Polls."

81 Posted by Nwhiker, October 22, 2010, in response to Caumont, "Post User Polls."

82 "Juan Williams Gets $2 Million, Three-Year Contract with Fox News: LAT," *Huffington Post*, October 21, 2010, www.huffpost.com.

83 Jack Mirkinson, "NPR's Juan Williams Firing Prompts Conservative Backlash," *Huffington Post*, October 21, 2010, www.huffpost.com.

84 Ibid.

85 Ibid.

86 Kevin Roderick, "NPR Memo to Stations: Why We Fired Juan Williams," *LA Observed*, October 21, 2010, www.laobserved.com.

87 Wendy Brown, *Undoing the Demos: Neoliberalism's Stealth Revolution* (New York: Zone Books, 2015), 176.

88 Bill Carter, "ABC to End 'Politically Incorrect,'" *New York Times*, May 14, 2002, www.nytimes.com.

89 Romano, "Mob Mentality."

90 Sarah Banet-Weiser, "Popular Feminism: The Scandal of the Comeback Story," *Los Angeles Review of Books*, May 25, 2018, www.lareviewofbooks.org.

91 Romano, "The Second Wave."

92 Ibid.

93 Christopher P. Campbell, "Commodifying the Resistance: Wokeness, Whiteness, and the Historical Persistence of Racism," in *Media, Myth, and Millennials:*

Critical Perspectives on Race and Culture, ed. Christopher P. Campbell and Loren Saxton Coleman (Lanham, MD: Lexington Books, 2019), 12–13.

94 Sarah Banet-Weiser, *Authentic™: The Politics of Ambivalence in a Brand Culture* (New York: NYU Press, 2012).

95 Sarah Banet-Weiser and Roopali Mukherjee, eds., *Commodity Activism: Cultural Resistance in Neoliberal Times* (New York: NYU Press, 2012).

96 "Section 4: Demographics and Political Views of New Audiences," Pew Research Center, September 27, 2012, http://pewresearch.org.

97 Archie B. Carroll, "A History of Corporate Social Responsibility: Concepts and Practices," in *The Oxford Handbook of Social Corporate Responsibility*, ed. Andrew Crane, Abagail McWilliams, Dirk Matten, Jeremy Moon, and Donald S. Siegel (Oxford: Oxford University Press, 2008), 20–21.

98 Carroll, "History of Corporate Social Responsibility." For more on corporate social responsibility, see Patrick Murphy, "An Evolution: Corporate Social Responsiveness," *University of Michigan Business Review* (November 1978); Henry Eilbert and Robert I. Parket, "The Current Status of Corporate Social Responsibility," *Business Horizons* 16 (August 1973): 5–14; David Vogel, *The Market for Virtue; The Potential and Limits of Corporate Social Responsibility* (Washington, DC: Brookings Institution, 2005); Inger Stole, "Philanthropy as Public Relations: A Critical Reception on Cause Marketing," *International Journal of Communication* 2 (2008): 21; Milton Friedman, "The Social Responsibility of Business is to Increase Its Profits," *New York Times Magazine*, September 13, 1970.

99 Carroll, "History of Corporate Social Responsibility," 21.

100 Banet-Weiser, *Authentic™*, 118.

101 Ibid., 43.

102 Ibid., 126–127.

103 Ibid., 148.

104 Alex Abad-Santos, "Why the Social Media Boycott over Colin Kaepernick Is a Win for Nike," *Vox*, September 6, 2018, www.vox.com.

105 Martha Kelner, "Nike's Controversial Colin Kaepernick Ad Campaign Is Most Divisive Yet," *Guardian*, September 4, 2018, www.theguardian.com.

106 Ibid.

107 Ibid.

108 Abad-Santos, "Social Media Boycott."

109 Malika Mitra, "Nike Won Its First 'Outstanding Commercial' Emmy in 17 Years for an Ad Featuring Colin Kaepernick," CNBC, September 16, 2019, www.cnbc.com.

110 Jonathan Berr, "Nike Stock Price Reaches All-Time High after Colin Kaepernick Ad," CBS News, September 14, 2018, http://cbsnews.com; Mitra, "Nike Won."

111 Banet-Weiser, *Authentic™*, 8–9.

112 Steve Almasy, "Curt Schilling Suspended by ESPN after Controversial Tweet," CNN, August 26, 2015, www.cnn.com.

113 Charles Kurzman, "Muslim-American Involvement with Violent Extremism," Triangle Center on Terrorism and Homeland Security, University of North Carolina, Chapel Hill, January 18, 2018, 6, http://sites.duke.edu.

114 Almasy, "Curt Schilling Suspended."

115 Ibid.

116 Daniel Martinez HoSang and Natalia Molina, "Introduction: Toward a Relational Consciousness of Race," in *Relational Formations of Race: Theory, Method, and Practice*, ed. Natalia Molina, Daniel Martinez HoSang, and Ramón A. Guttiérez (Oakland: University of California Press, 2019), 8.

117 Daniel Popper, "Curt Schilling Posts Anti-transgender Graphic on Facebook," *New York Daily News*, April 19, 2016, www.nydailynews.com.

118 Colin Campbell, "Four Things to Remember about House Bill 2," *News Observer*, September 13, 2016, http://newsobserver.com.

119 "'Bathroom Bill' to Cost North Carolina $3.76 billion," CNBC, March 27, 2017, http://cnbc.com.

120 Jasbir K. Puar and Amit S. Rai, "Monster, Terrorist, Fag: The War on Terrorism and the Production of Docile Patriots," *Social Text* 20:3 (2002): 117–148.

121 "ESPN Statement on Curt Schilling," *ESPN MediaZone*, April 20, 2016, http://espnmediazone.com.

122 Curt Schilling, "The Hunt to Be Offended . . . ," *Curt Schilling* (blog), April 19, 2016, http://38pitches.wordpress.com; Bob Raissman, "ESPN Fires Curt Schilling after Offensive Social Media Post," *New York Daily News*, April 21, 2016, www.nydailynews.com.

123 Gabriel Sherman, "Curt Schilling Joins Breitbart," *New York Magazine*, October 23, 2016, http://nymag.com.

124 Michelle A. Holling, Dreama G. Moon, and Alexandra Jackson Nevis, "Racist Violations and Racializing Apologia in a Post-Racism Era," *Journal of International and Intercultural Communication* 7, no. 4 (November 2014): 260–286, 261–262.

125 John Hartigan, *What Can You Say? America's National Conversation on Race* (Stanford, CA: Stanford University Press, 2010).

126 Ibid., 142.

127 Adam Ellwanger, "Apology as Metanoic Performance: Punitive Rhetoric and Public Speech," *Rhetoric Society Quarterly* 42:4 (2012): 307–329.

128 Christine Brennan, "Brennan: ESPN—at Long Last—Has Fired Curt Schilling, and We're All Better for It," *USA Today*, April 20, 2016, www.usatoday.com.

129 Roxanne Jones, "Curt Schilling Deserved to Get Canned," CNN, April 21, 2016, www.cnn.com.

130 Clay Travis, "On Curt Schilling," *OutKick*, April 21, 2016, http://outkick.com.

131 Teun A. van Dijk, "Discourse and the Denial of Racism," *Discourse & Society* 3:1 (1992): 95.

132 Sara Ahmed, *On Being Included: Racism and Diversity in Institutional Life* (Durham, NC: Duke University Press, 2012), 44.

133 Eva Cherniavsky, "Keyword 1: #MeToo," *differences* 30:1 (2019): 15–23, 16.

134 Ahmed, *On Being Included*, 44.

135 Michael Awkward, *Burying Don Imus: Anatomy of a Scapegoat* (Minneapolis: University of Minnesota Press, 2006), 5.

136 Junaid Rana, "The Racial Infrastructure of the Terror-Industrial Complex," *Social Text* 129 (34:4) (December 2016): 111–138.

137 Adrienne Matei, "Call-Out Culture: How to Get It Right (and Wrong)," *Guardian*, November 1, 2019, www.theguardian.com.

138 Loretta Ross, "I'm a Black Feminist. I Think Call-Out Culture Is Toxic," *New York Times*, August 17, 2019, www.nytimes.com.

CHAPTER 5. FLEXIBLE DIVERSITY

1 "Lounges," *Michigan Housing*, accessed September 9, 2020, https://housing.umich.edu.

2 I deliberately spell "antisemitism" without a hyphen or capitalization (i.e., "anti-Semitism") in line with the case made for this spelling by the book Jewish Voice for Peace, *On Antisemitism: Solidarity and the Struggle for Justice* (Chicago: Haymarket Books, 2017), xv. They cite Jewish studies scholar Yehuda Bauer, who argues that the term "Semite" was created through scientific racism and thus that the spelling "anti-Semitism" legitimizes the pseudo-science. See Yehuda Bauer, "In Search of a Definition of Antisemitism," in *Approaches to Antisemitism: Context and Curriculum*, ed. Michael Brown (New York: American Jewish Committee, 1994), 22–24.

3 Yazan Kherallah, "Viewpoint: Pineapple Express," *Michigan Daily*, March 10, 2014, www.michigandaily.com.

4 Adam Kredo, "BDS Leader Posts 'Overly Threatening' Photo to Facebook," *Washington Free Beacon*, March 26, 2014, www.freebeacon.com.

5 Adam Kredo, "University of Michigan Official Denounces Free Beacon," *Washington Free Beacon*, March 28, 2014, www.freebeacon.com.

6 Adam Kredo, "Palestinian Activists Violently Threaten Pro-Israel Students," *Washington Free Beacon*, March 21, 2014, www.freebeacon.com. Also see Adam Kredo, "Pro-Israel Students Called 'Kike,' 'Dirty Jew' at University of Michigan," *Washington Free Beacon*, March 24, 2014, www.freebeacon.com.

7 Kherallah, "Pineapple Express."

8 "The Palestine Exception: Campus Incidents," Palestine Legal, 14, http://palestinelegal.org.

9 Ibid., 15.

10 "The Palestine Exception."

11 Will Greenberg, "What Is Being Black at the University?," *The Michigan Daily*, February 3, 2014, www.michigandaily.com.

12 Kellie Woodhouse, "University of Michigan Renews Decades-Long Struggle to Increase Black Enrollment," *MLive*, February 2, 2014, www.mlive.com.

13 "Statement by the University of Michigan President and Provost Regarding the Proposed Boycott of Israeli Academic Institutions," U-M Public Affairs, December 23, 2013, http://publicaffairs.vpcomm.umich.edu.

14 Elizabeth Redden, "Boycott Battles," *Inside Higher Ed*, January 2, 2014, www .insidehighered.com.

15 "2015 Paris Terror Attacks Fast Facts," CNN, November 13, 2019, www.cnn.com.

16 VP for Student Life, "Support for students in troubled times," email communication to students at the University of Michigan, November 17, 2015.

17 The documents pertaining to the creation of the Islamophobia Working Group have been archived at the Bentley Historical Library at the University of Michigan.

18 This report served as a model for the IWG's report: Jihad Turk, Nan Senzaki, Tyrone Howard, and Armaan Rowther, "Muslim & Arab Student Campus Climate at the University of California Fact-Finding Team Report & Recommendations," President's Advisory Council on Campus Climate, Culture, & Inclusion, 2010.

19 Archived at the Bentley Historical Library.

20 Sara Ahmed, *On Being Included: Racism and Diversity in Institutional Life* (Durham, NC: Duke University Press, 2012), 97–98.

21 Benjamin B. Stubbs and Margaret W. Sallee, "Muslim, Too: Navigating Multiple Identities at an American University," *Equity & Excellence in Education* 46:4 (2013): 451–467.

22 Ibid.

23 Arshad Imtiaz Ali, "A Threat Enfleshed: Muslim College Students Situate Their Identities amidst Portrayals of Muslim Violence and Terror," *International Journal of Qualitative Studies in Education* 27:10 (2014): 1243–1261.

24 "Reflection Rooms on Campus," U-M Trotter Multicultural Center, http://trotter .umich.edu.

25 Kristen Brustad, Mahmoud Al-Batal, and Abbas Al-Tonsi, *Al-Kitaab Fii Ta'allum al-'Arabiyya: A Textbook for Beginning Arabic*, 2nd ed. (Washington, DC: Georgetown University Press, 2004).

26 Ibtihal Makki, "Op-Ed: Depoliticize Arabic Studies," *Michigan Daily*, January 29, 2017, www.michigandaily.com; Sophie Lehrenbaum, "The Politics of Language: Teaching Arabic in U.S. Colleges," *Tufts Daily* (blog), February 10, 2016, https://tuftsdaily.com; Madeleine Chang, "The Politicization of Learning Arabic," *Stanford Daily*, September 30, 2015, www.stanforddaily.com.

27 See Randa Kayyali, "US Census Classifications and Arab Americans: Contestations and Definitions of Identity Markers," *Journal of Ethnic and Migration Studies* 39:8 (2013): 1299–1318. Also see Sarah Gualtieri, *Between Arab and White: Race and Ethnicity in the Early Syrian American Diaspora* (Berkeley: University of California Press, 2009); Lubna Qutami, "Censusless: Arab/Muslim Interpolation into Whiteness and the War on Terror," *Journal of Asian American Studies* 23:2 (June 2020); Helen Hatab Samhan, "Not Quite White: Race Classification and the Arab-American Experience," in *Arabs in America: Building a New Future*, ed. Michael W. Suleiman (Philadelphia: Temple University Press, 1999).

28 Kayyali, "US Census Classifications."

29 On Arabs' shifting racial positioning in US history, see Sarah M. A. Gualtieri and Pauline Homsi Vinson, "Arab/Americas," *Amerasia* 44:1 (2018), vii–xxi.

30 Ella Shohat and Robert Stam, *Unthinking Eurocentrism: Multiculturalism and the Media* (New York: Routledge, 1994).

31 Zayna Syed, "ME/NA Identity Boxes Now Included in Rackham Applications," *Michigan Daily*, January 9, 2019, www.michigandaily.com.

32 John J. Mearsheimer and Stephen M. Walt, *The Israel Lobby and U.S. Foreign Policy* (New York: Farrar, Straus and Giroux, 2008). Also see Nadine Naber, Eman Desouky, and Lina Baroudi, "The Forgotten '-ism': An Arab American Women's Perspective on Zionism, Racism and Sexism," in *Color of Violence: The INCITE! Anthology*, ed. INCITE! Women of Color Against Violence (Durham, NC: Duke University Press, 2016), 97–112.

33 CLS Muslim Students Ass'n (@columbia.law.muslims), "The Muslim Law Students Association denounces all forms of professional retaliation against Arab, Middle Eastern, and Muslim students as well as against anyone doing Palestinian related human rights work," Instagram, July 1, 2021, www.instagram.com/p/CQyeGGDpKMR.

34 See Steven Salaita, *Anti-Arab Racism in the USA: Where It Comes From and What It Means for Politics Today* (London: Pluto Press, 2006).

35 Helen Hatab Samhan, "Politics and Exclusion: The Arab American Experience," *Journal of Palestine Studies* 16:2 (1987): 11–28.

36 Wajahat Ali, Eli Clifton, Matthew Duss, Lee Fang, Scott Keyes, and Faiz Shakir, "Fear, Inc.: The Roots of the Islamophobia Network in America (Washington, DC: Center for American Progress, August 2011), www.americanprogress.org.

37 Hatem Bazian, "The Islamophobia Industry and the Demonization of Palestine: Implications for American Studies," *American Quarterly* 67:4 (December 2015): 1057–1066, 1057. Also see Steven Salaita, "Beyond Orientalism and Islamophobia: 9/11, Anti-Arab Racism, and the Mythos of National Pride," *CR: The New Centennial Review* 6:2 (Fall 2006): 245–266; Sarah Marusek, "The Transatlantic Network: Funding Islamophobia and Israeli Settlements," in *What Is Islamophobia?: Racism, Social Movements and the State*, ed. Narzanin Massoumi, Tom Mills, and David Miller (London: Pluto Press, 2017), 186–214; Nathan Lean, *The Islamophobia Industry: How the Right Manufactures Hatred of Muslims* (London: Pluto Press, 2012).

38 Sunaina Maira, *The 9/11 Generation: Youth, Rights, and Solidarity in the War on Terror* (New York: NYU Press, 2016), 150.

39 For more on how Islamophobia and Zionism are connected, see Hatem Bazian, "The Islamophobia Industry and the Demonization of Palestine," *American Quarterly* 67:4 (December 2015): 1057–1066.

40 See, for example, Alice S. Cheng and Kristine E. Guillaume, "Hillel and Islamic Society Host Event against Islamophobia," *Harvard Crimson*, February 14, 2017, www.thecrimson.com.

41 See, for example, "ADL Saddened and Outraged at Supreme Court Decision Upholding Muslim Ban," ADL, June 26, 2018.

42 Salam Al-Marayati, "The ADL Cannot Have It Both Ways with Muslims," *Forward*, December 15, 2020, www.forward.com. The ADL, a core part of the Israel lobby in the US, has positioned itself as the premier civil rights organization in the US. However, many social justice groups refuse to partner with them. See "To Our Beloved Community: The ADL Is Not an Ally," #DropTheADL, August 2020, www.DropTheADL.org

43 Omar Barghouti, "Call for the Academic and Cultural Boycott of Israel," appendix 1, *Boycott, Divestment, Sanctions: The Global Struggle for Palestinian Rights* (Chicago: Haymarket Books, 2011), 35.

44 Sunaina Maira, *Boycott! The Academy and Justice for Palestine* (Berkeley: University of California Press, 2018).

45 Maira, *Boycott!*, 2; Barghouti, "Boycott of Israel."

46 Annie Robbins, " 'Shocked' by Tour of Occupation, 11 Feminists Led by Angela Davis 'Unequivocally' Support BDS," *Mondoweiss*, July 12, 2011, http://mondoweiss.net.

47 Selim Bulut, "Here's Why Artists Cancel Concerts in Israel," *Dazed*, January 17, 2018, www.dazeddigital.com.

48 Robin D. G. Kelley, "Another Freedom Summer," *Journal of Palestine Studies* 44:1 (Autumn 2014): 29–41.

49 On Ferguson and Palestine, see Kristian Davis Bailey, "Black-Palestinian Solidarity in the Ferguson-Gaza Era," *American Quarterly* 67:4 (December 2015): 1017–1026. For a longer history of Black-Palestinian solidarity, see Alex Lubin, "Locating Palestine in Pre-1948 Black Internationalism," *Souls* 9:2 (2007): 95–108; Alex Lubin, "The Black Panthers and the PLO: The Politics of Intercommunalism," *Geographies of Liberation: The Making of an Afro-Arab Political Imaginary* (Chapel Hill: University of North Carolina Press, 2014); Keith P. Feldman, "Black Power's Palestine: Permanent War and the Global Freedom Struggle," in *A Shadow over Palestine: The Imperial Life of Race in America* (Minneapolis: University of Minnesota Press, 2015), 59–101; Nadine Naber, " 'The U.S. and Israel Make the Connections for Us': Anti-imperialism and Black-Palestinian Solidarity," *Critical Ethnic Studies* 3:2 (2017): 15–30.

50 "A Threshold Crossed: Israeli Authorities and the Crimes of Apartheid and Persecution," Human Rights Watch, April 27, 2021, www.hrw.org.

51 "A Regime of Jewish Supremacy from the Jordan River to the Mediterranean Sea: This Is Apartheid," *B'Tselem*, January 12, 2021, www.btselem.org.

52 Loubna Qutami and Omar Zahzah, "The War of Words: Language as an Instrument of Palestinian National Struggle," *Arab Studies Quarterly* 42:1 & 2 (2020): 66–90, 74.

53 Normal Finkelstein, *Image and Reality of the Israel-Palestine Conflict* (New York: Verso Books, 1995).

54 Peter Bienart, "I No Longer Believe in a Jewish State," *New York Times*, July 8, 2021, www.nytimes.com.

55 "Our Approach to Zionism," Jewish Voice for Peace, www.jewishvoiceforpeace
.org.

56 See Feldman, *Shadow over Palestine*; Pamela Pennock, *The Rise of the Arab American Left: Activists, Allies, and their Fight against Imperialism and Racism, 1960s-1980s* (Chapel Hill: University of North Carolina Press, 2017); Loubna Qutami, "Transnational Histories of Palestinian Youth Organizing in the United States," *Journal of Palestine Studies* 50:2 (2021): 22–42, https://doi.org/10.1080/03 77919X.2021.1914938. For more on the politics of the BDS movement on college campuses, see Rabab Abdulhadi and Dana M. Olwan, "Introduction: Shifting Geographies of Knowledge and Power: Palestine and American Studies," *American Quarterly* 67:4 (December 2015): 993–1006. Also see the LA 8 case: Amy Goodman, "The Case of the L.A. 8: U.S. Drops 20-Year Effort to Deport Arab Americans for Supporting Palestinian Rights," *Democracy Now!*, November 2, 2007, www.democracynow.org.

57 Pennock, *Rise of the Arab American Left*, 55.

58 Ibid.

59 Sarah Banet-Weiser, *Empowered: Popular Feminism and Popular Misogyny* (Durham, NC: Duke University Press, 2018), 45.

60 Ibid.

61 Ella Shohat, "Exile, Diaspora, and Return: The Inscription of Palestine in Zionist Discourse," in *On the Arab-Jew, Palestine, and Other Displacements: Selected Writings of Ella Shohat* (London: Pluto Press, 2017), 173.

62 Thrall, "Battle over Israel."

63 Ben Lorber, "This Campus Will Divest! The Specter of Antisemitism and the Stifling of Dissent on College Campuses," in *On Antisemitism*: 159–171. Also see Jewish Voice for Peace, "Stifling Dissent: How Israel's Defenders Use False Charges of Anti-Semitism to Limit the Debate Over Israel on Campus," Fall 2015, www.jewishvoiceforpeace.org.

64 Lorber, "This Campus Will Divest!"

65 Nathan Thrall, "How the Battle over Israel and Anti-Semitism is Fracturing American Politics," *New York Times*, March 28, 2019, www.nytimes.com.

66 Lorber, "This Campus Will Divest!," 162.

67 Tom Pessah, "'Anti-Semitizing' Pro-Palestinian Activism Comes at a Price," *+972 Magazine*, August 21, 2016, www.972mag.com.

68 Tom Pessah, "On Bigotry and Solidarity," *+972 Magazine*, October 7, 2012, www.972mag.com.

69 Pessah, "Anti-Semitizing."

70 Umayyah Cable, "An Uprising at the Perfect Moment: Palestine in the 1990s Culture Wars," *GLQ* 26:2 (2020): 243–272, 245.

71 Mearsheimer and Walt, *The Israel Lobby*, 5.

72 Ibid., 9.

73 Ibid.

74 Thrall, "Battle over Israel."

75 Steven Salaita, "Normatizing State Power: Uncritical Ethical Praxis and Zionism," in *The Imperial University: Academic Repression and Scholarly Dissent*, ed. Piya Chatterjee and Sunaina Maira (Minneapolis: University of Minnesota Press, 2014), 217–235.

76 Amy Kaplan, *Our American Israel: The Story of an Entangled Alliance* (Cambridge, MA: Harvard University Press, 2018), 239, 241, 258.

77 Ibid., 240.

78 Ibid., 255, 266.

79 "The Six Words That Got Marc Lamont Hill Fired from CNN," *Al Jazeera*, December 9, 2018, www.aljazeera.com.

80 Marc Lamont Hill, "The Cost of Solidarity" (Palestine Writes Conference, Online, 2020).

81 Thomas Abowd, "The Boycott, Divestment, and Sanctions Movement and Violations of Academic Freedom at Wayne State University," in *The Imperial University: Academic Repression and Scholarly Dissent*, ed. Piya Chatterjee and Sunaina Maira (Minneapolis: University of Minnesota Press, 2014), 169–185.

82 Steven Salaita, *Uncivil Rites: Palestine and the Limits of Academic Freedom* (Chicago: Haymarket Books, 2015).

83 See, for example, "Israel Anti-Boycott Act," Senate Bill 720–115th Congress, March 23, 2017, www.congress.gov; "Combating BDS Act of 2017," Senate Bill 170, January 17, 2017, www.congress.gov.

84 Lara Friedman, president of the Foundation for Middle East Peace, outlines these two approaches in "Webinar: Legislating against Criticism of Israel—the Ongoing Assault on Americans' Free Speech," Foundation for Middle East Peace, April 14, 2020, www.youtube.com/watch?v=t4d-IvRmmhM. Also see "Opposing Efforts to Delegitimize the State of Israel and the Global Boycott, Divestment, and Sanctions Movement Targeting Israel," House Resolution 246–116th Congress, July 23, 2019, www.congress.gov; "Strengthening America's Security in the Middle East Act of 2019," Senate Bill 1–116th Congress, February 5, 2019, www.congress.gov.

85 Zack Beauchamp, "The Controversy over Laws Punishing Israel Boycotts, Explained," *Vox*, January 9, 2019, www.vox.com.

86 Jacey Fortin, "She Wouldn't Promise Not to Boycott Israel, So a Texas School District Stopped Paying Her," *New York Times*, December 19, 2018, www.nytimes.com.

87 Beauchamp, "Laws Punishing Israel Boycotts."

88 "Defining Antisemitism," Office of International Religious Freedom, Office of the Special Envoy to Monitor and Combat Antisemitism, US Department of State, 2016, www.state.gov.

89 Donald J. Trump, Executive Order on Combating Anti-Semitism, White House, December 11, 2019, www.whitehouse.gov.

90 See "Working Definition of Antisemitism," International Holocaust Remembrance Alliance, accessed May 15, 2020, www.holocaustremembrance.com.

91 Kenneth S. Stern, "Will Campus Criticism of Israel Violate Federal Law?," *New York Times*, December 12, 2016, www.nytimes.com.

92 Kenneth Stern, "I Drafted the Definition of Antisemitism. Rightwing Jews Are Weaponizing It," *Guardian*, December 13, 2019, www.theguardian.com.

93 "Palestinian Rights and IHRA Definition of Antisemitism," *Guardian*, November 29, 2020, www.theguardian.com.

94 "The Jerusalem Declaration on Antisemitism," March 25, 2021, www.jerusalem declaration.org.

95 "MESA Board Statement regarding the IHRA Working Definition of Antisemitism (and 'Contemporary Examples')," Middle East Studies Association, March 31, 2021, www.mesana.org.

96 See, for example, Alex Kane, "This University Claims to Be Pro-justice. So Why Is It Banning Palestine Activism?," +972 *Magazine*, February 25, 2021, www.972mag .com; "University of Illinois Faculty and Staff Reject Efforts to Suppress Palestinian Freedom and Solidarity," *Mondoweiss*, December 23, 2020, http://mondoweiss.net.

97 Kane, "University Claims to Be Pro-justice."

98 "President Donald J. Trump Announced Key Additions to His Administration," White House, October 26, 2017, www.whitehouse.gov.

99 Kenneth L. Marcus, "Standing up for Jewish Students," *Jerusalem Post*, September 9, 2013, www.jpost.com.

100 Ibid.

101 Ibid.

102 Ali Abunimah, "Trump Official Wants Students Prosecuted for Israel Protests," *Electronic Intifada*, September 19, 2018, http://electronicintifada.net.

103 "Webinar: Legislating against Criticism."

104 See comments by Lara Friedman and Dima Khalidi in "Webinar: Legislating against Criticism."

105 "The Palestine Exception."

106 Dylan Lacroix and Jordyn Baker, "Then and Now: The Struggle of Divestment at the University," *Michigan Daily*, November 13, 2017, www.michigandaily.com; Alex Kane, "U. Mich Student Government Move to Table Divestment Resolution Sparks Uproar," *Mondoweiss*, March 20, 2014, http://mondoweiss.net.

107 Kherallah, "Pineapple Express"; Kredo, "BDS Leader."

108 UM Divest Fan Mail, 2014, https://umdivestfanmail.tumblr.com.

109 Max Blumenthal, "'A Painful Price': The Escalating War on Palestine Solidarity at U of Michigan and Beyond," *Mondoweiss*, April 3, 2014, http://mondoweiss.net.

110 Will Greenberg, Michael Sugerman, and Max Radwin, "Administrators Meet with Sit-In, Hillel to Hear students' Concerns," *Michigan Daily*, March 22, 2014, www .michigandaily.com.

111 Ibid.

112 Jordyn Baker, Dylan Lacroix, and Rhea Cheeti, "#UMDivest Resolution Passes for First Time in U-M Ann Arbor Campus History," *Michigan Daily*, November 14, 2017, www.michigandaily.com.

113 Thrall, "Battle over Israel."

114 Jordyn Baker, "Student Body Reckons with #UMDivest Vote," *Michigan Daily*, November 16, 2017, www.michigandaily.com.

115 Baker, Lacroix, and Cheeti, "#UMDivest Resolution Passes."

116 Lacroix and Baker, "Then and Now."

117 Ashley Tjhung and Jason Rowland, "Re-centering the Struggle for #UMDivest," *Michigan Daily*, March 28, 2018, www.michigandaily.com.

118 Orian Zakai, "Antisemitism on the American College Campus in the Age of Corporate Education, Identity Politics, and Power-Blindness," in *On Antisemitism*, 173–180.

119 Baker, "Student Body Reckons."

120 Alexa St. John and Jordyn Baker, "CSG President Signs #UMDivest Resolution," *Michigan Daily*, November 21, 2017, www.michigandaily.com.

121 Derald Wing Sue et al., "Racial Microaggressions in Everyday Life: Implications for Clinical Practice," *American Psychologist* 62:4 (2007): 271–86.

122 Baker, "Student Body Reckons."

123 "'Resolution Regarding Divestment,' Statement from Several U-M Board Members re CSG Vote on Resolution A.R.7–019," U-M Public Affairs, University of Michigan, December 14, 2017, https://publicaffairs.vpcomm. umich.edu.

124 Lacroix and Baker, "Then and Now."

125 Lara Moehlman, "Schlissel Talks Student Debt, Diversity in Chat," *Michigan Daily*, December 3, 2015, www.michigandaily.com.

126 Ibid.

127 Regents Michael J. Behm, Mark J. Bernstein, Denise Ilitch, Andrea Fischer Newman, Andrew C. Richner, and Ron Weiser, "Statement Regarding CSG Vote on Resolution A.R. 7–019," U-M Public Affairs, University of Michigan, December 14, 2017, https://publicaffairs.vpcomm.umich.edu.

128 "Response to Those Writing about the CSG Resolution Regarding Divestment," signed by Rick Fitzgerald, U-M Public Affairs, November 17, 2017.

129 Roderick A. Ferguson, *We Demand: The University and Student Protests* (Berkeley: University of California Press, 2007), 69.

130 Josh Nathan-Kazis, "Revealed: Canary Mission Blacklist Is Secretly Bankrolled by Major Jewish Federation," *Forward*, October 3, 2018, http://forward.com.

131 Alex Kane, "'It's Killing the Student Movement': Canary Mission's Blacklist of Pro-Palestine Activists Is Taking a Toll," *Intercept*, November 22, 2018, http://theintercept.com.

132 Kane, "Killing the Student Movement."

133 Ibid.

134 Lacroix and Baker, "Then and Now."

135 Blumenthal, "Painful Price."

136 Zayna Syed, "Canary Mission Blacklists Students, Faculty for Pro-Palestine View," *Michigan Daily*, March 1, 2019, www.michigandaily.com.

137 Z. Zidan, "On Slander, Accountability and CSG Elections," *Scribd*, accessed July 14, 2021, www.scribd.com.

138 Lorber, "This Campus Will Divest!," 167.

139 Elizabeth Redden, "The Right to a Recommendation?," *Inside Higher Ed*, September 19, 2018, www.insidehighered.com.

140 Amir Fleischman, "Op-Ed: GEO's Fight for the Right to Boycott," *Michigan Daily*, May 18, 2021, www.michigandaily.com.

141 Mark Schlissel and Martin Philbert, "Letter: Important questions around issues of personal beliefs, our responsibilities as educators, and antisemitism," Office of the President, University of Michigan, October 9, 2018, http://president .umich.edu.

142 Safiya Merchant, "Schlissel Speaks Out on Professor's Refusal to Support Student Effort to Study in Israel," *University Record*, September 20, 2018, http://record .umich.edu.

143 Zakai, "Antisemitism on Campus," 180.

144 "Open Letter from Students Allied for Freedom and Equality (SAFE)," June 1, 2021, https://docs.google.com/document/d/1uTIy5lpoVhkLOumOTBRkjDqAPj6z 9rZYp7kLX9mLfr4/edit.

145 James M. Thomas, *Diversity Regimes: Why Talk Is Not Enough to Fix Racial Inequality at Universities* (New Brunswick, NJ: Rutgers University Press, 2020), 15.

146 Scott Jaschik, "Diversity Regimes," *Inside Higher Ed*, June 16, 2020, www.inside highered.com.

147 Thomas, *Diversity Regimes*, 47.

148 Peter Reinman, "It's Time to Name Anti-Palestinian Bigotry," *Jewish Currents*, July 10, 2021, www.jewishcurrents.org.

EPILOGUE

1 Glenn Greenwald (@ggreenwald), "GOP Leader Kevin McCarthy threatens punishment for @IlhanMN and @RashidaTlaib over their criticisms of Israel. It's stunning how much time US political leaders spend defending a foreign nation even if it means attacking free speech rights of Americans," Twitter, February 10, 2019, https://twitter.com/ggreenwald/status/1094727576013193216?s=20; JTA and Ron Kampeas, "Kevin McCarthy Promises 'Action' against Ilhan Omar and Rashida Tlaib," *Haaretz*, February 10, 2019, www.haaretz.com.

2 "Trump Calls for Omar to Resign over Israel Tweets," Minnesota Public Radio (MPR), February 12, 2019, www.mprnews.org.

3 Ilhan Omar (@IlhanMN), "Listening and learning, but standing strong," Twitter, February 11, 2019, https://twitter.com/IlhanMN/status/1095046561254567937?s=20.

4 Johnny Diaz, "Man Who Threatened to 'Put a Bullet' in Ilhan Omar Is Sentenced to a Year in Prison," *New York Times*, March 10, 2020, www.nytimes.com.

5 Ella Nilsen, "The House Easily Passed Democrats' Anti-hate Resolution, with Some Republicans Dissenting," *Vox*, March 7, 2019, www.vox.com.

6 Jamie Raskin, "H.Res.183—Condemning Anti-Semitism as Hateful Expressions of Intolerance That Are Contradictory to the Values and Aspirations That Define the People of the United States and Condemning Anti-Muslim Discrimination and Bigotry against Minorities as Hateful Expressions of Intolerance That Are Contrary to the Values and Aspirations of the United States" (116th Congress, 2019).

7 Yair Rosenberg, "'Jews Will Not Replace Us': Why White Supremacists Go After Jews," *Washington Post*, August 14, 2017, www.washingtonpost.com.

8 Jane Coaston, "Trump's New Defense of His Charlottesville Comments Is Incredibly False," *Vox*, April 26, 2019, www.vox.com.

9 "Statement from Reps. Ilhan Omar, Rashida Tlaib, Andre Carson on House Resolution," Representative Ilhan Omar, March 7, 2019, https://omar.house.gov.

10 Pamela Newkirk, *Diversity Inc.: The Failed Promise of a Billion-Dollar Business* (New York: Bold Type Books, 2019), 5.

11 Alana Wise, Jason Breslow, and Jaclyn Diaz, "'It's Time to End This Forever War.' Biden Says Forces to Leave Afghanistan by 9/11," NPR, April 15, 2021, www.npr .org.

12 Larry Buchanan, Quoctrung Bui, and Kugal K. Patel, "Black Lives Matter May Be the Largest Movement in U.S. History," *New York Times*, July 3, 2020, www .nytimes.com.

13 Wenei Philimon, "Not Just George Floyd: Police Departments Have 400-Year History of Racism," *USA Today*, June 7, 2020, www.usatoday.com.

14 Amy Harmon, Apoorva Mandavilli, Sapna Maheshwari, and Jodi Kantor, "From Cosmetics to NASCAR, Calls for Racial Justice Are Spreading," *New York Times*, June 13, 2020, www.nytimes.com.

15 Tiffany Hsu, "Aunt Jemima Brand to Change Name and Image over 'Racial Stereotype,'" *New York Times*, June 17, 2020, www.nytimes.com.

16 Jessica Bursztynsky, "Apple Announces Latest Efforts in Its $100 Million Racial Equity and Justice Initiative," CNBC, January 13, 2021, www.cnbc.com.

17 David Leonhardt, "Can Policing Change?," *New York Times*, April 20, 2021, www .nytimes.com.

18 Gabi Kirk, "Authors of California Ethnic Studies Curriculum Decry Cuts to Arab Studies," *Jewish Currents*, February 3, 2021, http://jewishcurrents.com.

19 Spencer Bokat-Lindell, "Why Is the Country Panicking about Critical Race Theory?," *New York Times*, July 13, 2021, www.nytimes.com.

20 John Eligon and Shawn Hubler, "Throughout Trial over George Floyd's Death, Killings by Police Mount," *New York Times*, April 17, 2021, www.nytimes .com.

21 Arun Kundnani, "Abolish National Security" (Amsterdam: Transnational Institute, June 2021), 5.

22 Mona Chalabi, "Terror Attacks by Muslims Receive 357% More Press Attention, Study Finds," *Guardian*, July 20, 2018, www.theguardian.com.

23 Michael D. Shear, David E. Sanger, and Thomas Gibbons-Neff, "In Forceful Defense of Afghan Withdrawal, Biden Says U.S. Achieved Its Objectives," *New York Times*, July 8, 2021, www.nytimes.com.
24 Kundnani, "Abolish National Security," 11.
25 Ibid., 23.

INDEX

ABOUT THE AUTHOR

EVELYN ALSULTANY is a leading expert on the history of representations of Arabs and Muslims in the US media. She is Professor in the Department of American Studies and Ethnicity at the University of Southern California's Dornsife College and author of *Arabs and Muslims in the Media: Race and Representation after 9/11*. She is the co-editor of *Arab and Arab American Feminisms* and *Between the Middle East and the Americas*. She has published op-eds in the *Hollywood Reporter*, *Washington Post*, and *Newsweek*.